French Poets and the English Renaissance

French Poets and the English Renaissance

Studies in Fame and Transformation

Anne Lake Prescott

New Haven and London   Yale University Press

1978

Copyright © 1978 by Yale University.
All rights reserved. This book may not be
reproduced, in whole or in part, in any form
(except by reviewers for the public press), without
written permission from the publishers.

Designed by John O. C. McCrillis
and set in Baskerville type.
Printed in the United States of America by
The Vail-Ballou Press, Inc., Binghamton, New York.

Published in Great Britain, Europe, Africa, and
Asia (except Japan) by Yale University Press,
Ltd., London. Distributed in Latin America by
Kaiman & Polon, Inc., New York City; in
Australia and New Zealand by Book & Film
Services, Artarmon, N.S.W., Australia; and in Japan
by Harper & Row, Publishers, Tokyo Office.

**Library of Congress Cataloging in Publication
Data**

Prescott, Anne Lake, 1936–
    French poets and the English Renaissance.

    Includes bibliographical references and index.
    1. French poetry—16th century—History and
criticism. 2. French literature—Appreciation—
England. 3. Literature, Comparative—French and English.
4. Literature, Comparative—English and French. I. Title.
PQ418.P7   841'.3'09   77–5482
ISBN 0–300–02140–2

For
Eleanor Hard Lake
and
Agnes Kirsopp Michels

Contents

Acknowledgments

In writing this book I have accumulated debts it is a pleasure to acknowledge. I owe my first interest in the topic to a conversation with Dr. A. L. Rowse during a visit to Cornwall twenty years ago when I had a year to spend in Paris and no very clear idea how to spend it. He showed me some D'Aubigné (a writer particularly appealing to his combative spirit) and urged on me the poetry of those others, then quite new to me, whose careers in England are the subject of this study. In pursuing my research and in the earlier stages of writing about it, I have been helped by Professor William Nelson, whose good-humored and patient common sense has provided firm ground for so many of us as we started on our various scholarly explorations.

I also thank my colleagues at Barnard, especially Eleanor Rosenberg, for her friendly challenges, and David Robertson, for gifts of time, energy, and affection. I am grateful to E. R. Gregory for sharing his thoughts and research on Du Bartas, and to Susan Snyder for her answers to my queries about Sylvester. I am sorry I was unable to make use of her forthcoming edition of his *Weeks*.

My sister, Lydia Lake, has given me more help with my translations from Latin than I quite like admitting and has saved me from more than one illiteracy. Any errors, of course, remain my own offspring and must not count as her nieces and nephews. My thanks also to Howard Schless for his encouragement, to my mother, Eleanor Lake, for taking time from her own work as an editor to check my manuscript, to my husband, Peter S. Prescott, for his expert advice on style, and to Orville and Lilias Prescott for their interest and support. Finally, I thank my Yale Press editor, Ellen Graham, for her smooth and sensitive guidance.

A.L.P.

Introduction

This book attempts to explore and clarify what intelligent or at least literate Englishmen during the sixteenth and much of the seventeenth centuries thought of the major French Renaissance poets and what they made of them—"made of" both in the sense of understanding or interpreting and in the sense of refashioning or reworking.

Such an investigation illuminates, I hope, English assumptions and attitudes during the Renaissance, for how we see people and things, which of them we prefer, how we transform them by new perspectives, helps sketch if only roughly the inner structure of our spirits. Just as the image on the retina does not merely reproduce what is really "out there" so our response to a friend, a poem, a public figure, is in part a "feigning," an act of the imagination. And the very fantasies we create, the sometimes astonishing distortions and selectivity of our perceptions, show in part who and what we are.

For this study I have chosen the five poets most familiar to Renaissance England: Marot, Du Bellay, Ronsard, Desportes, and Du Bartas. For evidence I have relied chiefly on published works of the time and to a much lesser extent on manuscript material,[1] so that most of what the English say in the following pages is limited to what they wished to be known to have said. I have as much as possible used only explicit reference, quotation, citation, and undoubted borrowings or translations. On occasion I refer to the possibility of "influence," but that is not my subject here.

My exploration has, of course, uncertainties of its own. If Renaissance Englishmen regarded the French from perspectives determined in part by geography, temperament, cultural and social imperatives, or literary requirements, it remains awkwardly true that a modern investigation of those perspectives is in turn angled by equivalent if dissimilar pressures. To think seriously about how we perceive perception or write about writing is very rapidly to enter infinitely regressing paradoxes. I can only hope to present the evidence and trust my reading of it is no more distorted than human readings must be.

Some inevitable distortions derive from the nature of the evidence. It is fragmentary, for many must have read these poets without committing what they felt to paper and much of what others did write is lost. Even what survives is inescapably bound by the limits of Renaissance critical vocabulary. Sooner or later in studying the literature of the time one senses a disparity between what poets did and what they could explicitly say they were doing. There was disappointingly little written about the numerical patterning of literary works, for example, perhaps because there was no clear classical precedent for such a discussion or perhaps because such techniques were supposed to be kept semisecret; yet Du Bartas evidently used them.

Or, to take another example, the available critical traditions did nothing to encourage a defense of love poems. One could call them "*nugae*"—trifles—and even speak of them with amused affection, but many of Ronsard's *nugae* seem to a modern reader more significant as well as more enjoyable than Du Bartas's *Sepmaines*. Did no one see that? Perhaps not; yet we might also suspect that what was said about "divine" and "sweet" Du Bartas was simply easier to say than what was not said about Ronsard's love poetry. The reasons for this are not merely linguistic, not merely a function of Du Bartas's relatively easy French and availability in translation. Desportes is an easy poet too and yet the English said little about him even as they read and pillaged his works.

Furthermore, what the English could say was often shaped, even more than modern comments would be, by the given rhetorical situation. For example, in an age to which later notions of sincerity or individual self-expression would have seemed unsophisticated, prideful, or simply incomprehensible, what one said in print about a poet may not have been a "personal opinion" at all but rather what the writer conceived to be the generally held view—and just because generally held then in some fashion his own. A stalwart like Jonson might scoff at Du Bartas but not to praise a widely admired figure would have struck some of the writers I quote as violating a decorum meaningless to modern readers. Such pressures to internalize a derivative estimate did not always operate, of course, or reputations would have been static and unvaried, but I think one can feel the tendency at work. Opinions on Du Bartas, especially, seem to have circulated almost like Petrarchist conceits—they were public property.

And whether one referred to Du Bartas's sweet *Sepmaines* or Ronsard's sweet conceits and what one said about them depended in part on the sort of text one was writing. Satire or repentance almost required a disabused rejection of love toys whereas one's mistress should be told she was prettier than Ronsard's Cassandre. The rhetoric of praise might entail telling a friend he had equalled Homer and Du Bartas. The purpose of eulogy, as Ronsard pointed out, is to praise the subject to the skies, and if such compliment requires hyperbole then hyperbole should flow like water from Helicon. I therefore ask the reader to view cautiously the many comments and references I quote. The final pattern is instructive, but the individual colors of rhetoric should not be read literally.

This study does not attempt very many large conclusions but it does offer a moral or two. First is the familiar but easily forgotten lesson that Opinion is shifty and elusive. Like Virgil's *Fama* she flies through streets and cities at will but what she says changes almost by the time she has reached the next town or even the last house in the row. After witnessing so many visions and revisions, improbable estimates, and vain prophecies of eternal glory it is even harder than before to take seriously attempts in our own age to settle on the "ten best" films of the year, to decide as if for all time whether or not "Four Quartets" is up to "The Wasteland," or to determine rigorously who belongs in the great tradition. Judgment and discrimination remain, but comparing what has been said of Ronsard by Gabriel Harvey, Boileau, and modern critics can bring humility and a useful deafness to Opinion's tattle.

Furthermore, the evidence will show, I hope, that English Renaissance attitudes were varied and complex. This point seems foolishly obvious, but it is always tempting to assume that although we ourselves are a pluralist and complicated lot our ancestors made a simpler sort of sense. It is easy to assume, for instance, that most Englishmen admired Du Bartas because they were Protestant and he was Protestant. Yet his Protestantism drew little comment and some who liked him were Catholic. Even our assumptions about the relationship of a writer to his words may oversimplify Renaissance attitudes. Many of the people who appear in this book, for example, seem to have felt that *sententia*, conceits, tropes, descriptions—detachable bits of discourse—had a life of their own distinct from the habits, beliefs, and behavior of their authors. Certain writers were useful to cite by name because of their reputations as learned, wise, good, or clever men; Du Bartas became such an authority. But since conceits and even whole sonnets are less tied down than tone, argument, or conviction, a poet could also search Ronsard's *Amours* for inspiration and admire the author in certain ways even while sympathizing with the Huguenots attacked elsewhere in the *Oeuvres*.

Or, to take another complexity, modern readers might understandably suppose that those who shared Du Bartas's hope for a "true" Christian masterpiece would also distrust fiction and allegory, but such was not always the case. Du Bartas appealed both to those who longed for discursive and unfeigned verse based on Scripture and those who wandered through the indirections of moralized landscape and fable. A liking for Du Bartas could and did accompany an affection for Chaucer, Ariosto, and Rabelais. The many references to these five poets, therefore, the translations of and borrowings from their work, will show if not the whole truth about the English Renaissance then something equally important: a rich and varied confusion which discourages swift generalization or summary conclusion but which was a source—and result—of the age's vitality.

1

Marot

Until a few years ago modern criticism thought Clément Marot (c. 1496–1544) securely placed in his own corner of the early French Renaissance. His particular niche was variously labeled "late Medieval," "precursor," or (always safe) "transitional," but whatever the words, the tone all too often suggested faint praise; genuine appreciation of Marot's easy charm and ironic humor seemed only to obscure his other accomplishments as chief poet at the court of François I. Such a view of Marot had, of course, been current for many years—it was Boileau himself who said at a time when few Frenchmen were willing to read the Pléiade, "Imitons de Marot l'élégant badinage." Recently, however, there have been objections to this diminished and diminishing view of Marot, although some might protest that the distorting lens has simply been reversed, not removed. We now have an excellent edition of Marot's poetry, recent and full biographies, a number of bibliographical studies, and new estimates of his importance and value.[1]

As his modern editor insists, Marot has too often been judged according to Romantic preconceptions and consequently found wanting in fire and high seriousness. Nor did the nineteenth-century revival of the Pléiade encourage a fuller understanding, for readers were apt to take at face value the group's boasts of poetic innovation and its celebration of victory over the giant Ignorance. In his *Deffence et illustration de la langue françoyse* (1549) Du Bellay scorned Marot for being unlearned and old-fashioned, but in fact he had done a great deal to liberate French poetry from the limits of the Rhétoriqueur tradition of verbal trickery and to "illustrate" it with new grace, flexibility, and wit. If in his work he shows his

1

inheritance from his father's generation he also helped introduce new genres like the elegy, eclogue, sonnet, and epigram; he even attempted some intriguing combinations of Petrarchan themes and diction with older French forms. Furthermore, although Marot was by no means so "docte" a poet as Ronsard, his assimilation and "imitation" of classical Latin poetry places him among Renaissance humanists, not merely among courtiers who wrote with ease. A few years after Ronsard's death, when poets were asked not to bore or puzzle their readers with bookishness or obscurity, Du Bellay's criticisms no longer seemed to matter and throughout the seventeenth and eighteenth centuries Marot remained fairly popular—popular, that is, for his by now entertainingly archaic diction and for his "badinage"; few seemed to relish his more serious poetry, his moments of real eloquence, or his darker satire.[2]

Marot's first important poems appeared in the 1520s.[3] In 1532 he published his *Adolescence clementine*, a collection that included a number of poems later imitated in England, and in late 1533 came *La suite de l'adolescence clementine*. There was an edition of the collected works in 1538, and another in 1544, the year of Marot's death. Many posthumous editions followed, and although these became fewer toward the end of the sixteenth century it is unlikely English readers, especially in London, would have found his works difficult to obtain.[4] Marot's translation of forty-nine psalms had a different and more complicated history, for they were made part of the Geneva Psalter.

Any Englishman who picked up one of these editions would have found a great variety of poems to explore. There were eclogues, "epigrams" (most of which are simply short lyrics, not the "pointed" verse later associated with the word), extraordinarily clever epistles and satires, epithalamia, *étrennes* (New Year offerings), occasional pieces, translations, some oddly impersonal elegies, and a few not very exciting sonnets. There were also older native forms: chants royaux, ballades, rondeaux, and chansons. For many readers throughout the years the chief value of this poetry has lain in Marot's witty grace and ironically assumed naïveté, his urbane control of compliment and insult, the clever modulations of tone in the epistles and the fresh simplicity of many lyrics. But there are also moments of genuine religious feeling and, in his attacks on some of the cruelties of the age, considerable courage. A few poems recount Marot's difficulties with the law (he wrote his bitter satire "Enfer" while in confinement) and with the Catholic Church. On several occasions Marot felt obliged to defend his religious position, although he did so in terms that leave room for speculation as to what that position actually was.[5]   In England some of this poetry was read, imitated, and commented upon, but the author was never very famous and when the English noticed him they sometimes did so with curious incomprehension.[6] Yet his career in England is well worth observing because of the very distortions in the picture he presented across the Channel; it provides an instructive example of how our "images" of people tend to be simplified, the modifying shadows lightened and the distracting lines erased. The English had a confused opinion of Marot, yet even those confusions did not allow for the far more disturbing and human multiplicity of his roles and the complexity of his thought and feeling.

Possibly the first poem by Marot recorded in England is an epigram copied into the Egerton MS of Wyatt's poetry. Not an example of Marot's satire at its subtlest, it tells how "Frere Thibault" tries to drag his girl all the way through the window and of his angry frustration when her bottom sticks.[7] The joke is typical of Marot's anticlerical epigrams, several of which were reprinted in England, although I can find few that were translated. Indeed it is at first surprising that Marot's verse on loose-living monks was quoted so seldom. Religious controversy of the day rejoiced in such scurrilities and many English writers paused in their often lurid descriptions of Catholic wickedness to regale their readers with lines on the Roman clergy from poets like Beza or Mantuan (among the most popular, so far as I can judge). Perhaps Marot seemed less useful for this purpose because his epigrams lacked the prestige of neo-Latin or because he himself lacked Beza's unambiguous position as a Calvinist leader and Mantuan's un-doubted Catholicism (so useful, under the circumstances, to a Protestant argument). And maybe his epigrams were simply too good-humored, too easygoing in their laughter at the familiar corruptions of lust and gluttony to compete with the angry and more clearly doctrinal witticisms of Beza.

In the 1570s two books were published in England that included

a number of Marot's poems. The authors, Thomas Vautrollier and
Jacques Bellot, were French in origin, but as a Protestant and a
printer Vautrollier probably hoped he knew something about
English taste and as a teacher Bellot probably hoped to improve it.

Of the two books Vautrollier's *Recueil du mellange d'Orlande de
Lassus* (1570) is the more extraordinary.[8] Vautrollier worked
quickly, for his collection is based upon an edition of Lassus's songs
published that same year. The *Recueil* nowhere mentions Marot,
but the treatment of the texts is interesting for what it suggests
Vautrollier thought about his readers' taste and attitudes. Several
texts come from Marot's translation of the psalms and two from his
epigrams—one tells of "Monsieur l'Abbé & monsieur son Valet"
who squabble at bedtime because the former must always have a
little wine by him at night while the latter can't get to sleep so long
as a drop remains undrunk. But in his preface Vautrollier says that
he has published Lassus for those who love music "conjoincte avec
une lettre grave, et eslongnée de toute impurité," so although he
welcomed the monk and his drinking problem he rewrote the love
poetry. Lassus had followed Marot's own words:

> Mon coeur se recommande à vous,
> Tout plain d'ennuy et de martyre;
> Au moins en despit des jaloux,
> Faites qu'àdieu vous puisse dire.
> Ma bouche qui vous souloit rire
> Et conter propos gratieux,
> Ne faict maintenant que maudire
> Ceux qui m'ont banny de voz yeux.

Vautrollier changes this to

> Mon coeur se rend à toy Seigneur,
> Tout plein d'ennuy et de martire,
> Helas! car j'ay de ta faveur
> Trop abusé, dont je soupire.
> Ma bouche qui se souloit rire,
> Et conter propos fabuleux
> Ne fera desormais que dire,
> Ton los en chant melodieux.[9]

Such washing of secular poetry in Jordan was not entirely new.

John Hall, for example, had revised Wyatt's love lyrics for his *Court of virtue* (1565) and in Scotland James Wedderburn had written parodies of popular ballads such as Gray of Reading's "The hunt is up." There were to be other versions of Lassus's texts, similarly freed from "ces puantises que beaucoup de poètes fransoys ont semées pour infecter le monde" (as one editor put it), and in England even Shakespeare's song was to be moralized; in a *Treatise on the true nature and definition of justifying faith* (Oxford, 1635) John Downe addresses not the ladies but the soul:

> Sigh no more soul, oh sigh no more,
> Despaire not thou thus ever,
> Thy God hath grace for thee in store,
> His mercy faileth never.
>> Then sigh not so,
>> Let sorrows go
>> Sing in the highest Hosanna
>> And change thy dolefull sounds of woe
>> Into Hallelujah.
>
> [sig. Fff2^v][10]

A taste for rewriting secular texts is not, however, to be dismissed as mere pious philistinism. Rather, such efforts can often be associated with a wider movement aimed at replacing "propos fabuleux" by the truth—not by the naked truth, necessarily, for here she is decked out in the Egyptian Gold of verse and imagery taken from the original poems—but by the truth as opposed to what Herbert perhaps half-seriously called "fictions only and false hair." To sing truly is to restore poetry itself to its original power.[11]

Jacques Bellot's *French grammer* was printed in 1578. Its author was a Norman from Caen, but the book is in English and some of his English friends contributed poems in his praise. Part Four of the book is a discussion of French poetry that illustrates a variety of poetic forms, rhymes, and meters, although the reader is disappointed to find here no mention of the French poets themselves. This section of the work seems oddly musty for 1578; I suspect it owes something to Sebillet's *Art poétique françoys*, published thirty years earlier. Some of the prefatory poems mention Du Bellay and Ronsard, but they are nowhere quoted, and although Bellot discusses the sonnet and the ode, he emphasizes those old-fashioned

forms and tricky rhymes which the Pléiade dismissed and which
Marot himself stopped writing as he grew older. At least, however,
the half-dozen selections from Marot are drawn from a broad
range of his tones and styles; Bellot chose the dignified chant royal
"Qui aime Dieu" and also an epigram on "mes beaux peres
religieux" who set a good table because they think their vow of
poverty exempts them from paying their bills (this is not in fact by
Marot, but it was widely supposed to be his).

There are also some lines from Marot in Abraham Fraunce's
Arcadian rhetorike (1588), a self-consciously modern handbook in
which a company of writers is mustered to illustrate various rhetorical devices and methods. Unlike Bellot, Fraunce was quite
interested in contemporary authors but he also seems to have
saved himself time by searching for illustrative material in *Les
bigarrures*, Estienne Tabourot's miscellaneous collection of essays,
verse, and quodlibets. Here he found a stanza by Marot which
struck him as a good example of the "half turn":

> Dieu des amans d'amour me garde,
> Me gardant donne moy bon heur,
> En me bienheurant prens ta darde,
> En la prenant navre son coeur,
> En le navrant me tiendra seur,
> En seuretè suivray laccointance,
> En laccointant ton serviteur
> En servant aura jouissance.

In his fascination with the clever twisting of the sentence Fraunce
failed to notice that as the stanza reads in the *Bigarrures* the first line
hardly makes sense—Marot's lover had more reasonably prayed,
"de mort me garde."[12] In any event Fraunce did not check the
original. Although careless, however, he was not quite so sloppy as
Simon Harward, preacher, doctor, schoolteacher, authority on
lightning and the propagation of plants, whose *Encheiridion morale*
(1596) defines the four cardinal virtues through a multitude of
extracts from Greek, Latin, Italian, Spanish, and French writers.
The French excerpts, says the preface, are from Marot, Du Bartas,
Tabourot, Ronsard, and other "viri eruditissimi," but to identify
them would make the book too long and anyway they are often so

proverbial they count as public property. Some passages are indeed from Tabourot and Du Bartas but I can find none from "eruditissimus" Marot, and it is possible that having read about him somewhere, perhaps in the *Bigarrures*, Harward decided his name alone would add weight to his collection.[13]

After Fraunce's treatise quotations from Marot's poetry are few or none, but English readers could have seen fragments in books translated from French. Thus a character in Estienne Pasquier's *Jesuites catechisme* (1602) quotes the "Romant of the Rose" in "the old language, with the newe of Marot, the first for his authoritie, the second for his grace" and *A world of wonders* (1607), translated from Henri Estienne's rambling and lively *Apologie pour Hérodote*, offers several passages from Marot including yet another epigram on thirsty clerics. Estienne calls Marot "the most famous of all the French Poets" (the original French says "le plus gentil") but this compliment dwindles to grudging acceptance in Charles Maupas's *French grammar and syntaxe* (1634)—explaining that word order in French is based on the "Naturall order of the understanding," the author quotes some lines on syntax by "Clement Marot (a French Poet of good esteeme in his time)."[14]

At least a few of Marot's poems, then, were published in Renaissance England. Most of them are short. Many have an obvious satirical flavor, although some are grave, even religious, and a few are love poems. The list offers considerable diversity, but the badinage of the epistles is missing.

Adaptations of Marot's poems show a different emphasis; almost all concern love, although the two most important are pastorals. English response to Marot's work in this regard illustrates, no doubt, the intense interest of the times (and all times) in the subject and in the opportunities love poetry offers for wit, pathos, rhetorical display, and oblique approaches to other less easily accessible realms of experience and imagination. Nor is it surprising that at the time of Wyatt and Surrey, and for some years after, writers attempting to innovate or at least to explore recent innovations and recoveries noted and borrowed from the work of a poet who had, after all, done the same in France. One can feel, however, a subtle modernization of Marot at work. The adaptations show a shift away from the fixed forms to the lyric "epigram," the eclogue, and the elegy (a shift paralleled in Marot's own poetry), while the treatment of the short lyrics shows a consistent tendency to maneuver the poetry toward an even sharper "point" at the end, sometimes by changing the conceit slightly, sometimes by changing the organization or structure.

Translations from Marot have usually been thought to begin with Sir Thomas Wyatt, who traveled in France, must certainly have heard about him, and could well have met him in person. A few poems probably owe something to him; "Ffor to love her," for instance, may derive its idea and refrain from Marot's rondeau "D'estre amoureux," and other parallels or echoes have been suggested. Usually, however, further research discloses an Italian source.[15] Yet reading Wyatt and Marot one is often aware, I think, of a kinship involving an occasional similarity of tone, an interest in fixed forms but also an openness to Petrarch and the Italians, a courtier's urbanity but moments of emotional depth or satirical force, and above all, of course, a similar role in the literary history of their countries in each case unannounced by the self-conscious claims and congratulations that accompanied the poetry of later decades. Although Wyatt preferred to imitate the Italians it seems fair to believe he read Marot with pleasure and recognition.

Wyatt was content some of the time to work with the fixed forms. Surrey, more "modern" in his experiments and translations, took a rondeau by Marot and made it into a short lyric which sounds as though it were trying to turn into a sonnet:

> Au temps passé, Apelles, Painctre sage,
> Feit seullement de Venus le visage
> Par fiction, mais (pour plus hault attaindre)
> Ton Pere a faict de Venus (sans rien faindre)
> Entierement la face & le corsage.
>
> Car il est Painctre & tu es son ouvrage,
> Mieulx resemblant Venus de forme & d'aage
> Que le Tableau qu'Apelles voulut paindre
>   Au temps passé.
> Vray est qu'il feit si belle son ymage
> Qu'elle eschauffoit en Amour maint courage;
> Mais celle là que ton Pere a sceu taindre
> I mect le feu & a dequoy l'estaindre.

> L'aultre n'eut pas ung si gros advantage
> > Au temps passé.

> Yf he that erst the fourme so livelye drewe
> Of Venus faas, tryumpht in paynteres arte;
> Thy father then what glorye shall ensue,
> By whose pencell a goddesse made thow arte!
> Touchid with flame, that figure made some rewe,
> And with her love surprysed manye a hart.
> > There lackt yet that should cure their hoot desyer:
> > Thou canst enflame and quenche the kyndled fyre.[16]

The translation seems to freeze a moment in the evolution of poetic forms, or at least in the development of English attitudes toward those forms. Surrey was willing to adopt Marot's conceit, although he simplifies its implications and saves the "point" for the very end. But he appears to have shared Marot's own increasing interest in structures that allow more flexibility than the "formes fixes" and that may have felt less old-fashioned to a young aristocrat familiar with the courts of England and France. Here instead of the modifications and accumulations encouraged by structural repetition there is a greater urgency of movement toward a sharply delineated conclusion. (In the next century the point of this same seductive logic emerges even more explicitly when William Cartwright borrows the conceit and marches his brisk couplets toward an overt invitation into bed. What Marot had hinted at and Surrey suggested Cartwright says openly—lest this triumph of nonfiction be mistaken for one of her father's works of art—"We two'l Embrace, and Love, and clear the doubt. / When you've brought forth your Like, the world will know / You are his Child; what Picture can do so.")[17]

Some poems by Wyatt and Surrey appeared in Tottel's *Miscellany* (1557), but not those which echo or adapt Marot. On occasion, however, the collection recalls his subjects or forms, although there are no ballades or rondeaux—by 1557 too passé for an anthology published, the printer says, "to the honor of the Englishe tong, and for profit of the studious of Englishe eloquence." One poem borrows a little from an epistle and another, a gracious tribute to Henry VIII's friend Sir Anthony Denny, adapts an elegant epitaph for Florimont de Champeverne in which Marot imagines that the king and Death contend to prove who bears the king's servant the greater love (the king offers Florimont all sorts of worldly honors but Death grants him Paradise). The anonymous translator follows Marot's line of thought fairly closely, but he arranges the rhyme scheme so he can sum up the poem in a final couplet, making the English version more epigrammatic than the original—and more like a Shakespearean sonnet.[18]

There is clear evidence, then, that a few English writers turned to Marot at least for models and "inventions." If the examples are not numerous, they do suggest an interest in Marot's work at an important time in the history of English poetry.

This interest then seems to lapse until the late 1570s. By now Du Bellay and Ronsard had long since published the poems for which they were to be known in England, Desportes was setting the fashion at the court of Henri III, and Du Bartas's *Premiere sepmaine* was in print. Yet some English writers seem again to have found Marot useful as well as pleasing. Translators of his poetry in the last decades of the sixteenth century were often attracted to the little lyrics—amused celebrations of pretty girls and sometimes frustrated, sometimes hopeful, hints at the elusive delights of "jouissance." But just as those who borrowed from him for the *Miscellany* had preferred the currently fashionable epigram and verse epistle, so Spenser, announcing himself as England's new poet in *The Shepheardes Calender* (1579), adapted two of Marot's eclogues: one on the death of Louise de Savoie and one a song from Marot to the king "soubz les noms de Pan et Robin."[19] His choice was particularly appropriate. As Spenser would have known, Marot was often and justly thought of as an innovator, the leading poet at a time of change and rebirth; yet he was also associated closely with the lesser "kinds" of poetry. By his imitation of Marot, Spenser in a sense furthered his claim to the same sort of role at this stage in his career—that of bringing to the vernacular a new voice and a new sort of poetry but not as yet attempting the higher strains of the *Aeneid*, of Ronsard's epic and hymns, or of the *Faerie Queene* still to come.

The eclogue lamenting the death of a queen and Marot's haunting evocation of mutability in his shivering old age are each

thematically related to the end of the *Calender* when the focus
moves, as one modern reader puts it, from man's harvesting of
nature to the inevitable and frightening reverse.[20] But Spenser's
aims in *The Shepheardes Calender* were far too multiple to allow a
simple translation of Marot's pastorals. And since neither of
Marot's eclogues is particularly obscure or dense, although the
poetry is often resonant and suggestive, they are all the more
susceptible to Spenser's further allegorizing. Each poem, then, is
thoroughly reworked and made to serve the larger structure and
many-vectored energies of the *Calender*. For instance, Spenser
could not retain Marot's "voice"; in each of the original eclogues
the chief speaker in effect represents Marot himself—not the full
human being, of course, but still a figure recognizable as Clément.
If Spenser's shepherd Colin is meant to recall the author, he is also
a character in his own right and what he says tells us more about
himself, such as his gloomy disillusion with love and the pastoral
world, than about his creator.

The "Eglogue sur le Trespas de ma Dame Loyse de Savoye,
Mere du Roy François" is occasional poetry, a public and ritual
performance of "dueil ordonné" written on behalf of an entire
nation about a well-known figure whose only pastoral disguise in
the poem is her position as mother of the "grand Berger"—and
there is no doubt about that shepherd's identity. Spenser's aim in
the November eclogue, on the other hand, has remained somewhat
obscured by the difficulty of knowing just who the dead "Dido" is
supposed to be. The extreme language with which Colin sings her
loss—not only does the natural world decay and fall but even the
"sonne of all the world is dimme and darke"—seems to push the
verse beyond seasonal exactitude toward a hidden meaning of
some sort that makes this death more mysterious than that of
Louise. In any event Spenser converts the pathos of a monarch's
physical subjection to death into Colin's more generalized dismay
at the "wofull waste of natures warke" and the "trustlesse state of
earthly things." He keeps much of Marot's somewhat strained
pathetic fallacy (which in a poem about a dead monarch, however,
acquires a certain mythic justification), but he eliminates some of
the preciosity—not for him the desolated sheep whose wool turns
black in mourning nor touches like the image of the dead lady in
heaven with the pet parrot who predeceased her. In November

Colin is in no mood for such fantasy, whatever the affirmations of his vision of Dido in the "Elisian fieldes so free."

In December Colin is even more disconsolate as he makes a complaint based in part on Marot's lovely appeal to the king for help in his troubled old age. Each shepherd recalls the spring days of "l'arondelle qui volle" and the pipings in summer, and each now observes the last days of autumn as the birds wheel in the sky and he finds his head "besprent with hoary frost." But Marot's lament for lost green seasons, melancholy in its mood of elegiac recollection, is lightened by a witty grace that begs a favor yet keeps its dignity.[21] Nor is Marot hopeless about the coming winter, for if the same Pan who first made the flute (a gracious compliment to François as patron of letters) will only help him protect his little flock he will pick up his pipes and play again. Colin's lament echoes many of Marot's phrases, his structure, and his comparison of a human life to the year, but his song is darker. Recalling the destructiveness of love and the ignorance of youth, Colin anticipates only silence. Even more than Marot, Spenser ties his images to a pattern of growth and decay, to the fact of mortality and its implications for shepherds and poets alike.[22]

A year after the publication of *The Shepheardes Calender*, Humfrey Gifford printed a lugubrious poem in his *Posie of gilloflowers* (1580) based on an elegy "Written in French, by Clement Marott" (sig. D3). Like his eclogues, sonnets, and epigrams, Marot's elegies are important in French literary history—the first of their kind—but this one, a sorrowful letter to her mother from a *mal mariée*, suffers in Gifford's *Posie* from being deprived of whatever interest its context among the other elegies could give it.[23] The sorrow of the phoenix "des Dames langoreuses" are unmodified by the pull of other investigations of love and Gifford's sad fourteeners do nothing to relieve the monotonous tears of the lady's "moyst and weeping eies." Gifford must have been drawn by the work's pathos—the anguish of the caged bird, the archetypal image of the captured girl and helpless mother—and the opportunity it gave him to "moane,/In dumps of deepe despite." But although a minor poet, perhaps even a minimal one, he was nevertheless forward-looking in attempting the elegy. In this attention to Marot's innovations, if in no other regard, he is like Spenser and the authors in Tottel.

During the next few years translations from Marot were all, so

far as I know, from the chansons or "epigrams." One is a brief
complaint to "Crueltye lodged in greate Bewtye" by Sir Arthur
Gorges, a minor but talented writer who knew Spenser, and in
1595 Spenser himself published two little lyrics borrowed from
Marot. Like earlier translators he changes the poems to make them
tighter and adjusts the rhyme schemes to give a more epigrammatic impulse. The result has great charm, although some of
Marot's humor evaporates and the tone and rhythms seem to me a
little flatter. In the following translation, for instance, Spenser
either did not observe or did not care to recapture the casual
reproach in the first line or the entertaining play on Cupid's
blindness in the last:

> Amour trouva celle qui m'est amere,
> Et je y estois; j'en sçay bien mieulx le compte.
> Bon jour (dit il) bon jour, Venus, ma mere.
> Puis, tout acoup, il voit qu'il se mescompte,
> Dont la couleur au Visage luy monte
> D'avoir failly, honteux, Dieu sçait combien.
> Non, non, Amour (ce dis je) n'ayez honte,
> Plus cler voyans que vous s'y trompent bien.

> I saw in secret to my Dame,
> How little Cupid humbly came:
>   and sayd to her All hayle my mother.
> But when he saw me laugh, for shame
> His face with bashfull blood did flame,
>   not knowing Venus from the other,
> Then never blush Cupid (quoth I)
>   for many have err'd in this beauty.[24]

Finally, in Francis Davison's *Poetical Rhapsody* (1602), there is a
poem in which this tendency to urge Marot's lyrics closer to a
sonnet form is fully realized. Davison changes the end of the poem
slightly to make the point more explicit—perhaps he found
Marot's version more fraternal than sexual in its implication:

> Estre Phebus bien souvent je desire,
> Non pour congnoistre herbes divinement;
> Car la douleur qui mon cueur veult occire
> Ne se guerist par herbe aulcunement;

Non pour avoir ma place au Firmament,
Car en la terre habite mon plaisir;
Non pour son arc encontre Amour saisir,
Car à mon Roy ne veulx estre rebelle;
Estre Phebus seulement j'ay desir
Pour estre aymé de Diane la belle.

Phœbus of all the Gods I wish to bee:
    Not of the World to have the overseeing
    For of all things in the Worlds circuit being,
    One only thing I alwaies wish to see.
Not of all hearbes the hidden force to know,
    For ah my wound by hearbes cannot be cured:
    Not in the Sky to have a place assured,
    For my ambition lies on Earth belowe.
Not to be Prince of the Celestiall quire,
    For I one Nymph prize more then all the Muses
    Not with his bow to offer Love abuses
    For I Loves Vassall am, and dread his yre.
But that thy light from mine, might borrow'd be,
And faire Diana might shine under me.[25]

These are the only poems I know about that are undoubted adaptations from Marot, although other traces of his phrasing or technique appear here and there.[26] The number of translations, borrowings, and echoes is too small for many confident conclusions, but it seems safe to say that English poets indebted to Marot were chiefly interested in his pastorals and love poems, that translations of his short lyrics are usually restructured to give them a sharper point (perhaps thus rendering them less old-fashioned or more decisive and dramatic), and that translators sometimes sacrifice, deliberately or not, Marot's witty lightness of touch and urbanity of tone. English poets, moreover, neglected Marot's satires and mocking epistles, maybe because such poetry is too specific in its application, or maybe because its flavor is not the sort that translates readily. There is nothing to be wondered at here, but it is likely this particular neglect limited and distorted Marot's reputation in England. What was best about him was simply harder to assimilate—perhaps harder, even, to understand—than the more conventional humor or sentiment his poetry exhibits when the original flavor has been leached out by translation or by the semicomprehension with which many of us read poetry in a foreign language.

Any discussion of Marot's reputation in England must also take into account the impact of the Geneva Psalter, to which he contributed and which in a sense he initiated with his translation of forty-nine psalms into French verse.[27] Marot began his translation in the 1530s and by 1539 had finished thirty psalms; during his exile in Geneva he revised them and wrote nineteen more. Together with the translations by Beza, they form the Huguenot psalter of 1562. Marot's versions had been popular at once, sung freely at court and praised even by the Emperor Charles. And although after a while many Catholics had second thoughts, Marot's psalms only grew in influence. In fact it is hard to exaggerate the role eventually played by the completed psalter in the spiritual life of Protestant Europe. Its immense impact was due in part to the melodies, which were considered quite lively, and to the virtuosity with which Marot, especially, shaped the poetry into an extraordinary variety of metrical patterns and rhyme schemes. There were some complaints that these meters were unfit for the Hebrew psalms, yet a good case can be made that Marot's success lay in his ability to retain much of the concrete diction and the syntactic parallelism of the original while delicately providing logical links and syntactical devices, such as subordination, that clarify the meaning and render the style less alien to his own language and culture. The result is not Hebraic (and in any event Marot worked from translations), but compared to other attempts Marot's poetry seems a sensitive compromise.[28]

What was to be the French Protestant psalter, then, was begun about the same time as the English Reformation and was in the process of development just as many English Protestants were fleeing to Geneva. Understandably, therefore, the English knew and often admired the translations of Marot and Beza. Some owned copies of the Psalter, others quoted it, and many English translations of the psalms that venture out of common meter show French influence on their metrical structures and rhyme schemes. Among those whose versions have striking similarities with at least some of Marot's are Sir Philip Sidney and his sister the Countess of

Pembroke, Joseph Hall, Francis Davison, George Wither, and George Sandys. There were also at least two English translations based explicitly on French models. One is *Al the French psalm tunes with English words*, printed in 1592 and reprinted in 1632, an enterprise that seems to have involved some interchurch cooperation, being "Perused and approved by judicious Divines, both English and Frenche."[29] It gives the "so celebrated tunes" and English texts which follow the French patterns of meter and rhyme. The other, not complete, is by the truculent Puritan John Vicars, who added "Divers of Davids Psalmes, According to the French Forme and Metre" to his *Englands hallelu-jah* (1631, sig. C8).

Marot's psalms were available in the original, too, and if an Englishman was curious to know them but lacked the sevenpence his bookseller would charge he might in some places hear them sung in Huguenot churches by the growing number of French refugees.[30] There was also an attempt to publish an English edition of the French psalter: an entry in the Stationers' Register for October 1, 1599, reads "A booke to be printed in Frenche onelye Called. les CL pseaumes de David mises in Rimme Ffrancoise per Clement Marot et Theodore De Beze." It seems reasonable, in sum, to suppose that a number of Englishmen knew the French versions of the psalms, and had they looked at the title page of the psalter they would have found Marot's name. Whatever the English thought of him, many must have been aware that he had contributed to one of the major texts of French Protestantism.

It would be an error, however, to conclude that those who read or imitated Marot's psalms did so only from that rigid and solemn piety sometimes associated with a strong taste for scriptural verse. It is true that for many people biblical translations and adaptations provided a welcome alternative to much secular literature; nor is there any question that for Marot and other translators their metrical versions were fruits of a duty to God and man. But we tend to forget that such efforts were often seen not as rejections of secular abilities but rather as their spiritual fulfillment. In his preface Marot had written that David was the real Apollo, the Holy Spirit his Calliope, that his "vers divins, ses chansons mesurées" surrounded the lovesick soul with a medicinal garden and had the power to affect even the Almighty. Much of what Marot says recalls not mainstream Calvinism but the Renaissance syncretism which was to be of increasing importance in France.[31] That the psalms were to be sung tied them all the more to current hopes for finding a marriage of words and music that would powerfully affect the hearers, much as had the songs of Hebrew and Greek antiquity, and thus restore harmony to the soul and to Christendom.

A similar complexity of motive would be found in a number of English translations indebted to Marot. Sidney, for instance, thought David a *vates* and his psalms "a heavenly poesy, wherein almost he shows himself a passionate lover of that unspeakable and everlasting beauty to be seen by the eyes of the mind only cleared by faith." Sidney was drawn to the psalms through strong religious feeling, no doubt, but like Marot and many others he believed Scripture scaled heights of *literary* accomplishment that surpassed even the Greek and Roman.[32] Sidney, probably, was particularly interested in the comments by Philippe Du Plessis Mornay, whose *Trewnesse of the christian religion* (1587) he helped translate: the ancient Greeks and Romans, Mornay says, sang "vauntings of men, counterfetted prayses, and discourses of Love Songs," so that now "it seemes unpossible for man to be a Poet, a Divine, and an Historiographer all togither. So farre are our mirth and songs estraunged naturally from God and from trueth." But in David's poetry we find victory chants, wedding songs, "songs of the very Love it self," and pastorals. "The arte of them is so excellent, that it is an excellencie even to translate them" (sigs. Dd5–Dd5ᵛ). And like Mornay, Sidney had a keen if restrained interest in Neoplatonism and in the mysteries of Pythagoras and Hermes. It is probable, in other words, that his rendition of the psalms, like Marot's, was an homage to the Creator but also and simultaneously an attempt to capture in the vernacular some of the visionary power, the *furor* leading to true Love, which characterized the greatest "divine poetry." The French psalms, then, were religious poetry and were read and sung as such in England, but they can also be seen as the culmination of other experiments in the "imitation" of ancient forms; English response to the Geneva Psalter is not unrelated to translations from Marot's elegies, pastorals, and "epigrams."

On occasion Englishmen referred to Marot. Some references merely mention a virtue; others attempt to place his poetry in a historical context; still others note some silliness or shortcoming.

To read these remarks is like looking at a double exposure of the
same actor in different costumes: two Marots appear, one a parody
of the other. Nor did one Marot simply replace the other, for
compliments to him continue into the seventeenth century and so
do suggestions of his failures and follies—his "image" remained
out of focus, as though the English were not quite sure what to
make of him.

One of these two Marots exercised his talent and wit as a protégé
of the great patron of learning François I, and in those days of
reform and revival, it was said, helped civilize the French language. An early if mindless reference to this Marot appears in some
lines Thomas Churchyard offered as an introduction to Skelton's
Pithy pleasaunt and profitable workes (1568). Time, Churchyard
observes, cannot "rust and canker worthy artes," so Englishmen
should emulate those other nations that have fostered writers able
to condemn vice and praise virtue:

> You see howe forrayn realms,
>   Advance their Poets all:
> And ours are drowned in the dust,
>   Or flong against the wall,
> In Fraunce did Marrot raigne,
>   and neighbour thear unto:
> Was Petrark, marching full with Dantte,
>   Who erst did wonders do. . . .[33]

This is barely coherent criticism, but the phrasing shows an
awareness of Marot as an important author, and the word
"neighbour," whatever the anachronism, implies he deserved to
keep some illustrious company. Many years later Churchyard still
admired Marot, and although time had brought no greater subtlety to his thought he now had more recent names to add. His
Musicall consort of heavenly harmonie (1595) hastily summarizes what
the reader should know about vernacular literature and its
triumphs:

> In France three more of fame we finde
> Whose bookes do well declare
> They beautifide their stately minde
> With inward vertues rare. . . .

[sig. E4]

A marginal note identifies these three as "Marrot, Ronsart, and du Bartas." Churchyard is silent as to what Marot's particular inward virtues might have been.

This first Marot was not only famous but talented. A poem contributed by one Jean Wrothe, "Gentilhomme Anglois," to Bellot's *French Grammer* explains why the reader should learn French (although he will have to know French to understand the explanation):

> En vain de veoir Marot tu seras curieux,
> (Ou de Beze, ou Bellay) les chants melodieux,
> En beau mettre françois deça, dela épars:
> En vain veoirras Froissard, Ronsard, Collet, Jodelle,
> Racontans l'un l'amour, l'autre Guerre cruelle,
> Sy tu n'as du françois parfaite Intelligence. . . .
>
> [sig. A6]

Essentially a puff for the book to follow, Wrothe's poem need not be taken seriously as a considered judgment, but it is interesting for its praise of Marot's melody and "mettre," his technical skill.

Marot was also charming and clever, or so says Claudius Holyband's *De pronuntiatione linguae gallicae* (1580). Holyband (who had been Desainliens in his native France) was a friend of Bellot and like him seems to have preferred Marot to the poets of the Pléiade. He urges his students to start with a French New Testament—advice still sometimes given beginners—and then to move to *Amadis de Gaule*, Belleforest, and Boaistuau's *Théâtre du monde* (a popular item with textbook writers, for it is moral enough to bend young twigs in the right direction yet bustles with interesting information and vivid anecdote). Then, says Holyband, as the consummation of their labor they should familiarize themselves with "our poet Marot, whose like France sees not nor will see, because of his charms [*lepores*] and witticisms [*sales*] and agreeable modes of expression" (sig. B3ᵛ). Holyband was himself an endearing writer whose bilingual dialogues show an affectionate and humorous observation of London life. Perhaps this temperament gave him a particularly close understanding of Marot, for his word *lepores*, with its connotations of wit, charm, grace, and humor, could not have been better chosen.

The same Marot appears briefly in Gabriel Harvey's marginalia; his copy of Dionysius Periegetes's *Surveye of the world* (1572) contains the appreciative note, "Sum not unlike astrological descriptions in the notablest French Poets: cheifly in livelie Marot, florishing Ronsard, admirable Bartas, etc."[34] Since there is little about the stars in Marot's poetry it is hard to see quite what Harvey meant by this reference, but in any case his word "livelie" is significant, for it suggests not only Marot's vivacity, the *sales* Holyband enjoyed, but also the quality known in the rhetoric books as *energia* and often translated in England as "spirit." Years afterward William Browne, a fine pastoral poet who had perhaps read Marot's eclogues, fleetingly complimented him on this *energia* in a passage telling "What wights should have their temples crown'd with Bayes." One of his shepherds (a well-read man) says that "Learn'd Ariosto," "holy Petrarch," and Tasso should "ascend the Muses hill." Most deserving is Du Bartas, but

> Marot and Ronsard, Garnier's buskind Muse
> Should spirit of life in very stones infuse.
> And many another Swan whose powerful straine
> Should raise the Golden World to life againe.[35]

For some who knew his works, then, or who wrote as if they did, Marot was a clever poet with charm and spirit. It is also true, however, that there was little direct focus on his particular talent for irony and mockery. Marot's thieving valet, about whom he wrote one of his most brilliant epistles, seems to have been known in Scotland, but the poem that recounts the story converts the original's sophisticated self-deprecation into amusing narrative:

> Gud Clemet Marit had a lowne—
> A knaif that cumbart all the towne,
> With spreitis employed to everie vice,
> As whoredome, drincking, cartis, and dyce;
> To sweir, to ban, to steill, and tak:
> Ane never my^t trow a word he spak;
> In everie ludgene whair he wald licht,
> Taking his leive without gud nych [t]. . . .[36]

(Marot had added dryly that his villainous servant was "Au demeurant, le meilleur filz du Monde" and a great favorite with the girls.)

A few Englishmen also commented upon Marot's relationship with François I, whose patronage of letters was useful to recall both as an example of liberality to open the hands and purses of modern noblemen and as one more answer to the scoffers and Momuses who thought poetry a waste of time at best, a lie at worst. Thus George Puttenham, who begins his *Arte of English poesie* (1589) with the familiar claim that poets, filled with divine fury, first brought civilization, soon moves to strengthen his case by citing those princes and statesmen who had rewarded good poetry. Among them is François I, who "made Sangelais, Salmonius, Macrinus, and Clement Marot of his privy Chamber for their excellent skill in vulgare and Latine Poesie."[37] More than a generation later the prolific and amusing Richard Brathwait repeated Puttenham's words to help clinch a similar argument in his *English gentleman* (1630, sig. Bb4). He even retained the sundering comma by which Puttenham or his printer had multiplied Salmon Macrin into two separate authors.

Marot the witty court poet was also a reformer of the vernacular, according to several tributes based on the yet widespread assumption that languages can in fact be improved, "illustrated," by conscious effort or degraded and mildewed by neglect and misuse. One such compliment is by Daniel Rogers, the diplomat and neo-Latin poet whose years in Paris and friendship with French poets provided a link between the French Renaissance and a number of English writers. Rogers knew Baïf and Ronsard, yet when writing of Chaucer he naturally recalled not the Pléiade but the precursor: "As great as was Boccaccio in Tuscan speech, as much as of old the Italian tongue delighted in thee, O Petrarch, and as discourse in the French language grows elevated now that Marot fits native words to the poet's lyre,—thus much and so wert thou, Geoffrey Chaucer, among thy Britons; by genius a poet no less powerful over English speech; under this master our tongue now lives with those graces which this man or that man gave to the Italians and the French."[38] Writing in the next century, however, James Howell was less impressed; "The French Language," he says, "began first to be polish'd, and arrive at that delicacy she is now come to, in the midst of the Reign of Philip de Valois. Marot did something under Francis I. (which King was a Restorer of Learning in general, as well as of Language); but Ronsard did

more under Henry II."[39] Like Rogers, Howell stresses Marot's
impact on the language itself, an impact here associated more with
polish than with power or eloquence.

This same faint praise ("Marot did something") was accorded
him in a series of remarks which derive from Du Bartas's "Babylone," a book in his *Seconde sepmaine* (1584), and from the commentary on Du Bartas by the Protestant scholar Simon Goulart.
Du Bartas explains that the "pillars" of the French language are
Marot, Amyot, Ronsard, and Mornay (chiefly for his persuasive
assaults on atheism). He regards the first, however, as a ruin:

> Mais qui sont les François? Ce terme sans façon,
> D'où la grossiere main du paresseux maçon
> A levé seulement les plus dures escailles,
> C'est toy, Clement Marot, qui, furieux, travailles
> Artistement sans art, et poingt d'un beau soucy,
> Transportes Helicon d'Italie en Quercy.
> Marot, que je revere ainsi qu'un colisee
> Noircy, brisé, moussu, une medaille usee,
> Un escorné tombeau, non tant pour leur beauté
> Que pour le sainct respect de leur antiquité.

Goulart adds, "Clement Marot, admirable pour son temps,
attendu l'ignorance et rudesse des siecles precedens, a fait passer
les monts aux Muses, et les a habillees à la Françoise: comme entre
autres sienes oeuvres, la translation de 49. Pseaumes de David
(laquelle durera autant que l'Oui et le Non) le monstre suffisam-
ment. Il n'a pas l'art ni les graces de quelques uns qui sont venus
depuis: mais il a fait merveilles en ces commencemens là, et en
suivant son naturel a monstré qu'il pouvoit beaucoup s'il eust
voulu: voire qu'en certains endroits il a si bien dit, qu'un autre
(quel qu'il soit) ne sçauroit dire mieux."[40] Du Bartas and Goulart
at least try to give Marot his due, whatever the latter's suggestion
that he was an underachiever and the tone of condescension in
both writers. The phrase "en suivant son naturel" is especially
interesting; this is not the only time that an older author's carefully
acquired technique has sounded to later readers like native wood-
notes wild. Marot is thus credited with some *furor poeticus*, but not
with art—a view of his talents and accomplishments diametrically
opposed to that of many critics in future centuries.

John Eliot's semisatirical textbook *Ortho-epia Gallica* (1593) is
much indebted to these passages.[41] Eliot praises Marot in his
introduction, including him among those wits "inimitable in
Poësie" who have written "Love-toies," but he seems (or pretends)
to have heard some unkind rumours about the man. He sets the
record straight in a dialogue on literature between a master and his
pupil which well illustrates the light-hearted tone of the whole
work. The master speaks first:

> First you have Clement Marot, that was King Francis
> Poet, who was admirable for his time.
>
> He was made the Kings foole, for since his time they call all
> fooles and idiots in France Marots, You are a Marot, say
> they, A vengeance of the Marot.
>
> You deceive your selfe greatly, he was the Poet Roiall, not
> a foole royall: of whom the fine poesies shall be read and read
> again, as long as Yea and Nay shall last amongst learned
> men.
>
> You will pardon me sir, for I speake no otherwise then a
> foole by heare say and at all adventure.
>
> They say that he transported the Muses beyond the moun-
> taines, and attyred them on the French fashion. He hath
> done marvellous well in his beginnings truly.
>
> Hold him of my word for a naturall Poet: when you shall
> understand French perfectly read me his bookes, if you have
> the leisure.
>
> [sigs. G4^v-H1]

Eliot is having fun. More seriously meant, or at least more
soberly expressed, is George Hakewill's *Apologie or declaration of the
power and providence of God* (Oxford, 1627), an important and
influential attack upon the belief in the world's decay. Hakewill,
too, had read "Babylone," and he seems to find Marot if not an
ancient then not quite a modern either. Writers like Ariosto, Tasso,
Du Bartas, and Sidney may be justly cited to match Virgil, he says,
and as for the very oldest authors it is true

> among the Greekes and Latines which Bartas hath of
> Marrot.
> Thee Marrot I esteeme even as an old Colosse
> All soyled, broke, overgrowen with mosse,

Worn picture, Tombe defac'd, not for fine worke I see,
But in devoute regard of their antiquity.
                                                                   [sig. Gg3]

The quotation comes from a translation of "Babylone" by the
scholar William Lisle, who later used the same lines himself in a
defense of Anglo-Saxon studies. Old English, he says in *Divers
ancient monuments* (1638), may seem archaic now, but "well saith Du
Bartas of that old French Poet. . . ." The passage from "Babylone"
follows (sig. F1). It is disheartening that in the time of Hakewill
and Lisle, less than a century after his death, Marot could have
been considered quite this antique. True, he had sometimes been
compared to Chaucer, but now he is pushed back, with the respect-
ful concern given valuable but dilapidated heirlooms, to the days of
King Alfred or even Hesiod.

Du Bartas may have found Marot worn and mossy, but there is
nothing seriously derogatory in what he says or in the comments of
those who quote him. Other references, however, are amused or
even disdainful. At his most foolish this second "Marot" was a sort
of court jester, whose antics were funny or scandalous and at whom
one could smile with little respect.

Two criticisms suggest Marot's limitations as a poet. One is a
complaint in the 1578 edition of *The Mirror for Magistrates* that by
using rhyme Churchyard, Buckhurst, Phaer, Turberville, Golding, and Gascoigne have failed to equal the ancients, "for al these
comming neare unto Marot whom they did imitate, did put a great
distance betwixt them and the Latines."[42] That Marot, not Du
Bellay or Ronsard, receives the blame for deflecting so many
English poets away from true "imitation" at least shows the extent
of his fame during the years which saw the translations by Spenser
and the quotations by Bellot and Vautrollier—although English
writers hardly needed foreign models to set them off rhyming. The
other denigration of Marot specifies no such particular shortcoming. E.K., the so far unidentified annotator of *The Shepheardes
Calender*, includes Marot among those "excellent both Italian and
French Poetes, whose foting this Author every where followeth,"
but when in his notes to the January eclogue he tells us that the
name "Colin" was "used of the French Poete Marot," he adds
ungraciously, "(if he be worthy of the name of a Poete)."[43]

It is at least possible E.K. meant that a man with Marot's

reputation was not a real maker or *vates*, for a number of other references show that some found him too silly to take seriously as an important poet. Marot's love poetry was known in England, for instance, but except for John Eliot I can find no one who praised him for it. Instead one finds George Gascoigne tolerantly if nervously reminding the reader of his *Posies* (1575) that after all most authors have written a few immodest works; Ovid did so, and so did Virgil and Ariosto—"And let not Marots Alyx passe, without impeach of crime." (Alyx was an insatiable peasant girl about whom Marot wrote some crudely funny epigrams.) Or there is the following poem in Kendall's *Flowers of Epigrammes*, based on a by no means derogatory original by Beza in his early frivolous vein:

> Apelles learned hand, so fine
>   did paint fair Venus Queene:
> That every one susposd that he,
>   had Venus vewd and seen.
> But workes of thine Marotus lewd,
>   of Venus savour so:
> That every one sure deemes, that thou
>   dost all of Venus know.[44]

When John Weever adapted the same insult for his *Epigrammes* (1599) he left out the reference to Marot, simply calling the poem *"In Spurium quendam scriptorem"* (sig. E2).

This reaction may be merely symptomatic of a more widespread uneasiness toward all love poetry, for while it is true that Petrarch was sometimes praised (often by fellow poets and not always for his sonnets) Renaissance England, especially toward the end of the period, found it difficult to discuss this sort of verse comfortably. The age was not unique in this feeling, of course; doubts about the value of nondidactic poetry extend from Plato to modern undergraduates searching for relevance or jobs. Nevertheless, one is impressed by the sheer number and virulence of sixteenth- and seventeenth-century attacks upon just the sort of "love toies" Marot wrote so well, love toys which lacked even a pretended claim to esoteric significance. "Tel me is Christ, or Cupide Lord? doth God or Venus reigne?" Those who write this garbage, declares one angry observer, are nothing but "Squitter–wits miscalled Poets."[45]

Luckily most squitter-wits were unabashed, but the attacks, reinforced by objections to the "Sinne-sweld Theatres," must have had some inhibiting effect on written and public praise of love poetry, especially since the poets themselves shared too many of their opponents' assumptions to carry a defense of non-philosophical love toys much beyond the casual humor with which Harington insists most of us really like the stuff or Sidney hopes that its dispraisers will fail in love for "lacking skill of a sonnet." Nor did Marot help matters by his frank admission that he wanted the lady's physical self in bed ("Suis je de fer, ou Ange?"). Nothing Platonic; nothing allegorical; not even a marriage. Astrophil had at least struggled against similar desires.[46]

Marot's career as a court poet seems also to have become distorted in some fashion. He seldom wrote of himself and his work as confidently as did later poets and he may have appeared undignified because his self-mockery was misunderstood or because the gracious humility with which he addressed the powerful was taken too literally. No doubt his difficulties with Church and State only enhanced this image, for his rapid exits and entrances at court and jail seem to have moved some members of a tough-minded generation not to pity or admiration but merely to a sort of contempt for his foolishness in getting himself into trouble. Marot had come close to martyrdom, but he did not actually suffer it and thus elevate his escapades to tragic prelude. Certainly there is little sympathy in Joseph Hall's image of this other, ridiculous, Marot. The satirist and future bishop writes in his *Virgidemiae* (borrowing a phrase from Scaliger) of how

> thred-bare Martiall turnes his merry note
> To beg of Rufus a cast winter cote;
> Whiles hungry Marot leapeth at a Beane
> Ands dieth like a starv'd Cappucien. . . .[47]

Just as unflattering is a story about Marot in John Wodroephe's *Marrow of the French tongue* (1623). Wodroephe quotes a French psalm (without credit) to illustrate the value of translating Scripture, but in a lesson on words ending in "alle" he says, "Clement Marot se cacha dans la malle grasse du Ray de France, estant dans ses malgraces (ou plustost mauvaises graces, mieuxdict:) Clement Marot hid himselfe in the king of France his great fat bag, or wallet, being in his disfavours etc." The margin explains the pun for the slow-witted: "Pour signifier Malgraces, pource qu'il y estoit aussi" (1625 ed., sigs. B6–B6ᵛ).

In this episode Marot is a clown, the French court's comic relief. Harvey, it will be remembered, had called him "livelie," but in another context he wrote: "Poggius was merry, and Panormitan wise: Marot was merry, and Bellay wise: Scoggin was merry, and the Lord Cromwell wise: Greene was merry, and Sir Christopher Hatton wise: Nash is merry, and there be enough wise, though his mothers sonne be Pierce Penniles."[48] Spirited and lively Marot has fallen in with a bad crowd: Poggio the indecent, Scoggin the court fool and jestbook hero, and two men Harvey claimed to find contemptible.

Still equipped with cap and bells Marot shows up in two mock encomia printed with *Coryats crudities* (1611), jokes that may explain the student's confusion in Eliot's dialogue. Thomas Coryate had for some years entertained the English court with his buffoonery, his odd looks, and his willing acceptance, even invitation, of good-humored teasing (one adventure found him, like Wodroephe's Marot, shut up in a trunk). When he hoped to publish a long description of his travels in Europe he asked his many acquaintances to write commendatory verses. This they did and the result is a very funny parody of the usual promotional material. One poem says grandly, "Thee of the Marrot worthy doe we deeme." Now, according to Cotgrave's dictionary the word "Marotte" meant a prince's scepter and also "a fooles bable"; the OED cites several instances of such usage in England. Coryate, however, who took this needling in good part and annotated the poetry with pretended incomprehension, says "That is the Lawrell, so called from one Marrot, a French Poet." With the same pun and the same tone of casual dismissal he explains a "sonnet composè en rime à la Marotte": "A scavoir selo[n] le style de Clement Marot vieil Poete Francois."[49]

At least, one would have thought, Marot's reputed Protestantism might have won him sympathy in England. It did not. In fact, although Marot was known in Europe as an anti-Catholic and although his modern editor says he was "pour ses contemporains un lutteur hardi qui s'en prend aux abus de son temps et aux institutions et doctrines qui avilissent l'homme," even some

Huguenots viewed him with impatience. Beza himself said in a work well known to Englishmen that Marot had helped the reformed church, made good poems, and suffered for his faith—but he also "consumed most of his life at court, the worst teacher of piety and virtue, nor ammended his hardly Christian habits even at the end of his life."[50]

In England Marot found little more sympathy than this. Sir John Wallop, for instance, told Henry VIII in a letter dated January 26, 1541, that "Francis sends ships and 500 or 600 footmen, to seek the 'trade of spicerey' by a shorter way than the Portingalles use, i.e. by the Mare Glasearum. Their pilot, Jacques Cartier, a Breton, thinks it will be navigable for three months in the year. The Captain of the footmen is Clement Marotte, who has been an exile for Lutheranism, and his men are malefactors and vagabonds, who can well be spared; so that if they never return it will be no great loss."[51] The passage is quite lacking in respect or pity, yet Wallop had known the French court well for some years and must have recognized the injustice to Marot. Was he simply passing along a dim witticism circulated by Marot's enemies? A passage in a letter from R. Jones to Richard Oseley, written in 1559 from Bar-le-Duc, is only a little more charitable. Jones is not altogether clear, but he seems to believe that Marot had been less heroic than indiscreet. The letter, which refers with grim humor to the persecutions in France and to the burning of heretics, is described as follows in the *Calendar of State Papers*:

> Thanks him for his dated the 4th inst. The Lord Ambassador and his family here have felt the extremity of the heats. Has been reading the follies of Amadis, and has studied so in Marot, that a companion has burned him for an heretic, as they would do the writer if he were no wiser than his book. Though the weather was hot, there has been as much roast meat in Paris without bread or drink as some have been dried up and consumed; and yet the seed springs so fast as there is good hope of mustard seed according to the Gospel. But he has bought a new Marot, and will study his follies, and so shall be out of danger, for vice is not so much punished here as virtue."[52]

Marot himself had almost been roasted in Paris.

Nor did the English often praise Marot by name for his versions of the psalms, although many must have noted at one time or another that he had written them. John Donne was probably thinking of the Geneva Psalter when he wrote that until Sidney's translations the psalms had been "So well attyr'd abroad, so ill at home," and Joseph Hall said of metrical psalms that "the French and the Dutch have given us worthy examples of a diligence and exquisitenesse in this kinde."[53] Neither man, however, mentions Marot. Almost certainly much of this neglect can be traced to the overshadowing reputation of the Protestant leader who completed the psalter and whose many learned books and political stature apparently won his efforts a more explicitly admiring and heartfelt response. Even Beza, however, did not escape censure—even contempt—for his translations.

Popular though the French psalms were, moreover, many disapproved of them. English reaction to Marot as a psalmist, particularly the image of him and his works that emerges in recusant writings, touches on and illustrates a much broader argument about how Christians might best use and interpret Scripture. At first Marot's psalms appealed not only to courtier and evangelical but even to Catholic poets who tried to continue what Marot had begun. Then the air chilled and Catholic attacks began in force, probably encouraged by the inclusion of doctrinal and didactic texts in the Geneva Psalter.[54] The objections varied but tended to revert to a few central claims: that Marot and Beza (chiefly Beza, whose other translations were subject to angry rejection by both Catholic and Lutheran scholars) distorted the meaning of the text; that the tunes and meters were too lively, too secular; that by their very popularity the psalms risked being "vulgar" in the worst sense; and that neither Marot nor Beza were qualified by their personalities and morals to translate the word of God.

Such scoffings were usually designed to add vigor and evidence to longer attacks on Calvinist theology and behavior, this last the subject of colorful slanders that would startle and perhaps reassure modern readers brought up to think "Puritans" a gloomy lot. Reformers lead vicious lives, claims one English recusant, Edmund Hill, in *A quartron of reasons* (Antwerp, 1600); among other misdoings "they season their errours with songes, and ballades in the vulgar tongue, to the end that the common people delighting to

heare and singe them, might thereby sucke theyr errours, as you
see them doe by the Geneva Psalmes, which women, children and
all sorts confusedlie sing, and so did the old heretiks, as historio-
graphers make mention" (sig. K6). (Hill's word "confusedlie" is
interesting since many Protestants, especially Calvinists, had
complained that older forms of church music had been in every
sense confusing, impossible to understand because of the complexities and mixtures of texts and musical lines. He also objects to
confusion but he finds consonance threatened not so much by
polyphony as by indecorous mixtures of people.) Beza himself
behaved shamelessly at the conference of Poissy in 1561, says the
Jesuit Parsons in *The warn-word* (Antwerp?, 1602), eating from
golden plates and then with his friends running "up and downe
woods, and feildes for recreation, sounding out your Geneva
psalmes, and other songs to refresh your spirits"—pastoral inter-
ludes one can only hope actually took place (sigs. V7^v–V8).

Many Protestants replied with strong denial, but others who
commented upon the psalms did so with unhappy awareness that
these rebukes existed and perhaps contained a little truth. Were
they really "Geneva Jiggs, and Beza's Ballets," as Wither says they
were sometimes called by Roman "sectaries"? (The insult is also
notable for its snobbery; jigs and ballads were "vulgar" as well as
profane.) Wither does not warmly defend the Marot–Beza version
but merely hopes in his own translation to "correct what deserves
amendment."[55] And a few years later William Vaughan, the sometimes dour author of *The church militant* (1640), who said he had no
liking for "Errant Knights" or the "Fairy Daunce," wrote of King
James's metrical versions

> His David Psalms our Belials so appall,
> None dare them now Geneva-jigges mis-call.
>
> [sigs. Z4, V5^v]

Earlier in the book Vaughan had written disparagingly of "Trivial
Tales, and sense-alluring Toyes," noting however that some poets
like Petrarch and Beza eventually give it all up, "Clozing their
Feast with Healths from Sions Fount" (sigs. A6, B2^v). In this
regard, except to some of his Catholic and Lutheran detractors,
Beza must have seemed very unlike Marot; whatever the latter's
contribution to psalmody he remained a court poet to the end, and

thus more vulnerable to ridicule and to exaggerated stories about his private life. Perhaps this vulnerability explains why in a discussion of poetry in *The golden grove* (1600) which borrows from Puttenham's line-up of royal patrons and their poets Vaughan omits Marot and Saint Gelais (sig. Y5^v).

Sensing this weakness, Catholic controversialists had sometimes mentioned Marot by name and urged his shabby morals (or what they thought were such) and his secular role as yet more reasons for rejecting the French psalter: "The Papists cast in the teeth of the Professors [i.e. Huguenots] in France, that they sing the Psalms translated in meeter by Clement Marot, a Courtly Gentleman," reported one Protestant, who added that during sixteen years on the Continent he "frequently did hear such scornful givings."[56] Marot was blasphemous, poisonous, ignorant, "Gascon de nation, Calviniste de Religion, bouffon de vacation, et de moeurs un vray bordelier. Qui . . . aussi apte à faire des vers, qu'un asne à joüer du violon, se voulut mesler de traduire ces Psalmes en vers François." Yes, he was a fine writer, wrote another Catholic, felicitous and clever, but also *ridiculus*, sarcastic, almost a clown (*scurra*), unable to break his bad habits, and he mutilated the psalms of David, destroying the majesty that once had shone from them.[57] The gossip recounted here and elsewhere had little truth but it is in the context of such remarks that one should see English reaction to Marot as a psalmist.

For some objections to Marot's work were made by Englishmen or at least aimed in part at an English audience. A few were offended by the very "literary" quality of the psalter that had commended it to Sidney and others. If the Word is inviolable, as even Calvin confesses, "pourquoy chantez vous en vos assemblées les Pseaumes de David, que Marot et Beze ont gastez et corrompus, y adjoustant et changeant tout ce qu'il leur a semblé, pour mieux faire leur rithme, quoy que le sens de l'Autheur deust estre perverti?" John Hay's question, asked in the French edition of *Certaine demandes* (1580), is indeed an awkward one, but other attacks went much further.[58]

In *Calvino-turcismus* (Antwerp, 1597), for instance, William Rainolds denounces the Huguenot psalter as a work of Mohammedan licentiousness. Some people claim, he says, that the metrical psalms are a good way to instill pure and simple truth.

And some have said Sleidan (the German Protestant historian)
praised them. But did he really? At this point Rainolds quotes
Sleidan's *Commentarii*: "Marot did not know much Latin but he
profited from his familiarity with the learned. Nor was there much
of anything in Tibullus, Propertius, and Ovid which escaped him;
some he put in his elegies. From Catullus he took his epithalamion
for Hercule of Ferrara and Renée the daughter of Louis XII and he
elegantly translated the first book of Ovid's *Metamorphoses*. By his
help was the whole psalter of David turned to French meters,
although after he had made only fifty psalms death took him."
Why, wonders Rainolds darkly, such a solemn introduction of
these Roman poets and praise for Marot's use of their "love-
flowers" (*venereis flosculis*) in his own poetry and then just at that
point the bringing forward of his metrical version of David's psalter? Probably to show that although Marot had little Latin he at
least knew enough Catullus and Tibullus to introduce their graces
(*lepores*) into his psalms, to scatter the ravings of Propertius and
Ovid over a work otherwise grave and severe so that he might more
greedily receive everything from the promiscuous multitude (sig.
S7^v).

Two years later Matthew Sutcliffe took on Rainolds passage by
passage in *De turcopapismo* (1599). He outlines the attack on
"Claudius Marottus" and objects, fairly enough, that Sleidan had
merely said Marot composed elegies in the manner of Tibullus,
Propertius, and Catullus. Rainolds, he explains, simply does not
want Scripture in the vernacular because he prefers people to read
"fabulous legends and Papal decretals" (sig. Dd3). Any confused
reader who wanted to check what Sleidan had in fact said could see
for himself in the English version, *A famouse cronicle of oure time*
(1560). Sleidan calls Marot the best poet of his day and after the
remarks which Rainolds quoted he adds that the psalms are "red
not without the admiration of hys excellent wit: for nothinge is
more pleasaunte than hys style, nothynge purer than his speache,
nothyng apter or more pleasaunt than hys Rythme. . . . in Fraunce
hys memoryal shal endure to the last posterytie, and most men be
of thys opinion, that it shall be ryght harde for anye man to matche
hym in thys kynde of vertue, and as Tullye reporteth of Cesar: he
maketh all wyse menne a frayde to wryte" (sigs. Nn2^v–Nn3).

Sleidan, however, was a foreigner. Unfortunately, the fullest
account of Marot by an Englishman was yet another "scornful

giving" on the psalms. This, by far the most interesting of them all, is the attack on Marot's character and competence in the recusant Thomas Harrab's *Tessaradelphus* (n.p., 1616). Harrab's angry outburst is worth quoting at length for its views on Marot and for the way it vividly illustrates a deep division, perhaps in theology but more probably in temperament, between those who wanted to infuse secular life with the sacred, to encourage milkmaids and plowmen to sing to the Lord while at work, and those who wanted to protect the holy, to keep some places and times free from daily sweat and smudge. To the latter Marot seemed not merely silly but irreverent, a careless dabbler in springs too pure for him, although from another point of view it is both natural and moving for a court poet to apply techniques learned in the service of king and mistress to the service of God and man.

There is nothing that hath drawne multitudes to be of therir [*sic*] Sects so much, as the singing of their psalmes, in such variable and delightfull tunes: There the souldier singeth in warre, the artizans at their work, wenches spinning, and sewing, apprentises in their shoppes, and wayfaring men in their travaile, litle knowing (God wotte) what a serpent lyeth hidden under those sweet flowers, what venom is in this pleasant liquor, and what distraction is in this Sirens songe: this craft and sbutilty [*sic*] did old Heretikes use. These divine psalmes are by them transported out of the Church, into the dwelling howse, out of the Quire into the shoppe, and as absurd it is for a shoomaker sowing his shooe, to sing one of these psalms, as it is to sing *Miserere mei*. or *De profundis*. in his petitions to God Almighty.

These Rithmes or Rimes in the vulgar, are rather Bezaes ballads, and Marots muses, then psalmes of David; for they vagary and goe out at their pleasure, from faithful translation, and from the sence of the holy Ghost, to make up their Rime: For it was hard, yea impossible, to fall right upon the feete of the Hebraicall poesie, being full of allegories and figures. They seeing this absurdity confuted in an assembly at Mountpeliere, put the psalmes into prose, and so to stop the mouths of Papists, by singing them in the old tune, and to leave of Bezaes and Marots Rimes; but for feare of condemning their former invention, they left the matter undecided. Marot in the very first psalme, inverseth the sence of the Prophet, Their Rimes indeed, are rather Paraphrases of their owne braine, then the text of Scripture, and so are nothing else but the ballads of Beza, and of Marot. As for Marot he was a wanton Courtier, a Poet, and a Musition, altogether unlearned but in the mother tongue; a man in regard of his ignorance and lose life, most unfit to medle in such divine matters, or affaires. At the first they were taken but for ballads, and divers sung them to what tune they liked best, some in hunting and hauking, some in other exercises, but they were not sung at sermons: In the end Marot fledde to Geneva, and there made up some fifty psalmicall ballads: But continuing his lose life, and it being known that he had debaunched his hostesse, for the which he was openly whipped, he fled from thence into Pyemont and there he died; after whose death Beza made up the rest of the psalmical ballads, and Calvin caused musitions to put ditties and tunes unto them, wanton, light, and whatsoever was delightful. [sigs. D2^v–D3]

That many Englishmen admired Marot or at least thought him a fairly well-known and able poet is not surprising, for that is what he was. Expressions of disapproval or faint contempt are more interesting, although they are not inexplicable. One reason for such a reaction is of course the mere fact of chronology: Marot wrote before the Pléiade, before Du Bartas, before the greatest period of English Renaissance poetry; he was old-fashioned by the time many English noticed him. Even his translators consistently "modernized" him, as though they enjoyed his conceits but, impatient with his particular ambiguity or irony, felt the need for a tighter and clearer form, a more showy mannerism of the sort they now knew in Du Bellay and Ronsard.

And yet there was probably more to the amusement or disapproval than that, more too than can be accounted for by Marot's biography or his career as a love poet. Marot was not alone in having a double reputation or at least in producing an ambivalent response in English readers. Rabelais, Cervantes, Skelton, even Chaucer and More, provoked comments that demonstrate a curious inversion, like those visual puzzles which suddenly shift

the direction of their perspective. Satire lends itself to this misunderstanding, of course, when the author and his work are first
collapsed into each other (hence, for example, Swift the would-be
Houyhnhnm) and then sometimes even reversed. One can see
something else at work, however, in the belief that, for instance,
Skelton was not worthy of his role at court, that he had been "a
rude rayling rimer and all his doings ridiculous."[59] Indeed the
parallels between his reputation and that of Marot are very suggestive. Each seemed to many of his contemporaries a man of talent
and at least some learning; each came to seem, in the view of a
number of later readers, entertaining but unpolished; each wrote
satires in which sharp political and religious commentary is hidden
in seeming nonsense or in which the poet assumes an ironic tone
easily confused with real naïveté or foolishness; and each eventually acquired so plausible a reputation for clowning that he
figures as the hero of a jestbook.[60]

Some of this process, this perversion of wit and irony into crudity
or silliness, was doubtless the result of time:

> Pasquels Conceits are poore, and Scoggins drie,
> Skeltons meere rime, once read, but now laid by.[61]

More important, however, must have been difficulties with tone,
for Marot's, especially, was often unlike that to which the English
were accustomed by the late sixteenth century. Even very sophisticated witty verse will seem to lose its urbane poise when a
culture's sense of humor—that delicately balanced piece of mental
equipment—undergoes a tiny adjustment. Now, it is often said
that Northern Humanist irony, with which Marot's work has close
affinities, was in many ways tied to popular comic traditions and
specifically to the figure of the fool.[62] The occasional simplification,
so to speak, of both Marot and Skelton into clever jesters and the
difficulty many readers in later years seem to have encountered in
hearing their irony were perhaps due in part to a shift away from these
older perceptions and uses of wit. This would explain, I think, not
only English response to Marot but the frequent misreading of
More's *Utopia* as either a mere joke or a serious desire (that it could
be both was a thought beyond such readers) and the reduction of
Rabelais to an "atheist" scoffer.

English writers, it is true, continued to create fools, but whatever their ventures into irony, playfulness, paradox, satire, or simple raillery, few were as happy as Skelton and Marot to *act* the fool. Sidney's and Donne's witty speakers are in overtly clever if not always fully comprehending command of their speech. Although star-gazing Astrophil can be shortsighted, he is himself no wide-eyed innocent or awkward victim. Shakespeare will play the untutored youth with his mistress—but he tells us what he is doing. The speaker, in other words, maintains control of his rhetoric and perceptions whatever his rueful admissions, self-delusion, or self-mockery. Rabelais, however, wandered into his own giant's mouth, More missed a good deal of his creature Hythloday's argument, and Marot can describe himself hustled off to jail by three "pendars":

> Et m'ont mené ainsi que une Espousée;
> Non pas ainsi, mais plus roide ung petit.[63]

Despite their sometimes high claims for poetry, then, Marot and Skelton were unconcerned to appear dignified, to make more than an occasional appearance in singing robes and laurel garlands, to show their wit as wit and not folly. They did not hesitate to speak through a cunning but possibly deranged parrot or coq à l'âne.

It is understandable, therefore, that the English responded more fully to Marot's pastorals, "epigrams," and lyrics than to his satires and epistles, that they preferred the Marot who as Robin described his vanished childhood with wry but pretty melancholy to the Marot who elsewhere wrote

> Mon beau printemps & mon esté
> Ont faict le sault par la fenestre.[64]

The poems they enjoyed are easier to grasp, for they rely on images and shapes that translate readily from one language to another. Even in them, however, the shades of tone, the humor, the attitude toward self and subject are easily missed by a reader deaf to ambiguity, in a hurry, or perhaps bringing with him a new set of expectations Marot's poetry cannot satisfy. How much more exciting and elevating, men like E.K. must have thought, were the poems of Du Bellay and Ronsard—more resplendent with visual images and emblematic descriptions, more cosmic and mythological even when addressed to a mistress, and more dignified, as befitted a new and learned age.

2

Du Bellay

Five years after Marot's death Joachim Du Bellay published a number of works which he hoped would show that French literature might now achieve the dignity and power up to then denied it by lazy centuries of ignorance and false modesty. Although such a claim was arrogantly unfair to Marot and his contemporaries, the publication in 1549 of Du Bellay's *La deffence et illustration de la langue françoyse* and of several collections of poetry unquestionably marked a significant change in sensibility and in the conception of a poet's privileges and responsibilities.

Du Bellay had been born in the early 1520s into a minor branch of a distinguished family.[1] After a melancholy childhood he studied law briefly and came in 1547 to the Collège de Coqueret, where he joined Baïf and Ronsard as a student of the humanist Dorat, a brilliant and compelling teacher. The next year he and his friends were irritated to read Sebillet's *Art poétique françoys*, a work that annoyingly anticipated some of what they themselves had already been thinking while it praised older poets—Marot, for example—and took seriously such dusty forms as the rondeau. Du Bellay's answer was the *Deffence*.

That same year he published *L'Olive*, a sequence of fifty rhetorically clever, richly descriptive, and allusion-filled love sonnets, many of which are based on Italian models. The following year he added sixty-five more. Du Bellay sings of the various aspects of his anguished devotion until toward the end he turns from Olive to the truer peace of Christ and to the heavenly Idea "de la beauté, qu'en ce monde j'adore."[2] At the close of the sequence we return at least part way from the empyrean, much as we do in *The Courtier* and in the *Symposium* itself, for Du Bellay ends with a pretty compliment to the "astre nouveau" of the Vendômois: Ronsard.

Although *L'Olive* was popular in Renaissance England, Du Bellay's conceits and inventions have a familiarity breeding contempt in modern critics quick to find the poetry artificial and derivative. Yet the verse may well be underestimated nowadays by readers chiefly interested in, say, the complexities of a poet's speaking voice or his originality of conception. These are worth admiring, but by stressing them one is apt to miss what Du Bellay does well in *L'Olive*: manipulate his dialectic to clever if anticipated purposes and create images not only of the natural world but of an inner vision of that world and what it may in turn, like Olive herself, symbolize or evoke.[3] The eros many readers cannot find in the Petrarchist lines to an uninterested and uninteresting girl flows instead through the images of the naiads in their "palais humides," the maternal but devouring ocean, the pull or flight of sleep and darkness, the embrace of elm and lascivious vine, the moving water and wind. Sometimes, like Ronsard, Du Bellay juxtaposes different textures, colors, and feelings. The poet will soar above the wild caves near the Loire as a swan flies to the green banks of the "recourbé Mëandre" and then to the lovers' woods in Hades to sing "au bord oblivieux." Or he invokes the river and the nearby "roc feutré d'un verd tapy sauvage," contrasting yet joining flux and hardness, resistance and soft invitation.

Published with *L'Olive* were the *Vers lyriques*. Du Bellay praises the Loire and the gods who haunt it, Love as order and generation, the three graces and the new year, Bacchus with his ivy, Spring and his own sorrows ("O que tout est muable / En ce val terrien," III, 38). In the *Recueil de poësie*, which appeared later that autumn, Du Bellay celebrates François I and Henri II who together undid "ce vil monstre Ignorance" and the "vray poëte" who flees the vulgar mob for "fontaines vives" and "cavernes profundes" (III, 70, 120–22). This sort of imagery is not merely decorative but a visionary insistence on re-creation and on the true poet's need to find the sources of inspiration hidden within himself and within the world, sources well symbolized by emergent water and an echoing cave. The cave is also the place of divine revelation (Apollo, lord of the sun, comes to Sibyl in the darkness) and the living waters recall both Helicon and Scripture.

In 1550 Du Bellay brought out a second edition of *L'Olive*. The somewhat agitated introduction repels attacks on the *Deffence* and excuses his borrowings and boastfulness ("ce n'est sans l'imitation des anciens"). To this new edition he added "La Musagnoeomachie," an allegorical war between Learning and Ignorance known to Spenser. Once more through this vision of a new age move the images that excited or comforted the author: the gods, the cave, the night and the ocean "qui reluit / Sous la tremblante lumiere" and whose heaving waves reach for "l'Astre pluvieux" (IV, 3). In 1551 he translated a Latin dirge for Marguerite de Navarre first composed by the Seymour sisters in England. The year 1552 brought the *Oeuvres de l'invention de l'autheur*. Du Bellay was ill and some of the poetry shows his sense of how "Chacune chose decline / Au lieu de son origine." Perhaps because of this "triste congnoissance" Du Bellay tried a little divine poetry, hoping for inspiration to sound an "Israëliade."

In 1553 came a second edition of the *Recueil de poësie*; the best-known addition is the witty "J'ay oublié l'art de petrarquizer." The humor, like that of Shakespeare's "My mistress' eyes," depends on a deliberate literal-mindedness which pretends, for instance, that the conventional lover really thinks he contains a globe of the four elements—a marvelous tribute, in fact, to the fascination of the Petrarchan poet with the nature and extent of the self.

In the spring of 1553 Du Bellay went to Rome with his learned cousin Jean Cardinal Du Bellay, ambassador to the Papal court. Upset by the corruption he found, bored by his job, homesick, he wrote the poetry that most appeals to modern readers.[4] Compared to his earlier works the *Regrets* (1558) seem strikingly personal, their grief and satirical humor the result of encounters with actual situations, not merely with books. Behind the poetry, however, move the depth-giving shadows of Ovid (hence the irony, it has been said, of an exile *in* Rome) and of other wanderers who "comme Ulysse, a fait un beau voyage" toward whatever Ithacas their spirits longed for. The poems had little success in England.[5] More readily imported were *Les antiquitez de Rome*, thirty-two sonnets on the monitory ruins and paradoxical survivals of the ancient city. This sequence is followed by a "Songe" which recounts in fifteen sonnets various allegorical visions of destruction or loss.

The *Divers jeux rustiques* (1558), probably written during the

same years, move in a different world. Many are beguiling little
poems, pagan in the original sense of the word—simple prayers of
rustic piety to the *numina* of the countryside. There are also satirical
verses, a paradoxical celebration of deafness, and erotic "baisers."
And in still another vein Du Bellay that same year published his
Poemata, a collection of clever neo-Latin verse. There were to be a
few more poems in 1559, but the next year Du Bellay died while
working at his desk. A collected edition appeared in 1568, then five
more before the turn of the century—and none again until the
nineteenth, although some continued to read him and even after
"Malherbe vint" he drew less scorn than Ronsard and Du Bartas.[6]

Since the early nineteenth century Du Bellay has been admired
for his "sincerity" and personal tone. It is easy to see why. In the
first "regret," for instance, he plays the introspective poet alone
with his feelings and his art:

> Je me plains à mes vers, si j'ay quelque regret:
> Je me ris avec eulx, je leur dy mon secret,
> Comme estans de mon coeur les plus seurs secretaires.
> Aussie ne veulx-je tant les pigner & friser,
> Et de plus brave noms ne les veulx deguiser
> Que de papiers journaux ou bien de commentaires.
>   [II, 52]

Furthermore, a romantic reaction finds easy encouragement in
some of the metaphors Du Bellay applies to himself. More often
than earlier poets he is airborne:

> Je voleray depuis l'Aurore
> Jusq'à la grand' mere des eaux,
> Et de l'Ourse à l'epaule more,
> Le plus blanc de tous les oyzeaux.
> Je ne craindray, sortant de ce beau jour,
> L'epesse nuyt du tenebreux sejour.[7]

Even Du Bellay's extensive use of classical myth accompanies and
provides symbols for a heightened awareness of interiority. The
ancient figures and stories, like the dancing maidens on Spenser's
Mount Acidale, seem to adumbrate an inner world accessible to
the poet's fascinated contemplation, a mental and spiritual kingdom in which

> De nuict, sur l'humide front
> Des fleurs de vermeil escrittes,
> Y viennent danser en rond
> Les Nymphes & Les Charites.[8]

It would be a mistake, however, to emphasize this aspect of Du Bellay and to ignore his pervasive reliance on traditional rhetoric, the solidity and balance provided by aphorism, antithesis, and anaphora, although it is likely that this very insistence on verbal order emanates from the same place in which the nymphs and graces dance.[9] So one should not be disappointed to find that in the main English writers did not much notice the Romantic Du Bellay. If the *Regrets* excited no comment and the swan flights little imitation, English poets found in Du Bellay what they wanted to find: conceits, mental pictures of the mutable or erotic world, and fine inventions to describe love, grief, and longing.

The "image" of Du Bellay that emerges from English comment, quotation, and choice of poems for imitation is blurred along the edges—not contradictory like that of Marot but simply vague.[10] Very roughly one can say that the English recognized for Du Bellay two closely related roles: the lyric poet who wrote of love and sorrow and the humanist who wrote ably about language and composed neo-Latin verse. This reaction, moreover, was exclusively literary. Du Bellay's poems touch on a number of matters of great interest in England from the nature of love to the corrupt glow of the papal court, but Englishmen seldom quoted him for his authority as they did Du Bartas, and even Ronsard, and nothing in his fairly uneventful life aside from his position as a writer provoked interest. Nevertheless he seems to have touched the imagination of some poets in ways that go well beyond liking or the gratitude owed a "source," and his career in England has importance if not clarity or splendor.

Although the following description of English response is not strictly chronological it will be clear that the most important decade for Du Bellay in England was the 1580s. It was then that his poetry on Olive and Rome was best known, his *poemata* first mentioned, his criticism first influential in published books. Furthermore, those who read and borrowed from him often did so in works associated with innovation and experiment. It is true that

few Englishmen explicitly commented upon Du Bellay as one who
helped start a movement or change a direction, and those who
wrote about French literature credited its refining to Marot or
Ronsard, not to him. Yet even more than Ronsard, Du Bellay turns
up in works that were early examples of their kind—the first
important miscellany, the first emblem book, an early study of
symbols, a collection experimenting with meter, and other efforts
at revival or importation. Marot, too, had appeared in some of
these places, but often with a slightly old-fashioned air quite unlike
the freshness Spenser, for one, found in Du Bellay.

The earliest borrowing from Du Bellay was almost certainly a
poem by Nicholas Grimald printed in the first edition of *Tottel's
Miscellany* (1557). Grimald apparently kept a sharp eye on what
was published abroad, for he was also the first to translate the very
popular epigrams of Theodore Beza and it is likely he was the
second Englishman to write blank verse. Here he turns Du Bellay's
"Face le ciel," a widely admired sonnet to Olive in *vers rapportés*,
into a celebration of Virgil's *Aeneid*. In the process much of Du
Bellay's wit evaporates (notice his phrase "l'oeil s'eçarte," which
because of its placement in the series must be applied to Homer);
the minimal drama of a poem addressed to a living listener dis-
appears; and a conceit that affirms the failure of the arts and the
power of the lady to create a true image or impression (all this said,
of course, in a very fancily worded poem) dwindles to a literary
compliment to another writer in which all paradox is lost.
Grimald's heavy poem, then, is not itself a triumph of art, but it is
worth quoting as the first English attempt to imitate Du Bellay.
The form is that of the Shakespearean sonnet:

> Face le ciel (quand il vouldra) revivre
> Lisippe, Apelle, Homere, qui le pris
> Ont emporté sur tous humains espris
> En la statue, au tableau & au livre.
> Pour engraver, tirer, decrire, en cuyvre,
> Peinture & vers, ce qu'en vous est compris,
> Si ne pouroient leur ouvraige entrepris
> Cyzeau, pinceau ou la plume bien suyvre.
> Voila pourquoy ne fault que je souhete
> De l'engraveur, du peintre ou du poëte

> Marteau, couleur ny encre, ô ma Déesse!
> L'art peult errer, la main fault, l'oeil s'ecarte.
> De vos beautez mon coeur soit doncq' sans cesse
> Le marbre seul, & la table, & la charte.
>
> By heavens hye gift, in case revived were
> Lysip, Apelles, and Homer the great;
> The moste renowmd, and ech of them sance pere,
> In gravyng, paintyng, and the Poets feat:
> Yet could they not, for all their vein divine,
> In marble, table, paper more, or lesse,
> With cheezil, pencil, or with poyntel fyne,
> So grave, so paynt, or so by style expresse
> (Though they beheld of every age, and land
> The fayrest books, in every toung contrived,
> To frame a fourm, and to direct their hand)
> Of noble prince the lively shape descrived:
> As, in the famous woork, that Eneids hight,
> The naamkouth Virgil hath set forth in sight.[11]

Grimald must have enjoyed Du Bellay's poem, or at least relished its possibilities, and it is fitting that a collection like the *Miscellany*, self-consciously designed to demonstrate English accomplishment, should draw in even this limited fashion upon a French poet similarly anxious to promote his country's letters. During the next few decades, however, several poets were to move beyond the casual adoption of a single pattern or conceit. The most important—and the most deeply moved—was Spenser. If his renderings sometimes falter, if no one would place them among his best poems, what he saw in Du Bellay was nonetheless central to his own sensibility; indeed it may have helped shape that sensibility, for Spenser came to Du Bellay young. Even more than other English writers he shared his sense of flux, his sharp anguish at the forward tread and cut of time and his ambiguous hope in the repeated circles of its larger movements. Like Du Bellay, Spenser was impressed by earthly glory, by noble service to Cleopolis—Fametown—but he, too, feared the pride that defies the gods above and ignores the ruinous undermining of the foundations below. And like Du Bellay he saw and made seen the mutable world largely through *poesis* which was also, in Renaissance terms, *pictura*.[12]

Spenser first worked with Du Bellay's poetry when as a school-
boy he was asked to translate most of the "Songe" for the Flemish
refugee and poet Jan van der Noot, whose *Theatre for worldlings*
(1569) had been published a year earlier in Flemish and French. It
was to be some years before he turned to the *Antiquitez* themselves.[13]

The "Songe"pushes to an extreme the visual tendencies of the
Antiquitez, for the fifteen allegorical dreams that appear to the
sleeping poet are in effect emblems of Rome's fall thickly veiled in
occult symbolism.[14] Less self-conscious than the *Regrets*, the
dreams take place not within the speaker's particular ego but in a
land of archetypes, ideas, and images, of falling oaks and eagles,
complaining nymphs, collapsing palaces, and monstrous transformations. The dreamer's very impersonality, furthermore, gives
his images the air of an inevitable revelation from the gate of horn,
and indeed the perspective is explicitly religious:

> Lors cognoissant la mondaine inconstance,
> Puis que Dieu seul au temps fait resistance,
> N'espere rien qu'en la divinité.

[II, 30]

Van der Noot recognized the power and usefulness of these
emblems of secular ruin, for his discourse on vanity was intended
to be a "theatre," a visually energetic image of earthly cupidity
offered to the understanding and memory of the Roman Church
and all proud "worldlings." After an epistle to Elizabeth praising
the religious freedom he has found in England come the "epigrams" from Petrarch, eleven of Du Bellay's sonnets from the
"Songe," and four sonnets based on the Apocalypse. Each poem
now has a picture, possibly by Lucas de Heere.[15] The bulk of the
book, however, is a long explanation of the emblems which pleads
for a charity mindful of how "vaine, transitorie, deceitfull,
unprofitable, and uncertain worldly things be" (sig. E1) and how
"authoritie ingendreth arrogancie" (sig. E3).

He also explains why he has borrowed from Petrarch and Du
Bellay: "And to sette the vanitie and inconstancie of worldly and
transitorie thyngs, the livelier before your eyes, I have broughte in
here twentie sightes or vysions, and caused them to be graven, to
the ende al men may see that with their eyes, whiche I go aboute to

expresse by writing." Some "ar described of one Joachim du
Bellay, Gentleman of France," who

> goeth about to persuade, that all things here upon earthe, are
> nothing but wretched miserie, and miserable vanitie, shewing
> also howe Rome hath bene destroyed, which of a base and low
> estate was lifted up, and become very hie, and that by none
> other means than covetousnesse . . . wheruppon folowed the
> oppression of other nations, through many great robberies,
> with great labour and paine, yea to the perill and losse of their
> owne men and Captaines, and so amplified and augmented
> above mesure their empires. . . . All whiche sumptuousnesse
> and superfluitie hathe oftentymes thoroughe dissention, dis-
> corde and sedition amongst them selves, also by their enimies
> privie conspiracy, hate, and Particular profite, and by child-
> ish and folish counsell ben to their great hinderaunce and
> damage. [sigs. F2ᵛ–F6]

Except for his simplistic assumption that Rome fell because of its
rejection of Christianity (although Du Bellay would have agreed
that pride is a declination away from the reason and love Christ
incarnated), van der Noot does not seriously misinterpret the
"Songe," and since he saves the task of excoriating modern Rome
for his commentary on the emblems drawn from *Revelation* the bulk
of his anti-Catholic diatribe is not directly related to Du Bellay. In
fact, despite its talk of "buggerous Cardinals, and lecherous Prelates," the *Theatre* may have been meant to promote broader Christian understanding, not merely to denigrate Rome.[16] The theology
is not particularly Protestant and the use of visionary poetry helps
make the book more than just an antipapal tract. It is, or means to
be, a mnemonic image of a world in which the spirit moves
mysteriously behind the literal and material surface of things.

Furthermore, van der Noot's own poetry and that written by his
friends to celebrate him is much closer in spirit to Du Bellay and
the Pléiade than to Luther and Calvin. A collection of his poetry in
various languages was published in London in 1570/71.[17] It offers
lyrics based on originals by Baïf and others, Pindaric odes in
evident imitation of Ronsard, and the sort of diction then fashionable in France (fame is "porte-nouvelle," van der Noot plays on
a "Lyre Antuerpienne"). A sonnet to van der Noot refers to Du

Bellay and an admirer says that as Ronsard is the father of French poets, so van der Noot leads the "bien-chantans" of the Low Countries. Finally, as if to stress the collection's openheartedness, van der Noot translates a number of psalms from the Marot–Beza psalter. No wonder a friend addressed the author as "Van der Noot pacifique." It was not for an enraged or bigoted partisan that Spenser translated the sonnets by Du Bellay, but for a man of fairly tolerant temperament deeply attached to the most advanced literature of his time.

Spenser wrote no comment on the "Songe," but one can see what he did to the original as he converted it into passable if not first-rate English. His most striking departure from Du Bellay is his use of blank verse, perhaps a deliberate effort to write of Rome and of religious mysteries (illustrated by strangely evocative images of occult truth) in a style free from modern rhyme and hence closer to the original music of the ancient poets.[18] The elimination of rhyme would be quite in keeping with van der Noot's own proclivities and even with the possibly eirenic aims of the *Theatre*: as the pictures of this theater recall to the sodden memories of the worldlings the extent of their danger, so the blank verse might have been meant to provide more compelling harmonies.

Spenser's eighth sonnet has one too many lines, a departure usually put down to carelessness, but for which I would tentatively offer another explanation. To begin with, Spenser's line is added to the eighth of fifteen sonnets, thus making the central poem of a series of fifteen into a fifteen-line structure.[19] The first result of the addition is, arithmetically, to give the sequence a central line— "When erst of Gods and man I worship was," says a "wailing Nimphe." But the extra line also calls attention to "fifteen" itself. Du Bellay may not have attached any importance to the number of sonnets in the "Songe," although in the *Deffence* he refers to the fifteen "signes du Jugement" and to Augustine's mention of the mystical text on which the signs were based.[20] Spenser, however, seems to be guiding our attention to the number in ways that anticipate his later use of numerical structures and symbols. Van der Noot himself had an interest in these matters; a close reading of the Apocalypse is apt to encourage even reasonable people to such speculations. Perhaps he was also interested, then, in a sequence of fifteen which ends in a vision of Judgment and the heavenly

Jerusalem, for that was the significance of "fifteen" as outlined by
Augustine and as described a few years after the *Theatre* by that
useful student of numbers, Petrus Bongus, whose discussion is at
times taken almost verbatim from Augustine.

Briefly, "fifteen" has two chief meanings, both relevant to the
Theatre. First, there were fifteen steps to the Temple, so that
"fifteen" represents spiritual ascent, an ascent providing an
answer to the problems set forth in Du Bellay's visions. Second,
"fifteen" combines "seven" and "eight," and it is to this property
of the number that Augustine turns several times and on which
Bongus concentrates. For Augustine the number "seven" sym-
bolizes the Law, the Old Testament, and the Sabbath "quies,"
while "eight" means the New Testament, resurrection, and the
New Law. Together they show the harmony of the two Tes-
taments, and since the waters of the Flood rose fifteen cubits above
the mountains "fifteen" also indicates baptism, a mystery beyond
the learning of the proud. Elsewhere, in a commentary on the sixth
psalm, Augustine says "seven" shows man in time, whereas "the
end of the world will admit us to life everlasting, and then the souls
of the just will no longer be subject to the vicissitudes of time. Since
all time advances by the repetition of the same seven days, the
octave may very well signify that eighth day which is beyond such
rotation."[21]

Du Bellay's "Songe" is about the effects of that rotation, about a
fallen world that despite its appearance of cyclical persistence
offers, as the first sonnet says, no real hope save in God. By
borrowing from *Revelation* van der Noot reinforces the lesson he
gives the worldlings, making more explicit Du Bellay's obliquely
presented eschatology and consolidating what has justly been
called a "climat de Patmos" into unmistakable picture and open
declaration.[22] Furthermore, if I am right that Spenser intended to
stress the "fifteenness" of the sequence, then he too was sharpening
the point—the number reminds us of the relationship of time to the
timeless and of the human carnality blind to the inner significance
of the world and its history.

Sometime in the 1570s or 1580s Spenser reworked his translation into smoother verse, replacing the Apocalyptic poems with
those by Du Bellay omitted in 1569 and providing a rhyme scheme.
He also drops the extra line. Perhaps while working on these

"Visions of Bellay," later published with the *Complaints* in 1591, he simply had more time to polish, but perhaps he also felt that the fifteenth line now lacked the symbolic meaning it had once had in the *Theatre*.

During the following decades other writers created emblematic visions of earthly vanity or impermanence, but usually it is impossible to determine if the author had been looking at the *Theatre*, the *Complaints*, Du Bellay, or Petrarch. Richard Rowlands, a Catholic expatriate who published *Odes in imitation of the seaven penitential psalmes* (Antwerp, 1601) under the name R. Verstegan, wrote for this collection seven "visions of the worlds instabilitie" which seem to owe a good deal to the *Theatre*—indeed his dream is specifically of a "spatious Theatre . . . hang'd with black to act some tragedie" (sig. H1). His own scenes of worldly vanity, however, chiefly concern the hubristic violence and negations of heresy. Henry Peacham's *Period of mourning* (1613) is in the same tradition, but there is no proof the author had studied Du Bellay's poetry before writing these six allegories on the death of Prince Henry. Even closer to Spenser's "visions" are those of William Browne, whose allegorical sonnets chiefly describe the destruction of various birds and plants in a countryside more familiar and English than the archetypal world of the "Songe."[23] Thanks chiefly to Spenser, then, a style first associated in England with Du Bellay was increasingly Anglicized.

Having translated the "Songe" Spenser turned to the *Antiquitez* themselves, although exactly when he did so is unclear. Like the "Visions of Bellay," the "Ruines of Rome" were published with the *Complaints*, but their quality indicates they were written when Spenser was still young.

Du Bellay's meditations on Rome's fall achieve more eloquence and complexity than the "Songe" which follows them. Much of the language is powerfully ritualistic, as though the poet were trying to work a summoning magic. He insists upon the ravages of time and upon the hubris of the ancient city, but he also affirms its rebirth as "le daemon Romain / S'efforce encor d'une fatale main / Ressusciter ces poudreuses ruines." This revival is itself ambiguous—Du Bellay had no love for modern Rome—and the cycles of history turn within an enclosed and solipsistic world, implying both the social and psychological effects of pride and Du Bellay's own poised balance between awe and repugnance. "Rome de Rome est le seul monument," for "Rome seule pouvoit à Rome ressembler, / Rome seule pouvoit Rome faire trembler."

It is easy to see why Spenser liked the *Antiquitez*, obsessed as they are with mutability and often emblematic in effect. His translation, however, is sometimes awkward and shrill—Renwick called it "noisy" (e.g. "mon cry" is intensified to "my shreiking yell")—and on occasion the rhythms bunch or sag.[24] Aside from his awkwardness and some simple errors, what most limits the translation is Spenser's inability to render fully the strange tone of the original. Du Bellay's poetry hovers between pain and quiet, its passionate distress at the sight of the ancient world's decay restrained by ceremonious patterning and controlled gesture. Du Bellay usually enjoins us not to complain but to "see." Much of this Spenser captures, yet he cannot always find English equivalents for the incantatory quality. Sometimes one can see him trying; "Rome was th'whole world, and al the world was Rome," for instance, retains the symbolic symmetry of "Rome fut tout le monde, & tout le monde est Rome" (although it lacks Du Bellay's perhaps significant shift in tense). In many ways the *Antiquitez* are "about" incantation, the poet's power to evoke the memory of the "peuple à longue robbe" and participate in Rome's mysterious survival by helping the "daemon Romain" in the work of restoration. But "Thrice unto you with lowd voyce I appeale" does not recapture the triple inner rhyme, the magical "fureur," of "A haulte voix trois fois je vous appelle."

At the end of the sequence Du Bellay confronts a painful question. If even ancient Rome could fall, what of poetry? Like stone monuments the sonnets are meant to memorialize, to recall. But people forget:

> Hope ye my verses that posteritie
> Of age ensuing shall you ever read?
> Hope ye that ever immortalitie
> So meane Harpes worke may chalenge for her meed?
>   If under Heaven anie endurance were,
> These moniments, which not in paper writ,
> But in Porphyre and Marble doo appeare,
> Might well have hop'd to have obtained it.

> Nath'les my Lute, whom Phoebus deignd to give,
> Cease not to sound these olde antiquities:
> For if that time doo let thy glorie live,
> Well maist thou boast, how ever base thou bee,
>   That thou art first, which of thy Nation song
>   Th'olde honour of the people gowned long.

The marvelously suggestive last line is itself a comment on mutability, for it probably refers to the "gens togata" to whom, says
Virgil, Jove promised empire without end.[25] At this point Du
Bellay moves to the "Songe," but Spenser instead adds an envoy in
praise of Du Bellay, the fullest compliment he received in England:

> Bellay, first garland of free Poësie
> That France brought forth, though fruitfull of brave wits,
> Well worthie thou of immortalitie,
> That long hast traveld by thy learned writs,
>   Olde Rome out of her ashes to revive,
> And give a second life to dead decayes:
> Needes must he all eternitie survive,
> That can to other give eternall dayes.
>   Thy dayes therefore are endles, and thy prayse
> Excelling all, that ever went before;
> And after thee, gins Bartas hie to rayse
> His heavenly Muse, th'Almightie to adore.
>   Live happie spirits, th'honour of your name,
>   And fill the world with never dying fame.

These gracious lines in effect reply to the doubts with which Du
Bellay had ended his sequence, doubts not wholly answered within
that final poem. In reviving Rome from her ashes he has indeed
won immortality for himself; such is the poet's power. Perhaps
there will be hope for Spenser too in raising this little memorial to
Du Bellay. The details of the memorial are interesting. Spenser
calls Du Bellay "first garland of free Poësie," implying, I think,
that he was not so much the first important French poet (Spenser
knew of Marot, after all) as the first writer of a new sort of poetry.
The words "free" and "garland" connote freshness and fame,
flowering and liberation; they show Spenser consciously perceived
in Du Bellay those elements of style and attitudes toward art we

tend to associate with the Pléiade. The "garland" is especially appropriate, for it specifically provides at the end of a work on mutability an image of perfection and recurrence, of immortality.[26]

Yet just as Du Bellay moved from a world of time to a "dream" obscurely presenting an apocalyptic significance, Spenser moves from the garland to an explicitly Christian reference to God and to the new poet now writing divine poetry—Du Bartas. Spenser knew that earthly garlands wither, offering frail protection against the terrors of one's own death and the pain with which one sees the present drawn inexorably into what Prospero called "the dark backward and abysm of time." To praise Du Bartas, who in this sense too comes "after" Du Bellay, is both to comment further on secular immortality and to move upwards with Urania, the muse of astronomy, away from the earthly circles of decline, fall, and temporary rebirth. Such a conclusion does not reject the garland of Du Bellay, for the poets are each enjoined to live happily and famously, but it does imply some limits to the vision of the *Antiquitez* taken by themselves and points to what many English writers were to consider a higher destiny for poetry itself.

It is at least possible, furthermore, that Spenser was again making symbolic use of number. Although not as important as "fifteen," "thirty-two" had attracted to itself an odd assortment of occult meanings. One, according to Bongus, was Justice, "since it is always divisible into equal parts and in equality is preserved the concern and integrity of justice." This meaning accords well enough with the *Antiquitez* and Du Bellay's vision of pride rebuked. I think (perhaps too fancifully) that by adding a thirty-third sonnet Spenser might have been providing a numerical parallel to his praise of Du Bartas; as Dante knew, "thirty-three" is a powerfully Christian number.[27]

Spenser made no other translation from Du Bellay, but his poetry shows his continuing interest. There are echoes here and there in the *Amoretti* and *Epithalamion*, although no convincing debts. Two poems in the *Complaints*, however, contain lines clearly based on passages in Du Bellay now fully integrated and re-imagined. One, *The Ruines of Time*, mourns the loss of Leicester, Sidney, and others in the visionary manner of the "Songe." We see again the emblematic pageant of earthly destruction, teaching that "all is vanitie and griefe of minde, / Ne other comfort in this world can be, /But hope of heaven, and heart to God inclinde," and here again the poet strives nevertheless to build a lasting "moniment" to the dead. Spenser is more explicit than Du Bellay both in his open weeping and in his religious consolations, but the kinship between the two poems is unmistakable.[28] So is that between *The Teares of the Muses* and *La musagnoeomachie*, although the former is a pessimistic vision of the sleepy yet destructive powers of ignorance in England and the latter a victory song describing the rout of those forces by modern French poets and their royal patrons. Euterpe's speech on Sloth and Ignorance echoes Du Bellay's similar allegory but, more important, both writers share the assumption that great poetry requires deep learning and that for a nation to lack either is a matter of moral, social, and political danger.[29]

After his "envoy" Spenser wrote nothing about Du Bellay. Yet even some lines in the *Faerie Queene* may remind a reader of him. It seems unlikely Spenser ever forgot Du Bellay's "free Poësie," the intensity of his inner vision, and the images in so many of his poems of those places, often green and hidden, where poets as well as dancing nymphs can find recreation and inspiration.

Sir Arthur Gorges was a "lover of learning and vertue," said Spenser when writing of him as "Alcyon," the bereaved lover of "Daphnaida."[30] He was also a lover of French poetry (his translations from Marot are mentioned above) and like Spenser he was particularly taken by Du Bellay, from whom at least twenty-three of his poems are derived. Gorges's adaptations, made mostly in the 1580s, show a lively and broad awareness of Du Bellay's work: many are from *L'Olive* and Du Bellay's other love poetry, six from the *Regrets*, one from the *Antiquitez*, and one from a sequence in honor of the queen of Navarre, now gracefully turned into a celebration of Elizabeth.[31] Gorges shared with Spenser a pleasure in Du Bellay's melancholy voice, but he responded less readily to the poetry of mutability and decay than to that describing the sorrows of a lover or victim of circumstance (and indeed Gorges's own circumstances were frequently painful).

In choosing which poems of this sort to translate Gorges was apparently guided not so much by a desire for striking pictorial effects as by an interest in enumeration, series, repetition, and anaphora—architecture that stiffens or clarifies verse otherwise

limp with sentiment. The qualities he found in Du Bellay, then, are
not altogether those Spenser emphasized in his own translations.
But neither did Gorges try to recapture Du Bellay's irony, sarcasm,
and satire, although he certainly knew the poems in which those
qualities predominate. Even when he translates a bitter original
the result is gentler:

> Si les larmes servoient de remede au malheur,
> Et le pleurer pouvoit la tristesse arrester,
> On devroit (Seigneur mien) les larmes acheter,
> Et ne se trouveroit rien si cher que le pleur.
> Mais les pleurs en effect sont de nulle valeur:
> Car soit qu'on ne se veuille en pleurant tormenter,
> Ou soit que nuict & jour on veuille lamenter,
> On ne peult divertir le cours de la douleur.
> Le coeur fait au cerveau ceste humeur exhaler,
> Et le cerveau la fait par les yeux devaller,
> Mais le mal par les yeux ne s'allambique pas.
> De quoy donques nous sert de fascheux larmoyer?
> De jetter, comme on dit, l'huile sur le foyer,
> Et perdre sans profit le repos & repas.
>
> [*Regrets* LII]

Gorges's twelve lines (he frequently expands or contracts the
original poems) keep the basic argument but not the tone. In place
of Du Bellay's swift and harsh conclusion he continues to describe
not the ugly fact of profitless weeping but the imagined relief tears
might provide, and adds to the witty alchemical conceit images of a
mourning dove and wounded deer that give the lines a sweet
prettiness quite different from the original's sense of futility:

> Yf teares avayle to ease the gryved mynde
>   or weepinge could our frowarde fate amende
> What under heaven mor praetious could wee fynd
>   then those deare dropps that from our eyes discend
> For yf in them such sweete effects weare fownde
> Amydste our cares our comforts wolde abounde.
>
> The waylinge turtle sone would ease hir griefe
>   and call againe hir mate shee loved so well
> The wounded deare would lykewise fynde releife

> by those moiste dropps that on his cheeks do swell
> And I poore soule would give myne eyes theyr fill
> Yff with my teares my harmes myght so distill.[32]

Although Gorges did not seek in Du Bellay the individual quality
modern critics find exciting, in part because it illustrates that
interiorization of experience some find characteristic of the Renaissance, he nevertheless understood Du Bellay well. His own poetry
is often simpler—the rendering of "J'ay oublié l'art de petrarquizer," for instance, sheds the qualifying irony of the original.
Sometimes, however, he not only finds concrete images to sub-
stitute for the subtler tonal qualities of the French but notices and
reproduces in his own way important details of the sort other
translators let go right past them. His fifty-seventh lyric, like the
fifty-seventh sonnet to Olive on which it is based, lists a series of
lovely things that man cannot count—drops of rain, flowers, stars,
and so forth. Into such sweetness Du Bellay introduces a small sour
detail: "les thesors, que l'Inde riche donne / Au marinier,
qu'avarice conduit." Gorges's adaptation is quite loose, but I think
he saw what Du Bellay was doing when he mentioned "avarice,"
adding to his own charming list of the innumerables the leaves that
fall in "wrathfull winters wyndes."

Gorges's twentieth lyric illustrates how he could find complexities of his own to replace those he was unable or unwilling to copy:

> Rendez à l'or cete couleur, qui dore
> Ces blonds cheveux, rendez mil' autres choses:
> A l'orient tant de perles encloses,
> Et au Soleil ces beaux yeulx, que j'adore.
> Rendez ces mains au blanc yvoire encore,
> Ce seing au marbre & ces levres aux roses,
> Ces doulx soupirs aux fleurettes decloses,
> Et ce beau teint à la vermeille Aurore.
> Rendez aussi à l'Amour tous ses traictz,
> Et à Venus ses graces & attraictz:
> Rendez aux cieulx leur celeste harmonie.
> Rendez encor' ce doulx nom à son arbre,
> Ou aux rochers rendez ce coeur de marbre,
> Et aux lions cet' humble felonnie.

[*L'Olive* XCI]

Du Bellay's last line provides a surprising finish to a series of languidly beautiful requests—after so much loveliness one is almost happy to encounter the lions. Except for a compliment to her mind Gorges does not complicate or deepen the nature of the beloved, but instead adds a couplet that replaces the change in tone with a change in the direction of the reader's attention, inviting us more overtly to consider the lover's situation and the final dissolution of the lady in his own memory:

> Restore agayne that colloure to the golde
>   that garnishte hath those haires like golden streames
> And lett those eyes so heavenly to beholde
>   resign unto the Sonn their borrowed beames
> And let those lyppes whose smyles so much delight
>   unto the corrall yeelde their lyvely hue
> And let those rancks of pearles retorne of ryghte
>   unto the Oryente whereas first they grewe
> And lett that snowe which shadoweth so her breste
>   dissolve it selfe and unto dropps distyll
> And lett that mynde which honoreth all the reste
>   surcease to use Mynervas sacrede skill
> And let that harte off hardened flynty stone
>   returne unto the rocks from whenc it came
> And then (oh love) if thow wilte heare my mone
>   teach me withall how to foregett her name.

Gorges's translation of the twenty-third sonnet in the *Antiquitez* appears to be in an experimental meter. Perhaps, as his editor remarks, the Roman subject suggested Roman numbers. I cannot identify the particular meter if any (each line has about eleven syllables, mostly long), but the combination of a "classical" imitation with the regular English sonnet form, rhyme and all, is an unusual mixture:

> How gravelye wise was that Senatours counsaile
>   who fearinge leaste Idlenes a foe to Courage
> Woolde breede unfitt people for warr and travayle
>   advysede nott to rase the walles off Carthage.
>
>   [no. 54]

If nothing else the poem illustrates Gorges's interest in language and its rhythms, but such verse rarely succeeds fully and these

efforts may be put with others of those years by writers like
Spenser, Harvey, and Fraunce that probably had a good effect on
English poetry without being very good poetry themselves. Some
who experimented with classical meters also knew Du Bellay's
work, but it is difficult to be sure whether reading him affected such
attempts; more relevant inspiration can be found in Ramus, Baïf,
and Italians like Tolomei. Yet the thrust of his criticism and
practice was toward the revival of ancient methods in vernacular
poetry, and in this sense Gorges and the others of that circle may
have thought they were following Du Bellay's example in "illustrating" their native literature.

While Gorges was writing his "vannetyes and toyes" another
Englishman, John Soowthern, was busy translating from several
French poets including Ronsard, Baïf, and Desportes. So far as I
know his debts to *L'Olive* have gone undetected.

To his modern readers (a small group) Soowthern is a miserable
incompetent, and indeed his fractured rhythms, the *franglais* into
which he sometimes laboriously forces his language, and a syntax
apt to float somewhere between England and France, combine to
make his *Pandora* (1584) a very odd collection of poetry. Yet these
sonnets, odes, elegies, and the like are so very bad it seems reasonable to ask if anyone could write like that except on purpose. Could
his cacophonous numbers derive from a mistaken ambition to
write quantitative verse? Perhaps so, but *Pandora* reads better (a
little better anyway) when one forgets English meters altogether
and reads along slowly with the rhythms as though Soowthern's
passion for French poetry led him to count by syllables, not stress
or quantity.[33] Thus the translations from Du Bellay work best as
unaccented fourteeners divided into alternating lines of eight and
six syllables with occasional feminine endings:

> When the eye of the world dooth washe,
>   his golden shining heaire,
> In the large Occean seas: and that
>   They have coverd the lyght:
> A murmuring repose, and a
>   Restfull and sleepy night,
> Is spreded both over the earth,
>   The waters and the ayre.

[sig. B2ᵛ]

This is from the second "elegy," a close translation of *L'Olive*
XXVII. Two other elegies, the first and third, adapt *L'Olive*
XXIV and L (which Gorges also borrowed), and the fourth and
fifth also recall Du Bellay. Each elegy in effect has fourteen lines
with the same rhyme scheme as many French sonnets. Like
Gorges, then, Soowthern was willing to combine nonaccentual
verse with conventional modern forms and rhyme.

Soowthern's most interesting experiment is based on the opening stanzas of Du Bellay's "Complaintè de Didon à Enée," which
Gorges had also translated. These are, he boasts, "New kinde of
verces devised by him: and are a wofull kinde of meter, to sing a
love, or death in," although in fact the meter and rhyme scheme
virtually reproduce Du Bellay's. Once again the poetry probably
should be read by the syllable and phrase, not the foot:

> Comme l'oizeau blanchissant,
> > Languissant
> Parmy l'herbette nouvelle,
> Chant l'hymne de sa mort,
> > Qui au bort
> Du doux Mëandre l'appelle. . . .
>
> > > > > > [VI, 307]
>
> Like the dolefull birde languishing,
> > the which dooth sing,
> Her fatall song in sweete accordes,
> Betaking her selfe to her death,
> > wearie of breath:
> On Meander her florie bordes. . . .
>
> > > > > > [sig. D2]

Gorges, realizing the difficulty of keeping Du Bellay's three
syllable lines, gave the short ones four ("Lyke as the swann snow
white / without delight"). Soowthern does the same, but perhaps
because he wanted to maintain the mathematical ratio his long
lines have eight—thus the musical phrasing is a little expanded but
basically the same as in the French. Indeed much of Soowthern's
interest in "new" meters may have derived from his experience as a
musician; no doubt he meant his subtitle quite seriously: "The
Musyque of the beautie, of his Mistresse Diana." It is hard to take

Soowthern himself very seriously. Yet one can be grateful to this
inept but hardworking follower of the Pléiade for his well-meaning
attempt to import some of the best of French poetry—conceits,
diction, syllabic meter and all—into England.

Samuel Daniel, too, was deeply interested in French and Italian
poetry.[34] Even before he joined the Pembroke household where
Mary Sidney encouraged such imitation he had adapted a number
of French love poems to be included in his *Delia* (1592). Daniel
reworked some of Desportes's facile sonnets, but like Spenser he
had deeper affinities with Du Bellay. He too tended toward melancholy, feared "the Darke and times consuming rage," created
resonant compound words as recommended in the *Deffence*, and
evoked images that link the lover's feelings to the energies of the
cosmos—images like the lady's "Summer smiles" or the tears that
flow for her as the ocean responds to the "nights pale Queene."
Sometimes, to be sure, Daniel's lover sounds less like Du Bellay.
The sonnets that urge the beloved to pluck the day and recite to her
the lessons of the rose resemble Ronsard's similar admonitions,
and the poet's power to eternize his love in "Arkes" and
"Tropheis" is claimed more insistently than in *L'Olive*.

Four poems to Delia derive from those to Olive. They have been
criticized as less imaginative and dramatic, less subtle in structure
than the originals.[35] Daniel knew how to rework a conceit but could
not always find equivalents for the ties between that conceit and
the poem's shape when he modified the original into a Shakespearean form. Thus a couplet designed to provide a summation or
artful surprise may diminish into anticlimax or simply feel dis-
connected. If not among his triumphs, however, Daniel's adaptations are pleasant to read. One, a sonnet published with the
pirated edition of Sidney's *Astrophil and Stella* (1591) and never
reprinted in *Delia*, is from *L'Olive* XXXVI. It tells the lady that like
the phoenix she can both burn and restore her ardent lover;
Daniel's couplet adds that thus to resurrect him would show her a
goddess in power. *Delia* XIV translates *L'Olive* X, which describes
in *vers rapportés* how his mistress has imprisoned her poet with her
hair, scorched him with love, and transfixed him with her eyes. Du
Bellay says he enjoys his pain too much to seek relief, but in a final
couplet Daniel begs Delia to "lose, quench, heale" him.[36]

Delia XXII, adapted from *L'Olive* XCII, complains of false hope. Once more Daniel appends a couplet, epigrammatic and gnomic in intention but a little banal in effect:

> Lookes feede my Hope, Hope fosters me in vaine;
> Hopes are unsure, when certaine is my paine.

This slackening and the omission of Du Bellay's protest that the lady laughs at him make the translation bland, always a temptation for well-languaged but unheroic Daniel. The eighteenth sonnet to Delia, based like Gorges's twentieth "vannety" on *L'Olive* XCI, works fairly well. Like Gorges, Daniel turns at the end to speak of himself, and he too banishes the lions, replacing them perhaps unwisely with adjective-encumbered tigers and bears. The ending of the poem spells out the meaning more clearly than Du Bellay cared to, and whereas Gorges praised his lady for her Athenian mind, Daniel finds her mind ferocious too:

> Restore thy tresses to the golden Ore,
> Yeelde Cithereas sonne those Arkes of love;
> Bequeath the heavens the starres that I adore,
> And to th'Orient do thy Pearles remove.
> Yeelde thy hands pride unto th'yvory whight,
> T'Arabian odors give thy breathing sweete:
> Restore thy blush unto Aurora bright,
> To Thetis give the honour of thy feete.
> Let Venus have thy graces, her resign'd,
> And thy sweete voyce give backe unto the Spheares:
> But yet restore thy fearce and cruell minde,
> To Hyrcan Tygers, and to ruthles Beares.
>> Yeelde to the Marble thy hard hart againe;
>> So shalt thou cease to plague, and I to paine.

Daniel probably looked at Du Bellay's other poetry. He tells Delia that though on a visit to Italy he has seen "those walles the which ambition reared" fallen and "intombd . . . Within themselves" the barbarians could not despoil the virtuous of their fame recorded in "Th'eternall Annals of a happie pen." This comforting reminder, here turned to the praise of his mistress, recalls the fifth "antiquité" (or Spenser). Other poems seem to echo the *Regrets*. Daniel says he writes not to seek bays "to deck my mourning brow" but "t'unburthen mine owne hart," a proud humility found in Du Bellay's opening sonnets, and while abroad he longs for "faire Albion, glory of the North," wishing her safe from "Muse-foe Mars" with a homesickness not unlike Du Bellay's desire for "France, mere des arts."[37] To Daniel, then, Du Bellay was a poet worth imitating, a source of argument and invention. Probably his response went further, though, so it is a pity he never recorded his opinion of a poet with whom, despite some differences, he shared feelings and tastes basic to his own nature and style.

No other poets in England or Scotland responded to Du Bellay as fully as Spenser, Gorges, Soowthern, and Daniel, but during the 1580s and for several decades after he won at least the passing attention of other writers, and to several of these he may have seemed important either as a creator of images and ideas to which they could respond warmly or as a fresh voice saying things they very much wanted to hear.[38]

A little poem by Du Bellay on François Gouffier, Seigneur de Bonnivet, enjoyed a remarkable career in England. Bonnivet had perished from wounds he received while fighting the emperor:

> La France & le Piemont, & les Cieux & les Arts,
> Les Soldats & le Monde ont faict comme six parts
> De ce grand Bonivet: car une si grand' chose
> Dedans un seul tombeau ne pouvoit estre enclose.
> La France en a le Corps, qu'elle avoit eslevé:
> Le Piemont a le Coeur, qu'il avoit esprouvé:
> Les Cieux en ont l'Esprit, & les Arts la Memoire:
> Les Soldats le Regret, & le Monde la Gloire.[39]

This minor but clever piece must have pleased English readers because it so handily magnifies the great soldier into a universe of admiration while simultaneously compressing him into one brief huitain; it thus appeals to two important tastes in Renaissance England—the desire to expand into sweeping gesture and a seemingly opposite liking for epitome and compact inclusion. (Du Bartas's popularity was to repeat this response on a much larger scale.) That Bonnivet is so finely partitioned may also have made the poem interesting to a generation fascinated by conceits, images, and tropes that first divide an experience or idea into particles and then arrange them into a pattern. Bonnivet suffers a' *divisio*, but then each bit is put in its proper place and we may feel both the grandeur of his destiny and the comfort of its order.

For these or other reasons Abraham Fraunce included the poem in his *Arcadian rhetorike* (1588). He probably came across it and some *vers rapportés* on "Un berger, un chevrier, et un bouvier" in Tabourot's *Bigarrures*, where they are credited to the "gentil du Bellay" and quoted "pour donner plaisir aux studieux de la Poësie." Through some slip, however, Fraunce identifies the author of both poems as Remy Belleau.

From this epitaph grew at least five English versions, most in memory of Sidney. One was an anonymous tribute some admirer set up in St. Paul's. This epitaph has long since vanished, but for some years it was an attraction to tourists and a reminder of the extraordinary outburst of feeling that greeted Sidney's death in 1586. John Eliot's *Ortho-epia`Gallica* (1593), for instance, includes a visit to "Powles to see the Antiquities." One "antiquity" is the epitaph for "the peerelesse paragon of letters and arms":

> England, Netherland, the Heavens, and the Arts,
> The Souldiors, and the World, have made six parts
> Of the noble Sydney: for none will suppose,
> That a small heape of stones can Sydney enclose.
> His body hath England, for she it bred,
> Netherland his blood, in her defence shed:
> The Heavens have his soule, the Arts have his fame,
> All Souldiors the greefe, the World his good name.
>
> [sig. X2]

Inevitably Camden knew the inscription, saying in his *Remaines* (1605) that "Sir Philip Sidney . . . hath this [i.e. as his epitaph] most happily imitated out of the French of Mons. Bonivet" and adding in a marginal note, "made by Ioach. du Bellay" (1614 ed., sig. Aaa4^v). A few years later Anthony Stafford quoted the verses in his *Niobe* (1611), a grumpy excoriation of half-dressed women, wanton poets, foolish youth, and the like which recovers its good temper when the author thinks of Sidney and Elizabeth ("Incomparable, immutable, inimitable Queene!"). He wishes for Sidney "a Quire of ancient Bardi" who "with their musickes melody, might expresse thy soules harmonie." Stafford could retrieve no bards, but he did know the lines "extant in S. Pauls Quire at London," which he gives in full (sigs. F8, E8^v–E10^v).

Stafford does not mention Du Bellay, but John Weever's *Ancient funerall monuments* (1631) both praises him and suggests the means by which his poem became known in England. Weever says that the Seigneur des Accords (Tabourot's pseudonym) "in his booke entituled, *Les Bigarrures* (a miscellanie or hotch-potch of sundry collections) amongst many choice Epitaphs, hath one, selected out of the works of Isaac [*sic*] du Bellay, the French Poet, excellently composed, to the memory of Sieur de Bonivet, a great Commander in the warres; which by some English wit was happily imitated." Weever gives the French, his own version in English, and then the epitaph on Sidney (sigs. Ee4^v–Ee5). Nor is this the only mention of Du Bellay in the *Monuments*, for in a passage about the vicissitudes of time he quotes the third sonnet by "Bellay in his ruines of Rome, translated by Spenser" (sig. B2).[40]

A version of Bonnivet's epitaph, meanwhile, had been imbedded in Ralegh's popular lament for Sidney. Illustrating that English tendency I have noted before to push a conceit even further, Ralegh splits Sidney not into six but into eleven or twelve parts:

> England doth hold thy lims that bred the same,
> Flaunders thy valure where it last was tried,
> The Campe thy sorow where thy bodie died,
> Thy friends, thy want; the world, thy vertues fame.
>
> Nations thy wit, our mindes lay up thy love,
> Letters thy learning, thy losse, yeeres long to come,
> In worthy harts sorrow hath made thy tombe,
> Thy soule and spright enrich the heavens above.[41]

It is difficult to know which version derives from which, but related somehow to this complex of poems are looser imitations by Constable and Gorges and one by Churchyard on Elizabeth's suitor the Duc d'Alençon.[42]

Toward the end of the 1580s in Scotland, John Stewart of Baldynneis, too, was reading Du Bellay. Somewhat sober of temperament, he nevertheless felt drawn to "L'Adieu aux muses," a good-bye to poetry in which lyric élan and satiric wit give the lie to

the writer's discouragement. Stewart keeps some of the original's
humor, including the image of frustrated poets:

> All solitar and sad thay do remaine
> Vith fervent furie for to flie aloft,
> Syn for to pen thair purpois prompt and plaine
> Both to and fro thay pouse the tabill oft,
> > And byts thair nails, And vreyis thair fingers vrang,
> > To thraw thair versis ether schort or lang.[43]

Stewart's countryman William Fowler preferred to borrow from
the *Regrets*. Fowler, who had lived in Paris and later worked as a
spy for Walsingham, joined the group of poets gathered around
James in the 1580s, although his own adaptation of Du Bellay was
probably written after the king came to England. Fowler's taste in
literature had a certain fashionable quality; he enjoyed psalmody,
Petrarchan sonnets, anagrams, *imprese*, and the Pléiade, even
adopting Du Bellay's motto *Coelo Musa Beat* (itself taken from
Horace). One of his "Miscellaneous poems" translates a procession of stereotypes urged with a relentless anaphora which
doubtless intrigued him:

> Je hay du Florentin l'usuriere avarice,
> Je hay du fol Sienois le sens mal arresté,
> Je hay du Genevois la rare verité,
> Et du Venetien la trop caute malice:
> Je hay le Ferrarois pour je ne sçay quel vice,
> Je hay tous les Lombards pour l'infidelité,
> Le fier Napolitain pour sa grand' vanité,
> Et le poltron Romain pour son peu d'exercice:
> Je hay l'Anglois mutin & le brave Escossois,
> Le traistre Bourguignon & l'indiscret François,
> Le superbe Espaignol & l'yvrongne Thudesque:
> Bref, je hay quelque vice en chasque nation,
> Je hay moymesme encor' mon imperfection,
> Mais je hay par sur tout un sçavoir pedantesque.
>
> > [LXVIII]

Du Bellay's phrase "un sçavoir pedantesque" probably refers to a
scholastic arrogance scornful of the learning the poet should work
for and express. Fowler makes the connection with pedagogy

plainer and narrower in his translation into heptameter couplets:

> I do detest the florentine his usuryce is so gritt;
> I do abhore the sienies for his unstable witt . . .
> I hate my self and all my faults, bot mair a pedant foole,
> quhase skill is nought and dois conduct the children to the
>   shoole.[44]

The catalogue does compel attention. Montaigne tells how as a child he was distressed to see schoolmasters laughed at, for he was then under their tutelage, but soon realized that "the choysest men were they, that most contemned them," repeating the last line of the poem by "our good Bellay."[45] In *De la sagesse* (translated by S. Lennard before 1612) Pierre Charron quotes the same line by "Sieur de Bellay" and adds four lines from the sestet of Regret LXV:

> Sayd I thou didst live but to eat and drinke,
> Then poore were my revenge, thy faults scantie:
> But that which most doth make thy name to stinke,
> Is, to be short, thou art a Pedantie.
>
> > [sigs. a5–a5ᵛ]

But Sir Thomas Browne says eloquently in *Religio medici* (1642), "There is another offence unto Charity, which no Author hath ever written of, and few take notice of; and that's the reproach, not of whole professions, mysteries and conditions, but of whole Nations, wherein by opprobrious Epithets we miscall each other, and by an uncharitable Logick, from a disposition in a few, conclude a habit in all.

> Le mutin Anglois, et le bravache Escossois,
> Le bougre Italian, et le fol François. . . .

It is as bloody a thought in one way, as Nero's was in another; for by a word we wound a thousand, and at one blow assassine the honour of a Nation."[46]

Understandably some Englishmen also knew Du Bellay as a critic, for though overstated and derivative the *Deffence* gave additional energy to a number of current thoughts on language, the craft of poetry, and the value of "imitation." Du Bellay's

confidence in the vernacular and the injustice done it by bad poets
on the one hand and narrow-minded pedants on the other, his
perception that no language is inherently inferior, and his insistence that a poet must work, imitating the ancients and enriching
his language, were often echoed in England. There can be little
doubt, I think, that a certain sort of English Renaissance criticism,
especially that published in the 1580s, derived considerable
impetus from Du Bellay and the Pléiade. One is apt to find traces of
the *Deffence* not in passages justifying the enterprise of feigning or
those exploring the relation of mimesis to philosophy but rather in
books or chapters explaining how to write poetry, celebrating the
vernacular, or discussing the nature of language itself. Much of
what Du Bellay says on these topics had been said by others, but
since his name is mentioned from time to time in England and since
the way or order in which he expresses these thoughts turns up on
occasion, it is probably fair to say that the *Deffence* was well read
among those concerned with the techniques of versifying and the
actual or future value of English. Furthermore, I suspect that his
authorship of the *Deffence* reinforced the association of his work
with literary restoration and experiment, although a desire for
such explorations was in the air anyway. Yet there was not much
comment on Du Bellay as a critic. Perhaps Englishmen who read
and borrowed from him felt his fame did not shine enough to make
him worth mentioning as an illuminating "author." Certainly
those who wrote on literary topics showed no reluctance to drop
well-known names, but just as those who had unquestionably read
Marot's psalms seldom referred to him, so some who must have
known the *Deffence* did not boast of that awareness with a quotation
or an "as learned Bellay saith."

Two chapters of Richard Mulcaster's *Elementarie*, published in
1582 but probably expressing convictions the author had long
taught at the Merchant Taylors' school where Spenser had been a
student, draw heavily upon Du Bellay.[47] Mulcaster insists that
English "hath in it self sufficient to work her own artificiall direction, for the right writing thereof." Not yet properly "founded," it
is already a viable and orderly language, underestimated by those
blind to its antiquity and the wit, learning, and inventiveness of its
speakers. "No one tung," says Mulcaster, is "more fine then other
naturallie, but by industrie of the speaker, which upon occasion

offered by the kinde of government wherein he liveth, endevoreth himself to garnish it with eloquence, and to enrich it with learning." We must admire Greek and Latin, but "did not those tungs use even the same means to brave themselves ear theie proved so beawtifull?" By that very precedent "let us understand, how boldlie we maie ventur, not withstanding the opinion of som such of our peple, as desire rather to please themselves with a foren tung, where with theie are acquainted, then to profit their cuntrie, in hir naturall language, where their acquaintance should be." Let us get to work. Imports and compounds, for example, if made judiciously and without too "manifest insolence," will improve our language (sigs. K3ff; Hh1ff; Kk1).

As he read the *Deffence* (which I think he must have done) Mulcaster may have felt for Du Bellay a fellowship based on more than his utility as a "source." There are differences between the two, to be sure—Mulcaster is less polemical and mean about the past, more commonsensical and even more interested in the texture of language itself—but the similarities are close. Each is particularly moving in his confidence that all languages are potentially equal, each relies, perhaps naïvely, on the power of a deliberate effort to polish and reform them, each adopts a sensible and flexible openness to lexical novelty, and each advocates that true humanism which imitates the ancients through writing like them in modern ways. Mulcaster was at once most himself and most a follower of Du Bellay when he said, "I love Rome, but London better, I favor Italie, but England more, I honor the Latin, but I worship the English" (sig. Hh1^v).

King James, too, had read the *Deffence* (there was a copy in his mother's library).[48] His *Schort treatise* on verse was published at Edinburgh in 1584 and in it he refers to Du Bellay, whose thoughts he echoes from time to time, as he does Ronsard's. The reference itself is a little obscure, for although he declines to discuss rhetorical figures because, among other reasons, "they are usit in all languages, and thairfore are spokin of be Du Bellay, and sindrie utheris, quha hes written in this airt," Du Bellay in fact nowhere describes the figures at length.[49] Mediocre and skimpy, James's little treatise is at least a further reminder that literary experiment and imitation were then accompanied by the unromantic belief that poetry and the arts would profit from a calculated, planned program of joint effort and that such optimism was sometimes linked to an awareness of Du Bellay.

The probable author of *The arte of English poesie* (1589), George Puttenham, may also have known Du Bellay. Fascinated by the patterned movement of rhetorical figures he was also, if temporarily, intrigued by anagrams and in some canceled pages provides examples of this "pretie conceit" drawn from Du Bellay or Tabourot's *Bigarrures*. A good courtier, he adds to Du Bellay's transformations of royal names his own variations on *Elissabet Anglorum Regina*—*Multa regnabis ense gloria* and *Multa regnabis sene gloria*—but he does not take such frivolities seriously. Du Bellay himself thought the anagram, like the acrostic, was an "antiquité," an invention of those Greeks whom the French were to follow in other paths. And he may well have suspected that verbal coincidence is more than chance, that it reveals something inherently true. One of his examples of the acrostic entails a supposed Sibylline prophecy of the second coming, and even the flattering anagram on "Françoys de Valoys"—"De façon suys royal"—might to a spirit so inclined seem proof that the political center of the kingdom was mysteriously validated by the country's very language. Puttenham, however, backs smiling away from such dangers; Dr. Dee, who owned a copy of the *Deffence*, might have been more sympathetic.[50]

It was during the 1580s, then, and probably even earlier, that attention was most clearly focused upon the *Deffence*. It is tempting, however, to detect in Daniel's *Defence of ryme* (1603) signs that he had read Du Bellay's criticism as well as his poetry, although by the early seventeenth century the assumptions behind the *Deffence* were so widely diffused that actual indebtedness is hard to prove, and in any case Daniel may have read Du Bellay's pamphlet many years earlier. He would have found little there on rhyme itself (although he would have noted the theory, which he mentions himself as a possibility, that rhyme was invented by the ancient "bards"), but he might have been pleased to read that rhymed poetry, too, has music and harmony, that languages have their own individual natures, that all men have been subject to the same nature within and without, and that it is "sotte arrogance"—Daniel says "arrogant ignorance"—to condemn the vernacular as barbaric. Daniel shares all these convictions, although he puts them more genially than did Du Bellay. "Suffer then the world to injoy that which it knowes, and what it likes," he says with a mellow ease not often found in the Pléiade's pronouncements.[51]

An actual quotation from Du Bellay appears in a textbook on French by the poet and grammarian John Sanford. Sanford's name was once linked to Daniel's by an admirer who called them the "two swans" of Somerset, but his drearily useful *Guichet françois* (Oxford, 1604) shows little elegance despite its references to modern poets like Baïf and Garnier.[52] Sanford knew, furthermore, that he was treading well-traveled ground; for the title page he took a somewhat inexact quotation from the *Deffence*: "Escrire apres tant d'excellentes plumes n'est que retistre [*sic*] la toile de Penelope. Joachim du Bellay de l'Illustration de la langue Francoise. Lib. 2. cap. 8." The mention of Du Bellay's name and the admirable precision of the reference are unusual.

Du Bellay had argued in the *Deffence* that since the ancients had sucked in their language with their very milk and "les femmes mesmes" aspired to eloquence and erudition, a wise modern will stick with the vernacular.[53] Nevertheless in 1558 he had published a collection of Latin poems, and to the English he was just visible on the edge of that crowd of Renaissance humanist poets which included writers like Marullus, Secundus, Buchanan, Beza, and in England Thomas More and John Owen. Perhaps these poems, like the *Regrets* and *Antiquitez*, served to give Du Bellay's image in England more gravity than that of Marot. This is true, I think, even though the *Poemata* are often light and funny. Some neo-Latin writers drew frowns for their licentiousness, but among the learned a reputation as an internationally important poet seems to have come more readily (other things being equal) to one who composed *basia* as well as "baisers," *epithalamia* and *elegiae* as well as sonnets and songs.

So far as I know the first Englishman to quote the *Poemata* was Geoffrey Whitney, whose *Choice of emblemes* (1586) was published at Leiden. As the first book of its kind in English, Whitney's collection was important and influential; once more in the 1580s Du Bellay found his way to the scene of that decade's many launchings. Whitney himself shared with Du Bellay a talent for creating suggestive images and a pressing knowledge that "The greatest oke, in time to duste doth turne./ The Raven dies, the Egle failes of flighte."[54] I can find no definite trace in his emblems of Du Bellay's other poetry, but if he did read the *Regrets* and *Antiquitez* he must have been touched. The poem he quotes at least comments upon some of the same dilemmas, for it tells how Death and Cupid reversed weapons, bringing no little confusion to the distressed human population:

> Mutarunt arma inter se Mors, átque Cupido:
>   Hic falcem gestat, gestat at illa facem.
> Afficit haec animum, corpus sed conficit ille:
>   Sic moritur juvenis, sic moribundus amat.
> Ut secat hic jugulos, oculos excaecat & illa:
>   Illa ut amare docet, sic jubet iste mori.
> Disce hinc, humanae quae sint ludibria vitae:
>   Mors thalamum sternit, sternit Amor tumulum.
> Tu quoque disce tuas, Natura, invertere leges:
>   Si pereunt juvenes, depereúntque senes.[55]

Whitney's much longer narrative is primarily based on Alciati's enormously popular version in which Love and Death bear golden and bone arrows and the old lover sports a garland, but the margin gives the first four lines of the poem by "Joachim. Belleius."

Two years after the publication of Whitney's *Choice* Abraham Fraunce brought out his *Insignium . . . explicatio* (1588), an often sensible introduction to insignias, *imprese*, heraldry, symbols, emblems, and hieroglyphs, somewhat dulled by the lack of pictures. Fraunce, it will be remembered, had that same year published a work on rhetoric which quoted lines from Du Bellay found in Tabourot's *Bigarrures*, but for his *Insignium* he preferred neo-Latin poetry. Emblems, he says, are songs learnedly explaining some clever invention, as witness those by Alciati, Sambucus, Beza, and others. He furnishes a few examples. The first is Giraldi's complaint by Niobe, weeping marble tears for her "Bis septem natos": "Sic mihi mors dolor est, sic mihi vita dolor"; two others are by Beza and one is the epigram on Death and Cupid by "Joachimus Bellaius," quoted in full (sigs. N2–N3). Fraunce may have enjoyed the paradoxical implications about life and death which it shares with that on Niobe and he may have liked the wry flavor, sharper than Alciati's.

English writers continued to note the odd habits of Death and
Love and to offer, sadly or satirically, the explanation they found in
Alciati, Du Bellay, or Whitney. Versions endowing Death and
Cupid with golden and bone arrows or the senile lover with a
garland probably derive from Alciati, but even in these poems
sometimes one finds traces of Du Bellay's wittily disquieting point
that such a disruptive interchange teaches Nature to subvert her
own laws. Francis Thynne, for instance, writes in his "Emblemes
and Epigrames" (*ca.* 1600) of the time when "hatefull Death"
switched arrows with Cupid's "goulden shaftes" so old fools now
wear "garlands fresh and gaye," yet he also complains that the two
archers now shoot "contrarie to kinde, and their nature." So, too,
for his very attractive emblem book *Minerva britanna* (1612) Henry
Peacham composed a fast-paced narration of the incident mod-
eled, he says, on Whitney, and also, I think, indebted to Du Bellay
for the line "Invert not Nature, oh ye Powers twaine."[56]

At least two other Englishmen found Du Bellay's epigram
penetrating enough to quote in their own moral observations,
although in both cases details from Alciati show they probably
read the line in Whitney, not the *Poemata.* They must have relished
its pithiness, its compression of such a large human problem into a
very few words. John Boys, soon to be dean of Canterbury, published an *Exposition of the dominicall epistles and gospels in our English
liturgie* (1610), filled with fragments and allusions collected from
wide and enthusiastic reading. He quotes Du Bellay in a passage
inspired by Luke's account of Christ's raising a young man from
the dead: "By birth," says Boys, "a man is greene in his flesh, by
youth he is white in his blossome, by death he is withered in the
dust. For death as a fisherman incloseth all kind of fish in his net,
great, small, good, bad, old, young: which the Poets insinuate in
the fable of Death and Cupid, who lodging at a time both in one
Inne, interchanged each others arrowes: and so from that day to
this, it comes to passe that sometimes old men dote, and young
men die: Sic moritur juvenis, sic moribundus amat" (*Works,* 1638,
sig. Tt3). The marginal note reads "Joachim Belleius." Writing
from Cupid's, not Death's, side of the reversal and perhaps for that
reason adopting a more cheerful tone, Robert Burton also noted
the silliness which leads people to fall in love even when they "have
more toes than teeth." "And 'tis no newes this, no indecorum, for

why? a good reason may be given of it. Cupid and Death met both
in an Inne, and being merrily disposed, they did exchange some
arrows from either quiver, ever since young men dye, and often-
times old men dote—Sic moritur Juvenis, sic moribundus amat."
Once more one reads Du Bellay's name in the margin.[57]

Other Englishmen knew the *Poemata* more directly. John Owen
probably borrowed and remodeled a snide little comment on a
fellow poet. Du Bellay had written,

> Paule, tuum inscribis Nugarum nomine librum:
>   In toto libro nil melius titulo.[58]

Owen applied this brief insult, itself of course a "trifle," to the man
Du Bellay calls "Paulus"—Nicolas Bourbon:

> In Borbonii Poetae Nugas.
> Quas tu dixisti Nugas, non esse putasti:
>   Non dico nugas esse; sed esse puto.
> > > [1633 ed., sig. A6^v]

Even those less learned than Owen could read of Du Bellay when
in 1634 Thomas Farnaby published his *Index poeticus*, not as popular as his *Index rhetoricus* but a useful guide to authors who had
written notably on subjects from "aborigines" to "zonae." Almost
all the citations are of Roman or neo-Latin writers like Beza,
Secundus, More, and others. "Joach. Bellaius," however, appears
twice in this multitude. He is mentioned along with Virgil, Ovid,
and Heinsius for having sung "patriae amor et desiderium," presumably a reference to an elegy on that theme in Book I of the
Poemata, and his epistle to Morel is listed under "Vita privata et
humilis."

Finally, in 1637, a brief sampling of Du Bellay's neo-Latin verse
appeared in Abraham Wright's *Delitiae delitiarum*, a collection of
the best modern European Latin epigrams found in the Bodleian.
Wright is or pretends to be a little hesitant about epigrams as such.
He fusses nervously with the thought that some may be frivolous
and even improper. So, says the dedicatory epistle, he has cas-
trated those requiring the operation, removing anything unchaste
that might offend the shamefast eye and ensuring that one may lie
down at this feast secure in the knowledge that the salt (*sales*) is
harmless. Indeed the poems he quotes from Du Bellay are hardly

salacious, if not quite the "lettuce and chaste lamb" Wright says he
will serve. One is the distich to the writer of "nuggets," one a
somewhat scrambled version of the "Mutarunt arma." Two others
had not, so far as I know, been printed in England before. One is to
a terrible poet and one an epitaph for a dog; both are funny:

Dum canit Euridicen, sylvaeque et saxa sequuntur,
    Et tenet immanes [Du Bellay has Detinet immaneis] Thracius
                                                                    ipse feras.

At tu dum horrisonis sylvas concentibus imples,
    Attonitae fugiunt in sua lustra ferae.

Latratu fures excepi, mutus amanti [Du Bellay has amantes]:
    Sic placui domino, sic placui dominae.
                                                    [sig. B6$^\mathrm{v}$][59]

Du Bellay's poetry, then, both French and Latin, was known to a
number of Englishmen and his criticism sometimes consulted.
Comments on him, however, are surprisingly few.

Some thoughts on Du Bellay's work were published in England
but written by Frenchmen. One such reference appears in Geoffrey
Fenton's translation of Estienne Pasquier's *Monophile* (1554), published in England in 1572. In the second book of this urbane and
aristocratic colloquy on love the fancy-free Glaphire argues that a
scholar should avoid Eros. Not so, says Philopole, who in Pasquier's words has a "coeur gay et François": many brave wits
"were kindled and set on fire by this brande of love whose drawing
violence as an adamant or loadestone, first entised the pen of
Petrarche . . . and in our tyme and countrie, was the original
bellowes which gave the first wind to the amorous e[x]ercises of
Consart [*sic*], Bellay, and Thart [*sic*, for Tyard?], whose singuler
perfection in their several phrase and methode of stile, hath
drawne unto them a name of ymortalitie." Monophile himself
doubts that in cold fact these writers have been as incandescent as
they claim, but he later adds tolerantly that such feigned trifles
may give promise of great poems to come and at least hold up a
mirror to the inward passions of the mind.[60]

A generation later English readers would find in Florio's Montaigne that "great Ronzarde and learned Bellay, have raised our
French Poesie unto that height of honour, where it now is," and

other references appear from time to time.[61] The fullest was that in Jacques Auguste de Thou's *Monumenta litteraria* (1640). After briefly recounting Du Bellay's life de Thou offers an evaluation of his poetry notable for its omission of *L'Olive*: "His *Regrets* which he wrote when he was at Rome in the household of his relative the Cardinal, as well as the *Jeux rustiques* and others to Marguerite the wife of Philibert Duke of Savoy, are especially praised. In Latin poetry, which he wrote at Rome in the same way, he was less happy (*faelix*)" (sig. L2). De Thou's readers would have seen similar estimates in books well known in England. Tabourot says in his *Bigarrures* that the sonnets to Olive are much inferior to the *Regrets* and *Antiquitez*, "Car les dernieres sont si belles, nettes et gentilles, que Minerve les advoüeroit pour siennes" (1662 ed., sig. V7ᵛ). Pasquier agreed with this estimate in his popular *Recherches de la France*: *L'Olive*'s popularity "fut plustost pour la nouveauté que pour la bonté: car ostez trois ou quatre Sonnets qu'il deroba de l'Italien, le demeurant est fort foible," whereas among his other poems "il n'y a rien de si beau que ses Regrets qu'il fit dans Rome, ausquels il surmonta soy-mesme" (1723 ed., I, sig. Yylᵛ). Many modern critics would agree.

Neither such praise, however, nor the appearance of Du Bellay's work at important moments in their literary history led many people in England to bother with compliment or comment. There were of course exceptions, such as the garland Spenser proffered him. John Wrothe, who contributed the poem for Bellot's *French grammer* (1578) quoted in the last chapter, praised Du Bellay's "beau mettre," and William Covell's *Polimanteia* (1595) cites several French poets spelled so strangely (e.g. "Master Barlasse" for Du Bartas) that it is difficult to know if in one passage he was thinking of "Bellay" or "Belleau"—his (or the printer's) muddled compromise between the two names could even indicate a hazy suspicion they were the same person. Covell rejoices at the splendor of English culture and the triumph of English poets like "divine Sydnay" and "Chrystallin Spenser": "let France-admired Bellaw, and court-like amarous Rousard confesse that there be of your children, that in these latter times have farre surpassed them."[62]

Why was there so little praise of Du Bellay? It cannot be that educated Englishmen did not know of him. Perhaps his reputation was so overshadowed by that of his more famous, long-lived, and productive friend Ronsard that he came less readily to mind when a name was wanted for a compliment or literary survey. Perhaps he seemed less dazzling than Ronsard and Du Bartas because he lacked their association with kings and great events; his career was never as close to stage center as theirs. And, despite his occasional boasts and high claims for France and poetry, he did not often strike such impressive or dramatic postures as the poet who told his critics "Vous estes tous yssus de la grandeur de moy" or the "divine" secretary of star-studded Urania.[63] Du Bellay's impression on the English, therefore, was less a matter of public glory than of individual moments when he struck a reader as having written something beautiful, exciting, or significant. Nor was this response confined to "debts" and "borrowings." Du Bellay touched some imaginations intimately, particularly those of Spenser, Mulcaster, and, I think, Gorges and Daniel.

I have found only one undoubted reference to Du Bellay in addition to those mentioned elsewhere in this chapter. It occurs in George Daniel's "Vindication of Poesie," a poem making the usual claims for the power of Orpheus and Amphion over the unconscious or uncivilized world and for the immortalizing architecture of poetry. Daniel honors the famous poets of the past and present, including Shakespeare, Samuel Daniel, Sidney, and Spenser ("He is my wonder; for who yet has seene / Soe Cleare a Poeme, as his Fairie Queene?"). Italy has produced "A noble Store" of poets,

> Nor shall the Muse, of that French Eagle dye,
> Devine Sire Bartas; and the happie writt
> Of Bellay, here shall live eternallie,
> Eternizing his Name, in his owne Witt.[64]

The "Vindication" is undated, but since Daniel lived from 1616 to 1657 this compliment must have been made well into the seventeenth century. And yet in spirit it is not unlike that early praise by Spenser, combining as it does the names of Du Bellay and Du Bartas in ways which both affirm the poets' conquest of death and distinguish between the "eagle" of the soaring "divine" poet and the "happiness" of the other living eternally "here." Daniel, one is not surprised to discover, was interested in landscape painting and in his verse wrote feelingly of mutability, flux, and change. Perhaps he was merely inspired to choose these two French poets by reading the envoy to the *Ruines of Rome*, but even so his choice was wise, for this serious and scholarly gentleman with artistic tastes seems, like Spenser and the other Daniel before him, to have visited the same realms Du Bellay found congenial.

3

Ronsard

Although to modern readers Pierre de Ronsard was beyond question the best poet of his age most Englishmen then preferred Du Bartas. Even in England, however, Ronsard found many willing to imitate or praise him, and unlike Marot and Du Bellay he was sometimes called "great." Born in 1524 into the minor nobility of the Vendômois, Ronsard spent his early years near the woods, caves, vines, and water with which he would long associate poetry itself. When still a child he was sent as a page to the court, remaining attached to it in one way or another for the rest of his life. In 1537 he made the first of two visits to Scotland with the short-lived Queen Madeleine. Had illness not left him half deaf he would have pursued a government or military career, but in 1543 he received the tonsure and was soon studying with Dorat.[1]

In 1550 Ronsard published the *Quatre premiers livres des odes*, introduced with magnificent scorn for the "rimeurs" and "courtizans" who "n'admirent qu'un petit sonnet petrarquizé."[2] The first book contains some Pindaric odes addressed to the great with much erudite hyperbole, but Ronsard also writes of the "vin qui rit dedans l'or," the "heurt du tens," and a mythology that expresses through fable the sexual energies of the cosmos. In the other three books one finds light lyrics as well as Ronsard's pride in being the first to "Pindarize" in France and his claims for poetry's ancient powers of prophecy and interpretation. Ronsard's faith in these vatic abilities was to be shaken during years of civil war and political decay, but he never lost it completely. It had an effect, I think, on what the English made of him and the sort of poetry he wrote.

The next year he published an ode to the Seymour sisters in England and, in 1552, a fifth book of odes and the *Amours*, a collection of songs and sonnets to "Cassandre." Here are the expected twin fires, the sun, the hairy nets, Pandora, Venus. The lady's beauty is splendid in jewels and metals, poignant in the rose flaming at dawn, gracious in the flight of birds and the dance of seanymphs. The lover is obsessed ("Cent et cent foys penser un penser mesme") and self-absorbed ("Je veulx darder par l'univers ma peine"). Other sonnets are loosely Neoplatonic: Love brings order to chaos, animates the atoms; the lady is the lover's "tout," his "Entelechie," with whom he makes "un petit monde." In Renaissance England these poems found a reception warmer than the sometimes disheartened reaction of modern critics; although one has called the sequence "un recueil rare, unique et pré-cieux . . . qui procurera toujours un singulier plaisir à ceux qui aiment," another is depressed by "such a density of outworn literary conventions, such a show of misplaced classical erudition, such a desert of lapidary images."[3] The language has seemed sensuous to some dismayed Huguenots and pleased moderns, yet others have denied the poems any strong sexual feeling; if one critic finds "Je vouldroy bien richement jaunissant" erotic in its vision of golden sperm, masculine bull and female pool, another finds it cold and confused.[4]

The "meaning" of these poems is to be found not only in the line of thought but in their dimmer recesses—the further but less readily expressed desires or praise to which the language points or in which it participates. Cassandre is the other who is as close as the self even though passion for her impels her lover into solitude and poetry; she is the pearl in the fountain, his half to whom he can say, "En toy je suis, & tu es dedans moy." Without her he is a salamander with no fire, a dolphin stranded. She is inspiration, completion, *anima*. But she is also the queen of Nature in whom its beauty and force may be summarized and seen; the very land "prend vigueur de sa main la touchant." Desire for her also brings dream and illusion, sometimes as disappointment "Comme l'esclair qui se finist en rien" and sometimes as conquest and delight when the dreaming lover finds himself "Changeant ma vie en cent metamorphoses." Amor is an ambiguous deity—if the lover imagines himself as Zeus he knows he is also Narcissus and if,

like Persephone, Cassandre brings the warm weather ("Vostre oeil
me fait un esté dans mon ame"), she is also Circe. The *Amours* of
1552 are not as nuanced as those Ronsard later wrote to Hélène but
the subtleties and multiple perspectives are already there.

The next year saw the *Livret de folastries*—"mignardes chan-
sonnettes" as Ronsard called these lighthearted and immodest
lyrics—a new and fuller edition of the *Cinqiesme des odes*, and the
Amours "nouvellement augmentées par lui, & commentées par
Marc Antoine de Muret." In 1554 came the *Bocage* and the *Meslanges*, both carefully read in England. One epistle in the *Bocage*
describes Ronsard's day in the country with a distanced landscape
and suspended infinitives not unlike those in Milton's *L'Allegro*. In
1555 Ronsard published his poems to Marie, the *Continuation des
amours*. Marie is less enameled than Cassandre. She is his "Belle,
gentille, honneste, humble, & douce Marie," as he called her the
following year in the *Nouvelle continuation des amours*. Yet her lover
can still be bookish, can tell her that "Pithon vous feit la vois à nulle
autre pareille." Here too are roses, aubades, warnings that "Le
tems s'en va, le tems s'en va, ma Dame," songs to the nightingale
flitting in the willow, lyrics on various subjects, and epigrams of a
less romantic sort.

Fifteen fifty-five also brought the first book of hymns; a second
followed the next year. Had they cared to, English readers might
have seen in them the grave magnificence and philosophical splendor they thought they saw in Du Bartas. Dorat himself was very
pleased, writing that after love poems and Pindaric odes Ronsard
now composes scientific poetry: "Naturae rerum cantica docta
sonas" (L. VIII, 4–5). He hopes Ronsard will turn next to divine
poetry, an ambition his pupil for a while shared. The hymns
concern justice, "philosophy," the "daimons," the heavens, stars,
death ("Je te salue, heureuse & profitable Mort"), gold, eternity.
Many passages propel the attention upwards to see the "merveilles
des Cieux," for instance, or to anticipate the Judgment. The
language itself is impressive and spacious, built with what one
modern critic calls "ces vastes vers . . . cosmiques."[5]

After a *Second livre des meslanges* in 1559 came the first collected
Oeuvres (1560), and in 1562 and 1563 a series of "discours" on the
civil wars. Here Ronsard is not the *vates* of the odes and hymns or
the lover of the sonnets but an engaged defender of crown and

church. Also in 1563, however, came *Trois livres du recueil des nouvelles poësies*, followed by a second edition the next year. They have, says Laumonier, an inspiration "païenne et voluptueuse" (L. XII, ix). In 1565 Ronsard published *Elegies, mascarades et bergerie*, dedicated to Elizabeth, and later that year another work known to some in England—the *Abbregé de l'art poëtique françois*. The first poets, he says, taught men to understand the divine majesty, for the muses are the daughters of God and "la Poësie n'estoit au premier aage qu'une Theologie allegoricque, pour faire entrer au cerveau des hommes grossiers par fables plaisantes & colorées les secretz qu'ilz ne pouvoyent comprendre, quand trop ouvertement on leur descouvroit la verité." Poets now must rely more on artifice and labor, but Ronsard feels some of the old glory still surrounds them (L. XIV).

There was a new edition of the *Oeuvres* in 1567, and two years later Ronsard published the sixth and seventh books of *Poemes*. One poem on cats (described with vivid dislike) opens with lines some-times quoted to prove Ronsard's pantheism: "Dieu est par tout, par tout se mesle Dieu . . . Come nostre Ame infuse dans noz corps" (L. XV, 39). Another demands a harvest of passion while the weather lasts, with a tone and movement anticipating Marvell:

> Cependant que ce beau mois dure,
> Mignonne, allon sur la verdure,
> Ne laisson perdre en vain le temps:
> L'age glissant qui ne s'arreste,
> Meslant le poil de nostre teste,
> S'enfuit ainsy que le Printemps:
> Doncq ce pendant que nostre vie,
> Et le temps d'aimer nous convie,
> Aimon, moissonnon noz desirs,
> Passon l'Amour de veine en veine,
> Incontinent la mort prochaine
> Viendra desrober noz plaisirs.

[L. XV, 204]

In 1571 came a new edition of the *Oeuvres* and then, the next year, the unfinished and largely unsuccessful *Franciade*, to which the English paid only slight attention.

Charles IX died in 1574, to Ronsard's great loss, for he never

was as close to Henri III as to his brother. He sometimes praised
Henri and his courtiers in public verse but privately he was
often discouraged and even sickened (his unpublished sonnets
on the king's homosexuality are unforgettably, obscenely, effec-
tive). Furthermore, the fashionable now looked increasingly to
Desportes, whose smoothly polished verses had just been printed.
In 1578, however, a new edition of the *Oeuvres* demonstrated what
Ronsard could still do. There are many new poems, including
those on the death of Marie and above all the sonnets to Hélène.
One finds in the once more fashionable Petrarchism much to
recognize: the fire and ice, the loving war, the eyes like lightning.
The lover has Neoplatonic aspirations as well—she is his
"Pasithee," his inspiration, the Idea unrecognized by the world.
The awareness of time is sharper than ever, the play of illusion
more disturbing. Sometimes sublimations give way to irritation at
cloud-embracing fantasy:

> Vous dites que l'Amour entretien ses accords
> Par l'esprit seulement: hé! je ne le puis croire:
> Car l'esprit ne sent rien que par l'ayde du corps.
>   [L. XVII, 212–13]

Like Donne's in a similar moment, the argument is as much
Scholastic as Epicurean—Christians as well as hedonists can reject
a Platonism that unties the subtle knot once binding God himself.[6]

It is among these poems that modern readers find Ronsard's
most powerful love poetry, such as "Quand vous serez bien vieille"
(L. XVII, 265–66), a seduction poem complicated by the self-
mocking vision of the lover as a boneless phantom in the myrtle
shades below and enlivened by the little symbolic drama of Hélène
and her servants at work near the evening candle. Time stretches
forward to include that scene and then backwards again as Hélène
remembers the lover who now warns her to gather today "les roses
de la vie." Other sonnets are even more disquieting. During one of
the "longues nuicts d'hyver" Hélène comes "toute nue" and com-
pliant to the dreaming lover; but this is a "joye menteuse" and in a
logical but unsettling extension of the lover's traditional quest for
secrecy the pleasure approaches the onanistic: "De toy fausse on
jouyst en toute privauté." The famous conclusion, "S'abuser en
amour n'est pas mauvaise chose," may be read in many ways, as

may that of a sonnet on the poet's loss of Charles and his passion for Hélène: "La vivante & le mort tout malheur me propose . . . Car l'Amour & la Mort n'est qu'une mesme chose" (L. XVII, 264–65; 294–95). Yet these poems to Hélène attracted much less attention in England than those to Cassandre, whether because of this same rich maturity or simply because the earlier sonnets had been around longer so Ronsard's reputation as Cassandre's lover and the fame of his poetry to her had had time to set.

The next edition of the works was that of 1584. One of the new poems laments the destruction of the forest of Gastine, once home of satyrs, nymphs, and silence. The final thought on mutability has sometimes been quoted to show Ronsard's Lucretian materialism, although it has parallels in the devout Du Bartas: "La matiere demeure, & la forme se perd" (L. XVIII, 147). In December of the following year Ronsard died at his priory of Saint-Cosme, writing verses until almost the end, debilitated ("Je n'ay plus que les os, un Schelette je semble") but able with mingled gaiety and sorrow to say good-bye to his "Amelette Ronsardelette" soon on its lonely way "là bas." In 1587 came another edition of the *Oeuvres* which now included Ronsard's "Tombeau" and Claude Binet's biography. There were other editions in 1597, 1604, 1609, 1617, 1623, and 1629/30.

Most English readers who mentioned him recognized in Ronsard a poet famous for his contribution to good letters and, more specifically, for his *amours*.[7] What first drew English attention, however, were his efforts on behalf of the dynasty he intermittently celebrated and the church he defended first with compassion, then with angry desperation.

Ronsard's early poetry often swells with political flattery for which the author claimed artistic reason: "C'est le vrai but d'un poëte Liriq de celebrer jusques à l'extremité celui qu'il entreprend de louer," says his preface to the odes. Furthermore,

> C'est un travail de bon heur
> Chanter les hommes louables,
> Et leur bastir un honneur
> Seul vainqueur des ans muables.
>
> [L. I, 43–50, 91–92]

The court Ronsard thus immortalizes shines with centered energy, knowledge, and fame, proof in its solar splendor of human achievement. Hence the mythical apparatus, for the court epitomizes a unified hierarchal cosmos in which the proportioned harmony of the muses helps maintain the political order Ronsard later begged the queen to restore through more forceful means.

Many Englishmen would have understood Ronsard's aims, in spite of the exaggerations or simple untruths they would have been ready to recognize. Nor would they have been surprised that the French government made use of its famous poet to impress the literate public at home and abroad. Elizabeth and Leicester came to know a good deal about such methods and doubtless read with some skepticism the encomia Ronsard sent them. They knew his greater loyalties lay with the queen's dangerous rival and cousin.

Ronsard apparently felt a lively affection for Mary Stuart, to whom he wrote several poems and who returned his esteem, although as queen and later as prisoner she would in any case have welcomed the attentions of France's leading poet. Concerning her sentiments there is considerable testimony.[8] Brantôme writes: "Tant qu'elle a esté en France, elle se réservoit tousjours deux heures du jour pour estudier et lire. . . . Surtout elle aimoit la poésie et les poëtes, mais sur tous M. de Ronsard, M. du Belay, et M. de Maisonfleur." In his *laudatio funebris* the Scottish Catholic George Crichton says that "Mary truly Queen of Scots did not cease to reward him even though captive for many years." And according to Ronsard's friend and biographer Claude Binet, Mary

> toute prisonniere qu'elle estoit, laquelle ne se pouvoit souler de lire ses vers sur tous autres, en recompense desquels et de ses loüanges y parsemées, l'an 1583 elle luy fit present d'un buffet de deux mil escus qu'elle luy envoya par le sieur de Nau son Secretaire, avec une inscription sur un vase qui estoit elabouré en forme de rocher, representant le Parnasse, et un Pegasse au dessus. L'inscription portoit ces mots:
>
> A RONSARD L'APOLLON DE LA SOURCE DES MUSES.[9]

Mary's generosity may have been prompted by political hopes as well: Ronsard's praise was another reminder of her support abroad despite destructive propaganda countenanced or inspired by the English government.[10]

In 1565, however, Ronsard directed his suavest flattery to

Elizabeth and her associates; Catherine asked him to do so, for she had recently concluded a treaty with England.[11] Earlier that year Thomas Smith, the English ambassador, had twice mentioned Ronsard or his work in dispatches to Cecil. There are, so far as I can discover, no other such references in English diplomatic correspondence from the French court, so perhaps one may infer some special effort that year to bring Ronsard's poetry to official attention.

On February the tenth Smith wrote Cecil in a postscript, "Bycause you should not want newes I send you Ronsarde our Archipoete of fraunce his Nues or Newes. Which be not unworthie the redyng they were sent me from Paris." Ronsard's "Nues, ou Nouvelles" was a verse pamphlet describing to Catherine how just as in winter the tumbling clouds rapidly divide into illusory shapes, so in the absence of the king, "nostre jour, Nostre Soleil," popular imagination projects a multitude of "nouvelles," gossipy news and novel fantasies, that only the royal presence can dissipate. The poem is indeed worth reading for its satirical portrait of an excited city and for the various "nouvelles" themselves, a crowded jumble of rumors about war, politics, and marriages in which Cecil would have seen a reference to Leicester: "un Anglois si fortuné sera / Que sa maistresse un jour l'espousera."[12] Two months later Smith sent him "thedict against killynge of flesh, thedict of layenge downe of armes, and a boke of our french poete to the Cardinall of Lorreigne." Smith probably refers to "Le procés," written several years earlier but published in 1565 as a pamphlet in which Ronsard pretends to sue the cardinal for neglect. The poem is unremarkable, but the English government was worried by the Guise faction and Smith may have thought Cecil would enjoy what Ronsard had to say about one of its leaders.[13]

Then, on August 23, the French ambassador De Foix sent Cecil a copy of *Elegies, mascarades et bergerie*, begging in polished Latin that it be presented to Elizabeth and complimenting the queen, the author, and poets.[14] These last De Foix credits with prophetic fury, no doubt a gracious way of authenticating his friend Ronsard's anticipations of lasting peace. Ronsard's preface to Elizabeth praises the recent treaty, the female sex, and this "Gynecocratie, sous laquelle l'estat publique est vertueusement policé." The *recueil* itself has charm, though it contains no major poetry. The first

hyperbolic and myth-filled elegy is to Elizabeth, the next to
"Mylord Robert Du-dlé." A third poem addresses William Cecil,
who perhaps set aside his sober prudence for a moment to imagine
himself as

> Docte Cecille, à qui la Pieride
> A fait gouter de l'onde Aganippide,
> A descouvert les Antres Cirrheans,
> A fait danser sur les bords Pimpleans. . . .
>   [L. XIII, 34, 39–74, 159]

The other poems make up a varied group; some of them may have
affected later styles in English political ceremony. The cartels, the
bergerie, and above all the several mascarades honor the throne
and its policies with an inlaid prettiness not unlike the masques of
Daniel and Jonson, although the mythology is simple and the plots
undramatic—nothing here approaches the complexity of Beau-
joyeulx's *Balet Comique de la Reyne.*

There is no clear record of the queen's response. According to
Binet, Ronsard "fut tant admiré par la Royne d'Angleterre, qui
lisoit ordinairement ses escrits, qu'elle les voulut comme comparer
à un diamant d'excellente valeur qu'elle luy envoya," but no other
evidence proves that the usually parsimonious queen gave him an
actual jewel. Even if the story is true, Elizabeth's public reaction to
the book Ronsard sent her and to his other works might well have
been a quasi-diplomatic matter.[15]

Two years later Thomas Jeney, then living in Paris, made a
translation of Ronsard's *Discours des miseres de ce temps.* The thin,
handsome volume purports to be from Antwerp, but *A discours of the
present troubles in France* was printed in Paris.[16] Dedicated to the new
ambassador Sir Henry Norris and festooned with complimentary
poetry in polished Latin and rough English, the work has, like
Ronsard's *Elegies, mascarades et bergerie,* the air of a political gesture.
That a group of English Protestants involved Ronsard's poetry in
making such a gesture raises an important issue requiring a short
digression.

Modern historians or critics have sometimes explained Ronsard's effect on the English in terms of his religion. "Partly it may
be," says one, "because of his violent anti-Protestantism, Ronsard
(except, perhaps, by Sidney) seems to have been far less widely

read in England than either Du Bellay or Desportes."[17] Yet most Englishmen who remarked disagreeably on modern writers' spiritual shortcomings objected primarily to frivolity and lust or to "atheism" like that of scoffing Rabelais. If Englishmen were seldom tolerant of "wrong" beliefs, many could nevertheless distinguish between writers as partisans and those same writers as artists one could read with pleasure and even with moral profit. It is useful to remember in this connection that English writers sometimes quoted as a moralist the devoutly Catholic Pibrac, to whom had been given the hardest public relations assignment in French Renaissance history—the justification of the St. Bartholomew massacre. Sidney was disturbed that Pibrac took the job, which he managed fairly well as such things go, but this willingness to make the worse appear the better reason seems to have had little other effect; Sylvester Englished his *Quatrains* as well as Du Bartas's *Weeks*.[18]

Among Ronsard's biographers and critics discussion of his religious views has usually taken quite another tack, exploring the extent to which he was "pagan" or "Christian" (his Calvinist enemies, of course, called him pagan and atheist both, but "atheist" was a common term of abuse in religious polemic). A recent statement that Ronsard's outlook in the "Hymne de la mort" was limited by "the clerical orthodoxy of a Catholic poet in minor orders" finds little support in most twentieth-century commentary, even that which considers him on balance Christian.[19] For Gustave Cohen, Ronsard was a materialist, pantheist, hedonist. For Paul Laumonier, he was "païen par son tempérament, par son imagination, par sa culture littéraire, par son esthétique," although among others Raymond Lebègue argues for Ronsard's orthodoxy broadly defined.[20]

Recently, however, the question has seemed less urgent, particularly because Ronsard's was an age when some Christians called each other Turk or "atheist" while others welcomed the "prisca theologia" of Hermes and Orpheus, an age when philosophers and poets could fuse the most disparate systems. And does "pagan" mean pagan like Pythagoras or like Lucretius? Epicurus or Calpurnia? As has been said, "Par méthode, nous posons peut-être des questions que l'homme du XVIe siècle n'aurait pas comprises. 'Es-tu chrétien ou païen'? Définir le christianisme ici, et là, le paganisme, tourne ainsi à un jeu qui ne tient pas compte de la réalité historique."[21] Nor, one might add, of psychological reality; for while it is increasingly clear there are many ways of being "Christian" it is easy to forget how many ways there are of "being" Christian or anything else. Certainly there were aspects of the Christian experience that if Ronsard did not neglect altogether he evidently de-emphasized. The numinosity of God's cosmos, for instance, seems to have moved him more than the drama of sin and redemption. The reasons for Du Bartas's greater popularity, then, certainly include the nature of his religious feeling, but to explain why he struck the English with greater force than did Ronsard must take one well beyond the categories "Catholic" and "Protestant" or even "pagan" and "Christian."

Ronsard had published his *Discours*, addressed to the queen mother, in 1562. The heart of the poem and of Ronsard's objections to the Reformers is expressed through the myth of Opinion, "nourrice des combats" and daughter to Jove and Presumption. By Opinion Ronsard means an arrogant and divisive confidence in one's individual power to evolve political and religious theory, especially scriptural exegesis, without reference to tradition, *consensus gentium*, or the mystery of God's "secrets." The *Discours* has no doctrinal argument against Calvinism nor any personal attack on the Huguenots themselves. The poem closes, however, with a prayer that if the dissidents persist the swords fail in their hands and they be blasted from above. Ronsard's next pamphlets were less conciliatory. His *Continuation du discours* lashes at the violence and pride of the Calvinists, especially Beza; the *Remonstrance* (1563) argues briefly for Catholic views and the *Responce aux injures* (1563) defends his habits and poetry. Meantime, of course, his Huguenot opponents had not been silent: Ronsard was an "atheist" whose "orgueil et . . . philautie" led him to turn theologian; one writer contemptuously calls him "jadis Poête et maintenant Prebstre."[22]

Thus by 1568 Ronsard was a controversial figure. In choosing to translate the *Discours*, however, Jeney was almost certainly trying not to promote Rome (although he later became a Catholic) but rather to recollect the earlier, more eirenic, phase of Ronsard's battle against opinion, novelty, and civil war. In any case Jeney knew how books could be designed to support quasi-official strategy. Several years earlier, probably encouraged secretly by the English government, he had written a pamphlet against Mary that emphasizes not only her immorality but also the "sour mishaps that discord doth reveal."[23]

Jeney's *Troobles* opens with the translator's "Passion"; he had been sunk in "grymm dispaire" when a friend gave him Ronsard's "mournynge verse," bidding him sing "Of hatefull warr, enforst by Envyes stynge." So, concludes Jeney, "My shaykynge hand, my plaintfull pen begann, / To wayle the Frenche, and present state of man." Next come some lines to Sir Henry Norris on the dangers of civil war, a catastrophe

> that Ronsard wayles in ryme,
> And I reduce, whith not resemblinge penne,
> To Englishe grace (though in unskilful verse)
> By frendes enforst to publish now abroade.

There follow seven Latin elegaic couplets in which Daniel Rogers, then living in Paris, tells Jeney that "if the Gallic muse of Ronsard deserves honor while he wept his country's fate in his country's language, Jeney's also is worthy his praise whose brief work he puts into the numbers of the English. For they have the same material, travel the same path, both learned in the Pierian lyre. He, sorrowing, sang of the fierce destruction of his disintegrating country and touched French words with Aeonian honey; Jeney as a priest following the steps of the Gallic muse stirs into motion the British plectra in learned measures. The pleasant grace which accompanies Ronsard as he sings shines out no less in Jeney's verse. Thus 'vatem vates vertens,' bard translating bard, those praises Ronsard deserves Jeney wins for himself."[24] Rogers's poem stresses Ronsard's learning, grace, and vatic power, ignoring the arguments that caused the conflict and his position as Catholic partisan.

The translation does not in fact flow with Aeonian honey, impeded as it is by heavy fourteeners and pushy alliterations (e.g. "such wrackes of woos, / By wynters wrathe y torne," which is at least cleverly chiastic). Jeney usually manages to be literal, only on occasion deviating from the original sense and stumbling back oblivious of his detour. He omits the prayer that unrepentant rebels be crushed, however, and ends merely with the long plea that Catherine

> Make cleare a bourde, in stormye seas
>   The master showes his skill,
> Reforme these franticke braines that thus,
>   Do ronne on headlonge will.

Although Jeney indeed wrote with a "not resemblinge pen" he was a better poet than Ferdinand Fyldinge, whose genuinely awful sonnet follows the translation. The association of Ronsard with epic writers is noteworthy, however, as is the horticultural metaphor: just as Homer and Virgil wrote vividly of war, says Fyldinge,

> So Ronsards blowminge grafte (from them as you may knowe
>   By ruthful mourners minde) doth wordes from parentes tame
> Wayling whith broken seighes the fyerie knightes of name,
>   That brave whith glitteringe sword in fielde to smyte the
>   blow.

The volume ends with some Latin poems from Rogers to Norris on the "perturbata christiana orbis republica."

On several occasions during the next few years Ronsard's name or extracts from his poetry appeared in tendentious works published in England or designed to attract English attention. The treatment of Ronsard is sometimes meanly clever, for his enemies soon learned to subvert his arguments through parody or misinterpretation. One brilliant set of distortions enlivens the satirical *Reveille-matin des françois et de leurs voisins* (1574), a pair of dialogues by the patently pseudonymous "Eusebe Philadelphe" (probably Nicolas Barnaud) printed in both Latin and French at Geneva with "Edinburgh" on the title page. The French edition is dedicated to Elizabeth, for Barnaud too seems to have been pressed into the propaganda war against Mary Stuart.[25] During a discussion of regicide Barnaud has one speaker, "Alithea," recite passages from the *Franciade* to show that while pretending to recount Merovingian history Ronsard had surreptitiously painted the hateful Catherine and her sons, even prophesying their assassination. The fragments are quoted accurately enough but ingeniously wrested into so lurid a political allegory that "Politique," astonished Ronsard dared publish it, exclaims "He que ces Poetes sont grands ouvriers" (sigs. G6^{v}ff.).

Perhaps inspired by this bitter foolery a Frenchman I have not identified wrote *A declaration concerning . . . peace in France* (1575), translated by G. Harte. The author urges Henri III (the text says Henri II, which must be an error) not to suppress religious dissent with violence, for if the present discord continues Henri might meet his own death through murder. Consider the example of King Childeric's assassin Bodille—and the "gentleman was for that deede commended . . . of Ronsard, where he speaketh of the king Childerick, thus" (fourteen lines from the Franciade follow, reworked into English heptameter). It is to be presumed, he adds, that "there be at this day a thousand Bandils," and "shall ye not as readily finde Ronsards to prayse and set them forwarde in such enterprises?" (sigs. F5ᵛ–G1). Ronsard, however, had not found Bodille praiseworthy, merely instructive.

Two years later Ronsard reappeared in a book intended like the *Reveille* to blacken Catholics, the Guise, and Mary Stuart. Again the authorship and title page are deliberately confusing, for *A legendarie . . . of the life of Charles, Cardinal of Lorraine* (1577), translated from a work published a year earlier in France, seems to have been quietly encouraged by the English government.[26] It was written by Louis Regnier de la Planche under the name de L'Isle and probably printed at Geneva (the word "legendarie" is of course sarcastic). Regnier says young Henri II had enjoyed reading the psalms of Marot, but the cardinal, alarmed by the king's delight "in these holie songs, which are the bulworkes of chastitie," began "first to reprove the translation, and then the Psalmes themselves, substituting in their steades the lascivious verses of Horace, together with other foolishe songs and abominable love matters of our French Poets whome he brought into credit. Then began Ronsarde, Jodelle, Baife, and other vile Poets to come into estimation. . . . The Psalmes, and Marot him selfe were together banished" (a peculiar chronology; sigs. D7–D8).

After the 1570s Ronsard tends to fade as a figure in religious and political battles, although lines from his *Responce* and the *Continuation du discours* illustrate the French version of John Hay's *Certaine demandes concerning the christian religion* (Lyons, 1583, sigs. M3ᵛ–M4). Other writers, too, particularly those interested in politics and history, continued to quote Ronsard as an authority on such matters or to reinforce their own discussions with excerpts from his poetry. Ronsard's comment that aristocrats thirst to be revenged over even tiny slights supports the argument of Jacques Hurault's *Politicke, moral, and martial discourses* (1595), translated by A. Golding; the passage is turned into one stanza of English rhyme royal and identified as Ronsard's in the margin (sigs. H3–H3ᵛ). Ronsard was not always thus credited. In *Titles of honor* (1614), a study of the origin and nature of names and symbols of power, John Selden says that engraved on Charles Martel's tomb are the words "Non vult Regnare sed Regibus imperat ipse." These are, says Selden, "imitated in more true verse thus:

> C'est ce Martel le Prince des François
> Non Roy de nom, mais le maistre des Roys."
>   [sig. F2ᵛ; L. XVI, 323]

Selden does not mention the author of the *Franciade*, from which the couplet is taken.

Ronsard's verse also ornaments André Favyn's *Theater of honour and knighthood* (1623), an impressive "chronicle and historie of the whole Christian world" in which one finds lines from Du Bartas, the *Roman de la Rose*, Saint-Gelais, and an explanation of crests "which the Prince of Poets hath learnedly noted, of Noble by Extraction, Science, and Learning, in his second Royall Boscage" (sig. A4ᵛ; L. XII, 241). A few pages later in a section telling how to fasten a helmet Favyn twice quotes "the Prince of French Poets Peter de Ronsard, in his Franciade," fragments the anonymous translator puts into blank verse. In the second quotation there is something odd about the meter—it reads better as decasyllables and I suspect it is meant to sound classical and heroic as befitting a high subject and "kind":

> That this Minion should become our prey,
> Let us fasten his nailed Murrian,
> Above the Temple, vowed to by my Father. . . .
> His Lance in hand, the Murrian on his head
> Well Crested, the tempest does resemble
> Sent downe from Jupiter in Summer monthes.[27]

Finally, Pierre Matthieu's *Remarkable considerations upon the life of M. Villeroy* (1638), translated by Sir T. Hawkins, records an exchange in which English readers may have been able to sense

Ronsard's lively intimacy with Charles IX. Among the king's verses, says Matthieu, are those "he addressed to Ronsard, wherein he sayth,

> Ronsard, thy wit more sprightly is than mine.
> My body younger, abler much than thine.

Ronsard's answer began in this manner.

> Such as I am you (Charles) shall be one day,
> Life hopeless of returne, still flies away."
>
>   [sig. C1; L. XVII, 49–50]

Even in the seventeenth century, then, echoes persisted (if often in translation) of Ronsard's position at court and of his activities as a political commentator. But by the 1570s Ronsard had also been established in England as a distinguished author involved, with varying degrees of commitment, in literary and philosophical movements that saw the arts as the means and result of studious but inspired apprehension and thus potential sources of religious and cultural regeneration. This aspect of Ronsard's career received little explicit recognition in England but some of what the English said about him, especially in the 1560s and 1570s or shortly thereafter, indicates an awareness of his participation in the French "academies" or at least a sense that he well filled the role they established for the poet. Thus a Neoplatonic aura glimmers about some of the early mentions of his name, an aura it is unlikely he would ever have rejected utterly, whatever the later readjustments and complications of his own views.

Probably the Englishman most conscious of Ronsard as a leader in the group of French writers and scholars already in the 1560s anticipating the establishment in 1570 of the "académie de poésie et de musique" was Daniel Rogers, the friend of Thomas Jeney, who came to live in Paris in that decade and for a while studied with Dorat. His unpublished Latin poetry contains precious evidence about the private meetings at Baïf's house, gatherings Rogers must have enjoyed all the more because like many he would have met there he was attracted to the Neoplatonic vision of poetry, to an eirenic approach to religious differences, and to metrical translations of the psalms.[28]

Several of Rogers's poems are to Ronsard or refer to him. One is not flattering, although from this distance the tone is hard to gauge: "You are wont to marvel," says Rogers, "that recently at Dreux Victory turned herself to the mighty Huguenots, who few in number on the field of battle withstood the force of innumerable soldiers, and this troublesome sorrow weighs down and grieves your mind. Doubtless you do not realize that God, on whom victory depends, favors the Huguenots because of their piety." This poem strongly recalls another unpublished epigram, written in red ink and dated 1562, ordering Ronsard to cease his amazement over the loss of Catholic leaders at Dreux. The author is harsher than Rogers, sneering at Ronsard's "plume mensongere" and his "foy . . . muable et legere."[29]

Other poems offer ecstatic praise. The hyperboles are not merely fashionable, however, for in their context Rogers's "ebriosus" rapture, Ronsard's "furor," and the poet's power to draw Phoebus down from the sky take on technical Neoplatonic meanings, while the flattering statement to Baïf that his recitations calmed a war-troubled mind would have had particular significance to a group longing to find through poetry a means to peace. In one poem Rogers writes Ronsard that he is the master of the Aonian art, the prince and arbiter of the native lyre, to which as a poet of Phoebus, better than Pindar, he sings varied measures. May he accept with kindly (aequo) favor the verses which Thalia sends with unequal (non aequo) feet, and may Ronsard look with benign face on what benign Love orders Rogers to write. Desiring his excellence and long since stirred by the well-known renown of his celebrated name he burns with love for the poet Ronsard. Nothing matters more to him than that he be known to him, see him more closely, and, drunk to the marrow, drink in his excellence. So that he may give recompense, he prays to be accepted as a novice in that troop which Ronsard leads, as though he were a more famous Apollo. May the muses favor Ronsard's frenzy, may they assist with their sacred liquor the unfailing river of his divine vein, and may they be willing when he calls.[30]

Elsewhere Rogers describes a meeting with Ronsard in Baïf's house. Certainly through kindly fortune a benign light shone on him, he says, when he recently sought Baïf's threshold and Baïf recited the charming delights of his muse. He so intoxicated Rogers with his learned charms and the witty delights with which he so abounds that the painful cares and anxious fears which had cruelly entangled the visitor recently because of the tumults of chaotic France fled away. He even had the joy of then seeing there the sacred face of the poet Ronsard, that very poet whom Phoebus loves more than his eyes. While Rogers saw and heard Ronsard recite Baïf's poems with a graceful sound, poems written with graceful style, then he thought that errant Phoebus, struck by the charming lines, had descended from the deserted sky to Baïf's dwelling. The rest of the poem asks what recompense would suffice for such a pleasure.[31]

One brief jeu d'esprit is in yet another mood. Rogers cannot be very serious, for his repetitions and case endings dance so lightly one may imagine a literary challenge, perhaps, or some event that demanded a friendly scolding:

> Si Ronsarde velut bonus poeta es,
> Tàm Ronsarde etiam bonus vir esses,
> Nullus te melior foret virorum,
> Nullus te melior velut poeta est.
> Nùnc verò optimus omnium poeta es,
> Sed vir pessimus omnium virorum,
> Tanto pessimus omnium virorum,
> Quanto es optimus omnium poeta.

[fols. 348b–49a]

(If, Ronsard, you were as good a man as you are a good poet no one would be a better man than you, just as no one is a better poet. Now certainly you are the best of all poets, but the worst man of all men, as much the worst of all men as you are the best of all poets.) The last two lines playfully echo the close of the forty-ninth poem in Catullus's *Carmina* ("tanto pessimus omnium poeta / quanto tu optimus omnium's patronus"); indeed in the manuscript the last line ends with the word "patronus" canceled to make way for "poeta."

After he went home Rogers established friendships that must have given him frequent opportunity to describe in person theories and hopes heard earlier in Ronsard's circle. He knew Sidney, for instance, as well as Dyer, Greville, and Harvey, who wrote Spenser commending him. He even knew Dr. Dee. Earlier in our own century there was speculation that members of this group had formed an unofficial "academy" designed to be in England roughly what the Pléiade was in France. The chief evidence for this association was a pair of good-humored references to an "Areopagus" in the correspondence of Spenser and Harvey. Spenser writes in 1579 that Sidney and Dyer "have proclaimed in their ἀρείῳ παγω, a generall surceasing and silence of balde Rymers . . . in steade whereof, they have by authoritie of their whole Senate, prescribed certaine Lawes and rules of Quantities of English sillables, for English Verse." Harvey replies, "Your new-founded ἄρειογ πάγον I honour more, than you will or can suppose: and make greater accompte of the twoo worthy Gentlemenne, than of two hundreth Dionisii Areopagitae, or the verye notablest Senatours, that ever Athens dydde affourde of that number."[32]

Few scholars now think this "senate" anything much more than a passing joke. In recent years, however, the "Areopagus" and its possible relation to Ronsard and his friends have received a tentative second look, although no one would claim there was an organized or formal group. Such a review has resulted not so much from new evidence as from increased awareness of who knew whom in England and abroad during the years before the flowering of Elizabethan poetry. In this network of friendships Rogers provides a clearly visible tie between the Continent and England. Furthermore, conversations among Harvey, Dyer, Spenser, and their friends very likely concerned more than a revival of classical meters, for in much European experiment with quantity those meters were themselves meant to serve larger syncretist and even hermetic aims.[33]

Admittedly, much of the evidence for what Spenser and Harvey really had in mind is circumstantial and oblique. Just as in the French academies there was that taste for the secretive ("obscuris vera involvens") which often accompanies belief in the revelatory power of myth and allegory, so too a conspiratorial atmosphere hangs over the Spenser-Harvey letters, not so thick as to hide their playfulness but dense enough to allow the suspicion that behind Harvey's deliberate obscurities lie concerns best kept from vulgar gaze.

In one postscript, for instance, Harvey tells Spenser to keep the letter private and adds, "Non multis dormio: non multis scribo: non cupio placere multis: Alii alios numeros laudant, praeferunt, venerantur: Ego ferè apud nos, ferè apud vos Trinitatem." After this boast of his indifference to the many and his capacity for discretion, and after the dark statement that while others venerate other numbers (does he mean poetical measures or literally other numbers or both?) he prefers the Trinity, Harvey concludes by saying, "Verbum sapienti sat: nosti caetera: et tres Charites habes ad unguem." (A word to the wise is sufficient: You know the rest: And you have the three Graces to perfection.)[34] That the letters containing these mysterious hints were shortly to be published only parallels the contradictions implicit in the hermetic approach to, for example, musical "effects": the people to be affected were themselves for the most part incapable of understanding the theory behind their experience—but then the stones and trees that crowded toward Orpheus did not understand either.

It is against this background, then, that the significance of Rogers's neo-Latin poetry should be seen. One is only sorry that despite some references to Ronsard and translations from his poetry Rogers's English friends had little that was clear, explicit, and unmistakable to say about a movement in France of which it seems fairly certain they were aware. Perhaps they felt that both French and English were simply following the Italians; in his letters to Spenser, Harvey nowhere mentions Ronsard, but he has high praise for Pico.

Harvey does, however, refer to Ronsard elsewhere. He makes no specific comment on him as a member of a group whose interests he in some ways shared, but the context in which Ronsard's name appears situates Harvey's esteem in the same general area as Rogers's ornate homage to "Phoebi . . . poeta." In *Smithus, vel musarum lachrymae* (1578) Harvey calls on each muse to weep the recent death of Sir Thomas Smith. The *lachrymae* stream with famous names, some appropriate to the particular muse—Urania refers to Copernicus—and some meant to add their luster to Smith's own. Melpomene summons "loftysinging bards and tragic poets" who "dwell near the Loire, the Rhône, Saône, and Ebro, the Rhine and Thames, and however many everywhere flourish skilled in song, whose roster Ronsard heads."[35] To many Englishmen, especially in later decades, Ronsard was a love poet, but here he is a *vates*, found among muses and bards ritually lamenting a scholar and statesman.

Harvey mentions Ronsard again in a passage I have already quoted—the remark in the margin of Dionysius Periegetes' *Survey of the world* (1572) that there are "astrological descriptions in the notablest French Poets: cheifly in livelie Marot, florishing Ronsard, admirable Bartas, etc." As he said, Harvey enjoyed "astrological descriptions in anie language," and his library and writings show he also felt the lure of the occult. Probably he thought Ronsard's starry poems flourished not only with beauty but with the mysterious *frisson* that animates them at their best; he must have found in them the sense that much Renaissance "scientific" poetry tries to give of approaching those inner workings which the enraptured poet may apprehend, if then veil in fable.[36] If, as seems likely, Harvey looked at the "Hymne des astres" he would have read with sympathy and admiration a passage from the opening lines:

> Il me plaist en vivant de voir souz moy les nües,
> Et presser de mes pas les espaules chenües
> D'Atlas le porte-ciel, il me plaist de courir
> Jusque au Firmament, & les secretz ouvrir
> (S'il m'est ainsi permis) des Astres admirables.
>
>   [L. VIII, 150]

For Harvey these "secretz" were central to the learning and mental order necessary for the artist. True poets, he says in the same note on astronomy, must not be "superficial humanists" but "curious universal schollers."

At about the same time Harvey wrote his *Smithus* one of his countrymen paid a similarly fleeting compliment to Ronsard, a brief tribute again more interesting for the setting around the praise than for the worn conceit itself. The author, Richard Willes, had spent some years on the Continent as a Catholic but returned in the early 1570s to Protestantism and England, where he soon published a *Poematum liber* (1573), together with a Latin oration on poetry and copious notes to his own compositions. The oration is an early example of its kind in England, an organized Neoplatonic discussion of poetry as inspired and informing power, but when addressing Cecil in the introduction to his *Poemata* he lowers his voice. He is not, he says, thirsty for fame or an "inaurata . . . statua." Yet in these times afflicted terribly by "libidine ac voluptatibus" the learned may find great pleasure in true poetry. His own poems he made when sailing around the islands of the Sirens (that is, he explains heavily, the flower of his youth) as an antidote to the furies of lust. The opening poem offers Cecil these "nugae" and "ludicra" as recreation if he "will set by the writings of weightier men" (sigs. A3–4, A8^v).

Many of the hundred poems that follow are indeed "nugae" more in keeping with the humility of the dedication than with the loftiness of the oration. There are shaped poems: a sword, a set of wings (to symbolize the fame of the poem's subject), an altar, and the like. One page illustrates the fall of Rome with a meditation on that city's *ruina* forming an inverted pyramid. Some poems contain hidden messages in their capital letters; two on the Redemption make quincunxes; most are solemnly annotated. These intriguing oddities are easily dismissed as childish, but the philosophy behind them may have been quite serious. In one poem ten little hiero-glyphic creatures march enigmatically off to the left, exemplifying the author's youthful taste for "ludicra" yet also providing what he probably thought was a glimpse into the occult world of Eastern wisdom.

In the middle of this collection at least half seriously presenting shards of hermetic mystery and in the same volume as a Neo-platonic oration Willes makes an otherwise banal reference to Ronsard. The poem honors "Stephanus," the first and last letters of each line creating additional words. Its *mythos*, according to the notes, shows that "any region bears up to the sky with highest praises men of outstanding erudition." Thus, says the poem, their countries flattered Nestor, Orpheus, Amphion, Homer, and Lucan, Rome thinks itself happy and shining in the name of Hortensius (the orator), the Arpino celebrates the Ausonian rivers of Cicero's speech, and Ronsard is the honor of his native soil and Petrarch of polished Italy."[37] Willes does not mention the recently formed "Académie" or tie his taste for the hermetic to the French poets (although he does have a poem to the occultist Postel), but the entire thrust of his criticism and practice makes it likely that for him Ronsard was the sort of *vates* described in his oration, fit to be mentioned with Orpheus, Homer, Lucan, and Cicero (no poet but deeply learned in rhetoric, ethnic wisdom, and, it was thought, the art of memory). One would like to know if while fighting off the earthly Venus by making anagrams and pentangles he read Ronsard's love poetry, and what he thought of it.

During the next few decades Ronsard was to be quoted, translated, praised, even laughed at. Seldom, however, does his name again appear in surroundings so clearly marked by the syncretist and hermetic interests also found in the French academies, seldom was he so specifically honored as a *vates* even though some of those with concerns like Willes's or Harvey's borrowed from his poems or had a word or two to say about him. One exception is Henry Reynolds, whose often eloquent *Mythomystes* (1633?) pushes the theories behind Willes's oration to a fervid extreme. Opposing to the inspired wisdom of the ancient poets the lazy ignorance of the moderns, Reynolds guides his readers over terrain well surveyed before but still offering views of undiminished fascination to the seventeenth century: poets are inspired by one of Plato's *furores*; the poet-prophets of Greece and Egypt (whose hieroglyphs contain hidden significance) received knowledge imparted fully to Moses but found also in the Cabala and the mysteries of number; myths veil—and reveal to the wise—the workings of the universe. Few modern poets retain these orphic capacities, says Reynolds, because they live in an age which sees in myth merely moral truth, not the secrets of Nature, and indeed which does not understand "scarse the lowest and triviallest of Natures wayes." Thus discouraged, Reynolds warms to a mere handful of writers: Ariosto, Tasso, Marino, Sidney, Spenser, a few others. As for the French, he exempts from his condemnation "a Ronsart or Des-Portes, but chiefly their Salust, who may passe among the best of our modernes."[38] The reference to Ronsard is brief, even tepid, but Reynolds clearly assumes he understands the vital mysteries.

The fullest recognition of this sort, however, was given Ronsard by a Scot, William Drummond. Drummond knew Ronsard's poetry well. In 1609, say some notes he made, he read the *Amours*, hymns, odes, elegies, eclogues, even the *Franciade*, and his poetry shows the impact of this reading.[39] Drummond was particularly drawn to Ronsard's longer poetry. His unfinished "Shadow of the Judgement" strongly recalls Ronsard's "Hymne de la justice," "Forth Feasting" memorializes a visit of James home to Scotland with the exaggerated energy of the "Panegyrique de la renommée," and the "hymn of the Fairest Faire" owes a great deal to

Ronsard's "Hymne de l'éternité"—both poems evoke the divinity's incomprehensible splendor in "those vaste Fieldes of Light" and the deep gulf between a world fallen into mutability and the transcendent unmoved mover.

Because his praise is more directly addressed to God and perhaps because he wanted a more explicitly Christian tone, Drummond adds sections of his own to what might otherwise be called a loose translation. These tend to be Christian Platonist in color: ranks of angels emanate downwards, the trinity above is reflected in triplicity below, and there is more about love. Yet the spirit of the two poems is in many ways alike and Drummond probably saw himself as expanding the original, not as redirecting it. In any case Ronsard's opening flight must have appealed to an imagination fed also by the books he owned on cosmology and the occult; one can see why he wanted to follow:

> Remply d'un feu divin qui m'a l'ame eschauffée,
> Je veux mieux que jamais, suivant les pas d'Orphée,
> Decouvrir les secretz de Nature & des Cieux,
> Recherchez d'un esprit qui n'est poinct ocieux:
> Je veux, s'il m'est possible, attaindre à la louange
> De celle qui jamais pour les ans ne se change,
> Mais bien qui faict changer les siecles & les temps,
> Les moys, & saisons & jours inconstans.

> I feele my Bosome glow with wontlesse Fires,
> Rais'd from the vulgar prease my Mind aspires
> (Wing'd with high Thoghts) unto his praise to clime,
> From deepe Eternitie who call'd foorth Time;
> That Essence which not mov'd makes each thing move,
> Uncreat'd Beautie all-creating Love.[40]

On occasion Drummond refers to Ronsard. He does not say much about the love poetry, although in the notes he made following a visit from Ben Jonson he remarks that Ronsard celebrated his mistress after her death. He writes to Arthur Johnston in an undated letter, "Neither do I think that a good Piece of Poesy which Homer, Virgil, Ovid, Petrarch, Bartas, Ronsard, Boscan, Garcilasso (if they were alive and had that Language) could not understand." In a history of the reign of James V he says of the king

that "Ronzard, who with his Queen came to Scotland, and was his
Domestick Servant, describeth him . . . to the Life," and quotes the
passage in *Le tombeau de Marguerite de France* beginning "Ce Roy
d'Escosse estoit en la fleur de ses ans." And he cites Dorat's
anagram "Pierre de Ronsard—Rose de Pindare," a flattering witticism, seductively reminiscent of stronger alphabetical magic,
found in Tabourot's *Bigarrures* and among the prefatory materials
sometimes published with Ronsard's poetry.[41]

Drummond's greatest tribute to Ronsard, and that which shows
most vividly the connections in his mind between an appreciation
of Ronsard's poetry and loosely Neoplatonic and syncretist
enthusiasms, is a Scots poem printed posthumously but probably
written when he was much younger:

> Great Paragon, of Poets richest Pearle,
> Beneath the artick circles statlie pole
> Abut quoes point the sphears of knouledge role,
> The magnes of al mynds, ear-charming Mearle;
> The perfumd cabinet quher muses duel,
> Enameling neu-found skyes vith starres of gold,
> Quher Pallas vith the free-borne queens enrold,
> And beutie, stryffs it selff for to excel.
> Farre-virthier Orpheus then they quho suel
> Vith sacred Pegasus azure streames,
> Or he quho brocht from Heaven the fyrie beames:
> Mor fit for Phǫbus Bay then Phebus sel.
>   Thy perfyt praises if the vorld vold vrit
>   Must have againe thy selff for to endit.[42]

Here, as in the estimation of Rogers, Willes, and Harvey, Ronsard
is Orphic, learned in the mysteries, drawing to himself the hearer's
mind, and associated with stars and sky and Promethean fire.

Throughout the Renaissance many had affirmed the power of
musical harmonies, their various if elusive effects on human minds
and bodies. Although Englishmen often shared the ancient
assumption that through music, based as it is on number, the mind
more nearly apprehends the structure of the cosmos, I can find
little to indicate they thought French theories and practice
required much notice. The ancients and Italians provided models
enough. John Dowland, to be sure, says in his preface to *The first*

booke of songes (1597) that he had visited France fifteen years before and found it "a nation furnisht with great variety of Musicke" and in the dedicatory epistle to his *Principles of musik* (1626) Charles Butler refers to the academy of Charles IX, but neither mentions the poets who worked with the musicians.

A few compositions written for Ronsard's poetry found their way to England. Elizabeth's virginals book had the music for "Bonjour mon coeur," one item in Robert Dowland's *Musicall banquet* (1610) derives from that by Guillaume Tessier for "Le petit enfant Amour," and Adrien Le Roy's *Briefe a. plaine instruction* (1574) gives the setting for some songs.[43] Vautrollier's *Recueil du melange d'Orlande de Lassus* (1570), however, offers both the music for "Ren moy mon cuoeur" and a sacred parody of the words:

> Ren moy mon cuoeur, ren moy mon cuoeur, pillarde,
> > Que tu retiens dan ton sein arresté:
> > Ren moy, ren moy ma doulce liberté
> > Qu'à tes beaulx yeux mal caut je mis en garde.
> Ren moy ma vie, ou bien la mort retarde,
> > Qui me devance au cours de ta beaulté,
> > Par ne scay quelle honneste cruaulté,
> > Et de plus pres mes angoisses regarde. . . .
> > > > > > > [L. IV, 156]

> Rends moy Seigneur, Rends moy et plus ne tarde,
> Le bien qui est de moy tant escarté
> Ren moy, ren moy la douce liberté
> Qu'Adam mal-caut m'a perdu par mesgarde:
> Ren-moy la vie ou bien la mort retarde,
> Qui me devance, ô Dieu par ta bonté,
> Retire-moy de mon iniquité,
> Et de plus pres mes angoisses regarde.
> > > > > > > > [sig. C4ᵛ]

Perhaps, as I suggested earlier in connection with Marot, Vautrollier thought that music would be more effective if married to overtly religious verse.

For some Englishmen, then, especially during the first half of Elizabeth's reign, Ronsard was associated with French political and philosophical movements or events in ways that rendered him a more complex and interesting figure than the singer of wine, roses, and girls to whom modern anthologies have sometimes limited themselves. As the decades passed Ronsard was still praised, often in the highest terms. Yet, with some important exceptions, I think one can see a thinning out of his reputation, not so much a decline from the high esteem in which he had been held as a greater conventionality or narrowness in its expression. One notices, for instance (and again there are exceptions) that borrowings or quotations tend to be from his early love poetry and that many complimentary references float about in generalities so featureless that neither the praise itself nor the context hints at how and why he was admired. That is not to say that those who mentioned Ronsard in the later years of the English Renaissance had nothing at all in mind, only that for the most part their reaction was less complex and knowledgeable than Rogers's, less engaged than Jeney's, less specific than Harvey's. As far as conscious, definable, English response to him is concerned, Ronsard became primarily a source for other writers, especially love poets, and a name—a famous name—to be awarded a place with or without a reason given in the poetical galleries many enjoyed constructing for celebrated authors in antiquity and modern Europe.

On the other hand it seems likely that Ronsard's actual influence on English poetry of the late Renaissance went well beyond the conventional. The Anacreontic delicacy of his little odes, the spaciousness of his hymns, the numinosity and freshness of his natural descriptions, the dramatic shifts of his speaker's voice, his attitudes toward himself as a poet and toward inspiration—all these must have had an effect on English poets, however hard it is now to follow the wandering channels through which such influence flowed. To read Elizabethan and Stuart verse soon after putting Ronsard down is to catch echoes of his style, his voice, his tone, even when there is no mention of his name or any sign the English author knew him at first hand. Ronsard's effect on the history of English poetry certainly transcended the response to his work as expressed in explicit comment or quiet expropriation. That effect, however, is not the subject of this chapter.

In the 1580s Ronsard's love poems drew particularly careful attention, and his other poetry did not go utterly unnoticed.

Thomas Watson's *Hekatompathia* (1582), for instance, seems to
have been designed to reproduce in England the sort of sequence
Petrarch and Ronsard had written abroad. A highly "artificial"
work in both the Renaissance and modern senses of that word, it
bears signs that Watson hoped its publication would be an important literary event. The hundred "passions," usually eighteen-line
lyrics, are heavily annotated—perhaps Watson was thinking of
Bembo's commentary on Petrarch or Muret's on Ronsard—and
prefaced by rapturous commendations. One of these, a Latin
epigram by a certain C. Downhale, refers to Ronsard. Like many
who mention French poets, Downhale places the subject of his
flattering *comparatio* in a continuous line of good poets. "Fecund
Greece," he says, "brought forth many poets whose fame has
lasted across the lapsed ages; next Italy rivalling Greece in praise
transported learned Helicon to the protection of Latium, which
held and cherished welcome poetry and daily increased your
laurels, Apollo. The French language starts to become rich with
Parnassus and to luxuriate in the new works of Ronsard." England
has thus far lacked a "vates" but now Watson "has taught the
Muses to speak the words of Britain."[44]

Watson based many of these quasi-sonnets on foreign models
which he acknowledges in his notes, often giving a few words of the
original. Four derive from Ronsard's *Meslanges* (1554), a collection
that offered him what he also sought in other poets for "these his
English toyes"—varied attitudes toward love and witty conceits
expressing them in a manner obviously learned but not obscure.
The twenty-seventh passion combines "Celuy qui n'ayme," in
which Ronsard reproaches the greediness of modern women, with
"Quand au temple," a sensual piece about disintegrations beyond
the Styx and the solace of physical love. Watson's method illustrates how detachable, how like discrete particles, many English
poets found the valuable bits they adopted from others. Two other
translations are even more interesting, however, for their depar-
tures from Ronsard's tone.

In the twenty-eighth passion Watson "doth very busilie imitate
and augment a certaine Ode of Ronsard" ("Plusieurs de leurs
cors"). Both poems envisage the metamorphoses by which the
lover might attain intimacy, but whereas Ronsard is content to
proceed through several images of surrounding or enclosure

toward a final kiss, leaving the reader with an imagined consummation, Watson reverts to his own sorrow: "But woe is me, my
wishing is but vaine, / Since fate bidds Love to work my endlesse
paine." Whether from incomprehension, a more commonsensical
approach to love, or a different feeling for the shape of the lyric,
most English adapters seem to have ignored in Ronsard and other
French poets the literary possibilities of this particular conquest—that in which the enfranchised imagination of the poet rests
in satisfied fancy upon the woman lost in actuality but won either
in hope or within the mind's theater. Ronsard was not forever
content with love achieved in the subjunctive mood or future tense,
but more often than his adapters, at least in his earlier poetry, he
allowed the fantasy to survive unshattered and thus affirmed not
his prowess as a lover but his victory as a poet safe from the lady's
denial.[45]

This reluctance on the part of some English love poets to leave
the vision intact finds an interesting analogue in Watson's eighty-
third passion. Ronsard's witty allegory about the subjection of
sexuality to the imagination is, in Watson's good-humored version, made to suggest the death of love:

> Les Muses lierent un jour
> De chaisnes de roses Amour,
> Et pour le garder le donnerent
> Aus Graces & à la Beauté,
> Qui voyans sa desloyauté
> Sus Parnase l'emprisonnerent.
>
> Si tost que Venus l'entendit,
> Son beau ceston elle vendit
> A Vulcan, pour la delivrance
> De son enfant, & tout soudain,
> Ayant l'argent dedans sa main,
> Fit aus Muses la reverence.
>
> Muses, déesses des chansons,
> Quand il faudroit quatre ransons
> Pour mon enfant, je les aporte:
> Delivrés mon fils prisonnier.
> Mais les Muses l'ont fait lier
> D'une autre chaisne bien plus forte.

> Courage donques, Amoureux,
> Vous ne serés plus langoureux,
> Amour n'oseroit par ses ruses
> Plus faillir à vous presenter
> Des vers, quand vous voudrés chanter
> Puis qu'il est prisonnier des Muses.
>
> [L. VI, 253–55]

The Muses not long since intrapping Love
In chaines of roases linked all araye,
Gave Beawtie charge to watch in theire behove
With Graces three, lest he should wend awaye:
    Who fearing yet he would escape at last,
    On high Parnassus toppe they clapt him fast.
When Venus understoode her Sonne was thrall,
She made posthaste to have God Vulcans ayde,
Solde him her Gemmes, and Ceston therewithall,
To ransome home her Sonne that was betraide;
    But all in vaine. the Muses made no stoare
    Of gold, but bound him faster then before.
Therefore all you, whom Love did ere abuse,
Come clappe your handes with me, to see him thrall,
Whose former deedes no reason can excuse,
For killing those which hurt him not at all:
    My selfe by him was lately led awrye,
    Though now at last I force my love to dye.[46]

Two years later John Soowthern published his odd verse. Soowthern certainly knew other French poets well, but his love for Ronsard, I think, led him to make *Pandora* an epitome or condensation of the latter's work (luckily, the epic is missing). The collection begins with a Pindaric ode to the Earl of Oxford not based on any one original by Ronsard but borrowing lines here and there. Jouncing along in rhythms which cannot have been intended as ordinary English meter and scattering imprudent neologisms, Soowthern evidently hoped to reproduce not only Ronsard's structure but also his hyperboles, self-congratulations, claims for poetry, and invocations. Whatever he thought he was doing in these strange lines Soowthern was proud of it, reaching the end of the last epode in a posture also imitated from Ronsard:

> Vaunt us that never man before,
> Now in England, knewe Pindars string.[47]

The next few pages contain very self-conscious and self-extolling sonnets to Diana, several indebted to the first book of *Amours*. Again the rhythms are ametrical. There are also elegies, including those based on sonnets by Du Bellay, another frantic Pindaric flight, some epitaphs, and fragments, Soowthern says, of other elegies and hymns. Then come the "new kinde of verces" quoted earlier, several "odellets" (lines of which echo the *Meslanges*) and finally a "stansse" and two "quadrans" in French. The whole collection is thus an anthology of those genres in which Ronsard had worked. Furthermore, Soowthern tried in this verse to include many of his master's tones and moods: the grandiloquence of the ode, the Petrarchist woe of the love poetry, the sententiousness of the elegy and hymn, the gaiety of the odelets (these last straining for a ghastly hedonism devoid of Ronsard's charm: "But like the olde Poët Annacron, / It pleases mee well to be Biberon").

Soowthern nowhere mentions that he lifted his own lines from French poets but he does refer several times to Ronsard, adopting toward him an unlikable tone of jolly admiration or impertinent sympathy. In one sonnet he promises Diana the company of famous beloveds and himself that of their poets:

> And he that soong the eldest daughter of Troye,
> In Fraunce hath made of her, an astre Divine. . . .
> I the peane of Soothern will my fayre Diana,
> Make thee immortall: if thou wilt give hym favour:
> For then hee'll sing Petrark, Tien [Anacreon], Ovide, Ronsar:
> And make thee Cassander, Corine, Bathyll, Laura.
>
> [sig. B1]

An "ode" in Soowthern's wine-and-roses vein invites Simonides and Anacreon to drink with him and wishes that "our olde Ronsard of Fraunce, / With his Cassandra too were here" (sig. D2^v). And a French "stansse" commiserates with Ronsard on his "Casandre implacable" (sig. D4). This is ridiculous stuff, but together with Watson's more important work Soowthern's *Pandora* may have had some impact on English awareness of Ronsard as a major innovative poet and specifically on his reputation as a love poet. Soowthern borrows from a broad range of Ronsard's verse, but the "image" of Ronsard in his poetry is that of Cassandre's lover.

Soowthern's debts to Ronsard's odes did not go unnoticed. George Puttenham in 1589 cited them as an outrageous example of theft and "mingle mangle" diction:

> Another of reasonable good facilitie in translation finding certaine of the hymnes of Pyndarus and of Anacreons odes, and other Lirickes among the Greekes very well translated by Rounsard the French Poet, and applied to the honour of a great Prince in France, comes our minion and translates the same out of French into English, and applieth them to the honour of a great noble man in England (wherein I commend his reverent minde and duetie) but doth so impudently robbe the French Poet both of his prayse and also of his French termes, that I cannot so much pitie him as be angry with him for his injurious dealing (our sayd maker not being ashamed to use these French wordes *freddon*, *egar*, *superbous*, *filanding*, *celest*, *calabrois*, *thebanois* and a number of others . . . . And in the end (which is worst of all) makes his vaunt that never English finger but his hath toucht Pindars string which was neverthelesse word by word as Rounsard had said before by like braggery.

Puttenham quotes some examples of Soowthern's mingle mangle and then adds, "this man deserves to be endited of pety larceny for pilfering other mens devises from them and converting them to his owne use, for in deede as I would wish every inventour which is the very Poet to receave the prayses of his invention, so would I not have a translatour to be ashamed to be acknowen of his translation."[48] Interestingly, Puttenham limits Soowthern's faults to dishonesty, boasting, and Frenchified language. He says not a word about the deformed rhythms, indeed credits Soowthern with a "reasonable good facilitie in translation." And he must have known Ronsard's odes fairly well himself to have recognized the "pety larceny," although he is evidently unimpressed by the author's self-promotion.

Ronsard had other imitators in the later sixteenth and earlier seventeenth centuries, most of whom followed Watson in borrowing only from his love poetry. Yet within the broad category "love poetry" English poets adopted from Ronsard more than one way of expressing their various passions or inventions, finding in him the usual Petrarchist complaint or compliment but also light Anacreontic treatment of Eros, admonitions to consider mortality, and refashionings of Greek myth.

Sir Arthur Gorges confined himself to translating two sonnets from the first book of *Amours*. A very pretty "vannetye," written during the 1580s and later published in the *Phoenix nest* (1593), translates one of Ronsard's loveliest poems to Cassandre:

Je vouldroy bien richement jaunissant
En pluye d'or goute à goute descendre
Dans le giron de ma belle Cassandre,
Lors qu'en ses yeulx le somme va glissant.

   Puis je voudroy en toreau blanchissant
Me transformer pour sur mon dos [or "pour finement"] la prendre,
Quand en avril par l'herbe la plus tendre
Elle va fleur mille fleurs ravissant.

   Je voudroi bien pour alleger ma peine,
Estre un Narcisse & elle une fontaine,
Pour m'y plonger une nuict à sejour:

   Et si voudroy que ceste nuict encore
Fust eternelle, & que jamais l'Aurore
Pour m'esveiller ne rallumast le jour.

Woolde I were changde into that golden Showre
   that so devynly streamede from the Skies
To fall in droppes upon my daynty flowre
   when in her bedd Shee sollytarye lyes
Then woulde I hope such showers as richly shyne
Sholde pearce more deepe then thes waste teares of myne

Els woolde I were that plumed Swann snowhite
   under whose forme was hydden heavenly power
Then in that River woolde I moste delighte
   whose waves do beate against hyr Stately Bower
And on those bancks so tune my dyinge Songe
That hir deaffe eares shoulde thinke my plaints to longe

Or woolde I were Narcissus that sweete Boye
  and Shee her selfe the fountayne cristall cleare
Who ravishte with the pryde of his owne Joye
  drenchede his lymmes with gazinge over neare
So shoulde I brynge my Sowle to happie reste
To ende my lyfe in that I lovede Beste.[49]

Some might find Gorges's poem a little less sensuous than Ronsard's; thus "goute à goute descendre" becomes "devynly streamede," mythologically more informative but not as languorous; there is no equivalent for the quasi-phallic "y plonger"; and the swan is less obviously masculine and ravishing than Ronsard's bull. Gorges, rather, stresses his woeful failure, his "waste teares."

That his friends Gorges and Harvey admired or borrowed from Ronsard makes it all the more likely Spenser knew his poetry. There are many analogous passages in their work and despite the obvious temperamental differences some deeper affinities as well.[50] On at least two occasions one can find direct imitation, although what Spenser took was put to new use. In the March eclogue of *The Shepheardes Calender* (1579) young Thomalin says he has seen Love flitting through the bushes and has shot at him, only to be wounded himself. Bion had written of this strange bird but Spenser's version owes more to Ronsard's "Un enfant dedans un bocage," a lyric in the *Nouvelle continuation des amours* (1556).[51] Ronsard's effect depends in part on the contrast between the naïve "enfant" and the older woman who explains that someday he will know Love too well. Spenser's shepherd, however, discovers during the eclogue what it is he has found—the scene (which has considerable humor) allegorizes an awakening to sexual experience thematically related to the rest of the *Calender* and appropriate to a month which, like Love himself, offers "Hony" and "Gaule."

"Astrophel" (1595) also suggests that Spenser had been reading Ronsard. This elegy on Sidney loosely follows Ronsard's "Adonis" (1563), itself in part an adaptation of Bion's great lament for the lover of Aphrodite.[52] To a certain extent Ronsard retains the ancient implications of the tragedy (interpreted by some Renaissance mythographers as a vegetation myth); the boar is compared to winter and the mischievous ending whereby the goddess forgets

Adonis to love Anchises is analogous to Bion's reminder that she must weep for Adonis again next year—for Bion the cycles of generation attain their own eternity; for Ronsard, as he said elsewhere, "La matiere demeure, & la forme se perd." Venus must ever receive new lovers. Spenser's quite actual hero is a noble figure whose chaste Stella is no Venus forgetful of the ideal in her descent to the lower world and whose sister, not mistress, is the chief mourner. The original significance of the story adds resonance to Spenser's poem—Sidney was a "pattern" whose loss was deeply felt in England—but naturally Spenser recognizes not only the flower into which Astrophil changes but the happiness of his soul in Heaven, a reward more readily available to English captains than to a demigod. Spenser, it seems clear, knew and used Ronsard; but it was Du Bellay he called the garland of free poesy.

"Astrophil" himself would have had every reason to read Ronsard's poetry, yet he never mentioned him and despite many parallels his verse shows little if any actual indebtedness. Probably his reasons were as much a matter of literary strategy as of personal or ideological distaste. More than most Elizabethan lovers Astrophil swears he speaks only from his heart, and although such declarations, themselves conventional, usually lead to hyperbolic flattery (who needs divine *furor* or a foreign model if he has Stella?) the claim is quite seriously meant, not as a modern affirmation of sincerity but as a demand that poetry imitate an inward truth:

> Let daintie wits crie on the Sisters nine,
> That bravely maskt, their fancies may be told:
> Or Pindare's Apes, flaunt they in phrases fine,
> Enam'ling with pied flowers their thoughts of gold.

Astrophil's scorn for the poet who "his song in Jove, and Jove's strange tales attires, / Broadred with buls and swans, powdred with golden raine" refers to common Renaissance images, but like the words "Pindare's Apes" may be meant to recall Ronsard.[53] If so, Astrophil's dissociation of his love from tired tradition does not prove much about Sidney's own settled opinion of Ronsard. The rhetoric of praise requires such stress on the superior reality of this particular passion.

During the next decade many other English love poets adopted themes and images from the Italians and French; two in par-

ticular—Giles Fletcher the elder and Thomas Lodge—took from
Ronsard not merely phrases but whole poems. Fletcher's *Licia*
(1593), his introduction speculates entertainingly, could symbolize almost anything: the courtesy of his patroness, perhaps? or
even a college? Some denigrate such verse, but in Italy and France
"men of learning and great partes" have written "Poems and
Sonnets of Love." Too many of his countrymen, he says, have
obtained "from Italie, Spaine, and France their best and choicest
conceites," yet Fletcher's own poems are almost all borrowed;
most derive from the neo-Latin poets, and two from Ronsard's
Amours. He translates "Quand au premier" fairly literally (adding
a compliment to Licia's chastity), but like many English adapters
he makes the ending more epigrammatic:

> Quand au premier la Dame que j'adore,
> Vint embellir le sejour de noz cieulx,
> Le filz de Rhée appella tous les Dieux,
> Pour faire encor d'elle une aultre Pandore.
>
> Lors Apollin richement la decore,
> Or, de ses raiz luy façonnant les yeulx,
> Or, luy donnant son chant melodieux,
> Or, son oracle & ses beaulx vers encore.
>
> Mars luy donna sa fiere cruaulté,
> Venus son ris, Dione sa beaulté,
> Peithon sa voix, Ceres son abondance.
>
> L'Aube ses doigtz & ses crins deliez,
> Amour son arc, Thetis donna ses piedz,
> Cleion sa gloyre, & Pallas sa prudence.

> When first the Sunne, whome all my senses serve,
> Began to shine upon this earthly round,
> The heav'ns for her, all graces did reserve,
> That Pandor-like, with all she might abound.
> Apollo plac'd his brightnesse in her eyes,
> His skill presaging, and his musicke sweete.
> Mars gave his force, all force she now defyes.
> Venus her smyles, wherewith she Mars did meete.
> Python a voyce, Dyana made her chaste,
> Ceres gave plentie: Cupid lent his bowe:
> Thetis his [*sic*] feete: there Pallas wisdome plac't.

> With these she Queene-like kept a world in awe.
> Yet all these honours deemed are but pelfe.
> For she is much more worthie of her selfe.[54]

The last sonnet translates "O doulx parler" (L. IV, 49), increasing the already insistent anaphora and once more compressing Ronsard's poem to make room for Fletcher's own conclusion.

Lodge was Ronsard's most tireless adapter in the 1590s. A pleasant and facile poet, not of the first rank but often delightful, he found in Ronsard fine inventions, clever tropes, a mannered loveliness, and self-conscious grief exactly suited to his own requirements. Images of metamorphosis, morning freshness, and inward sorrow seem especially to have touched him.

Even before 1590, however, Lodge had been reading Ronsard, borrowing lines that he did not translate but merely rearranged into a commendatory poem for Robert Greene's *Spanish masquerado* (1589). His chief source was "A sa muse," Ronsard's tribute to his own fame and accomplishment first published at the end of his odes.[55] Lodge transforms self-congratulation into compliment by changing the pronouns and adjectives but the result hovers between sense and confusion (the italicized words are from "A sa muse"):

> *Le doux Babil de ma lire d'ivoire*
> *Serra ton front d'un laurier verdisant:*
> *Dont a bon droit je te voy jouissant,*
> (Mon doux ami) *eternisant* ta *gloire.*
> Ton nom (mon Greene) anime *par mes vers*
> Abaisse l'oeil de gens seditieux,
> Tu de mortel es compagnon de Dieux:
> N'est ce point grand loyer dans *l'univers?*

> [sig. A2ᵛ]

With less effort Lodge could have written a better poem in English. Did he hope the lines would be recognized and his cleverness admired? Or, his sources too obscure to spot, that he would be praised for his bold-mannered French?

At least seven sonnets in *Phillis* (1593) derive from the first book of *Amours*, translated about as literally as the rules of the sonnet allow. On occasion, though, Lodge edges toward greater subjectivity and woefulness or heightens the conceit a little, dimin-

ishing somewhat the subtlety of tone or detail. At times he elaborates on the original mythology, at times sharpens the final point.
Some of these tendencies can be seen in his pretty rendition of "Je
vouldroy bien richement," the sonnet attired in "Joves strange
tales" Gorges had already adapted:

> I would in rich and golden coloured raine,
> With tempting showers in pleasant sort discend,
> Into faire Phillis lappe (my lovely friend)
> When sleepe hir sence with slomber doth restraine.
>   I would be chaunged to a milk-white Bull,
> When midst the gladsome fieldes she should appeare,
> By pleasant finenes to surprise my deere,
> Whilest from their stalkes, she pleasant flowers did pull:
>   I were content to wearie out my paine,
> To bee Narsissus so she were a spring
> To drowne in hir those woes my heart do wring:
> And more I wish transformed to remaine:
>   That whilest I thus in pleasures lappe did lye,
>   I might refresh desire, which else would die.[56]

Lodge's *Life and death of William Longbeard* (1593) describes in
euphuistic prose the career in Plantagenet days of a "most famous
and witty English Traitor." Unlike most of his contemporaries,
who borrowed either openly or with, one assumes, the realization
that many literate readers would recognize their debts, Lodge
seems almost to go out of his way to confuse those who might
wonder where he found a conceit. Perhaps he thought such back-
tracking or evasion increased the plausibility of his crime story by
concealing an anachronism. Once, he says, when William and his
friends "discoursed of love, shewing all the idolatrie of their pens,"
he remembered "a sonnet in an ancient French Poet" and "on
sudden wrote this imitation." The lyric, "As soone as thou doost
see the Winter," is a close paraphrase of a poem Lodge could have
found in the *Meslanges* or, later, among the odes ("Si tost que tu
sens arriver").[57]

Before the law catches up with William, as of course it must, he
writes some other poems that show his "high spirite and deepe
invention." One demonstrates how "even in those daies, Poecy
had hir impugners, and industrie could not be free from detraction." If he must die, the poet asks, why write verses? Fame is

neither sure nor lasting. Can he do better than the great Greeks?
Even their poetry was long lost:

> No, no: tis farre more meet
> To follow Marchants life,
> Or at the judges feet
> To sel my toong for bribes to maintaine strife.
>
> Then haunt the idle traine
> Of poore Calliope,
> Which leaves for hunger slaine,
> The choicest men that hir attendants be.[58]

William has been reading the *Meslanges* again:

> Non, non, il vaut mieux, Rubrampré,
> Son age en trafiques despendre,
> Ou devant un Senat pourpré
> Pour de l'argent sa langue vendre,
>
> Que de suivre l'ocieux train
> De ceste pauvre Caliope,
> Qui toujours fait mourir de faim
> Les meilleurs chantres de sa trope.

[L. VI, 197]

That Lodge may for some reason have been nervous about his
borrowings is further indicated by a little slip he made years later.
In his translation of Goulart's *Learned summary* (1621) he says
Ronsard was "rich in the spoiles of the Grecians, and Latines, as
his divers Poems, Odes, Elegies, and Hymnes do verifie" (sig.
Vvvl[v]), omitting the "amours" which Goulart had included and
which of all Elizabethans Lodge had best reason to remember.

Other convincing Renaissance adaptations of Ronsard are few,
whatever his possible influence on writers from Lyly and Barnes to
Shakespeare himself.[59] Michael Drayton's odes, however, some
first published in 1606 and others in 1619, are at times quite like
Ronsard's in their debts to Horace and Anacreon and, occasionally, in their self-conscious tone of lyric elevation. "To Himselfe, and the Harpe" advances the assertions found in similar odes
of Ronsard: a poet like Pindar is able "The Soule with power to

strike"; there is a line of such inspired singers stretching from David to Orpheus, Hermes, Amphion, Pindar, Horace, the druids, and the Irish bards; the speaker himself will now join this group and "Th'old Lyrick kind revive." Drayton nowhere mentions Ronsard, the greatest of the moderns to revive that kind, but he has a surprisingly good word for Soowthern, "Who me pleased'st greatly, / As first, therefore more rare, / Handling thy Harpe neatly"—he must have found results where we can perceive only intentions.[60]

Several passages in Donne strikingly resemble similar moments in Ronsard's poetry. Because he seems so original one tends to resist finding in these similarities evidence that Donne had been looking elsewhere for inventions and arguments. Furthermore, Ronsard's great lines often achieve classical finality rather than the intellectual compression of Donne at his best, and the latter's pyrotechnic displays of paradox and religious intensity are remote from the crystalline amplitude of, say the "Hymne de l'éternité" (although Ronsard of course was not without his own doubts and ironies). Yet Donne might have recognized in Ronsard a writer particularly fascinating, like himself, for a carefully modulated voice and sense of self, an often dramatic relationship to the hearer within the poems, varying rhetorical poses, and radical inconsistencies. Many parallels in their verse may be dismissed as the result of a common heritage—the soul's journey upwards after death, the rock on which truth (or "philosophie") is found, the defense of inconstancy and of the flesh—but some of the borrowings that have been suggested are worth considering.

Donne, like Ronsard, contemplates with philosophy and amusement a flea trying to bite his mistress. "Batter my heart" shares with Ronsard's sonnet "Foudroye moi le cors" the image of a warring city betrayed by Reason, a violent tone, and a plea for God's overpowering force to do for the speaker and his inner divisions what his own defective will cannot. And whatever the precedents in Theocritus' twelfth idyll and elsewhere, Donne could have found in an elegy to Marie published first in 1560 ("Marie, à celle fin") one source for "The Canonization"; Ronsard describes how when they are dead lovers will build them a temple where they will be worshiped: "Et par voeux nous serions invocquez tous les jours / Comme les nouveaus dieux des fidelles amours."[61]

There seems to be, in fact, little doubt that Donne had read some of Ronsard's love poetry. In a canceled passage before a paradoxical "problem" exploring "Why is there more variety of Greene than of other Colours," he says "Konsard [*sic*] and all his Cuntrymen since are inraged with greene eyes." Donne could be thinking (a bit confusedly) of any number of lines in Ronsard's verse, such as those on what the lover would like in a girl—"Noir je veux l'oeil, & brun le teint / Bien que l'oeil verd le François tant adore."[62] That the allusion is obscure does not diminish its importance as evidence he knew a poet whose work so often resembles his own, however much those resemblances are disguised by the many obvious differences and especially by the more embroidered or enameled surface of Ronsard's style and the greater smoothness of his rhythms.

During the next two generations or so one can often feel the effects, immediate or at several removes, of the Pléiade. Some of Carew's poetry, for instance, recalls Ronsard so strongly it is tempting to believe he had read the *Amours*. Unlike Ronsard's earlier adapters, however, Carew moved away from the sonnet and its rhetoric, reversing a long-standing tendency among the English that started as early as Surrey to urge French lyrics closer to an epigrammatic structure. One of his "perswasions to enjoy" may expand the opening quatrain of a poem to Hélène, although others had made the same logical if speciously seductive argument that mortal girls should make love while they have time and immortal girls have nothing to lose.[63]

Thomas Stanley, a young man familiar with continental poetry, adapted a poem by Ronsard and took the unusual step of crediting his source. In his collection of lyrics (1647) he reiterates the old hope that Time and Venus will bring the lover revenge:

> Jeune beauté, mais trop outrecuidée
> > Des presens de Venus,
> Quand tu verras ta peau toute ridée
> > Et tes cheveus chenus,
> Contre le tens, & contre toi rebelle
> > Diras en te tansant,
> Que ne pensoi-je alors que' j'estoi belle
> > Ce que je vai pensant?

Ou bien pourquoi à mon desir pareille
    Ne suis-je maintenant?
La beauté semble à la rose vermeille
    Qui meurt incontinant.
Voila les vers tragiques, & la plainte,
    Qu'au ciel tu envoiras
Tout aussi tost que ta face dépainte
    Par le tens tu voiras.
Tu sçais combien ardamment je t'adore
    Indocile à pitié,
Et tu me fuis, & tu ne veus encore
    Te joindre à ta moitié.
O de Paphos, & de Cypre regente
    Déesse aus noirs sourcis,
Plus tost encor que le tens soi vangente
    Mes dédaignez soucis,
Et du brandon dont les cueurs tu enflammes
    Des jumens tout au tour,
Brusle-la moi, afin que de ses flammes
    Je me rie à mon tour.
              [L. II, 33–35 with 1587 variants]

Fair Rebell to thy self, and Time,
    Who laughst at all my tears,
When thou hast lost thy youthfull prime
    And age his Trophie rears,

Weighing thy inconsiderate pride
    Thou shalt in vaine accuse it,
Why Beauty am I now deni'd
    Or knew not then to use it?

Then shall I wish ungentle Fair
    Thou in like flames may'st burn;
Venus, if just will hear my prayer
    And I shall laugh my turn.[64]

Stanley's approach differs greatly from that of most earlier translators. Where they would elaborate he simplifies; where they
would stress the agony of the narrator he remains wittily detached.
Gone is Ronsard's richness of surface, but in its place reposes a

dispassionate clarity that may even improve upon the original. Some years later the Earl of Rochester adapted Ronsard's translation of an Anacreontic plea to Vulcan for a drinking cup.[65] He too sought clear rather than florid wit, although by adding a homosexual touch and a final obscenity he gives a more desperate gaiety to Ronsard's smiling *voeu*.

I do not know of any other obvious adaptations during the seventeenth century, although one hears echoes of Ronsard from time to time. Long before Marvell's "Garden" and "Mower's Song" Ronsard had referred to his "pensers tous vers" in a passage describing how he wanders "Par les prez non frayez de nulle trace humaine" and in his lady's absence embraces the erotic trees (elsewhere he lies beneath "umbrages vers," but that phrase is less arresting). And a poem asking "Que sert aus hommes de suivir / Apollon, & les neuf pucelles" (L. VI, 44) sounds to me quite like the lines beginning "Alas! what boots it" in Milton's *Lycidas*.[66]

During the decades in which Englishmen were reading and translating Ronsard's poetry some also referred to him. After the first quasi-political response to his poetry and the slightly later vision of him as a bard it is hard to sense any particular direction or shape in English remarks. Most are brief if complimentary; some associate Ronsard primarily with love poetry; few attempt an intelligent estimate. Yet even the silly or trite notices illustrate the extent to which Ronsard came to be seen as his nation's chief poet (or one of them), taking his place as he himself prophesied among authors of whom his country could boast, and the banal *comparationes* share with more thoughtful comments an interest in "placing" Ronsard, situating him in the increasing group of modern authors one had heard of, or in relation to those long dead. For behind the desire to clutch these wilting flowers of rhetoric lay a larger impulse to define modern poetry with regard to antiquity, to affirm its achievements while establishing an emotionally satisfying continuity with the past. The result is a sort of grid in which an author may be related to those like him in other countries, usually because of the mere fact of accomplishment, and to those classical figures grouped in the distance against which the set of moderns is seen. Sometimes distinctions are made, but usually one feels more strongly the impulse to compare, to parallel, to locate a name among others in European space and along a perspective reaching back in time and forward in fame. The group is thus given a sort of unity, while the concomitant myth of national and personal competition adds an interesting tension.

Some such appearances of Ronsard's name in flattering comparisons or similar structures into which a flock of authors may be readily shepherded and "placed" have already been quoted—Fylding's inept panegyric, Downhale's poem to Watson, the Latin celebrations by Harvey and Willes. Another early inclusion of Ronsard swells the crowd of famous names to which "R. W. G. A." adds that of Jacques Bellot in a sonnet prefaced to *The french grammer* (1578). The poem shows the company Ronsard was thought worthy to keep, and although R. W. G. A. seems less certain than Willes and Harvey precisely why, aside from their fame, the authors he chooses belong together, the names are chiefly of those connected in some way with myth, secret learning, and the upward reach for mystery and wisdom. Thus Greece boasts of Pythagoras, Hesiod, Homer, and Plato, Tuscany of Petrarch and Bembo, Sion of Josephus,

> Et de Ronsard, bruit en France le Loire.
> De son Bocace aussy se gloriffie
> L'Italien, France, se fortiffie
> De Des-Essarts, & maint autre françois.
>
> [sig. A5ᵛ]

The next poem commending Bellot's *Grammer* is that by the English gentleman "Jean Wrothe" who, it may be remembered, praised Marot, Du Bellay, and the writings of "Froissard, Ronsard, Collet, Jodelle. / Racontans l'un l'amour, l'autre Guerre cruelle" (sig. A6).

The 1580s saw few direct English references to Ronsard besides those by Soowthern and Downhale, the not wholly flattering remarks of Puttenham, and the acknowledgments by Watson. For his *Lawiers Logike* (1588) Abraham Fraunce quoted a few lines of Propertius "by Ronsard translated into French"; he must have taken them from Ramus's *Dialectique* (1555; in L. X, 383). In Scotland, however, one finds another example of the list as hyperbolic compliment. "E. D.," who may have been Elizabeth Douglas, Countess of Erroll, wrote an awkward sonnet for William

Fowler's translation of Petrarch's *Trionfi* (1587) in which Ronsard
makes an appearance a little dimmed by the author's preference
for Du Bartas. Greece, of course, glories in Homer and Italy in
Virgil; Sulmo boasts of Ovid, Spain of Lucan,

> And France for Ronsard stands and settis him owt;
> The better sort for Bartas blawis the horne,
> And Ingland thinks thair Surrye first but dout.
> To praise thair owen these countreis gois about . . .

but of course now all "yeild Sen foular doith arrywe."[67]

In the 1590s one finds the method of sorting out authors by their
nationality used at its tiresome worst in Churchyard's *Musicall
consort* (1595), quoted in an earlier chapter. Churchyard, it may
be recalled, had identified as "Marrot, Ronsart, and du Bartas"
those three famous poets in France who "beautifide thier stately
minde / With inward vertues rare" (sig. E4). John Eliot, however,
gave Ronsard a fuller if derivative discussion, like Churchyard's
only in the familiar method of traveling country by country to note
and cluster the best-known writers. The student in *Ortho-epia Gallica* (1593) whose misunderstanding of Marot has just been cor-
rected asks, "Who is the second French Poet in your opinion?" (He
means second in time, not in merit.) Eliot himself earlier in the
book had listed Ronsard among those who wrote "Poësies and
Love-toies" (sig. B1), but here the teacher elaborates: "It is Peter
Ronsard, rich in the spoiles of the Greekes and Latines; as his
Loves, his divers Poesies, his Odes, Elegies and Hymnes do testifie,
in the which we read all kind of verses, all kinde of Arguments in all
kind of stiles" (sig. H1). This encomium, like the more qualified
tribute to Marot, is taken word for word from Goulart's commentary on Du Bartas's "Babylone." Du Bartas had written (I
quote Sylvester's English):

> That is, great Ronsard, who his France to garnish,
> Robs Rome and Greece, of their Art-various varnish;
> And, hardy-witted, handleth happily
> All sorts of subject, stile, and Poësie.[68]

Eliot, however, must have read Ronsard himself. During a very
funny scene in a bookstore a customer asks for "The Butterflie of
Bellauius. The flie of Lucian. Ovid of the Flea and the Nut-tree.

Ronsard in praise of the Ant his booke of the Frog, and of the Waspe. Phavorin of fevers quartane." He also wants the "description of the West Indies in Spanish," Du Bartas's *Sepmaines* in French, Petrarch and Boccaccio in Italian, Caesar in Latin, the Koran in Arabic, the Talmud in Hebrew, and the New Testament "in the Assirian tongue." He needs these, he explains, for his return to the university (sig. i2). The works by Ronsard, light odes praising small or unworthy subjects in a manner popular during the Renaissance, are all found in the *Meslanges*, as is the "Papillion" of Belleau.

A decade later Robert Dallington, too, surveyed French literature, like so many others finding it best to arrange modern writers according to their nation and the most analogous figures in antiquity. In *The view of France* (1604), a pleasant and detailed guide for the English traveler, he writes,

> If you aske me what Authours of the French I most approove? I durst commend Commines, Bodin, Plessie, Bertas, for Historie, Policie, Divinitie and Moralitie, with the best: and great pitie it is, that the Historie of the first is written in no better French. But if you demand the best Authours, for the language it selfe, I thinke, as Tuscaine hath a Dante and a Petrarch, Greece an Isocrates and a Demosthenes, Rome a Cicero and a Caesar, we a Sydney and a Chaucer: so, France hath a Bertas and a Romsart, in this kinde most recommendable. [sig. V4]

To Dallington, apparently, Du Bartas shared with Ronsard a supremacy in style, in using the language well (not a judgment modern readers would endorse), but he did not care to put Ronsard in his category of authors to "approove." One would not have expected him to find much substance in the *Amours*, granted the assumptions of his time, but some of Ronsard's work might reasonably have been commended for "philosophie" had Dallington so wished (and as Harvey might have suggested).

Less sophisticated than Dallington but not without charm was I. or J. G., author of *An apologie for women-kinde* (1605), who begs the muses to infuse him with high thoughts while he writes "The sacred honours of your fellowe Sexe, / Which mens unlawfull tirannye doth vexe." Rightly modest about his capacities

(although his Petrarchist portrayal of Eve is rather pretty), I. G.
says he wishes better writers would take on the task:

> Full well I wot, this subject was more fitte
> For peerlesse Homers or for Virgils witte,
> The Florence-Petrarkes, Tassoes, or Ronsardes,
> Sidnyes or Spencers; unto whome, rewardes,
> Garlands of Bayes by Poets graunted are.

[sig. A4ᵛ]

I have already quoted William Browne's catalogue of such
laurel-worthy authors in *Britannia's pastorals* (1616). That Marot
and Ronsard "Should spirit of life in very stones infuse" recalls the
old tale of Orpheus and his vivifying *energia*, but Browne does not
elaborate.[69]

A more extended comment appears in George Hakewill's
Apologie or declaration of the power and providence of God (1627).
Hakewill's admiration of Ronsard and Du Bartas is particularly
significant since to him the triumphs of Ronsard and the others he
"places" in time and merit offer further evidence the world has not
decayed. Poetry in fact has improved since the days of those
"Monkes or Fryars" who "for the most part . . . only delighted in
rhyming, without either sharpnesse of wit, or neatnesse of stile, and
sometimes . . . wanted all three." Among the "infinite number" of
good modern poets he "will onely instance in two, Ronsard and
Buchanan," and he then quotes and translates a Latin epigram on
Ronsard by Pasquier which plays gracefully upon the by now
familiar comparisons:

> Whether thee Maro's number please,
> Or elegant Catullus vaine,
> Or Petrarchs Thuscan gracefulnesse,
> Or Theban Pindars lofty straine:
> Ronsard doth Maro's rimes expresse;
> And elegant Catullus vaine,
> And Petrarchs Thuscan gracefulnesse,
> And Theban Pindars lofty straine.
> He so expresseth Pindars stile,
> So doth Catullus emulate,
> Virgil and Petrarch, that the while

They all seeme him to imitate.
Grave Maro he resembles so,
None would him thinke Catullian:
So elegant Catullus too;
None would him thinke Maronian,
Though all Catullus, all Virgill,
All Pindar he and Petrarch be,
Yet the same Ronsard is he still.
Maro, Catullus might we see,
Pindar or Petrarch live againe,
And all th'old Poets more or lesse
All joyntly hit not Ronsards vaine,
Who onely doth them all expresse.

To this praise of Ronsard's work in so many genres Hakewill adds Pithou's "Epitaph upon the same Ronsard," for which he again provides the English:

Greatest of Poets whom old or present times,
Or future to thy French shall ere bring forth,
Pardon, these are not rights fitting thy worth.
But to thy great ghost like some sprinkling rimes.[70]

At about this time Richard James, librarian to Sir Robert Cotton, wrote a letter in Latin that compares Jonson to the ancients. He believes, he says, "that if the fathers were now to return they would look with delight on the wit of the most fecund Ben Jonson, whom I judge as Thuanus does Ronsard to be comparable to all antiquity if we consider his elegant [*compta*] and weighty [*plena sensibus*] poetry and plays."[71] (Jacques De Thou's *Monumenta litteraria* were published in England in 1640. De Thou offers a brief biography of Ronsard and says that after much hard work Ronsard came to equal the best of the ancients and to surpass many, the most outstanding poet since the flourishing age of Augustus, although ruining his health by self-indulgence, sigs. Ii1–Ii2.)

"E. D." had been quite right to say that each country vaunted its own writers, for such was the myth behind much compliment of this sort. And in fact during the Renaissance Englishmen would have read a number of works, mostly translated from French, linking Ronsard not to a literary tradition but to a place. Thus E.

Grimestone's translation of Jean de Serres's *Generall historie of France* (1624 ed.) describes Ronsard's tomb: Joachim de la Chétardie

> finding great Ronsards boanes to lie in a base, mute and illiterate coffin, more just then they that had beene advanced by his rich spoyles, he would not suffer his Ghost to lie any longer neglected, causing a stately Tombe of Marble to bee made for Ronsard, and a lively Image to bee cut by the Phideas of Parris, with a short inscription; for it was sufficient to admonish Passengers that there lay Ronsard; neither did he need this care and charge of mortall men, who in his life time saw his owne eternity, whose glory after death cannot exceed that, which hee did reape lyving: yet this goodly and boun-tifull Councellor, by this good Office hath deserved much of all them that honour learning. . . :

> > Cave Viator sacra hec humus est
> > Abi nefaste quam calcas humum
> > Sacra est Ronsardus enim jacet
> > hic Quo oriente oriri Musae et
> > occidente Commori ac secum in-
> > humari volverunt Hoc non invi-
> > deant qui sunt superstites nec-
> > parem sortem sperent Nepotes.[72]

Grimestone also translated Pierre d'Avity's *Estates, empires, and principalities of the world* (1615), which says of the Vendômois in words close to the original French that they "are of a milde disposition, courteous, and given to all things that are most neat: yea borne to be excellent in some thing, as Peter Ronsard a gentleman of this countrie was, whose works are wel known to all Europ, and have made him not only the honour of this countrie, but also the ornament of France" (sig. G2).

Englishmen might also have read of Ronsard's geographical setting in two different translations of Mercator's great *Atlas*. One, by H. Hexham (Amsterdam, 1636) reports that Vendôme saw the birth of "that famous Poet Peter Rondsard" (sig. 6Q2^v). The other, Wye Saltonstall's *Historia mundi* (1635), quotes an epitaph for Remy Belleau by "Ronsard the Prince of French Poets," and says of Tours that "It containeth the ashes of that great Poet P. Ron-

sard, who they call the French Homer, and Pindar."[73] At least one
Englishman visited that grave, noting surroundings he may have
recognized as poignantly appropriate. John Evelyn records in his
journal that on June 7, 1644, while on a trip through the country
around Tours, "we walked about 2 miles from the Citty to an
extraordinary agreable solitude Calld Du Plessis, The house
belongs to the King, & has many pretty Gardens, the fullest of
Nightingalls that ever I saw: In the Chapell lyes buryed the famous
Poet Ronsard."[74] More than either Marot or Du Bellay, then,
Ronsard was "placed" in a particular locality, not only in his
boastful nation but in his own countryside.

Almost all these references, perfunctory or considered, situate
Ronsard somehow in space and time. Others, however, specifically
concern his love poems. A great many Englishmen must have read
the *Amours* with delight, but comments on Ronsard as the author of
such poetry lack the reverence accorded him by Willes, Harvey, or
Reynolds. Other poets had on occasion written of women in ways
that implied one of the *furores*, the thirst of the soul for beatitude or
wisdom, the pursuit of the mind for the world of Ideas or the poet
for the laurel. Ronsard's love poetry is by no means without such
aspiration, whether found openly in Neoplatonic ascents or hidden
in the complexity and suggestiveness that expand the *Amours* beyond the limits of sensuous desire; but he is often vigorously
opposed to the more rarefied sublimations of passion and remains
unallegorical except in the profoundest sense. English readers who
mentioned him were not tempted, so far as I can discover,
explicitly to consider his *Amours* much more than the "love-toies"
Eliot praised him for creating.

Many English readers would have seen comments on Ronsard's
love poetry in books translated from French like Pasquier's *Mono-
phylo* (1572), Regnier's *Legendarie* (1577), and Montreux's *Honours
academie* (1610). But English writers, too, referred to "court-like
amarous Rousard," as William Covell called him in *Polimanteia*
(1595, sig. R2^v). On occasion such notice takes in not only the lover
but the beloved, particularly Cassandre. Soowthern, it will be
remembered, complained that she was mean to Ronsard, and it
was her name Ben Jonson used when he cited the most famous
modern mistresses in a light ode asking why he should not sing of
Celia, since so many others had sung such praises:

> Hath Petrarch since his Laura rais'd
> Equall with her [i.e. Corinna]? or Ronsart prais'd
> His new Cassandra, 'bove the old;
> Which all the Fate of Troy foretold?

When he visited Drummond in 1619 Jonson told him that "the best pieces of Ronsard were his Odes," but Drummond does not say whether he meant all the odes or only those Horatian lyrics at times not unlike his own. He also claimed to regret that Petrarch had imprisoned his sentiments in the sonnet, so his preference for the odes may have entailed a similar discomfort with most of the *Amours*. His host was skeptical: "All this was to no purpose," he says, for "he neither doeth understand French nor Itallianne." Jonson owned a copy of Montaigne in French and the *Balet comique de la reyne*, however. Perhaps Drummond exaggerated.[75]

Drummond's brother-in-law, Sir John Scot, was a man of considerable learning, well traveled and well read, generous for many years to Scottish writers and scholars. He too knew of Ronsard's love poetry, writing in his *Serenissimi regis Jacobi Sexti* (Edinburgh, 1619) of celebrated ladies like Laura, Lesbia, Julia, Delia, and "necans oculis Cassandra petulcis"—Cassandre killing with wanton eyes (sig. C3^v). And in England Richard Brathwait, author of many cheerfully moral works, wrote in his *Schollers medley* that a disappointed Italian lover could cry out, "Our Italian Dames had never beene acquainted with such disdaine, nor entertained their Servants with such contempt, nor rejected them with such Self-content, had they not beene instructed by inconstant Cassandra to love in jest and loath in earnest." The moral, says Brathwait with mock solemnity, is that "nothing could more prejudice either publique or private Estates; then to be fraughted with Forraine vices" (1638 ed., sigs. Pp4–Pp4^v).

Ronsard the lover also appears in two longer passages, each quite funny. *Tarltons newes out of purgatorie* (1590; Tarlton was a clown) tells of a region in the underworld "where sat a crew of men that woare baie garlands on theyr heads." There we find Ennius, Virgil, Juvenal, Propertius, Ovid, Martial, Horace, and "many moe: which had written lascivious verse, or other heroicall poems." Like those in Virgil's "myrtea . . . silva" such shades still suffer their ancient malaise, so "ould Ronsard" finds in this pur-

gatory not the repose he had anticipated when describing to
Hélène his future in the "ombres Myrtheux" but, as a sort of
refining fire, the torture of reading a poem that is in fact a parody of
his own work (or possibly that of an imitator such as Thomas
Lodge). There he sits "with a scroule in his hand, wherin was
written the description of Cassandra his Mistresse, and because his
stile is not common, nor have I heard our English Poets write in
that vaine [surely a bit of sarcasm], marke it, and I will rehearse it,
for I have learnd it by heart." The poem that follows glides
smoothly through many of the commonplace images and phrases
for which Ronsard and others could be parodied: the red and
white, Cupid and Apollo, Flora, art and nature, the bewitched
gazer, the moon, the dawn, the starry eyes, even the metrical
invention and rhetorical patterning, here reduced to an indeed
tormenting banality:

> Downe I sat,
> I sat downe,
> > where Flora had bestowed hir graces:
> Greene it was,
> It was greene
> > Far surpassing other places,
> > > For art and nature did combine
> > > With sights to witch the gasers eyne.
>
> There I sat,
> I sat there
> > viewing of this pride of places:
> Straight I saw,
> I saw straight
> > the sweetest faire of all faire faces:
> > > Such a face as did containe,
> > > Heavens shine in every vaine.
>
> I did looke,
> Looke did I,
> > and there I saw Appollos wyers,
> Bright they were,
> They were bright,
> > with them Auroras head he tiers,

> But this I woondred how that now
> They shadowed in Cassandras brow.

Still I gazde,
I gazde still,
   spying Lunas milke white glase:
Comixt fine,
Fine comixt,
   with the mornings ruddie blase:
      This white and red their seating seekes
      Upon Cassandraes smiling cheekes. . . .

This was Ronsards description of his Mistres, and he is forct
to hold it in his hande, that every time hee casts his eies on it,
he may with sighs feel a secret torment, in that he once loved
too much being alive.[76]

That many saw in Ronsard a love poet fashionable to have read
is amusingly illustrated in two of the clever university plays known
as the Parnassus trilogy, acted in Cambridge around the turn of the
sixteenth century. In the first part of *The return from Parnassus* we
meet the boastful dilettante Gullio, a pretender who hopes to awe
his hearers with his reading and erudition. He quotes Homer (in
Latin), cites "prating Tullie," and says "True it is that Ronzarde
spake, Chi pecora si fa il lupo la mangia, which I thus translated,
Quisquis amat ranam, ranam putat esse Dianam, and thus extem-
pore into Englishe,

> What man soever loves a crane
> The same he thinkes to be Diane.

A dull universities heade would have bene a month about this
muche." Gullio, of course, is scornful of "base English witts," but
explains that it is his "custome in my common talke to make use of
my readinge in the Greeke, Latin, French, Italian, Spanishe
poetts, and to adorne my oratorye with some prettie choice extra-
ordinarie sayinges." His choice saying from Ronsard is in fact a
garbled version of an old proverb (qui pécore se fa / Il loup la
mangera"), which he translates into another but unrelated
proverb.[77]

In the next part of the *Return* the foppish lover Amoretto,
superficial braggart and nearly illiterate sonneteer, illustrates his

shallow pretention through the orders he gives his servant: "Sirrah boy remember me when I come in [to] Paules Churchyard to buy a Ronzard and Dubartas in French and Aretine in Italian, and our hardest writers in Spanish, they will sharpen my witts gallantly. I doe rellish these tongues in some sort. Oh now I do remember I heard a report of a Poet newly come out in Hebrew, it is a pretty harsh tongue, and [doth] rellish a gentleman traveller."[78]

In neither *Tarlton* nor the Parnassus trilogy is Ronsard mantled in Orphic power or even courtly grace, but for the most part his "image" in Renaissance England was dignified and on occasion luminous. In France, however, his work was to be treated with widespread if not unanimous disdain and then mere indifference. The English, particularly before the Restoration, often followed European shifts in taste at many years' remove, so statements that at first seem old-fashioned are not, in their context, very dusty or quaint. Nevertheless, as the seventeenth century wore on references to Ronsard, like adaptations or borrowings from his work, become fewer. In 1642 James Howell suggested in his *Instructions for forreine travell* that "There bee some French Poets will affoord excellent entertainment, specially Du Bartas, and 'twere not amisse to give a slight salute to Ronzard, Desportes, and the late Theophile" (sig. C11)—hardly an enthusiastic recommendation. A few years later Howell located Ronsard historically in an epistle quoted earlier: "Marot did something under Francis I . . . but Ronsard did more under Henry II."[79] Howell's tribute, certainly deserved, is unusual in its citation of Ronsard as a figure in the development of his language, although Robert Dallington, it will be recalled, thought him praiseworthy for his style and on at least one occasion he was mentioned in a discussion (translated from French, however) of syntax and poetic license.[80] In fact, toward the end of the seventeenth century the few comments on Ronsard tend to concern his use of French, for increasingly it was his language that disturbed critics in France itself.

During these years news of Ronsard's decline could be heard not only from visitors abroad but in at least two works published in England. One was Trajano Boccalini's *I ragguagli di Parnasso* (1656), a satirical work set on Parnassus which in one chapter describes how Dante, "being assaulted by night in his Country-house, and ill used by some disguised Vertuosi; is relieved by the great French Ronsard." Here Ronsard is still "The Prince of French Poets, who had a Country-house not far from that of Dante" (a good neighborhood), but the humiliations to which he is subjected in the episode are at least undignified (sigs. Dd2^v–Dd3). More damaging, because closer to the heart of recent assumptions about style, would have been the exchange between Jean-Louis de Guez de Balzac and his friend Jean Chapelain, published in English in 1658. In July 1641 he writes Chapelain, "But are you serious, when you speak of Ronsard, and give him the title of Grand? . . . As for me, I esteem him not great, except in the sense of the old proverb, Magnus liber, magnum malum; and I have declared as much in one of my latin Letters, which you suffered to passe, without making any opposition. Since the thing is done, there is no place left for denial; and Monsieur de Malherbe, Monsieur de Crasse, and your self, must come into the number of small Poets, if he be allow'd to passe for great" (a prescient warning). Later that summer he wrote again to say that he would reread Ronsard, but that "upon the last reading, I thought him rather the matter and beginning of a Poet, then one accomplish'd; and in the fire wherewith his imagination was heated, there was much lesse of flame, then smoak and soot. You know the fancy of the late Monsieur de Malherbe, that blotted out a whole Volume with his own hand, and did not pardon one syllable; I do not approve his rigour so universall. But if all the Sonnets, all the Franciade, and all the Odes were lost, I think, I should not need much comfort against my sorrow."[81]

The last decades of the seventeenth century saw Ronsard's image gradually fade. A few traces lingered. Sir William Temple wrote condescendingly in 1690 of how poetry emerged from the dark ages dressed "in Rhyme, after the Gothick fashion," yet "not without some Charms, especially those of Grace and Sweetness, and the Oar begun to shine in the Hands and Works of the first Refiners. Petrach, Ronsard, Spencer met with much Applause upon the Subjects of Love, Praise, Grief, Reproach." Ronsard is again "placed," but further back in the development and polishing of French than Howell, Hakewill, and others had once put him. For Thomas Rymer, Ronsard (and by now even Malherbe) had not been so much reformers as objects of reform; he wrote in his preface to Rochester's poems (1691) that "The French have ordinarily compar'd their Ronsards and their Malherbes with Virgil and Horace; Boileau understands better. He has gone farthest to purge out that Chaff and Trifling so familiar in the French Poetry, and to settle a Traffick of good Sence amongst them."[82]

Ronsard's name does not disappear from library catalogues even in the next century, although there is no way of telling the degree of enthusiasm with which heirs or buyers read these volumes or if they read them at all.[83] Few would have been encouraged by comments such as Warburton's remark in a footnote to Pope's *Dunciad* that of many authors "who have the most boldly promised to themselves Immortality, viz. Pindar, Luis Gongora, Ronsard, Oldham, Lyrics; Lycophron, Statius, Chapman, Blackmore, Heroics; I find the one half to be already dead, and the other in utter darkness." At least Ronsard's name is still, as he had prophesied, linked with Pindar's. And later yet Warton said in his notes to Pope that Malherbe was the "first *correct* Poet of France, to whom their language had inestimable obligations. . . . Ronsard had a more vigorous imagination than Malherbe, but not so true a taste and judgment; his style is harsh, and full of barbarisms and foreign idioms." Elsewhere he wrote concerning overblown hyperboles "there are many such in Rotrou and in Ronsard."[84]

Comments on Ronsard's style, then, move from Dallington's assumption that Ronsard was superlative in his use of French, to Howell's acknowledgment of his role in its later development, to Temple's inclusion of him among the "first" refiners, and finally to Warton's conviction (perhaps derived ultimately from Boileau) that he was barbaric and harsh, not "correct." Only after the historical and linguistic assumptions that propped up this inhibiting condemnation had themselves collapsed was the way once more open for unabashed admiration of Ronsard as prince of poets, "aeoniae magister artis."

4

Desportes

In the fall of 1605 Malherbe came to Paris, where he was soon invited by Mathurin Régnier to visit the latter's distinguished and aging uncle, Philippe Desportes. Although they arrived after soup was on the table, Desportes offered to fetch a copy of his recently published translation of the psalms. No, said Malherbe, he had already seen them, they were not worth the trouble, and the soup was better. Desportes died shortly thereafter, probably unaware that Malherbe's ruthless incivility anticipated the criticism and then neglect in store for his poetry.[1] Yet before this shift in taste, before "Malherbe vint," Desportes had enjoyed a popularity and prosperity given few authors in any age. Editions flowed steadily from the press, compliments piled up at his feet, the powerful admired his work, and during the second half of his career, except for an anxious time as a member of the rebellious Ligue, money and abbeys accumulated comfortably around him. Nor was this popularity confined to France, for a number of Englishmen read his poems and borrowed his conceits or patterns (themselves often taken from the Italians); if never mentioned with the honor sometimes given Du Bellay and Ronsard or the adulation heaped on Du Bartas, his name was certainly known.

Desportes had been born in 1546 at Chartres, the son of a prosperous bourgeois who provided him with a good education. Once in Paris he knew swift success, attaching himself to usefully important figures like the Duc d'Anjou and writing gracious verses that soon circulated in manuscript to his increasing renown. Among those pleased by the poems and by what must have been considerable personal charm was the Maréchale de Retz; at her salon Desportes participated in a revival of Petrarchism and there he would have known other poets, among them the surviving members of the Pléiade. In 1573 he published his *Premières oeuvres* and left for Poland with its new and reluctant king, the Duc d'Anjou. He was, wrote Dorat pleasantly, the bard of the French Argo—PHILIPPUS PORTAEUS is, rightly rearranged, PUPPI TALIS ORPHEUS.[2] He stayed in Poland a while, working with the king's chancellor Pibrac, and returned when Anjou inherited the French throne as Henri III. Home in France he wrote on the death of "Diane" (the king's adored Marie de Clèves), helped organize the Académie du palais, composed more verses, and made more friends, such as the future cardinal Du Perron. As money and responsibilities gathered to him, however, he devoted his hours to government work; he was particularly close to the Duc de Joyeuse until the latter fell at Coutras in 1587.

In 1582 Desportes acquired the abbeys of Tiron and Josaphat, took minor orders, and collected almost all his verse for a new and major edition the next year. The edition of 1583 was by no means his last but it was in some ways a farewell to secular poetry. Penitence and piety were in the air, as well as "academic" experiments with music and verse, so Desportes's chief literary effort from now on was directed to translating the psalms (a project that did not discourage him from what certainly seems like opportunism during the final stages of the civil wars nor from feminine solace—and rumor said the pox—in his last years).[3] In 1603 he published the complete Psalter, not wholly successful as poetry but welcomed by many Catholics as a persuasive answer to the Marot–Beza version. He died in 1606, rich, famous, the owner of a magnificent library, the friend of scholars like Casaubon and respected by the king himself. The poetry written upon his death would have touched but not surprised him: he was, said his mourners, a sun, a French Apollo, who wrote with sweetness and "belle sciance."[4]

One friend called the *amours* an "ouvrage inimitable," but as the English soon discovered, Desportes was about as easily copied as a poet can be. The first works of his to which they would have had ready access were his smooth imitations of Ariosto, published in 1572, and for the next several decades there were many editions of the *Premières oeuvres*.[5] Probably most English readers knew

Desportes's earlier poetry best, for imitations of poems to Cléonice (added in 1583) are few. Whether they knew the early or the late Desportes scarcely matters, however, since the various "amours" show little evolution.[6] The sonnets are individually facile, adept, and sometimes charming—"mignon"; but they seem to have been mass produced in some interior workshop by an artisan with a few good tools and a limited if ingenious imagination. The English image of Desportes, the response he provoked, would not have been much affected by familiarity with this or that part of his secular work.

Of all Desportes's poems, those to Diane were the most popular in England. In them one finds the usual themes: the poet's thoughts ascend, he speaks on a multitude of matters to Cupid, he suffers but enjoys it, he is "en mesme temps tout de flamme et de glace," he sails, burns, sighs, invokes, weeps ("Les pleurs et les sanglots sont fleurs de la tristesse"), wakes, dreams ("Helas! somme trompeur, que tu m'es inhumain!"), and above all compares—the lady is like the sun, his thoughts are like Acteon's hounds, his condition is like a jail.

Second only to these in popularity were the poems to Hippolyte. Here are the same subjects, the same rhetorical patterns, the same tone, the same Petrarchist conceits that flutter around the sequence like a cloud of putti. Perhaps the stress on the sun and on the poet's doomed flights (he is Icarus, Phaeton) is even greater, and there is more about death. Desportes almost certainly addressed many of these poems to the king's sister, Marguerite de Valois, probably on behalf of Bussy d'Ambois, which would explain his trembling respect. At the same time he is proud of his heroic surge sunwards. The monument of this Icarus should read:

> Il mourut poursuivant une haute adventure,
> Le ciel fut son desir, la Mer sa sepulture:
> Est-il plus beau dessein, ou plus riche tombeau?
>
> [no. i]

For the most part, though, these *amours* are like those to Diane—clever, facile, pretty, and accompanied by songs which if no deeper than the sonnets are more successful in their gracious and musical perfection.

Had they read the *Diverses amours* the English would have noted some reproaches to a treacherous lady probably given their unusual energy by a real love affair, but they tended to neglect these poems. Apparently easier to enjoy or use were the "Bergeries"; here readers would have found the exquisite "Rozette, pour un peu d'absance" which complains of the girl's infidelity in a tone of gay mockery ("Nous verrons volage Bergere, / Qui premier s'en repentira").

Desportes in many ways continued the work of the Pléiade, but perceptive English readers might have noticed how very different he was as well. Like his predecessors he knew the Greek myths, but he usually confined himself to the best-known figures and stories. He was, as his friends said, "docte," but his Platonism ("Aussi l'Amour n'est rien qu'un desir de Beauté") is unlikely to have long puzzled the ladies he knew and his diction at its most difficult is not more obscure than "Aussi l'amour en moy n'est point par accident; / Il est de ma nature et ma propre substance." (Nevertheless, Malherbe criticized Desportes for writing this way to women.)[7] Even when he ventures into philosophy or difficult subjects the topics often serve merely to further the sonnet's wit, not to suggest other dimensions or modify what is said. Desportes dreams and like Ronsard can enjoy the deceit ("J'aime une telle tromperie," he says in a prayer to sleep), but this remains almost a matter of taste, not a disturbing suggestion about love and illusion. He is more than willing to die, blasted to ashes by the various suns he worships, but "death" in his poems is often a useful hyperbole rather than one way of getting at otherwise indescribable psychological or sexual experiences. Even faith subserves conceit and compliment. In *Diane* II, xlvi the lover goes to church on Easter, praying with some force, "Seul Sauveur des humains, sauve ta creature!" Then he sees *her* praying and merely wonders "Se repent-elle point du mal qu'elle m'a fait?" Spenser's sonnet "Most glorious Lord of lyfe," also an Easter love poem, shows what a greater poet can make of a Petrarchan theme here bleached pale by Desportes's pleasant frivolity.

English readers might also have noticed Desportes's chastity. In life he was not particularly repressed—he made an illegitimate son and a few obscene verses—but his poetry is usually reticent about just what the lover is after. Of course many of the poems were written on behalf of others who for one reason or another might not want to spell out the "jouyssance" usually sought, and the Platonism would be undercut by too earthy a desire crying for some food. Still, this tendency to minimize the sexual has results that further separate Desportes from Ronsard and even Du Bellay—there is only a little about seizing the day or the revenge of time, little description of what the lover would do if he could do or dreams of doing in that land of desire, illusion, or anticipation where the poet can achieve delight and union. In one sonnet copied in England Diane arrives in a dream to "cure" the lover, but he awakes while trying to kiss her eyes. This poem, unusually sensuous for Desportes, is ice itself compared to Ronsard's similar vision when "Rien ne m'est refusé."

The lover himself seems oddly inactive in these poems. Much love poetry involves some sort of passivity, of course, which may be one reason passionate lovers have sometimes struck their unafflicted friends as unmanly; although actively masculine in sexual desire, male love poets are often submissive to the experience itself, even to the point of equating love and drowning, love and death. Desportes seems more passive than most. Furthermore, the chaste quality of the verse accompanies a certain indifference to texture, to the wind on the skin, the light on the leaves, the wine's color in the cup, or the curves of stream and hollow. Compared to older poets Desportes preferred sharp and stable outlines. English readers would have found much less in his poetry about metamorphosis or mutability; nor did he often describe water, being less drawn than Du Bellay to the winding Meander or than Ronsard to the pool of Narcissus and the sea of Aphrodite. His talent was for what is clear-edged and glittery, intellectually clever rather than resonant and haunting.

After 1575 English readers could have seen some religious poems, penitential in content and a little facile in manner. The depth of Desportes's religious feeling is hard to measure. According to one story he turned down an archbishopric, explaining he did not feel qualified for a cure of souls. That he was an abbot, he added cheerfully, gave him no qualms—monks have no souls.[8] Probably he thought he was as pious as decency required, but neither his religious verse nor his position as an ecclesiastic was much noticed in England. Nor did his Catholicism bother anyone. In any case, like Ronsard, he had Huguenot friends.

During the 1580s and 1590s, when the fashion for sonnet sequences was at its height, English writers leafed through Desportes's poetry with more than ordinary attention.[9] The most striking fact about the adaptations that resulted is simply their number; more than thirty of the *Amours de Diane* were rendered into one or more English versions during a short period. Many are typical of Desportes—wittily mannered, elegantly phrased, arranged by repetition and anaphora into clear if static patterns. They must have appealed to a taste for structures that gather and interrelate particles of discourse—enumerations, lists of anatomical parts, series of paradoxes, particularized allegorical comparisons, syllogistic propositions suspended in the air until the final conclusion, collections of divinities, reiterated words or phrases. Many are arguments, many rely on figures of repetition; a few are emblematic, providing allegorical details out of which one may construct an inner picture of the lover's ship on the sea of passion, the lover as hermit, even (in a rare moment of broad humor) the often-shot lover as Cupid's quiver.

But English poets in search of new toys and trifles found in Desportes, more often than is statistically probable, images of metamorphosis or evocations of time, water, dream, flowers—that which does not long keep its shape or that which invites immersion. Even when they do not seek out those poems in Desportes that express flux or change, many English translators, particularly the good ones, alter details here and there to make the verse conform more closely to such a taste. This tendency is sometimes subtle, sometimes hardly worth mentioning, but it is there, and suggests that English readers found or created in Desportes's poetry elements they knew already in the Pléiade, making of Desportes a figure just as mannered as ever and just as fascinated by pattern but not quite so nearly neoclassical.

Not surprisingly, one of the first to imitate Desportes was John Soowthern. Filled like Desportes with "audâce" and "haultaines" thoughts, he too named his mistress Diane. The third sonnet in *Pandora* (1584) tells, like *Hippolyte* xlix, how Death thought of killing Diane but was persuaded by the archer Cupid that more people would die if the lady remained alive and inhabited by Love. The ninth, based on *Diane* I, lxi, anticipates the joys of Hell; she will suffer for her cruelty but he will be happy in her presence.

Desportes evokes death and Hades with none of the shudder
Ronsard could elicit, but these poems are undeniably clever.
Soowthern follows them slavishly. He also admired *Diane* I, xxxiv,
however, a poem unusual for its description of metamorphosis and
lost outline. It was popular in England:

> Celuy que l'Amour range à son commandement
> Change de jour en jour de façon differente;
> Helas! j'en ay bien fait mainte preuve apparente,
> Ayant esté par luy changé diversement.
>
> Je me suis veu muer, pour le commencement,
> En cerf, qui porte au flanc une fleche sanglante;
> Depuis je devins cygne, et d'une voix dolente,
> Je presagé ma mort, me plaignant doucement.
>
> Apres je devins fleur languissante et panchée,
> Pius, je fu fait fontaine aussi soudain seichée,
> Espuisant par mes yeux toute l'eau que j'avois;
>
> Or je suis salemandre et vy dedans la flame;
> Mais j'espere bien tost me voir changer en Voix,
> Pour dire incessamment les beautez de Madame.

Soowthern renders this in his usual style: he was "Metamorphosd"
into a "wandering Harte," a swan, "a Flowre, and since withred
away," a "Fountaine, and since, I am drie," and now a "Salamander, live in my flame," but maybe someday "a well singing
voyce: / And there in louange, the fayre eyes of Ma-dame" (sig.
C2).

Two better poets, Sir Arthur Gorges and Thomas Lodge, knew
Desportes's work well; at least twenty of Gorges's "Vannetyes and
Toyes," written in the 1580s, are unmistakably based on it, and
Lodge not only borrowed from it but mentioned its popularity.

Gorges's taste in some ways resembled Desportes's. He too liked
extended and static comparisons, elaborately developed conceits
and figures of repetition; he too tended to avoid the sensual. Yet he
had, I think, a closer kinship with earlier French poets. Desportes
dies and burns with some regularity, but Gorges's sober and
melancholy temperament was more like Du Bellay's. Furthermore, an interest in dream, mutability, and images of the
natural world, although not so acute as that of the Pléiade or his
friend Spenser, sometimes led Gorges to imitate poems by

Desportes that include just those elements. One fresh song recre-
ates a springtime "Complainte":

> La Terre, nagueres glacée,
> Est ores de verd tapissée;
> Son sein est embelly de fleurs,
> L'air est encore amoureux d'elle,
> Le ciel rit de la voir si belle,
> Et moy j'en augmente mes pleurs. . . .

[Diane II, 244]

> The gentell Season of the yeare
> hath made the bloomynge braunch appeare
> and beautyfied the landes with flowers
> The ayre doth savor with delyghte
> the heavens doo smyle to see the syghte
> and yett myne eyes augment theyr showers. . . .[10]

On another occasion the lady arrives in a dream ("Oh sweet
Elusion straunge"), and elsewhere in a rare Epicurean mood the
lover laughs at "good fame" while demanding "the sugred fruite"
of love. "Nothinge is constant here belowe / sometymes the Ebbe
sometymes the flowe," as the lady herself will learn, for

> when Shee sees her selfe so wrackte with age
> and farr unlyke to that before Shee was
> Lo then as one afright, twixte griefe and rage
> even with her fyste shall breake her flattringe glase.[11]

And, like Soowthern, Gorges found among many intellectual and
clearly outlined conceits Desportes's tale of metamorphosis:

> Whom love commaundes and holdes as humble thrall
> Transformed is each daye to sundry formes
> I lyke ytt nott but cannott doo with all
> For he that loves must needes endure those stormes
> I first of all was chaungde into a harte;
> Within whose flancke the murtheringe shafte did lye
> Then to a swanne that syngs the dolefull parte,
> Which doth presage the tyme that he muste dye
> Then to a springe as cleare as cristall glasse
> And by myne eyes I dyd unlade the same

The Salamander after that I was
   Who loves to bath amydste the burninge flame
But laste of all a flower moste fayre to see
   No soner spronge butt quayled on the grounde
And now I fynde my selfe a voice to bee
That to the worlde my mistresse praise muste sownde.

                                [no. 51]

A small detail illustrates how intelligently Gorges reworked
Desportes. The latter had "hoped" to become a voice, which
Gorges translated as "wishe" but then changed to "fynde." His
editor considers this illogical (taking "laste of all," I assume, to
include present time), but Gorges may have thought "fynde" an
ingenious piece of logic, referring as it does to this very utterance.
The storm of love has now metamorphosed him into a poet.

  More typical of Desportes, however, are the dozen or so poems
Gorges probably enjoyed for their mannered if unresonant cleverness:

   Si j'aime autre que vous, que l'honneste pensée,
Qu'Amour loge en mon coeur, s'en puisse departir
Et que vostre beauté, qui m'a rendu martyr,
Ne me soit jamais plus que fiere et courroucée!
   Si ce n'est de vostre oeil que mon ame est blessée,
Jamais d'allegement je n'y puisse sentir;
Qu'à regret je vous serve, et taschant de sortir,
Que de plus pesans fers ma raison soit pressée.
   Si j'aime autre que vous, Amour, tyran des Dieux,
Les feux croisse en mon ame, et les pleurs en mes yeux,
Et que vostre rigueur mon service rejette!
   Las! Je n'aime que vous, ny ne sçaurois aimer;
Je dépite autre amour qui me sceut enflamer:
Mon coeur est une roche à toute autre sagette.

                                 [*Diane* II, lxix]

Yff other love then yours do lodge within my Breste
   let never pleasinge thought henceforth frequent my mynde
Or iff my constante hope elsewhere do seke for reste
   let my desyres in vayne still stryve agaynst the winde

Or if my vowed faith be ever founde untrue
  let all the fruits I reape be rygor for good will
Or yf I doe adore another Saynte then yow
  let me in restles toile loose all my labour still
Or iff that daungers dreade my lykinge can decaye
  let then my faintinge harte be shrynde in fowle defame
Or yf with tracte of tyme my fancye were awaye
  let some untymely ende shute upp my dayes in shame
But yow it is I love and yow I serve alone
Agaynste all other lookes my harte is hardned stone.

[no. 52]

Gorges's translations are, of course, marked by his own taste and feeling, particularly his liking for pattern and clarity. Thus, although retaining the sonnet form did not always interest him, he sometimes adds couplets to give a greater sense of a destination achieved or a point made. Sometimes, as in the poem just quoted, he makes the original verbal pattern even clearer. Sometimes the conceit itself is made more precise, sharper. The twenty-eighth "vannetye" translates *Diane* I, xlvi, in which the lover says he freezes far from her yet burns when near; Gorges omits from Desportes's list of discomforts those irrelevancies of speechlessness and pallor which detract from the distinct antitheses of cold and heat. Yet Gorges's imagination was concrete as well as clear. If Desportes mentions that Nero sang during the fire Gorges adds that he sang "the burnynge off Troye." When Desportes says "C'est l'extreme desir qui de force me prive" Gorges ties the statement down with a gnomic phrase: "Alas that sweet I doubte will breede my sower."

The result of these changes, I think, is to move Desportes back a few years. Gorges's poetry has elements of mannerism, but his verse sounds more old-fashioned than Desportes's; the urbane poet whose smoothness made him closer kin to Malherbe than the latter wanted to admit is here comfortably transformed into an English Renaissance poet whose verse, while sometimes fluid and nuanced, is no longer quasi-neoclassical. The point is worth stressing. During the 1580s a number of English poets were consciously striving for a mannered, ornamented, and metrically stable language. No doubt French poetry had some impact on this development and there were connections in one way or another between most of the significant poets of this crucial period and writers like Du Bellay, Ronsard, and Desportes. But that Desportes is gently nudged back toward the Pléiade through selection and modification illustrates the limits of his "influence" on that generation.

Thomas Lodge shared Gorges's fascination with Desportes, although he, too, often chose poems to translate that show feelings or concerns closer to those of Du Bellay and Ronsard.[12] This tendency is not surprising. Lodge was not as deep and rich a poet as Ronsard, but in several of his many manners he shows a similar impulse toward images of metamorphosis and retirement. His taste for "artificial" language with high gloss, intricate order, and balance accompanied a desire for the nymph-haunted world that recalls one aspect of Ronsard's imagination. Thus, Lodge's poetry is often wetter than Desportes's. He loves the "sacred Sea-nimphes pleasantly disporting, / Amidst this watrie world" and delights in an old legend uniting water, song, and oblivion:

> The rumor runnes·that heere in Isis swimme,
> Such stately Swannes so confident in dying;
> That when they feele them selves neere Lethes brimme,
> They sing their fatall dirge when death is nighing.[13]

Lodge's published translations from Desportes began in 1589 with some poems printed after *Scillaes metamorphosis*, an Ovidian tale of love, sea, and change. One, from the "Bergeries," praises the country life in heavy hexameters; another, a sonnet rigid with anaphora, wittily describes the lover's struggles with Cupid:

> If that I seeke the shade, I sodeinlie doo see
> The God of Love forsake his bow, and sit me by:
> If that I thinke to write, his Muses pliant be:
> If that I plaine my griefe, the wanton boy will crie.[14]

The prettiest is based on that charming song to Diane which Gorges had already translated ("La Terre, nagueres glacée"):

> The earth late choakt with showers
> Is now araid in greene:
> Her bosome springs with flowers,

> The aire dissolves her teene,
>> The heavens laugh at her glorie:
>> Yet bide I sad and sorie. . . .

[I, 46]

Lodge also translated a sonnet to Diane that was to prove very popular in England: Desportes's vision of himself as a hermit. This hope for what is a sort of metamorphosis winds through one of those extended comparisons Desportes so enjoyed:

> Je me veux rendre Hermite, et faire penitence
> De l'erreur de mes yeux pleins de temerité,
> Dressant mon hermitage en un lieu deserté,
> Dont nul autre qu'Amour n'aura la connoissance.
>> D'ennuis et de douleurs je feray ma pitance,
> Mon bruvage de pleurs; et par l'obscurité
> Le feu qui m'ard le coeur servira de clairté,
> Et me consommera pour punir mon offense.
>> Un long habit de gris le corps me couvrira,
> Mon tardif repentir sur mon front se lira,
> Et le poignant regret qui tenaille mon ame.
>> D'un espoir languissant mon baston je feray,
> Et tousjours, pour prier, devant mes yeux j'auray
> La peinture d'Amour et celle de Madame.

[Diane II, viii]

Lodge turns this into fourteeners even more old-fashioned sounding because of the occasionally heavy alliteration ("My dolefull drinke my drierie teares") and the thumping rhythms:

> I will become a Hermit now,
>> and doo my penance straight
> For all the errors of mine eyes
>> with foolish rashness fild.

[I, 43–44]

The next year Lodge published *Rosalynde*, a pastoral romance flourishing with "som leaves of Venus mirtle" and written, he says, during an ocean voyage "when everie line was wet with a surge." Shakespeare transformed the story into *As You Like It*. Four or five of the poems in this prettily costumed tale of disguise and

retreat are quoted or borrowed from Desportes. One is a looser
version of the sonnet to Diane complaining of Love as a perpetual
companion ("Turne I my lookes unto the Skies, / Love with his
arrowes wounds mine eies"); the French poem "Helas Tirant" to a
snowy-breasted girl is simply lifted with a few inaccuracies from
Diane I; "If it be true," closely translated from *Diane* I, xli, con-
trasts the wheeling and mutable world with the lover's painful
constancy; and poor Phoebe's love poem to the disguised heroine
tells with elaborately built comparisons how her "boate doth passe
the straights / of seas incenst with fire," blown by sighs through
the starless dark.[15]

In 1591 came *The famous, true and historicall life of Robert Second
Duke of Normandy.* The story follows the career of "Robin the
Divell" from his early days as a rapist and murderer to his triumph
as a Christian champion, offering as it does so an entertaining
mixture of euphuism, medieval romance, crime story, and late
Renaissance love poetry. Before a regenerate Robert wins the
heroine, however, a sultan longs for her in elegant poems meant to
accompany emblems of his passion. One of these is drawn loosely
from the sonnet on metamorphosis already translated by Soowthern and Gorges. Lodge omits the flower and voice but adds a ship
and a "Nimph of craggie rock" (II, 53). He must have been
particularly touched by this poem, for he included a translation of
it in his sonnets to Phillis (1593):

> Who lyves inthrald to Cupid and his flame,
> From day to day is chang'd in sundry sort:
> The proofe whereof my selfe may well report,
> Who oft transformd by him may teach the same.
> I first was turnd into a wounded Hart,
> That bare the bloodie arrow in my side:
> Then to a Swanne that midst the waters glide,
> With pittious voyce presagd my deadlie smart.
> Eft-soones I waxt a faint and fading flower,
> Then was I made a fountaine suddaine dry,
> Distilling all my teares from troubled eye:
> Now am I Salamander by his power,
>   Living in flames, but hope ere long to be
>   A voice, to talke my Mistresse majestie.[16]

Most of Lodge's translations follow Desportes closely. If sometimes he diminishes the mythology to suit the speaker, at other
times he makes the learning a little more obvious. On occasion,
however, although not so often as Gorges, he seeks a local or
concrete precision. Desportes sees that "les oiseaux cherchent la
verdure," Lodge that "The Thrushes seeke the shade." Desportes
says "la terre en Hiver ne resemble à l'Esté," which Lodge turns to
"If earth in winter summers pride estrange." Lodge's Desportes,
then, bears a strong resemblance to the original, but, like Gorges's
Desportes, his features have been retouched. He seems here a little
more like Ronsard in theme or imagery and from time to time more
old-fashioned in his diction and rhythm.

Although Lodge nowhere mentions Desportes in these four
books, he refers to him elsewhere in two very different contexts.
Fashionably euphuistic, *A margarite of America* (1596) tells of love,
violence, and betrayal. Chief villain is the murderous Arsadachus
who, when courting the heroine, takes his feigned passions from
the Italian but not, says Lodge, from Desportes: "All other of his,
having allusion to the name of Diana, and the nature of the Moone,
I leave, in that few men are able to second the sweete conceits of
Philip du Portes, wose Poeticall writings being alreadie for the
most part englished, and ordinarilie in everie mans hands,
Arsadachus listed not to imitate" (III, 79). Lodge's remark has
sometimes been quoted to illustrate Desportes's popularity, for
although exaggerated it does show how widely read his *amours* had
become and why (his "sweete conceits"); but the statement does
not prove any deep impact on English sensibility or any profound
admiration.

Published the same year, *Wits miserie, and the worlds madnesse*
satirizes the various "incarnate devils" and their progeny who
afflict the age. One offspring of Lust is modishly dressed For-
nication, who spies out pretty women in the day then courts them
at night with masques and music, telling them adultery is just "A
fit of good fellowship"; as for a sonnet, "Du Portes cannot equall
him, nay in the nice tearmes of lechery he exceeds him." He knows
the stories of Bandello better than his Paternoster but of all things
"he will not heare of death" (IV, 52–53). As Phillis's lover, then,
Lodge looked through the *Amours de Diane* with hopeful liking. As a
satirist he finds Desportes plying the same trade as a devil. Perhaps

in the past several years Lodge had sobered or, more likely, the rhetoric of satire simply required laughing at love poems.

No other writers gave Desportes quite the devoted attention of Gorges and Lodge, but Daniel, Constable, and Spenser all borrowed from him.

It has been said that Daniel learned from Desportes "the virtues of simplicity and grace"; certainly he found in the French poet much that pleased him.[17] Not surprisingly, therefore, modern scholars have stressed the debts or similarities of *Delia* (1592) to Desportes's love poetry and noted how both poets, for instance, avoid frank sensuality and often focus on the lover's psychology. Yet the knowledge of time ("When thou surcharg'd with burthen of thy yeeres, / Shalt bend thy wrinkles homeward to the earth") and the imaginative belief in ancient deities like Apollo ("O cleer-eyde Rector of the holie Hill") sound much more like the Pléiade than like Desportes in his most typical moments.[18]

Sometimes one meets familiar themes or styles in Daniel's poetry without being able to point directly to a source in Desportes. Thus the famous "Care-charmer sleepe, sonne of the Sable night" (no. 45) recalls Desportes's "Sommeil, paisible fils de la Nuict solitaire" in *Hippolyte*, but Daniel could be remembering similar poems. And sometimes it is difficult to know whether Daniel is imitating Desportes or one of the latter's many Italian models. It seems unlikely he took all of the sonnets that sound like Desportes directly from the Italian, and in some cases details more nearly resemble the French.

Several poems Daniel borrowed are typical of Desportes: witty, highly patterned, more impassioned in statement than pressing in language.[19] Two, however, strike a different tone, and here Daniel is both closer to the originals and, I think, more intense, as though more deeply stirred. *Delia* 29 adapts *Hippolyte* xviii in asking the lady to look at him, not at her mirror, for unlike Narcissus she is turned to stone by her contemplation of self. Daniel may have liked the poem in part for its concern with metamorphosis and in part for the intriguingly Neoplatonic implications of the lover as mirror. The next sonnet in the sequence follows *Cléonice* lxii, itself from Tasso. Here Desportes, as in only a few other poems, anticipates the cruelties of time:

Je verray par les ans vangeurs de mon martyre
Que l'or de vos cheveux argenté deviendra,
Que de vos deux Soleils la splendeur s'esteindra,
Et qu'il faudra qu'Amour tout confus s'en retire.
  La beauté qui si douce à present vous inspire,
Cedant aux lois du Temps, ses faveurs reprendra:
L'hyver, de vostre teint les fleurettes perdra,
Et ne laissera rien des thresors que j'admire.
  Cêt orgueil desdaigneux qui vous fait ne m'aymer,
En regret et chagrin se verra transformer,
Avec le changement d'une image si belle:
  Et peut estre qu'alors vous n'aurez deplaisir
De revivre en mes vers chauds d'amoureux desir,
Ainsi que le Phenix au feu se renouvelle.

I once may see when yeeres shall wrecke my wronge,
When golden haires shall chaunge to silver wyer:
And those bright rayes, that kindle all this fyer
Shall faile in force, their working not so stronge.
  Then beautie, now the burthen of my song,
Whose glorious blaze the world dooth so admire;
Must yeelde up all to tyrant Times desire:
Then fade those flowres which deckt her pride so long.
  When if she grieve to gaze her in her glas,
Which then presents her winter-withered hew;
Goe you my verse, goe tell her what she was;
For what she was she best shall finde in you.
  Your firie heate lets not her glorie passe,
But Phenix-like shall make her live anew.

The verse here and elsewhere seems more forceful than Desportes's, more condensed as well as more concrete, in part because (as Du Bellay advised) Daniel skillfully uses what could loosely be called "mots composés" like "winter-withered." Indeed, despite his very real liking for Desportes's conceits and figures of repetition Daniel aimed at another feeling than the former's smooth grace. Daniel was undoubtedly well languaged, his verse flowing clearly between well-mowed banks, but at its best his love poetry also has a metaphoric compression and hence an energy Desportes may not even have wanted. "Hunger-starven thoughts," "Vultur-gnawne hart," "mercy-wanting storme," and "cloath me with darke thoughts" all appear in sonnets indebted to Desportes, but the tone is not his. In other ways, too, one senses a movement to another sensibility; it is Daniel, not his probable model, who asks "Care-charmer sleepe" to let him dream forever, "imbracing clowdes in vaine; / And never wake, to feele the dayes disdayne." Daniel must have read Desportes with great pleasure but even he, I think, sometimes refashioned him not only according to his own taste but very specifically to that taste he shared with Du Bellay and Ronsard.

The relationship of Henry Constable to Desportes seems quite different. Here Desportes found an Englishman who imitated his spirit as well as—indeed more than—his letter. Few of Constable's poems paraphrase Desportes directly, but his secular poetry includes many reminders not only of Desportes's conceits but of his style and his vision (such as it was). Because of his reluctance to copy entire sonnets Constable did not borrow Desportes's sometimes highly patterned structures; unlike Gorges, Lodge, and Daniel, he was not particularly drawn to figures of repetition and relied little on anaphora or extended comparisons. Otherwise, and granted his lesser variety, Constable's poetry is strikingly like Desportes's. Thus in *Diana* (1592) he writes of himself as Icarus, burns in the beauty of the sun by which, like Desportes, he is fascinated, irradiates his verse with a light Neoplatonism, avoids almost all mention of the lover's earthly hopes, worships in paradox, and as his editor notes tends to neglect the mythology, natural world, and expressions of mutability he apparently found less interesting than witty turns of thought or language. Constable's poem to the lady's "sweet hand," for example, probably owes its conclusion to *Diverses amours* xviii (Malherbe said of these lines, "Si froid qu'il fait pitié"):

> Mais puis qu'un si grand prix à ma foy n'est promis,
> "Au moins baisons son gand. Il est tousjours permis
> "De baiser le Dessus d'un sacré reliquaire.

> And I thy glove kisse as a thinge devine
> Thy arrowes quiver and thy reliques shrine.[20]

In 1594 there was a second edition of *Diana* with many more sonnets. The spirit of these additional poems is sometimes unlike

Constable's—Epicurus shows his face from time to time and there
are lines to "You secrete vales, you solitarie fieldes, / you shores
forsaken, and you sounding rocks." That these newcomers are not
his is confirmed, if confirmation were needed, by the response to
Desportes they show. Here are imitations of entire sonnets and
here are precisely those anaphoric structures, series, repetitions,
and parallels Constable neglected for argument or description.
Two poems adopt both Desportes's conceit and structure and two
others are fairly close paraphrases. All the originals are in *Diane* I.
One example will illustrate the sort of poem the author (or
authors) admired in Desportes:

> Mon Dieu! mon Dieu! que j'aime ma deesse
> Et les vertus qui l'elevent aux cieux!
> Mon Dieu! mon Dieu! que j'aime ses beaux yeux,
> Dont l'un m'est doux, l'autre plein de rudesse!
> Mon Dieu! mon Dieu! que j'aime la sagesse
> De ses propos, qui raviroyent les dieux,
> Et la douceur de son ris gracieux,
> Qui me remplit d'une heureuse allegresse!
> Mon Dieu! que j'aime à l'ouir deviser
> Et tout ravy baiser et rebaiser
> Sa blanche main alors qu'elle n'y pense!
> Mais sans mentir doy-je pas bien aymer
> Le rare esprit qui l'a fait estimer
> Mesme de ceux qui n'ont sa cognoissance?
>
> [*Diane* I, xxvi, 1583 version]

> My God, my God, how much I love my goddesse,
>   whose vertues rare, unto the heavens arise,
>   my God, my God, how much I love her eyes,
>   one shining bright, the other full of hardnes.
> My God, my God, how much I love her wisdome,
>   whose words may ravish heavens richest Maker,
>   of whose eyes-joyes, if I might be pertaker,
>   then to my soule a holy rest would come.
> My God, how much I love to heare her speake,
>   whose hands I kisse, & ravisht oft rekisseth,
>   when she stands wotlesse whom so much she blisseth.
> Say then what mind this honest love wold breake,

Since her perfections pure withouten blot,
Makes her belov'd of them shee knoweth not?[21]

Unlike Constable, Spenser had little in common with Desportes. They shared the taste of their age for elaborately developed conceits, series and repetitions, embroidered language, and a vague Neoplatonism, but otherwise the two poets differed profoundly—in their conception of poetry, in the seriousness of their moral and political convictions, in the genres they were willing to try, in the very nature of their sensibilities, and of course in their talents. Spenser's greatness, however, lay partly in his power to assimilate an extraordinary variety of readings into his own capacious imagination. Not surprisingly, therefore, he borrowed some conceits from Desportes for his *Amoretti* (1595). The eighteenth sonnet, for instance, repeats with more humor the puzzled complaint in *Hippolyte* li that one may eventually soften all hard objects except the lady's heart, and the twenty-second shares with *Diane* I, xliii the construction of an inner temple to the beloved. The fifteenth probably paraphrases *Diane* I, xxxii:

Marchands, qui voyagez jusqu'au rivage More
Du froid Septentrion et qui, sans reposer,
A cent mille dangers vous allez exposer
Pour un gain incertain, qui vos esprits devore.
    Venez seulement voir la beauté que j'adore,
Et l'objet qui a sceu ma jeunesse embraser:
Et je suis seur qu'apres, vous ne pourrez priser
Le plus riche thresor dont l'Egypte se dore.
    Voyez les filets d'or de ce chef blondissant,
L'eclat de ces rubis, ce coral rougissant,
Ce crystal, cet ebene, et ces graces divines,
    Cet argent, cet ivoyre; et ne vous contentez
Qu'on ne vous monstre encor mille autres raritez,
Mille beaux diamans et mille perles fines.

                                        [1583 version]

Ye tradefull Merchants that with weary toyle,
    do seeke most pretious things to make your gain:
    and both the Indias of their treasures spoile,
    what needeth you to seeke so farre in vaine?

> For loe my love doth in her selfe containe
>   all this worlds riches that may farre be found,
>   if Saphyres, loe her eies be Saphyres plaine,
>   if Rubies, loe hir lips be Rubies sound:
> If Pearles, hir teeth be pearles both pure and round;
>   if Yvorie, her forhead yvory weene;
>   if Gold, her locks are finest gold on ground;
>   if silver, her faire hands are silver sheene:
> But that which fairest is, but few behold,
>   her mind adornd with vertues manifold.[22]

More than Desportes Spenser evokes the centeredness of these treasures, their containment in his lady's epitomizing self, and it is typical of both his seriousness and his sense of that lady's own reality that he should turn at the end from the precious splendor of her body to the *invisibilia* of her mind.

Other poets in the 1590s studied Desportes's "sweet conceits." The anonymous E. C., whose present obscurity conceals a real if minor charm, borrowed several for his *Emaricdulfe* (1595).[23] He is Icarus and she the sun; she is Pandora; he will build her a temple of loving thoughts and sacrifice his heart; and like Desportes he lists those impossibilities which must happen before he will change his affection ("First shall the Sea become the continent, / And red gild Dolphins dance upon the shore," sig. B8ᵛ). He shares Desportes's liking for anaphora, allegorical items organized into quasi-emblems, and detailed comparisons. Yet if usually conventional he can also describe how Emaricdulfe welcomed him indoors with wine and beer and he consoles her touchingly on the death of her little girl. Like some of his betters, if with more truth, E. C. claims never to have drunk "Of learnings spring, bright Aganippe fount," but he brings a pleasant grace to his own sonnet on his lady's wealth. Why do our merchants plow the seas, he asks, since all treasures lie in her—the gold and silver of India in her hair and brow, "More Diamonds then th'Egyptian surges folde" in her eyes, Arabian honey in her breath, and "pearles more worth then all America" in her mouth (sig. B3).

The same year there appeared a rather odd sequence of love poems, J. C.'s *Alcilia, Philoparthens loving folly*, prefaced by a letter congratulating the author on his inspiring farewell to passion. J. C. is or pretends to be nervous about his offering, as though he sensed some inner Stephen Gosson frowning at his lascivious page. "Nil Amor," he says ruefully in a prefatory poem, "est aliud quàm mentis morbus, et error," but now he has put aside such "nugae" for more useful matters "ut Ratio monet." There seems to be no doubt, however, that while afflicted with his "mentis morbus" or its literary facsimile J. C. diligently read and copied Desportes. Among his many "sonnets," sixains that briefly express some loving conceit, readers of Desportes would recognize the allegory of the ship (closer to the French than to Petrarch), the anaphoric syllogism "If it be love," the complaint that blind Cupid aims too well, the paradox that the lover melts when absent from his sunlike lady, the claim that he is immune to death while she has his heart, and so forth. The lines are at least smooth:

> If it be Love, to waste long houres in griefe;
> If it be Love, to wish, and not obtaine;
> If it be Love, to pine without reliefe;
> If it be Love, to hope, and never gaine:
> Then may you thinke that he hath truely lov'd,
> Who for your sake, all this and more have prov'd.
>
> [1613 ed., sig. B3]

Eventually Philoparthens's failure to move the beloved cools his fever and rectifies his mind. Luckily Desportes had written on this topic too, so J. C. was able to find in *Diane* I material for "Loves Accusation at the Judgement-seate of Reason."[24] E. C. and J. C., then, "use" Desportes as he was perhaps best used—as a pastry cook might consult a collection of recipes or a petit-point worker a pattern book. He did not, one suspects, reach the inner chamber of their spirits as Du Bellay did with Spenser or Ronsard with Drummond. Fine knacks for ladies were wanted, and those Desportes could offer.

Several other adaptations of Desportes are more surprising, not because of their technique, which is moderately adept if quite conventional, but because of their author's later career. Joshua Sylvester, who as Du Bartas's translator was to be England's chief "divine poet" for two generations, left some unpublished juvenilia which his printer collected for the 1633 edition of his works.

Perhaps anticipating a few raised eyebrows, he says in a letter to
the reader, "I durst not conceale the harmlesse fancies of his
inoffensive youth, which himselfe had devoted to Silence and
Forgetfulnesse; it is so much the more glory to that worthy Spirit,
that hee who was so happy in those youthfull strains . . . would yet
turne and confine his pen to none but holy and religious Dities."[25]
At least three fancies are close translations of sonnets to Hippolyte.
When exactly they were made I am not sure; despite some awkward spots their style seems more developed than Sylvester's
earliest translation from Du Bartas, which would put them after
1590. And it is possible that the printer was mistaken about their
authorship, for he includes as Sylvester's the lovely "Thou art not
fair for all thy red and white," which is almost certainly by Thomas
Campion.

Less easy and fluid than Desportes, Sylvester (assuming the
author was he) is nevertheless faithful to his flavor. It is pleasant to
think of him dallying with a few mannered love-toys before pressing on to fame and virtue with Urania. One sonnet follows *Hippolyte*
lvii:

> Autour des corps, qu'une mort avancée
> Par violence a privez du beau jour,
> Les Ombres vont, et font maint et maint tour,
> Aimans encor leur despouille laissée.
>
>   Au lieu cruel où j'eu l'ame blessée
> Et fu meurtri par les fleches d'Amour,
> J'erre, je tourne et retourne à l'entour,
> Ombre maudite, errante et dechassée.
>
>   Legers esprits plus que moy fortunez,
> Comme il vous plaist vous allez et venez
> Au lieu qui clost vostre despouille aimée,
>
>   Vous la voyez, vous la pouvez toucher,
> Où las! je crains seulement d'approcher
> L'endroit qui tient ma richesse enfermée.

Sylvester lurches a bit when he reaches the couplet, but otherwise
he stays as close to Desportes as he can, even in his own way
recreating the restless pacing of line 7. That he was intrigued by
this description of ghosts (his few changes add to the poem's
spectral quality) may indicate that like some others he sought out

those lyrics in which Desportes offers at least a minor *frisson* as well
as glittery cleverness:

> They say that shadowes of deceased ghosts
> Doe haunt the houses and the graves about,
> Of such whose lives'-lamp went untimely out,
> Delighting still in their forsaken hostes:
> So, in the place where cruell love doth shoote
> The fatall shaft that slue my love's delight,
> I stalke and walke and wander day and night,
> Even like a ghost with unperceived foote.
> But those light ghosts are happier far then I,
> For, at their pleasure, they can come and goe
> Unto the place that hides their treasure, so,
> And see the same with their fantastick eye.
> Where I (alas) dare not approach the cruell
> Proud Monument, that doth inclose my Jewell.[26]

During these years adaptations of several sonnets by Desportes
turned up in English anthologies and songbooks. Probably the
most popular source was *Diane* II, viii, in which a discouraged
lover plans to turn hermit. The poem must have touched some
chord in England—Lodge translated it into the mechanical fourteeners already mentioned, an "uncertain author" expanded it
into a long vision of "A Hermites lief," also in fourteeners, and
Ralegh wrote a much better version anthologized and quoted for
many years to come:

> Like to a Hermite poore in place obscure,
> I meane to spend my daies of endles doubt,
> To waile such woes as time cannot recure,
> Where none but Love shall ever finde me out.
> My foode shall be of care and sorow made,
> My drink nought else but teares falne from mine eies,
> And for my light in such obscured shade,
> The flames shall serve, which from my hart arise.
> A gowne of graie, my bodie shall attire,
> My staffe of broken hope whereon Ile staie,
> Of late repentance linckt with long desire,
> The couch is fram'de whereon my limbs Ile lay,

> And at my gate dispaire shall linger still,
> To let in death when Love and Fortune will.[27]

Perhaps readers of Desportes or Ralegh were taken by the wittily developed comparisons, the metaphors gathered into an easily visualized emblem. And some must have been pleased by the contrast, common in this sort of poetry, between the pastoral melancholy of the speaker's proposal and the urbanity of his style; Desportes's sonnet is a worldly poem about isolation and refuge, readily borrowed and readily understood.

Probably it was this emblematic or at least visual quality as well as the patterned enclosing repetitions that charmed readers of *Diane* I, xv, a little story about an archery contest between the goddess Diana, Love, and the poet's mistress. Desportes's own sonnet was based on a lyric by Gil Polo in the latter's addition to the *Diana* of Montemayor, itself translated by Bartholomew Yong in the early 1580s but not published until 1598. The most famous version of the conceit is Lyly's beguiling "Cupid and my Campaspe," but a poem in *Brittons bowre* is more evidently from Desportes. The fast-paced English adaptation reverses Amor's gender, thus surrounding the poor lover with dangerous females:

> Un jour, l'aveugle Amour, Diane et ma maistresse,
> Pour sçavoir qui aurait plus de dexterité,
> S'essayerent de l'arc à un but limité,
> Et mirent pour le prix leur plus belle richesse.
>
>   Amour gaigea son arc et la chaste deesse
> Qui commande aux forests, sa divine beauté;
> Ma maistresse gaigea sa fiere cruauté,
> Qui me fait consommer en mortelle tristesse.
>
>   Las! Madame gaigna, remportant pour guerdon
> La beauté de Diane et l'arc de Cupidon,
> Et le rocher cruel dont son ame est couverte.
>
>   Pour essayer ses traits, elle a percé mon cueur;
> Sa beauté m'eblouit, je meurs par sa rigueur:
> Ainsi sur moy, chetif, tombe toute la perte.
>
> [1583 version]

> To trie whose art and strength did most excell,
> My Mistresse Love and faire Diana met,

The Ladies three forthwith to shooting fell,
And for the prize the richest Jewell set.
Sweete Love did both her bowe and arrowes gage,
Diana did her bewtie rare lay downe,
My Mistresse pawnde her crueltie and rage,
And she that wanne had all for her renowne:
It fell out thus when as the match was done,
My Mistresse gat the bewtie and the bowe,
And streight to trie the weapons she had wonne,
Upon my heart she did a shaft bestow.
  By Bewtie bound, by Love and Vigor slaine,
  The losse is mine where hers was all the gaine.[28]

Other poems by Desportes inspired imitation, although sometimes it is impossible to know if the English poet followed the
French or an Italian source. For the most part the sonnets that
seem to haunt the anthologies are patterned and glossily mannered
conceits or little dramas like *Diane* I, xxxvii ("Amour, quand fus-tu
né").[29] Collections of lute songs and madrigals, too, include many
lyrics vaguely reminiscent of him. The stock quality of the individual conceits makes tracing sources virtually impossible, yet one
goes through Fellowes's *English Madrigal Verse* often nodding at
faces that seem familiar. John Wilbye, for instance, probably owes
the idea of a poem in *The first set of English madrigals* (1598) to *Diane*
I, xv—or to Spenser's similar admonition; the riches are more like
the former, the geography more like the latter:

What needeth all this travail and turmoiling,
  Shortening the life's sweet pleasure
  To seek this far-fetched treasure
In those hot climates under Phoebus broiling?
O fools, can you not see a traffic nearer
In my sweet lady's face, where Nature showeth
Whatever treasure eye sees or heart knoweth?
  Rubies and diamonds dainty,
  And orient pearls such plenty,
Coral and ambergris sweeter and dearer
Than which the South Seas or Moluccas lend us,
Or either Indies, East or West, do send us.[30]

It was during the 1590s, then, that Desportes's poetry drew considerable attention.[31] In 1607 Gervase Markham published *Rodomonths infernall*, a lively story "Written in French by Phillip de Portes" telling how the pagan champion goes down to defeat in battle only to raise impious war in Hell. The dedicatory letter, however, says that the work was finished more than a dozen years earlier, which would place it, too, during the height of Desportes's popularity as a source for conceits and inventions. In fact Markham apologizes for what he fears may be an old-fashioned quality in his poetry, written when "bumbasted breeches, and straite whale-bon'd doublets had neither use nor estimation." He nevertheless admires Desportes and seems impressed not only by his qualities as a writer but by his worldly position: "The Noble Frenchman Monsieur Portes, who was the first Author of this worke, was a man of great wit, famous learning, and Noble place; each of which carrie in them, defence sufficient to shield him from imputation."

The story that follows expands one of Desportes's early imitations of Ariosto (and Aretino), "La mort de Rodomont." Much is paraphrase, some is translation, and Desportes's steady couplets have been regrouped into stanzas. The chief difference between the two poems lies in Markham's greater liking for funny and even grotesque details. He encourages his characters to boast longer, inflates the hyperboles and comparisons, and welcomes an indecorum Desportes avoided. He gives Rodomont slangy lines— "Packe hence then crooked lozzell, hide thy head," the angry pagan says to the ferryman of Hades—and pushes the action further into the mock heroic so that, for instance, while Pluto chairs a sort of great consult to determine what should be done about this unwanted newcomer we are told that Rodomont "all this while upon the bridge did stand, / Tearing the yron barres up with his hand." Markham was not much of a poet, but surely it was humor and not ineptitude that led him to say breathlessly (there is nothing like this in Desportes) that the hero's spear broke "& with a breach so sound, / That both the horses buttocks kist the ground" (sigs. C4, D3, B6). Markham's rough verve, then, is far from the poised urbanity of his model. His Desportes, like that of Daniel and Lodge, has stepped back several decades from the verge of neoclassicism—he is now less witty and more rambunctious, his ear less finely tuned but his eye for the ridiculous more appreciative.

In Thomas Carew's hands, however, Desportes seems once more himself, although certainly "Englished." When Carew visited the French court in 1619 he might have sensed that Desportes's reputation had slipped, but his poems nevertheless show he read him and found a few lines worth borrowing for his own love poetry. One poem in particular seems indebted to *Hippolyte* x (although the quiver could be from *Diane* II, xii). The vogue for love sonnets was over by now, so Desportes's conceit here supports a briefer and lighter lyric, a poem of no great significance, of course, but with the same worldly yet "mignon" grace, the same sophisticated and assumed innocence with which Desportes had so pleased his aristocratic friends more than a generation earlier:

> Amour, qui vois mon coeur à tes piés abbatu,
> Tu le vois tout couvert de sagettes mortelles,
> Pourquoy donc sans profit en pers-tu de nouvelles,
> Puis que je suis à toy' pourquoy me poursuis-tu?
>
> Si tu veux, courageux, esprouver ta vertu,
> Décoche tous ces traits sur les ames rebelles,
> Sans blesser, trop cruel, ceux qui te sont fidelles,
> Et qui sous ton enseigne ont si bien combatu,
>
> Quand tu tires sur moy tu fais breches sur breches:
> Donc sans les perdre ainsi, garde ces belles fleches
> Pour guerroyer les Dieux, et m'accorde la paix:
>
> Ah! j'entens bien que c'est, Amour veut que je meure:
> Je mourray, mais au moins ce confort me demeure,
> Que la mort de moy seul luy couste mille traits.

> No more, blind God, for see my heart
> Is made thy Quiver, where remaines
> No voyd place for another Dart;
> And alas! that conquest gaines
> Small praise, that only brings away
> A tame and unresisting prey.

> Behold a nobler foe, all arm'd,
> Defies thy weake Artillerie,
> That hath thy Bow and Quiver charm'd;

A rebell beautie, conquering Thee!
If thou dar'st equall combat try,
Wound her, for 'tis for her I dye.[32]

Carew's friend John Suckling characteristically found in an
anthology of French poetry one of Desportes's few off-color poems,
written just before his death but not published with his works. The
translation (made in the mid 1630s) is moderately elegant, the
brutality of spirit tamed or at least smartened by the ease and
speed of the language. Desportes's epigram had been less self-
consciously cynical, its satirically precise equations of sex and
money less nastily made, but both versions of this parodic bar-
gaining are a long distance from the pretty gallantry of the sonnets:

> Il y peut avoir quatre annees,
> Qu'à Philis j'ai voulu conter
> Deux mille pieces coronnees,
> Et plus haut j'eusse peu monter.
> Deux ans apres elle me mande
> Que pour mille elle condecent;
> Je trouvay la somme trop grande,
> Je n'en voulus donner que cent.
> Au bout de six ou sept semaines
> A cent escus elle revint;
> Je dis qu'elle perdoit ses peines
> S'elle en pretendoit plus de vingt.
> L'autre jour elle fut contente
> De vertir pour six ducatons,
> J'en trouvay trop haute la vente,
> S'elle passoit quatre testons.
> Ce matin, elle est arrivee,
> Gratis voulant s'abandonner,
> Et je l'ay plus chere trouvee,
> Que quand j'en voulois tant donner.

> It is not four years ago,
>   I offered Forty crowns
> To lie with her a night or so:
>   She answer'd me in frowns.

Not two years since, she meeting me
    Did whisper in my ear,
That she would at my service be,
    If I contented were.

I told her I was cold as snow
    And had no great desire;
But should be well content to go
    To Twenty, but no higher.

Some three moneths since or thereabout,
    She that so coy had bin,
Bethought herself and found me out,
    And was content to sin.

I smil'd at that, and told her I
    Did think it something late,
And that I'de not repentance buy
    At above half the rate.

This present morning early she
    Forsooth came to my bed,
And *gratis* there she offered me
    Her high-priz'd maidenhead.

I told her that I thought it then
    Far dearer than I did,
When I at first the Forty crowns
    For one night's lodging bid.[33]

Charles Cotton, somewhat younger than Suckling, was also entertained by the lady's deflationary offers, coarsening Desportes's gay cynicism into a bit of quasi-pornography:

Epigramme de Monsieur Des-Portes
Some four years ago I made Phillis an offer,
    Provided she would be my whore,
Of two thousand good crowns to put in her coffer,
    And I think should have given her more.

About two years after, a message she sent me,
    She was for a thousand my own.
But unless for an hundred she now would content me,
    I sent her word I would have none.

> She fell to my price six or seven weeks after,
>   And then for a hundred would do;
> I then told her in vain she talk'd of the matter,
>   Than twenty no farther I'd go.
>
> T'other day for six ducatoons she was willing,
>   Which I thought a great deal too dear.
> And told her unless it would come for two shilling,
>   She must seek a chapman elsewhere.
>
> This morning she's come, and would fain buckle gratis,
>   But she's grown so fulsome a whore,
> That now methinks nothing a far dearer rate is,
>   Than all that I offer'd before.[34]

Often Desportes had been made to seem more old-fashioned than he appeared in the courts and salons of France. For a time—in Constable's verse, in the additions of 1594, even in Carew—he was more or less himself in English dress. But here he moves ahead of his time, approaching the Restoration.

Lodge exaggerated when he wrote in 1596 that Desportes's works had been for the most part Englished and were ordinarily in everybody's hands. There was, however, some truth to what he said. Desportes was read, imitated, certainly widely known, probably widely liked. And yet few Englishmen mentioned him in what they wrote. It is true that more writers imitated Marot, Du Bellay, and Ronsard than cared to say so, just as they did classical and Italian poets. It seems to me, however, that the contrast between Desportes's evident usefulness as a source and the near indifference to him as a literary figure worth a comment or even a compliment is quite striking. Marot had his curiously double image in England, Du Bellay won from Spenser eloquent and deserved tribute, Ronsard was at least occasionally recognized as "great," and Du Bartas was compared to Homer. On Desportes there was virtual silence.

This silence was not, of course, complete. Several references have already been mentioned—Lodge's ambiguous and satirical remarks, Gervase Markham's praise, Cotton's acknowledgment of his source. The most intriguing comment, hitherto unnoted, is that of Sir Edward Stafford, ambassador to France during most of the

1580s. Stafford was greatly concerned with France's policy toward the low countries and wrote Walsingham on January 25, 1585, to tell him how he gauged the wind. His theories on how the king could be persuaded are of particular interest for the illumination they throw on Desportes's political influence over the Duc de Joyeuse, a matter still not wholly clear. As reported in the *Calendar of State Papers* (Foreign Series) the letter says:

> I have caused the two kings that rule our King [i.e. Joyeuse and Epernon] in this matter of the Low Countries; to feel how they are affectioned to it, and "egged by hope of ambition and profit," the two things which would move them to further it. The instrument to Joyeuse was Desportes . . . who rules him as he lists, and who propounded to him the great commodity it would be to the realm, whereof he would have the honour, every body knowing how he governs the King, as also the dishonour, if it went not forward and perchance the King should miscarry, or he fall into disgrace and the hindrance of so great a matter laid to his charge.
>
> Also, how greatly his office of the Admiralty would be enlarged and he himself "like enough to be much enriched by it, besides that they of the Low Countries . . . could not for a gratuity be so smally liberal to him but that it would be worth to him better than a hundred thousand francs a year."
>
> These things he marvellously bit at, and promised to egg the King on all he could.

The 1590s saw a few literary remarks. In a passage quoted before, John Eliot said Desportes wrote sweet "Poësies and Love-toies," and Michael Drayton complained in a sonnet published with his sonnet sequence *Idea* (1594) that his contemporaries knew these "Poësies and Love-toies" all too well. His own rhymes, he says with some truth, are more original:

> Yet these mine owne, I wrong not other men,
>   Nor trafique further then thys happy Clyme,
>   Nor filch from Portes nor from Petrarchs pen,
>   A fault too common in thys latter tyme.
> Divine Syr Phillip, I avouch thy writ,
> I am no Pickpurse of anothers wit.[35]

This proud and patriotic statement needs to be interpreted cautiously. Sidney and Drayton, if not apes or thieves, wrote securely in a tradition stretching back at least to Petrarch and coming to them through France as well as modern Italy. The notion of not stealing feathers or coin refers to something like Du Bellay's distinction between external servile copying and imaginative imitation shaped by what Sidney called an "inward tuch." A phrase, a theme, an image, an attitude—these are part of one's tradition. An entire "fore-conceit" should come from one's own vision whatever the provenance of its component parts or the antiquity of its significance.

Except for a fleeting reference to the "feu Mr Desportes" as Régnier's uncle in one of Francis Davison's papers and the somewhat surprising approbation by Henry Reynolds, I can find no other mention of Desportes until James Howell's *Instructions for forreine travell* (1642) which, it may be remembered, suggests giving a "slight salute" to Ronsard and Desportes.[36] English readers might also have seen Desportes's name in translations. Tofte's *Honours academie* (1610), for instance, cites the "Diana of courteous De Reports" (sig. Ii2), and many years later *A discourse of women* (1662), which illustrates "their imperfections alphabetically" from Avarice to Zeal, quotes Desportes (a "brave Poet") on women's false faith, rendering *Diverses amours* xxxi and *Cléonice* lxxxvi into what one could in an irresponsibly generous mood call blank verse (sigs. E2–E3). Nor, so far as I can tell, were many Englishmen taken by Desportes's psalms, although they might have found them praised in St. Francis de Sales's *Treatise of the love of God*, translated by M. Car: "I have often cited the sacred Psalmist in verse, and it was done to recreate thy mind, and through the facilitie which I found in it by reason of the sweete translation of Philipe de Portes, Abbot of Tiron" (Douai, 1630 ed., sig. b4). And others might have noted in Charles Maupas's *French Grammar* a reference to Desportes as a "learned exact writer" who translated the psalms "most elegantly" (1634, sig. B7).

Desportes, then, stirred no great interest in England beyond his usefulness and the pleasure he must have given his readers. Few tried to locate him in his country's history of letters, fit him into a tradition, or place him among relevant moderns. He had a lively presence in England, one must assume from the many translations, but no "image" of his own, no visible or describable "figure," no reputation except—if one may judge from the references by Lodge and Drayton—as the author of love toys everyone knew. The reasons for his seeming indifference are probably several. Chronology may have had something to do with it, for during the vogue for love sonnets in England Ronsard and Du Bellay had simply been around longer, having arrived earlier on the scene in an age when lists of names, collections, or *comparationes* tended to assign a famous name to a particular genre or literary function as *the* name one knew in that context. The niche of "French author of conceited love toys" was by the 1580s and 1590s already well inhabited, as were those of "French author or authors who polished the vernacular" and "French writer plausibly compared with the ancients"; in a friendly moment Dorat (who must have known better) found Orpheus mystically residing in Desportes's name, but such a comparison was more reasonably made with Ronsard and Du Bartas. There was no niche for Desportes except that of provisioner, where he was twice placed.

Furthermore, English readers may have sensed in Desportes (all the more because his conceits were so exportable) a lack of personality or character, a self-effacement in the verse accounted for in part by the circumstances of its composition and in part by the author's attempt at smoothness and grace rather than force or depth. It is true that the poems in which Du Bellay was most "himself" and the hymns and odes in which Ronsard reached the furthest were the least imitated of their major works, but they were there in the same volumes and doubtless read. In this poetry, and even in that more often translated into English, Du Bellay and Ronsard insistently draw our attention to themselves not only by the power of their language but by their explicit boasts of priority, triumph, and access to realms beyond time's reach. Desportes adopted the pose of the immortalizing poet as he adopted most fashionable stances, but one can feel that despite his success his heart was not in this particular claim, whereas it lay at the very center of Ronsard's conception of poetry. Du Bellay, and especially Ronsard, were thus louder, more unmistakable, in what they said about themselves— and rightly so, for their assertions and hopes were not merely self-promotion but a vision of poetry thinned and diminished by the courtly elegance of Desportes. No wonder, then, that they presented themselves more vividly to the English imagination.

Finally, the same hesitancy about love poetry which, I am persuaded, limited the praise given that aspect of Marot's, Du Bellay's, and Ronsard's careers also limited the admiration Desportes could in any case have won in England, for unlike these three, unlike Petrarch, unlike the "Tiphys . . . Amoris" Ovid himself, Desportes wrote virtually nothing except the very sort of poetry often dismissed as toys, trifles, *nugae*, even by those who wrote it. Compared to the poems for Hélène or to *Astrophil and Stella* Desportes's sonnets really do seem toys, although shiny and delicate ones. Yet even had they shimmered with more genuinely Neoplatonic emanations, expressed a more truly complex psychology, suggested more wrenching dilemmas or more exalted meanings, hinted at occult significance, or arrayed themselves numerologically, it still is unlikely Desportes would have been much discussed in England. As I have argued earlier, the genre of the love sonnet was hard to handle critically. It was much easier to introduce one's "passions" or trifles with humor and even apology, much easier for a printer like Sylvester's to assume that this was pleasant verse a good poet would outgrow.

Some, of course, had more serious reservations. If we are to give an account of every idle word what shall we say of Desportes? Perhaps simply that he wrote well, as one anonymous schoolmaster said of Anacreon:

> Anacreon was a wanton Epicure,
> A glosing Poet, but lewd Moralist:
> He sould his soule to Venus and her sonne,
> Such writers we for stile, not matter reade.[37]

Probably few of Desportes's English readers, except those severely hampered by what at times appears a neurotic fear of idleness and temptation (a fear that gives to the written word a power even beyond what Ronsard had claimed for poetry), felt a genuine contempt for love sonnets or were deeply troubled by reading and writing them; most knew that no girl was ever ruined by a Petrarchist or even Ovidian compliment. But because of this hesitation, this focusing of critical attention elsewhere on poetry more evidently didactic or of a higher "kind," Du Bellay and Ronsard could be praised only slightly as love poets and Desportes could not appear—even had his sonnets possessed more fire and pro- fundity—as much more than a pleasant writer of popular trifles about whom there was simply not much one could say.

English silence on Desportes is disappointing to one seeking to define his reputation but it is not, upon reflection, surprising; nor, probably, was it unjust.

5

Du Bartas

Guillaume de Salluste, Sieur Du Bartas (1544–90), said Gabriel
Harvey, was the Christian Homer, majestic in style and heavenly
in matter, wiser than Euripides, the "only brave poet" in the
"Sacred vein," the treasurer of humanity and jeweler of divinity.[1]
Most of Harvey's contemporaries and the two generations that
followed would have agreed. Not so their posterity. Douglas Bush,
for instance, called the *Divine Weeks* "a kind of Albert Memorial of
encyclopaedic fundamentalism," a clever analogy that makes Du
Bartas's efforts sound at least noticeable, if only as an eyesore to
tourists unprepared for such structures.[2] Yet far from seeming an
inescapable monstrosity, Du Bartas's work as Englished by Joshua
Sylvester has slipped below the horizon of many historians and
teachers of Renaissance English poetry. A recent handbook on
Elizabethan and Stuart literature has no entry for Sylvester, only a
brief inaccurate mention of him under "translations."[3] Spenser,
Daniel, Sidney, Burton, Walton, Milton, and many others would
be astonished.

Guillaume de Salluste was born in Gascony into a Huguenot
merchant family.[4] He studied law in Toulouse, won a prize for
poetry, and at the suggestion of Queen Jeanne d'Albret composed
an epic on the heroine Judith. This, together with "Le triomfe de la
foi" and "L'Uranie," he published at Bordeaux in 1574 as *La muse
chrestiene*. Although Du Bartas joined the civil wars he had Catholic
friends, belonged to the academy at Navarre, and like Ronsard,
whom he admired, had ties to the syncretic and eirenic movements
of his time. Probably, therefore, his *Muse* was meant not to replace
but to complete the work of his elders, to fulfill their own attempts
to revive Orpheus. Ronsard himself was dismayed.[5]

"La Judit" tells how Judith murdered Holofernes and saved the
Israelites, a story Du Bartas expands with descriptions, epic similes and lofty speeches, sometimes soaring uncontrollably ("La
parole me faut, mes poils d'horreur se dressent") and sometimes
effectively vivid. The verbal trickiness shows already and, in an
attempt at literary and philosophical syncretism, Du Bartas incor-
porates Greek fable and metaphysics:

> Mais Judit au milieu de la troupe reluit
> Comme Phoebé par-mi les lampes de la nuit;
> Car il semble que Dieu ait ses beautés moulées
> Sur le moule plus beau des plus belles idées.
>
> [Book I, 135–38]

"Le triomfe de la foi," dedicated to the Catholic Pibrac, recounts a
dream from the "porte de corne" in which Faith progresses in
allegorical majesty across the poet's inner vision. Riding on
Ezekiel's many-eyed wheels, she brings with her a multitude of
conquered gentile kings, pagan philosophers, and ethnic theologians (they are not crushed, merely subject—a matter of some
importance). After these come the heroes of God. The poetry has
few set pieces, for the effect derives chiefly from the names and the
range of thought or action they evoke.

"L'Uranie" describes how during the poet's "April" days when
he thought to write eulogies, classical tragedy, an epic on French
history, or songs of "le mal dous-amer," he was visited by the muse
of astronomy and exhorted to sing of God. Urania is crowned with
seven obliquely turning folds of seven metals, dressed in blue with
fires spangled like the zodiac, and "sa bouche à neuf vois imite en
ses accors / Le son harmonieus de la dance celeste." Her sisters,
she says, are now given to "feints souspirs, de feints pleurs, de
feints cris, / D'impudiques discours, et de vaines quereles," but
probably Urania is not so much rejecting them as insisting upon
her greater sincerity and nobler subject, just as Sidney and other
love poets who evidently "feigned" somewhat liked to say that *their*
verses were truer than those others' uninspired flatteries.

The source of true poetry, Urania tells Du Bartas, is the divine
"fureur" that inspired Homer, Orpheus, Hesiod, David, and
Ovid; Plato only exiled poets who betrayed their gift; a great
subject will bring "Graves et masles motz" and win laurels. So sing

of Noah, not Deucalion (although when Du Bartas did so he
borrowed from Ovid), and leave the old fables and the "insolent"
archer. Du Bartas means, I think, that myth should serve truth,
not that it has no place in poetry. Urania herself is, after all, a
Greek fiction, however Christianized, and an allegorically costumed one at that.

"L'Uranie" expresses forcefully what was to be a powerful
thrust toward verse based overtly upon Scripture, literature some
welcomed as godly matter one could put into the hands of wife or
children without leading them the primrose way. Yet distressed
though she is by the recent shabby behavior of her sisters, Urania's
own movement is up to the firmament, not inside to the Sabbath
parlor; she offers an increased delight as well as spiritual profit.
And more than "Le triomfe" this poem is a work of Renaissance
syncretism. Urania knows the Bible—according to some she
helped write it—but she has also read Plato's *Phaedrus*:

> D'autant que tout ainsi que la fureur humaine
> Rend l'homme moins qu'humain; la divine fureur
> Rend l'homme plus grand qu'homme, et d'une sage erreur
> Sur les poles astrés à son gré le pourmene.
>
> [ll. 53–56]

Under Urania's guidance Du Bartas set to work and in 1578
published *La creation du monde ou premiere sepmaine*, an encyclopedic
hexameron describing the Creation day by day with many invocations, lists, anecdotes, comparisons, arguments, and as much
erudition as the author could muster. The poem is not so much a
narrative as an expatiation on the whole multiple universe lying
enclosed within the creating Word.

In "Le premier jour" Du Bartas prays that he might show forth
"Les plus rares beautez de ce grand univers." These beauties
please both soul and body, for God's universe is a school, a store, a
theatre and book available to the senses yet leading the mind to
rapture. One should love reverently, however, and even as Du
Bartas urges the reader upward to observe the nature of things he
urges his reason down to humility. From the primordial elements
Du Bartas moves to anticipate that day when "La mer deviendra
flamme, et les seches balenes, / Horribles, mugleront sur les cuites
arenes," then to a celebration of day and night and to a con-

sideration of angels. The second day tells of the elements and of
mutability:

> Rien n'est icy constant: la naissance et la mort
> President par quartier en un mesme ressort.
> Un corps naistre ne peut qu'un autre corps ne meure,
> Mais la seule matiere immortelle demeure.
>
> [11. 199–202]

Matter, he says in a passage typical for its rhetorical play, is a Lais
always ready for a new lover:

> Et dans un mesme temps, elle reçoit à part
> Figure apres figure, en sorte qu'une face
> S'efface par le trait qu'une face efface.
>
> [11. 224–26]

Yet this changeable world dances to number and measure, creating variations on the basic "four." We read of the bride Earth, the
winds, the seasons, the waters above the earth, and the Flood when
dolphins brushed against mountain treetops.

On the third day come the division of the waters from the land,
the rivers, and then the earth dressed with the plenitude of plants,
the "pesche velu" and "figue jette-laict." Du Bartas invokes the
fully clad earth and, as usual when hoping to elevate or intensify
his language, clusters the *mots composés*:

> Je te salue, o terre, o terre porte-grains,
> Porte-or, porte-santé, porte-habits, porte-humains,
> Porte-fruicts, porte-tours, alme, belle, immobile,
> Patiente, diverse, odorante, fertile,
> Vestue d'un manteau tout damassé de fleurs,
> Passementé de flots, bigarré de couleurs.
>
> [11. 851–56]

In the fourth day the sky dances for earth like the courting peacock,
the zodiac blazes across our view, and the heavenly spheres roll by.
In the next day we read of "les nageurs citoyens de la venteuse
mer" whose variety demonstrates the astonishing *energia* with
which God wrote his book of creatures: "la diversité des oeuvres de
ses mains" shows "sa force." We hear of the moral and immoral
behavior of the fish and birds, the dolphin "Ayme-naux, ayme-

humains, ayme-vers, ayme-lyre" and the little bees and flies who show that God glories even in "un obscur ouvrage." The sixth day brings the animals and the microcosm Man with all his powers of memory and contemplation, his arts and inventions, and the woman with whom he forms an "amoureux Androgyne." God tells the couple to have babies. As he rests on the last day the Lord "s'esgaye" like a painter reviewing his finished landscape; and Du Bartas tells us to study the Creation and its lessons.

In 1579 Du Bartas published a new edition of the *Muse chrestiene* (the version known in England). Fifteen eighty-two brought a hymn to peace and some sonnets, and 1584 saw the first two parts of the *Seconde sepmaine*, introduced with the praise of Dorat, Henri Estienne, and others. This was to have been an enormously long history of the world from Genesis to the last Sabbath divided, as Augustine had suggested at the end of *The City of God*, into "days." Each "day" would have four sections to make a total of twenty-eight, a powerful and interesting number, but Du Bartas found his own *quies* before he could finish.

The first "day" describes a lush and varied Eden in which the first pair is given just enough labor to prevent idleness, knowledge of everything except the actual experience of evil, and religious ecstacy which leads them up to "l'Archetype unique." Adam lies on roses arranged by angels into love knots, triangles, and lozenges; but his Paradise, says Du Bartas, was no ineffable allegory. In "L'imposture" Satan seduces Eve like "un amant ruzé" and then come "Les furies," shattering "l'amour qui regnoit durant le premier age." Man's fall untunes the rest, for he was the "principale corde / Du luth de l'univers." In "Les artifices" the repair work begins with clothes, houses, fire, agriculture, horse-taming; Tubal invents metallurgy and Jubal hearing the hammers on the anvil finds music in the "accords" of his "nombreux esprit," a happy discovery usually ascribed to Pythagoras.

The "Deuxieme jour" begins with "L'arche," the story of Noah. There is considerable arguing in this section as Noah replies to his son Cham's sulky atheism. In "Babylone" human languages diverge, and Du Bartas describes their history, nature, and triumphs with great delight. Hebrew is the first and still the most magical tongue, filled with anagrams and numerical meanings. "Les colonies" follows human migrations and invasions, the races and their traits, men's trade and travel. Once more, however, thunder the lengthy arguments against those who doubt Scripture's letter, a hectoring (and perhaps an unconscious anxiety) which, I think, creates problems of "belief" not raised by better authors even when expressing the same convictions. "Les colomnes" describes huge pillars on which are carved symbols of the quadrivium. Du Bartas discourses on arithmetic, presented chiefly as numerology; geometry, based on the "loy qui forma l'univers"; and astronomy. The starry figures he says were given false identifications by the Greeks, so he names them anew—Hercules becomes David, Taurus the Golden Calf, and so forth. The pagan experience of the heavens is thus folded into the Christian. The book closes with a discussion of "la sacree harmonie, / Et la nombreuse loy."

By 1584 Du Bartas had translated the "Lepanto" of James VI, who invited him to Scotland in an adulatory letter. In the spring of 1587 he came, sent by Henri de Navarre to arrange a marriage between the king's sister and James. The negotiation failed, but Du Bartas impressed the Scots, and when he returned home in August James accompanied him to the ship, pressing gifts and further invitations upon him.[6] He continued to work on the *Seconde sepmaine* and in 1590 wrote a "Cantique d'Yvry" to celebrate this crucial battle. Later that year he died. In 1591, however, appeared some unpolished segments of his *Seconde sepmaine*: the "Pères," "Jonas," "Trophées," and "Magnificance." In 1593 came "La loy" and in 1603 the "Vocation," "Capitaines," "Schisme," and "Décadence," less popular than the earlier poetry.

Although some objected to Du Bartas's language and a few to his organization, his poetry was nonetheless immensely successful, frequently reprinted (often with the learned commentary by the Huguenot scholar Simon Goulart), and translated into many languages.

The verse so widely read and greatly admired is filled with disjunctions, variety, movement, subjective intrusions, strange images and ornaments, a passionate sense of ordered beauty yet also a perception of multiplicity and violence; understandably, it has been called "baroque." For Du Bartas, who loved the word "tout," any subject, any metaphor, any item in the world of the many was suitable in a celebration of the One, the All. The resulting style has disturbed many readers, especially the French, because of its sudden dips or rises, the mixture of preciosity and naïveté, the juxtapositions of mean and high (justifiable theologically but apt to jar or amuse, as when we are told to take faith for our "lunettes"), the impacted ornamentation, the reckless neologisms, the disparity between the recherché language and the often conventional thought, and the mélange of abstract sophistication and anthropomorphism in the treatment of God—Noah calls him a mystic circle but Du Bartas can also say that Eden pleased "l'oreille, l'oeil, le nez du Tout-puissant." Yet even these very oddities can breed an affection for the *Sepmaines*, and in recent years Du Bartas has been cogently defended.[7]

More damaging (and less perceptible to those of us who cannot hear French as well as we can English) is a lack of musicality and despite the inflation an absence of vigor in Du Bartas's language itself, although it was precisely his *energia* that the English once admired. The *mots composés* are meant to intensify or compress and sometimes they do, but often like the asyndeton of which his English translators were so fond, they merely compress words, not thoughts or emotions, and the result is flaccid in feeling while stiff or strange in rhythm. To illustrate Du Bartas's inadequacy French critics have on occasion set passages like his praise of the earth against those by Ronsard which move with greater fluidity and power.[8] More relevant to his career in England is a comparison with Milton. Du Bartas describes how in the beginning

> comme l'oiseau qui tasche rendre vifs
> Et ses oeufs naturels et ses oeufs adoptifs,
> Se tient couché sur eux, et d'une chaleur vive,
> Fait qu'un rond jaune-blanc en un poulet s'avive;
> D'une mesme façon l'Esprit de l'Eternel
> Sembloit couver ce goufre, et d'un soin paternel
> Verser en chasque part une vertu feconde,
> Pour d'un si lourd amas extraire un si beau monde.
>
> [*PS*, I, 297–304]

The simile itself is not inherently foolish (nor original with Du Bartas), but here it lacks Milton's wise reticence, resonant intensity, and rhythmic tension:

>   Thou from the first
> Wast present, and with mighty wings outspread
> Dove-like satst brooding on the vast Abyss
> And mad'st it pregnant.
>
> [*Paradise Lost* I, 19–22]

Until Milton's day and for a little time after, however, Du Bartas's popularity in England was virtually unmodified by doubt or reservation, a vogue for which literary historians have in our own century tried to account. Most have concluded that his fame derived in large part from his rhetorical flashiness, since this sort of extremism was "one of the ways in which the exuberance of spirit released at the Renaissance found an outlet," or from his "Protestant zeal." "Catholic readers were undoubtedly put off by Du Bartas' Protestant bias, but it suited most English readers very well," says one. Even C. S. Lewis, who enjoyed Du Bartas's verve, seems to have assumed the *Weeks* were primarily "Sunday reading." Du Bartas's popularity has, of course, been tied to the vogue for divine poetry, and some point to his combination of Platonism and Protestantism, to a conservative and encyclopedic vision of the cosmos comforting to people nervous about new threats to older views, or to his reverent skepticism, which responded to such threats by denigrating human reason.[9]

These explanations of Du Bartas's career in England are all plausible, although I doubt strongly that except at first he appealed much to a specifically Protestant bias. What most comments on the English reaction to him and to his work miss is the tone, the flavor, the deeper assumptions or feelings behind the praise. The rest of this book will, I hope, not so much disprove as qualify what is often said about his long triumph through Renaissance England. Before looking at the translations published there or the many encomia, references, and quotations, however, two further comments should be made about the works thus honored. First, as is by now obvious, Du Bartas hoped if not to reconcile pagan learning and Christian verity then somehow to include the former in the latter. In certain moods, it is true, Du Bartas triumphs over gentile error, and he is quick to argue that explicitly Christian poetry will reach a grandeur not allowed mere fantasy. No Orpheus could equal his David, no Apollo his Christ. Yet his use of the "prisca theologia" and Greek myth, his modified Platonism and traces of the Cabala, all show he was both a sober Huguenot and one of those many who found in the wisdom of the ancients not only moral guidance and literary example but mystic learning.[10]   Second, and not unrelated, is the tendency of Du Bartas to shape his work according to an inner outline which can be best indicated through number. Modern readers are apt to wonder if he had any principle of selection at all, for as narrative the *Sepmaines* are mostly distraction and interruption.[11] Yet the English and even the French could praise Du Bartas for his powers of composition. Clearly for them his organization grew from something other than event or argument. Although his works have nothing like the complicated number symbolism found in Spenser's *Epithalamion*, for instance, the larger structures of the two *Sepmaines* are of course based on "seven" and, in the second *Week*, on "four" and "twenty-eight" as well. The first edition of "Le triomfe" has four books and seven hundred lines. Within these patterns Du Bartas insists upon similar patterns in the cosmos, the four of the elements, seasons, humors, winds, the seven planets, ages, "days."

This kind of arrangement must have affected English perception of Du Bartas in interesting ways. Philip Sidney, in defending poetry, had distinguished among three sorts of poets—the divine *vates*, versifiers of nonfiction, and the "right" poets, who feign and whom he chiefly defends. I suspect that had he excluded him from the third category Sidney would have put him in the first, not the second, but Ben Jonson was perverse enough to say that Du Bartas was not a poet "but a Verser, because he wrote not Fiction." Du Perron, whom Jonson met in Paris, had said the same.[12] Which sort of poet was Du Bartas? What he wrote was "true" yet the English did not often classify him with, say, Lucretius. He was certainly "divine," yet often the English associated him with secular if serious writers like Sidney. Du Bartas may have appeared a "right" poet loosely defined thanks to his energy and rich ornamentation, but perhaps some of the more thoughtful English readers also felt he escaped being a "verser" because like the angels arranging Adam's bed of roses he made a mystically significant shape, a Pythagorean (and Christian) structure. If Du Bartas's poetry imitates scriptural story and natural history it also illuminates the inner truth they, even more than Greek fable, contain as a gift and imprint from that God who worked by number, weight, and measure. Despite the absence of a fictional plot or feigned setting, then, he had a worthy "fore conceit" which allowed him in much English compliment the company of Chaucer, Ariosto, and Spenser as well as that of Orpheus and David.[13]

Du Bartas soon found translators in England and Scotland. The first was Thomas Hudson, an English musician at the court of James VI who explains in the preface to his *Historie of Judith* (1584) that once when he rashly claimed it was possible to put Du Bartas's "exquisite" verse "succintlie, and sensibly in our owne vulgar speech" his skeptical king told him to try "La Judit." With a sober gait and an occasional misstep Hudson closely follows the prose sense of the 1579 edition, attempting a few compounds—"Mars le rase-tours" is now "Mars towremyner"—but usually restraining the language (although he should have thought twice before describing dawn as that time when "The Snoring snoute of restles Phlegon blewe, / Hote on the Ynds").[14]

That same year James VI published *Essayes of a prentise*. The young king had surrounded himself with poets who would, as he might have put it, lead the muses yet further north, so it is not surprising he translated "Uranie"; its piety well suited a pupil of Buchanan, and a translation would also, the king must have thought, give his own court some of the glory Du Bartas had won in France. His pentameter couplets show more daring and energy than Hudson's *Judith*, if only because even more than his model James reaches for the concrete and homely; where Du Bartas's Plato "chassoit" poets, for instance, James's bids them "pack." Despite his awkwardness, moreover, he has imaginative touches of his own:

> For even as humane fury maks the man,
> Les then the man: So heavenly fury can
> Make man pas man, and wander in a holy mist,
> Upon the fyrie heaven to walk at list.[15]

In the late 1580s James translated the "Furies," soon published in *His Majesties poeticall exercises* (Edinburgh, 1591). His original, says the king, is a "vive mirror of this last and most decreeped age.

Heere shalt thou see clearlie, as in a glasse, the miseries of this wavering world." The words are banal but they describe qualities in Du Bartas others were to remark—*energia* or forcefulness in "imitating" and *enargia* or the power to make a vivid image. James's invocation presses even further, honoring Du Bartas for virtues Englishmen were to admire over and over again: the starry splendor of a poet "Who Azure Skie doth decke / With blazing lights"; his fame; the power of this "Alluring Orpheus" who crowns the muses' "Ethnique heades" with "holie twists and faire / Of Liban Cedres tall"; his style "loftie," "golden," and varied. James prays he himself may "vivelie paint him forth," and his translation into fourteeners is not without flair. A fragment of the "second jour" in yet more fourteeners remained unpublished, however, as did a fervent compliment in French:

> O divin du Bartas, disciple d'Uranie
> L'honneur de nostre temps, poëte du grand Dieu
> Tes saincts vers doux-coulants pleins de douce manie
> Distillés des hauts cieux volent de lieu en lieu
> Comme esclairs foudroyants du grand esprit tonnant
> Postillonent tonnants du levant au ponant.[16]

James never lost his admiration for the "poëte du grand Dieu," and would long quote little tags from his poetry like the fragment he found in the "Capitaines" for his *True lawe of free monarchies*, published at Edinburgh five years before he left to apply his theories in England. James, of course, takes a conservative line on the dangers of political reformation, "For as the Divine: Poet Du Bartas sayeth: Better it were to suffer some disorder in the estate, and some spots in the commonwealth, then, in pretending to reforme, utterly to overthrow the Republicke" (1603 ed., sig. D6^v). Like Elizabeth, James sympathized with a religious movement that had a dangerous streak of revolutionary sentiment, so it must have pleased him that Du Bartas was so sound politically.

It was not long before references to the royal literary prowess began to appear, not all of them, one hopes, inspired by prudence or ambition. With his usual hyperbole, for example, Harvey calls James "a Homer to himselfe, a Golden spurre to Nobility, a Scepter to Vertue, a Verdure to the Spring, a Sunne to the day," citing "his heavenly Urany, and his hellish Furies." Inevitably, the king ascended his new throne amid a flurry of such homages. John Savile's *King James his entertainment at Theobalds* (1603), for instance, says he "doth excell / As his Lepantho and his Furies tell / In Poesie: all kings in Christendome" (sig. C4), and at Oxford James learned he had indeed translated "vivelie": JACOBUS STVARTVS equals VIVÈ SCOTUS BARTAS. The chorus went on. James, says Drummond in *Forth feasting* (1617), was an Orpheus "garlanded with all Uranias Flowres," and in 1625 William Vaughan's *Cambrensium Caroleia* recalls the "Furies" of the new king's father (1630 ed., sig. C4). Du Bartas was thus in an enviable position as political tensions in England tightened; Puritans might read him for his moral profit, but to praise him was also to flatter the Stuarts' taste.[17]

While James labored over the "Furies," Sir Philip Sidney was putting the *Premiere sepmaine* into what one would assume was the best English version of Du Bartas. The stationers' register for 1588 records his "translation of Salust de Bartas," and there are several early references to the poem. From time to time Du Bartas's other translators would mention that, as Sylvester put it, England's Apelles "This Lovely Venus / First to limne beganne." But, Sylvester adds, the poem is now "close lockt from common light," and there it has stayed, with no evidence as to what became of it or why Sidney's family did not want it published. Perhaps it was unpolished; perhaps as Sidney worked with the material he became dissatisfied with the original or with himself. One wonders how he handled Du Bartas's neologisms and the odd metaphors. That he wanted to translate Du Bartas is itself interesting, furthermore, for the light it may cast on his views of poetry. During the past few years it has been argued that Sidney's true opponents were not those who mistrusted poetry but the "divine" poets like Du Bartas who preferred scriptural and hence true verse to make-believe. The point seems well taken. And yet Sidney translated the psalms and like many of his friends admired Du Bartas. Did he change his feelings toward divine poetry, sobering in thought as he got older? Was he talked into the project by devout friends like Mornay?[18] Probably we will never fully know his reasons or the evolution of his convictions. I would, however, add that Du Bartas's rejection of the fictional and secular must not be exaggerated; despite his own faith in Urania he praised writers like Ariosto and

Ronsard with little reservation. Furthermore, his insistence on the value of divine poetry sometimes seems to exclude other "kinds" chiefly because the rhetoric of praise and blame in the Renaissance virtually required overstatement. Urania celebrates only divine poetry, for that is her job; in "Babylone" Du Bartas is more catholic. Last, some English readers dissociated Du Bartas from authors of fiction, while others linked him with Sidney and Spenser—there was simply no consensus on the matter.

Sidney's was not the only translation of Du Bartas since lost. Thomas Churchyard says in *Churchyards challenge* (1593) that he has written several manuscripts now lent to various acquaintances, among them "a great peece of work translated out of the great learned French Poet Seignior Dubartas, which work treated of a Lady and an Eagle, most divinely written on by Dubartas, and given by me to a great Lord of this land, who saith it is lost" (sig. A5). The story of the eagle and the girl, from the end of the "premier jour," is not a "great peece," but Churchyard's poem puts him among Du Bartas's earliest translators and one may regret with him the absentminded ways of book borrowers.

Even more interesting might be an item in the 1609 catalogue of the Lumley library: "Sir William Herbertes translation of the Urania or Coelest Muse of Salust de Bartas, out of French into English, dedicated to my lorde Lumley. manuscript."[19] John Lumley, ·said his contemporaries, was a pious man much given to recondite learning; his library included works by Hermes, Lull, Vitruvius, Agrippa, and Dee, as well as books on mythology and the art of memory. He had little modern literature besides this lost "Urania." Who its author was I am not sure. The most plausible candidate, I imagine, is Churchyard's friend Sir William Herbert or Harbert (*c.* 1552–93), who according to his son-in-law Lord Herbert of Cherbury liked books, divinity, astrology, and alchemy. He wrote some verses and like Lumley he knew Dee. Whoever Sir William was, however, he gave his manuscript to a man whose interests involved the Pythagorean and hermetic learning which Du Bartas from time to time absorbed into his Christian vision.

Published translations in England began with Robert Ashley's *Urania sive musa coelestis* (1589), one of several attempts to encase Du Bartas in the permanence of Latin. In an elegant preface, Ashley says he read Du Bartas as a student at Oxford and a friend compliments him on his own divine *furor*. He gives both languages so that readers can compare lines like "De la molle Cipris, et le mal doux-amer" with "Et Veneris cantare malum, tam dulce, et amarum" (sig. B1). English translations soon followed. Joshua Sylvester's *Canticle of the victorie . . . at Yvry* (1590) was not, however, an auspicious start; the alliterations only emphasize the already thumping rhythms of his hexameters (e.g. "O God! what glorious sun, beams bright about our bounds?"). Perhaps he worked in haste, for English readers followed Navarre's career closely and publishers were quick to produce battle reports in both prose and verse. Since Ivry was an important triumph, many must have been curious to read how, as Sylvester says on his title page, "After the dawne, comes day."

In 1591 there was a Latin translation of the *Premiere sepmaine*, Gabriel Lermeus's *Hebdomas*, already published in Paris in 1583 and dedicated to Elizabeth. This is the poem, Lermeus tells her, whose unexpected splendor has stunned the world of letters; while others idly composed trifles and sighed out love complaints Du Bartas alone dared penetrate the bosom of Nature. It is possible that the London edition, like Sylvester's *Yvry*, was in part designed to gather more sympathy for the Protestant struggles; the poem signed "Th. B. V. F." which follows the dedication must be by Beza, the French Calvinist leader. Meanwhile Sylvester had finished *The triumph of faith* (1592), published with fragments of the *Seconde sepmaine* (the "Sacrifice of Isaac" and "The ship-wracke of Jonas") and *Yvry*. "The argument," he says, "is excellent and the author honorable," while to describe the language he searches for images of wealth and rarity—"rich and sumptuous French garments," the "robe of Salomon" and "riche mans purple." His own verse improves upon *Yvry*. Vivid passages like the storm in "Jonas" have a force if not depth that understandably pleased the age and perhaps the author of *The Tempest*:

> Strike saile the maister cries, strike saile amaine,
> Vaile misne and sprit-saile: but the winds constrain,
> With boistrous blasts that beate upon his face,
> His sea-shápt speech to fly before their chace. . . .
> The easterne wind drives on the roring traine

Of white-blew billowes, and the clouds againe,
With fresh seas crosse the sea, and she doth send
In counter-change a raine with salt y-blend.
The heavens do seeme in Thetis lap to fall,
The sea scale skies, and God to arme this Al
Against one ship that skips from stars to ground. . . .
  Like idol pale one stands with armes a-crosse:
One moans himself: one moorns his childrens losse
One more then death, this forme of death affrights:
Another cals on heavens unviewed lights:
One fore his eies his ladies looks beholds:
Another thus his fainting feare unfolds,
Curst thirst of gold!

[sigs. C2–C2^v]

After several years came an anonymous *First day of the worlds
creation* (1595), written earlier, we are told, but not published in
hopes Sidney's own Week would see print.[20] Just as Du Bartas's
poem affords France a sunshine, the translator prays with
ridiculous charm, may this version "be Englands moonshine." A
friend congratulates him and, as many others were to do, admires
the poet's capacity to gather into a single epitome "the world, the
earth, the heaven above, / The elements, and sense-deceiving
skies." The verse, unusual in its stanzaic form, is not unpleasant:

Even as the Sunne (earths fairest husbandman)
Annexed to the wheeling firmament,
Descendeth not from his pavilion;
But sends from thence his fruitful increment,
Cheering the love-sicke earth with meriment:
Although he list not come, yet doth he send
Garlands of plentie to his distant frend.

[sig. C1^v]

Whoever the author was he admired Spenser (whom he praises)
and sometimes tries to capture his diction and rhythms. He had
imagination, I think, and it is too bad he went no further in
Englishing Du Bartas.

That same year, William Lisle published *Babilon* with the commentary of Goulart. A dedicatory epistle says the poem will lead

the young "from the wanton and faining Cantoes of other Syren-
Poets . . . unto a further acquaintance with this heavenly-poeticall
writer of the truth." Du Bartas is particularly happy to be in
England, furthermore, because of that realm's peace and "free
course of the Gospell," a specifically Protestant note not often
sounded in later references. Fifteen ninety-six saw a new edition
and in 1598 came *The colonies*, again with Goulart's commentary.
Like others, Lisle was less astonished by Du Bartas's expan-
siveness than by his ability to compress: "In lesse roome then
might be thought able to containe so great and sundrie matters, are
plainlie set downe, and even tabled-out unto us, the severall partes,
peoples and policies of the whole earth" (sig. A2^v). His affection for
Du Bartas survived the decades, for in 1625 he published the entire
second day of the *Seconde sepmaine* in both French and English; there
was another edition in 1637. Lisle's verse is stiffer than Sylvester's
and probably the hexameter was a mistake:

> Sith every Sphere (they say) hath some Intelligent,
> Or Angell musicall, for Lady president,
> Appointed by the Word: to th'end of those above
> These lower things may learne the perfect cord of love,
> And that with Angell-queers a dauncing Set be seene
> To revell on his praise in temple fyrie-sheene.
>   [Column., 1637, sig. L13]

In 1598 Sylvester published *The second weeke*, which offered
sections of the first two days. The translator hopes Essex, to whom
he dedicates "Eden," will take a "few turnes in this delightfull
garden." He calls the poem "a sacred feast" and prays that by
equaling "the divine Sunne of these learned dayes" he may draw
ears away from "Ovids heires, and their unhallowed spell." Sylvester's stance here is pious and moral, yet even while beckoning us
away from Ovidian concupiscence he points to Du Bartas's festive
fertility. A Latin poem by "Georg. Burgh." of Cambridge tells how
Sylvester outsings his country's neriads just as Du Bartas with
grandiloquent song excels the druids of the French forests, not an
utterly silly compliment if one remembers the fashion for those
sages as ethnic theologians in the tradition of Hermes and
Orpheus. Another friend writes of Du Bartas's divine *furor*, range

of vision, wealth of style, and fame—impressive in itself to an age that respected glory and light more than misunderstood or alienated obscurity.

In 1600 English readers would have found many quotations from Du Bartas's translators in two anthologies, Robert Allott's *Englands parnassus* and John Bodenham's *Belvedere*. The *Belvedere*, says Bodenham, is a garden with winding walks and herbs for both medicine and recreation, yet his flowers do not in fact grow beside sinuous garden paths but are marshaled into rank on rank of topics disposed into sententiae, similes, and examples by well-known but here anonymous poets. A commendatory poem calls the *Belvedere* an "Abstract of knowledge, Briefe of Eloquence" and that is clearly its aim—to summarize as pithily as possible already compressed commentary on subjects from God to death, abundance to zeal. The result has a curious sameness of tone; so that even Marlowe's "Who ever lov'd, that lov'd not at first sight" here seems no less moral and gnomic than the lines from Sylvester, Hudson, and James.[21]

Allott's *Parnassus* gathers a multitude of descriptions, similes, tags, examples, tropes—"the choysest flowers of our Moderne Poets," as the title page says. There are many passages by Spenser, Shakespeare, Drayton, and others. More than a hundred come from Sylvester and some from James and Hudson. This garden has more variety and life than Bodenham's, if only because the fragments are longer and less dispirited by conscription into an alien rhetorical scheme. The quotations from Du Bartas are sometimes moral ("Let sobernesse be still thy wisdomes end, / Admitting what thou canst not comprehend"), but even more Allott loved his patterns, vivid descriptions, ingenious comparisons, and emblematic images.[22]

The same year there appeared in Edinburgh a translation of the entire *Premiere sepmaine*. Like Ashley's *Urania*, Hadrian Damman of Bysterveldt's *De mundi creatione* illustrates how Du Bartas was welcomed as a learned humanist whose work deserved marmorial transformation into Latin. Du Bellay might have regarded the process with some misgiving. Dedicated to James, of course, the poem arrived with Greek and Latin encomia in the expected style—Du Bartas scatters ambrosial song in his native land,

Damman pours out Ausonian nectar, and so forth. A prose summary ends with Paul's reminder to the Romans that God's power
and godhead are clearly seen in the things he has made, a conviction that explains much of the pleasure Du Bartas inspired in
England. The translation probably pleased the king; certainly his
Stuart heart must have warmed to the additional lines in which the
sun proceeds like James amid his courtiers: "Rex Scotorum, com-
plura per oppida Regni / Arduus invehitur" (sig. N7).

So far, in deference to Sidney, there had been little attempt to
publish the *Premiere sepmaine* in English. In 1603, however,
appeared Thomas Winter's *Second day*. After a letter to Ralegh that
calls Du Bartas noble for his birth, famous for his learning, and ·
admirable for his inventions, several poems praise the translator
("Winter yeelds a spring of Poesie") and his author. A poem by
John Davies of Hereford sounds that mingled Christian and
Neoplatonic note one hears so often in English comment on Du
Bartas; he admires that fire

> That did enflame the rarest poets wit,
> That ere in France (worlds garden) did respire.
> Bartas, the bosome of whose blessed Muse
> With Homers sacred fire (refin'd) did burn.
>
> [sig. A4^v]

The following year Winter published his *Third day*. He opens with
an epistle to Prince Henry interesting for some of the assumptions
amid the clichés. Though Du Bartas's "subject be verie excellent,
and consequently verie difficult," he says, "yet he hath made such
an insensible mixture of profit and pleasure, and so artificially
compounded them together, that when the reader thinks perad-
venture but to tickle his eare, with the sweete measure and delicate
cadencie of a majestical verse; he finds that both Divinity and
Philosophy do steale upon him unawares" (sig. A2). No wonder
James delights to "beautifié his books and speeches with such
pithie sayings, as do abound in this incomparable Poet." That
Winter can find Du Bartas's cadence delicate (there were many
other compliments he could have chosen) is an intriguing reminder
of how what readers *hear* can vary, and the reference to his pithiness
fits the recurrent admiration for his compactness—a response
quite unlike that of modern readers, who are apt to notice not his

ability to summarize but his seemingly uncontrollable passion to include.

Winter is usually clear and at times even anticipates the limpid banalities of a later age; thus "the scaly traine / Divide the surges of the watrie plaine." In his hands the compounds are often syntactically modified so that, for instance, the invocation to Earth quoted above subsides into "Haile mother Earth, that bearest men and corne, / Gold, houses, health, fruites, garments to be worne." The resulting verse is not daring or intense, but fairly pretty, despite some lax or stiff rhythms. For example, in the *Second day* the four elements dance:

> As when the shepheardesses chaunce to meete,
> Trampling the flowers with their tripping feete,
> Marrying their pitches to the oaten sounds,
> And sportfully do daunce their rusticke rounds
> Under the branches of some shadie tree,
> By joyning hand in hand so coupled be.
>
> [sig. C2ᵛ]

After his *Third day* Winter fell silent, but Sylvester continued to publish. *Bartas: his devine weekes and workes* (1605; the title recalls Hesiod's "Works and Days") included the *First week*, much of the second, and the *Triumph of faith*. The next year brought a new edition with *Urania*. *Posthumus Bartas* (1606 and 1607) gave more of the *Second week*, and in 1608 came a complete translation of the two *Sepmaines*. There were new editions in 1611 and 1613. Sixteen fourteen saw a translation of "La Judit," and more editions of Sylvester's works arrived in 1621, 1633, and 1641. Even by 1605 these had become inflated with the puffery nowadays relegated to advertisements or jacket copy. There are the inevitable anagrams like "Josua Sylvester—Vere Os Salustii," a series of pillar poems to the mighty, and an impressive array of verses by Jonson, Daniel, Hall, and others. Probably much of the praise was sincerely meant, for the themes one finds in such adulation are found also in less promotional commentary.

Some contributors are awed at the extent of Du Bartas's fame:

> Witnesse Du Bartas (that rare Master-peece
>   Of Poetry) to past and future Times:

> By whose mellifluous, sugred, sacred Rimes,
> Thou got'st more fame, then Jason by his Fleece.[23]

Others, of course, celebrate Du Bartas's morality or his choice of
truth over pagan fable, but even here the stress is on the pleasure
and *energia* that make that piety effective:

> If profit, mixt with pleasure, merit praise,
> Or works divine be 'fore profane preferr'd . . .
> Shall not Du Bartas (Poets Pride and glorie)
> In after Ages bee with wonder heard,
> Lively recording th'Universall Storie?
>
> [by "R. N."]

Elsewhere abound images of treasure, gold, and light. Du Bartas is
acclaimed for the eloquence of his style, his *cultissima lingua*, and
well-wrought "inventions," and as expected some call him
inspired, a *vates*.

No one seems to find his style unusual, however, and there is
virtually nothing about his Huguenot faith. Indeed the apparatus
of the major editions suggests a nearly royal enterprise: the focus is
upon the sunlike James and his zodiac of aristocrats and the
ideology is as much political as religious. Du Bartas is praised for
recreating a plentiful and spacious universe, for daringly epitomizing it to the astonishment not only of Protestants but of all Christians. His compass, says Davies of Hereford, "circumscribes (in
spacious words) / The Universall in particulars." And Joseph Hall
follows the progress upwards of Du Bartas and his Urania:

> I Dare confesse, Of Muses more then Nine,
> Nor list, nor can I envie none, but thine.
> Shee, drencht alone in Sion's sacred Spring,
> Her Makers praise hath sweetly chose to sing,
> And reacheth neerest th'Angels notes above;
> Nor lists to sing or Tales, or Wars, or Love.
> One while I finde her, in her nimble flight,
> Cutting the brazen spheares of Heaven bright:
> Thence, straight shee glides, before I be aware,
> Through the three Regions of the liquid Ayre:
> Thence, rushing downe, through Nature's Closet-dore,
> Shee ransacks all her Grandame's secret store;

> And, diving to the darknesse of the Deepe,
> Sees there what Wealth the Waves in Prison keepe:
> And, what shee sees above, below, between,
> Shee showes and sings to others eares and eyne.

Sylvester's translations soon found an enthusiastic welcome, although a few doubted he was much of a poet himself. According to Michael Drayton he made Du Bartas speak "naturall English" but was poor in his own "invention." William Drummond agreed.[24] For the most part, however, vociferous admiration rendered such cavils barely audible.

Modern scholars have usually judged that on balance Sylvester translated Du Bartas faithfully, although unlike Drayton they are apt to find his language too often precious, eccentric, and stiff.[25] He is, to be sure, more vigorously Protestant, more concrete and familiar than his original, and on occasion he interpolates some patriotic lines on England. His syntax is often simpler than Du Bartas's, and while he usually retains the antithesis and balance of the French couplets he often calms the rhetorical play and changes the compounds to fit ordinary English. Du Bartas's amorous androgyne is a wince-giving "he-shee-coupled-one" but the "figue jette-laict" is now a mere "milky fig" and "L'Aquilon chasse-nue" a "cloud-chasing Boreas." I suspect this tendency helped promote his extraordinary popularity in England; had he allowed himself very many "spurt-milk figs," "chase-cloud winds," or the like (and he allowed himself a few) his verse might have been greeted with more surprise and less pleasure. The following lines (based on passages quoted earlier) illustrate both how he tried to recreate Du Bartas's verbal wit and how he acclimatized the French:

> Here's nothing constant: nothing still doth stay;
> For, Birth and Death have still successive sway.
> Here one thing springs not till another die:
> Onely the Matter lives immortally. . . .
> Or like a Laïs, whose inconstant Love
> Doth every day a thousand times remove . . .
> Because the Matter, wounded deep in Heart
> With various Love (yet, on the selfe-same part,
> Incapable, in the same time, at once
> To take all figures) by successions,

Form after Form receives: so that one face
Another's face's features doth deface.

[Day II, 219–48]

All-hail fair Earth, bearer of Towns and Towrs,
Of Men, Gold, Grain, Physick, and Fruits and Flowrs;
Fair, firm, and fruitfull, various, patient, sweet,
Sumptuously cloathéd in a Mantle meet
Of mingled-colour; lac't about with Floods,
And all imbrod'red with fresh blooming buds,
With rarest Gemmes richly about embost,
Excelling cunning, and exceeding cost.

[Day III, 1016–23]

After 1621 those who wanted a useful and erudite commentary in English could read Thomas Lodge's translation of Goulart. In this *Learned summary*, says Lodge, "The learned shall meete with matter to refresh their memories; the yonger Students, a Directory to fashion their discourse; the weakest capacity, matter of wit, worth and admiration." Like others who loved the *Sepmaines* Lodge was fascinated by the amount of material not merely included but contained and arranged within the poetry. In this work "you may gather the Subjects and Principles of all Sciences, delivered by such a spirit, that I may justly speake of him as Picus Mirandula did of Philip Beroaldus: that he is a certaine living and speaking Library of all Learning" (sig. *2).

In addition to these translations there was one other English version of Du Bartas. Robert Barret, author of *The theorike and practike of moderne warres* (1598), translated some minor works and those parts of the *Seconde sepmaine* available by 1600, but for some reason—the length of the manuscript perhaps, or the odd language and the competition from Sylvester—the work was never published. Except that he was a military man, spent some time on the Continent, and liked to compose verse, not much is known about Barret. His enormous unpublished epic "The sacred warr," written early in the seventeenth century, describes the conquest of the Holy Land in about sixty-eight thousand lines. As Barret says in his preface, it is filled with "Poetical fictions, phrases, narrations, digressions, reprizes, ligations, descriptions, representations, similes, and poetical figures, with Epithetes, Motti, and Names agreeable," a copiousness he claims he learned from his "sweet patterne the perennall-famouzed Salustius, Sieur du Bartas, and sundry his long-long fore-runners, in their eternal-during fabriques . . . Hee in his Saincted Judith, and Great-worlds byrth and Chieldhood; they in their Troian and Latine Warrs."[26]

Barret probably translated his "sweet patterne" Du Bartas before he went to work on "The sacred warr," for in a digression on Elizabeth he says she has reigned forty-two years (p. 127). The manuscript includes all the *Second week* Barret knew about, the "Lepantho" retranslated into English, "Yvry," "Judith," and some pages from Goulart. The verse is in pentameter, all of it except "Yvry" shaped into double quatrains. On occasion Barret intrudes his own opinions or interrupts to expound on some subject dear to his heart. Thus, when Du Bartas mentions Ireland in passing, Barret cannot resist a few words on that "elvish, hellsprong-broode," and he breaks into the "Artifices" to praise England and Elizabeth. His two most interesting additions, probably, are another paean to England in the "Colonies" and his treatment of mathematics and music in the "Pillars." The former mingles piety and patriotism much as Sylvester does in similar exclamations. England is the "feconde Mother deere / of Mars his Dearlings, and Minerva's Babes." Long may this "Nurce of Christs deere Agonistes" harbor the true religion, made safe by "an Ocean Asylum, / Encurtayn'd rounde withe Thetis mantle blew" and teeming with "Silke-fleeced sheepe, fishe, foule, and fruit at fill" (pp. 127–28). In the "Pillars" Barret elaborates on arithmetic, devoting eleven stanzas to fractions, roots, squares and cubes, surds, and even algebra ("knowen to few, but spirits delicate, / Whose braynes, by Uran'e, and hir sisters fayre / Quintessenc't bee," p. 136). Other stanzas describe geometry with many marginal diagrams, and the section on music praises modern composers like Lassus, "our English Burde, and Bull, with sundry moe" (p. 153).

Barret was an odd poet—if a poet at all. Convõluted, almost insanely asyndetic, his disheveled verse deserves its outcast state. Here he is on Sidney:

> And worthy Sydney, whose sweet swan-like songs,
> Have so allur'd Thamesis sea-proude-waves,

> That, honor-childe Bigge, beares his famous leaves
> To Thetis Lappe, Thetis to world alongs.
>
> [from "Babilon"]

Yet for all his incoherence at times Barret has an angular appeal, and because his verse was never to see print despite his work and learning I will close this description with his hopeful but unanswered prayer:

> And Spir't, spir't-giver, which diddst so Inspire
> My Salust deere, with such saint accents sweet;
> Inspire my spirit, enwarme me with thy fyer,
> Thy sacred-fyer, as shall to thee seeme mete:
> That I may warble out, in native toung,
> His native Accents to my Countrey-men;
> And that they may, by mee, as I by hym,
> Reape spirits-musike from my rustike song.
>
> [p. 209]

In addition to their homage of time and effort many translators (or their printers) added marginal notes that provide glimpses into their assumptions about Du Bartas's poetry. They are, of course, particularly interested in his rhetorical figures, especially the example, simile, and description, often calling them "lively" when the image is strikingly visual. Sometimes just where modern readers would shake their heads the margin says "a fit comparison" or "a fit simile." Thus Sylvester notes approvingly that the likening of the angry jangle of languages at Babel to birdsong at dawn is a "fit comparison." Apparently the one similarity of the situation, the variety of voices, makes the figure "fit." On occasion he and the others also identify Du Bartas's transitions or explain his organization. Sylvester, for instance, points out that "Babylon" opens with a description of a tyrant which "the Poet very fitly proposeth as his introduction to the life and manners of Nimrod." Later there is a "Prayer fitted to the former discourse, and giving entry to that which followeth." And Winter notes in the Argument to the *Second day* that Du Bartas "assumes a fit occasion to mention the generall flood."

Sylvester, Lisle, and Barret frequently call attention to Du Bartas's skepticism and piety. They seldom mention his Prot-

estantism, for the enemies in these marginal comments are not
Catholics but false reason and the prying "atheist." Yet one can
see that these translators, like Du Bartas, enjoy and linger over the
very speculations they find dangerous. When, in "Eden," Du
Bartas disowns frivolous quibbles while nevertheless carefully
describing the various issues he refuses to consider, Barret first
duly numbers them in the margin (heading the list "curious questions") and then praises the "christianlike Care of our Poet for not
overcuriously to run into the searching of difficult questions" (p.
17); the next page contains the undeniable truth that "Curious
questions breede confusion in the brayne." Sylvester agrees. Du
Bartas had elaborated some theories on how Noah got all those
animals into the ark and then, having satisfied his imagination,
had reminded us that the real answer to such questions is not to ask
them in the first place. Sylvester robustly calls this statement "an
un-answerable answer to all profane objections."

Most of those who discuss Du Bartas nowadays assume he
somehow affected English Renaissance poetry, although how
much he created the atmosphere that enabled his influence to
spread and how much that atmosphere derived from other causes
and simply facilitated his English welcome is hard to say. It seems
reasonable to suppose, for instance, that he had a great impact on
the vogue for biblically inspired poetry that culminated in *Paradise
Lost*, and there can be no doubt Milton not only read Du Bartas but
borrowed phrases from the *Weeks*.[27] On the other hand, the impulse
toward a modern vatic poetry and the thirst for explicitly religious
themes had sources so deep in the spiritual and social energies of
the time that the word and indeed the concept of "influence" are
here more seductive than enlightening. About his effect on the style
and subjects of particular writers there is less of a puzzle, and
various biographers, critics, and historians have found signs of his
presence in the work of many poets and dramatists. Such an
impact, however, is matter for a different study. Instead I will
explore the crowd of references and quotations to see what they
reveal about conscious or semiconscious reaction to this famous
poet.

It was sometime in the mid to late 1580s that the attention of the
English poets and scholars turned to Du Bartas, perhaps impelled

by the translations of James and certainly encouraged by Sidney's admiration. Thus whereas in 1578 a poem before Bellot's *French grammer* included the line "De Des-Essarts, et maint autre fran-çois" the edition of 1588 says "De des Essarts, Saluste, et maint françois." Some of the references to him that then accumulated rapidly merely show how much, as Joseph Hall wrote in 1603, "the yeelding world" admired his "sacred layes." The dropping of his name by a showoff in *The return from parnassus*, a citation of his poetry in a book of paradoxes, a joking comment in *Coryats crudities*, and the implausible suggestion that a translation of William Alexander's *Doomesday* might be welcomed in France "yea even as well as a second Du-Bartas" say little about English feelings.[28] Many other remarks, luckily, give some clue as to how he was perceived.

I will not proceed chronologically through this mass of material until the end of the story, however, for after the initial discovery of Du Bartas the pattern of comments on him does not shift much, except in two important respects. At the start of his popularity most major and many minor writers—Spenser, Sidney, Daniel, Drayton, Nash, Campion, Lodge, and others—knew and appreciated his work, whereas in the seventeenth century there was little said about him by the poets we call "cavalier" (in this sense, too, they were of the tribe of Ben, for Jonson was one of the very few English writers with doubts about Du Bartas). Nor did many "metaphysical" poets mention him, although Donne may have parodied him and Herbert's "Jordan" would have pleased Uranie.[29] Du Bartas's popularity did not diminish in intensity until the late seventeenth century, but it became less universal and also less associated, I think, with a sense of literary renewal and adventure. On the other hand, there is a specifically Protestant flavor to a few of the early references or translations that tends to broaden later into a general religious or moral acclaim.

One approach to Du Bartas, inevitably, was to find a place for him among the illustrious and long since categorized ancients while at the same time defining, if only with clichés, his modern company. Some *comparationes* and groupings have been mentioned in earlier chapters, such as "E.D."'s comment in 1587 that in France "the better sort" blow the horn for Du Bartas or Churchyard's banal compliments in *A musicall consort* (1595).[30] Thoughts of Chaucer readily provoked such clusters of names. In the preface to Speght's Chaucer (2nd ed., 1602) Francis Beaumont mentions the many interpreters of classical, Italian, and French poets like "Guillaume de Salust, that most divine French Poet," and a little later a poem by Francis Thynne runs through a list of famous writers among whom Chaucer will forever live, giving "life and light" to "unborne Poëts"; his colleagues include Socrates, Cicero, Petrarch, Tasso, Montemayor, Gavin Douglas (so Scotland will not be left out), and Du Bartas, who has won fame for "proud France ... By seven daies world Poetically strained" (sig. b1).

There are similar lists by John Taylor the Water Poet. Du Bartas is among those to be quoted, he wryly suggests in *The sculler* (1612), if a poet wants to overwhelm someone (all the others he mentions except Petrarch are ancients). Elsewhere Taylor says he has stored his works away in memory along with Homer, Virgil, Chaucer, and Spenser.[31] In *Britannia's pastorals* (1613–16) William Browne lingers at greater length over Du Bartas's triumph in a long procession of laureates:

> Divinest Bartas, whose enriched soule
> Proclaim'd his Makers worth, should so enroule
> His happy name in brasse, that Time nor Fate
> That swallows all, should ever ruinate.
> Delightfull Salust, whose all blessed layes
> The Shepherds make their Hymnes on Holy-daies;
> And truly say thou in one weeke hast pend
> What time may ever study, ne're amend.[32]

Some of this celebration merely moves dutifully through the conventional steps, yet Browne's festive tone is a reminder of the *pleasure* many found in Du Bartas, and his admiration of the poem's compactness, although jestingly put (all time may study this one week) touches on a major cause of the *Sepmaine*'s popularity.

Such compliments persisted. Some years later, it may be remembered, George Daniel praised "Devine Sire Bartas" and Du Bellay in a poem citing the best poets from Amphion and Orpheus to Waller and Denham (an evolution that apparently did not alarm him), and James Howell's *Instructions for forreine travell* (1642) especially recommends Du Bartas among French poets. Evidently

Du Bartas was soon and long remained a "generall allowed moderne Writer," as Thomas Nash called him.[33]

To vary his *comparatio*, however, a writer can modulate to the
negative, and recalling the myth of rivalry on Parnassus say that all
those other great writers now realize they are beaten. Let them
weep or blush, let them hand over their wreaths. Thus around 1591
Thomas Campion urged English poets to cast off rhyme and
summon Apollo:

> Call him with numerous accents paisd by arte,
> He'le turne his glory from the sunny clymes,
> The North-bred wits alone to patronise.
> Let France their Bartas, Italy Tasso prayse;
> Phaebus shuns none, but in their flight from him.[34]

England produces witty and happy conceits, says Anthony Chute
in an epistle before *Beawtie dishonoured* (1593), "though Italie
sleepes in the charme of a sweet Hierusaleme, and France waxes
proud in the weeke labours of her toyling-mused Bartas (the first as
conceiptively Allegoricall, as the other is laboursome significant)."
Du Bartas and Ariosto, says Joseph Hall, must "Yeeld up the
Lawrell girlond" to Spenser, and Charles Fitzgeffrey agrees, telling Du Bartas to triumph no longer now that England has in
Spenser a *vates* with no equal.[35]

Much of this sort of compliment is enforced by the rhetoric of
praise; perhaps Hall and Fitzgeffrey would have told Spenser to
ungarland himself had Sylvester's printer urged them enough.
Several "placings" of Du Bartas, however, indicate a deeper interest in his position.

Gabriel Harvey's estimate of Du Bartas would seem hyperbolic
if applied to Orpheus himself:

> The afore-named Bartas (whome elsewhere I have stiled the
> Treasurer of Humanity and the Jeweller of Divinity), for the
> highnesse of his subject and the majesty of his verse nothing
> inferiour unto Dante (whome some Italians preferre before
> Virgil, or Homer), a right inspired and enravished Poet, full of
> chosen, grave, profound, venerable, and stately matter, even
> in the next Degree to the sacred and reverend stile of heavenly
> Divinity it selfe; in a manner the onely Poet whome Urany

hath voutsafed to Laureate with her owne heavenly hand, and worthy to bee alleadged of Divines and Counsellours, as Homer is quoted of Philosophers and Oratours. Many of his solemne verses are oracles; and one Bartas, that is, one French Salomon, more weighty in stern and mighty counsell then the Seaven Sages of Greece. Never more beauty in vulgar Languages; but his stile addeth favour and grace to beauty, and in a goodly Boddy representeth a puissant Soule. How few verses carry such a personage of state? or how few argumentes such a spirite of majesty? Or where is the divine instincte that can sufficiently commend such a volume of celestiall inspiration? What a judgement hath the noble youth, the harvest of the Spring, the sapp of Apollos tree, the diademe of the Muses, that leaveth the enticingest flowers of delite, to reape the maturest fruites of wisdome?[36]

Time after time in his copious marginalia Harvey returns to the topic, citing Du Bartas's various works and comparing the French poet to other writers.[37] Together with Homer, Plutarch, and Virgil he is a great teacher; his poem on Ivry is better than anything similar "but sum inspired Pageants of Homer"; his similes may be compared with lesser passages in the ancient epics. Harvey admires his "life" and *enargia*, his capacity to elicit a compact inner image. "Yvry" is only nine pages, he notes, "sed rosa Solis," and of one line he says in the margin, "Spiritus vividus, et animosús; splendidus, et magnificus. Nec ullus stylus penetrantior; nec ulla Musa potentior." "Quae pictura tam conspicua?" he asks near a description of Henri's forces. Struck by Du Bartas's political acumen, he also admired the "furor" of this companion to "Orpheus, Homer, Pindar, and the rest of the inspired divine Poets."

Inevitably, Harvey compares Du Bartas to the moderns. Like Petrarch, Ariosto, Tasso, he deserves "curious comparison with Chaucer, Lidgate, and owre best Inglish, auncient and moderne"; he is the "french Dant," and his "Yvry" better than any "heroical Canto of Ariosto, Tasso, Aretine, or anie of owr late heroical Muses." Harvey also enjoyed Rabelais and apparently spent a little time sorting out his feelings about these two dissimilar writers. One comment in the margin of a joke book sums up his conclusion: "Addo Bartasium ob divinum furorem: Rabelaesium, ob humanum: Chaucerum ob mixtum." A bit later he says, "In jest, Rabelais: in earnest, Bartas singular."

Harvey, then, devoted many hours to defining this shining presence in his imagination, drawn more than his contemporaries to Du Bartas's political and military moods, fascinated by his power and fame, less consciously given than many to finding him "delightful," yet awed by his flights to places he himself longed to visit but perhaps had trouble reaching. For another note sounds faintly in the marginalia. Harvey was in some ways a neurotic man, obsessed by success as only a very ambitious academic can be and cursed with an ego particularly vulnerable to insult and self-doubt. "I am sorie for him," he writes of someone, for "he dyed withowt a plaudite." A certain ambivalence toward Du Bartas, therefore, shows when he notes his unhappiness that Ramus is more renowned, Tycho more skillful, Du Bartas more divine.[38]

To Harvey, Du Bartas was a radiant example of fairly recent glory; to George Hakewill, author of *An apologie or declaration of the power and providence of God* (Oxford, 1627), his triumphs had an even greater significance as offering further disproof of entropy. He uses many excerpts from the *Weeks*, sometimes quoted in French but usually in the English of Sylvester or Lisle, to reinforce his conviction that this world still manifests its ancient beauty and power. Like Du Bartas, Hakewill knew about flux; his proof that there has been no decay in Nature, arts, manners, or "wits" relies on a sense that cultures rise and fall. Yet he also perceived an architecture whose persistence belies "the fictions of Poets, the morosity of old men, the over-valuing of Antiquity, and the disesteeming of the present times" (sig. d1).

It is this vision of the pattern sustaining the world, I think, that drew Hakewill to Du Bartas. He concedes that faith teaches us the world has a beginning and end, quoting Du Bartas in the *Premiere sepmaine* as a witness. He admits that nations conquer and are conquered "As when the winde the angry Ocean moves, / Wave hunteth wave, and billow billow shoves" (sig. c3). Yet beneath all lies the elemental quaternity. Hakewill was moved by the thought that although, as "Divine Bartas" sang "sweetly and truly," "Heere's nothing constant, nothing still doth stay," matter nevertheless remains "Changelesse in essence, changeable in face." Another excerpt tells how as soon as God spoke, all four elements leaped to their "proper place" and now dance "As countrie-maidens, in the moneth of May, / Merrily sporting on a holy-day." From this basic four, says another passage, God brings infinite variety like a musician working with only six strings or a poet with only twenty-four letters (sigs. N1^v–O2^v).

Du Bartas is not merely useful to quote; like Ronsard, Ariosto, Tasso, and Spenser he is a modern Hakewill can set against the ancients (sig. Gg3). Some disagreed with this and other claims in the book, however, so in a later edition Hakewill answers his critics in a long appendix. Again he puts Du Bartas among those who show the world has not degenerated, and later gives a long passage from the *First Week* on God's inexhaustible creativity and unflagging diligence (1635, sig. Xxxx5). Hakewill was impatient with those who yearned for the gold of a fictional past, but he had no desire to join Lucretius and others in denying involvement to God or a significant pattern and end to time. He must have appreciated Du Bartas's effort to combine an affirmation of matter's imperishable "eternity" in the created universe of space and time with faith in a divine and shaping scheme. The logic is misty but the intention clear—to preserve a Christian sense of a fallen yet redeemed Creation pressing toward God's great Sabbath sight and simultaneously to feel the solidity, the trustworthiness, of a cosmos not subject until that final day to serious tarnish or fatigue. As in other ways, Du Bartas provides a means of having two visions at once. Ronsard, too, spoke of matter that remains and form that perishes, and he too thought himself a Christian, but his assurances were less consistent and explicit than those of Du Bartas—and to the English explicitness was both comforting and quotable.[39]

The *Sepmaines* are not formal epics, yet Harvey and Hakewill both compare Du Bartas favorably with Virgil and place him with other Renaissance "epic" writers like Ariosto, Tasso, and Spenser. Inevitably, though, there came a time when English definitions of the epic dwindled into neoclassical correctness. Sir William Davenant, writing a preface to his own heroic *Gondibert* (1650), is forced to exclude most modern authors. Even Tasso and Spenser made grievous errors, he says, and "I will yeeld to their opinion who permit not Ariosto, no, nor Du Bartas, in this eminent rank of the Heroicks."[40] Du Bartas, is once more placed, but this time he is merely expelled with the other moderns from the narrowing inner circle. Soon he was to be detached from even that company.

But until that day the praise continued. Some references to this modern Homer set him among the learned, for more than any other poet who wrote in French Du Bartas was welcomed into the fellowship of Renaissance humanists and was admired in the universities. Belief in his learning, however, in no way diminished his reputation as a "ravished" singer, because central to his (and to the Pléiade's) conception of the poet was an inspiration that worked through the encyclopedia of knowledge. It was appropriate on several counts, therefore, that one of the earliest references to him in England appeared in an Oxford anthology of Latin epigrams and elegies for Sidney, *Exequiae illustrissimi equitis* (1587). In this collection Matthew Gwinne urges Mornay and Du Bartas to lament the slain captain (a marginal note says of them "E Gallico in anglicum versi"), another poem mentions the author of "opera septem . . . dierum," and Thomas Lodington paraphrases the compliment to the English "pillars" in "Babylone" (sigs. D3, E2^v, K1). Nor did this popularity at Oxford soon decline. In *Oxoniensis academiae funebre officium in memoriam . . . Elizabethae* (1603) Edward Evans recalls in dreadful French Du Bartas's lines to the queen:

> Muse, donne salut Guillaume de Saluste,
> Et vous luy en prie, de donner beau lustre
> À ton dire François pour le los derniére
> De la Roine des Anglois, en fame premiére.[41]

In later years Gwinne quoted the *Weeks* in Latin, borrowing a passage on "lucifer, aestifer ignis" ("le feu donne-clarté . . . jette-flamme") for his *In assertorem chymicae* (1611, sig. C1), and two of the age's most erudite scholars referred to Du Bartas, John Selden quoting a fragment on deluded philosophers in *Titles of honour* (1614, sig. D1) and Robert Burton admitting that although most aristocrats care only for hunting, sex, gambling, and drink, he "may not deny but that we have a sprinkling of our Gentry, here and there one, excellently well learned, like those Fuggers in Germany, Du Bartas, Du Plessis, Sadael in France."[42]

Du Bartas became so established an author that schoolboys would have found his name in handbooks. Simon Harward's *Encheiridion* (1596) offers the little "tirunculi" for whom it was written moral and descriptive lines like those on the good prince in "Babylone" and the drunk in "L'arche" (sigs. C7^v, H7^v–H8). John Clarke's popular *Formulae oratoriae* repeats the anagram "Josua Sylvester—Vere os Salustii" (1632, 1637 ed., sig. R6), and Thomas Farnaby's *Index poeticus* (1634), which relies almost exclusively on ancient and neo-Latin poets, advises the student to consult Du Bartas on "mundi creatio," "Zodiacus," the rustic life, and several living species including dolphins, elephants, and roosters.

To the English, then, Du Bartas was learned. He was also a stylist, praiseworthy for his handling of language. In fact his poetry was first introduced to the English in Abraham Fraunce's *Arcadian rhetorike* (1588), which illustrates the "Braverie of speach" produced by tropes and figures with excerpts from the classics, Sidney, Tasso, Du Bartas, and Boscán. In choosing them Fraunce tends to neglect description for fragments demonstrating control of language seen as the effect of a logical process. "Brave" speech leads to delight, but these rhetorical intricacies are not merely pretty; they express definable relationships. Thus "La terre de tout temps n'est ceinte de Neptune" illustrates, says Fraunce, a metonymy in which the efficient cause stands for the thing caused. The same year saw Fraunce's *Lawiers logike*, the other part of what in a less Ramist scholar might have been a single book. Here, too, Du Bartas appears as an artist who shapes language according to an inner mental structure: "Reade Homer, reade Demosthenes, read Virgill, read Cicero, reade Bartas, reade Torquato Tasso, reade that most worthie ornament of our English tongue, the Countesse of Penbrookes *Arcadia*, and therein see the true effectes of natural Logike" (sig. B3).

Renaissance poets seem sometimes to have attended more closely to the coherence of small units of discourse than to larger organizations. Nevertheless some comments on Du Bartas suggest a sense that his poems were deliberately shaped wholes. In the notes to his *Orlando Furioso*, for instance, Harington remarks that Du Bartas "contrived" the story of Judith into an excellent poem (1591, sig. Cc1^v), and in *Origens repentance* (1619) Stephen Jerome defends his own expatiations by the example of Homer, Virgil, Spenser, and that "which the exquisite Poete Silvester useth in his Dubartas; and in his owne little *Dubartas*, running all descants and

Poeticall divisions (in this best minde musick of numerous versifying) from some positive, reall (or else only fictious or
imaginarie) grounds" (sig. B2). Even when the focus is on Du
Bartas as a Uranian poet with "positive, reall" grounds for his
descant, praise sometimes touches on his sense of direction. Sir
John Stradling pauses in his *Divine poemes* (1625) to defend the
"graceful exercise" of "poetizing on the Sacred Word," citing Du
Bartas:

> He that by weekes and dayes his worke divides,
> First on the worlds-creation poetizeth:
> Then forwards to succeeding Ages slides,
> The choisest matters in his Verse compriseth.
>
> [sig. G2]

Other comments seem less concerned with Du Bartas's ability to
"slide" from one part of the work to another than with what was
often called spirit or liveliness, the power to make a strong impression on the imagination. Thus *Sir Thomas Smithes voiage and entertainment in Rushia* (1605) says of the bloody doings there, "he which
would lively, naturally, or indeed poetically delyneate or enu-
merate these occurrents, shall either lead you thereunto by a
poeticall spirit, as could well, if well he might the dead living,
life-giving Sydney Prince of Poesie; or deifie you with the Lord
Salustius devinity" (sig. K1ᵛ). It was this vigor Abraham Darcie
meant when in his dedication to *The honour of ladies* (1622) he
referred to "Dubartas spirit and Hanibals powers."[43] This "spirit"
dresses language brightly. One author who objects to versifying
Scripture "like the Battle of Troy" absolves Du Bartas,

> Who, be it spoken to thy lasting praise,
> Gav'st Sunday rayment to the Working Dayes.[44]

The capacity to clothe the truth vividly produces a lively image.
Charles Fitzgeffrey's *Blessed birthday* (1634) opens with a poem by
Henry Beesley, who says "noble Bartas"

> Adorn'd Gods works, and like another light,
> Pictur'd the whole creation to our sight.

Pleasurable adorning and picturing in turn persuade the reader.

Richard Zouch's *Dove, or passages of cosmography* (1613) praises the learning of "Spencer, having as well delivered Morall, and Heroicall matter for use and action, as Du Bartas (now ours) Naturall and Divine, for study and meditation," adding that this instruction was effective because it pleased, whereas some "have returned exceeding empty from Systems and Commentaries."[45]

Many English readers were also attracted by Du Bartas's compounds and tried their own hands at combining words. "Spenserian" poets like William Browne were particularly drawn to the technique, but the sound of separate morphemes collapsing into new units, so familiar in Du Bartas's descriptive passages, may be heard also in a diversity of usually minor writers (and on occasion in French—a mourner in Charles Horne's *In obitum G. Whitakeri* (1596, sig. E4ᵛ) hopes his friend is now with "L'Eternel darde-feu, roule-ciel, lance-foudre"). Such compounds, to be sure, are also found in Sidney and Spenser, as well as Ronsard. Indeed, any Renaissance poet with a taste for the classics and verbal experiment might be tempted to find vernacular equivalents for lines like "ubi cerva silvicultrix, ubi aper nemorivagus." The technique was, however, specifically associated with France, or so Joseph Hall's complaints about its overuse seem to show. In his satirical *Virgidemiae* (1597–98) a would-be poet implores the heathen deities, steals from Petrarch, and glitters with compounds:

> He knows the grace of that new elegance,
> Which sweet Philisides [Sidney] fetch't of late from France,
> That well beseem'd his high-stil'd Arcady,
> Tho others marre it with much liberty,
> In Epithets to joyne two wordes in one.[46]

Du Bartas's translators often unjoined these epithets, but Lodge enjoyed them when adapting the lines on War for *Wits miserie* (1596):

> Next marcheth war, breake-law and custome-breaker,
> Race-fort, spil-bloud, burne-hostry, loving-teares. . . .[47]

And at least one writer complimented Du Bartas in his own style. The Cambridge scholar Thomas Goad, writing in *Threnothriambeuticon* (Camb., 1603), calls him

Bartas le verse-miel, treshaut, entasse-mots . . .
O si vivoit ores cil chanteur grave-dous.

[sig. I2]

Many others found Du Bartas "sweet."[48] The word now seems
wholly inappropriate, whatever Du Bartas's other merits, but both
"sweet" and "grave" had for some time lost concrete significance
and indicated a general pleasingness of style and weightiness of
subject. To be "grave-dous" is to mix delight with profit.

Du Bartas was so admired for his style that Robert Dallington's
View of Fraunce (1604) could recommend him both for "moralitie"
and, together with Ronsard, "for the language it selfe." Textbooks
on French were apt to agree.[49] Eventually, however, English
readers became deaf to Du Bartas's "sweetness." As a boy, Dryden
reported in 1681, he had been "rapt into an ecstasy" by lines like

Now, when the Winter's keener breath began
To crystallize the Baltick Ocean;
To glaze the Lakes, to bridle up the Floods,
And periwig with Snow the bald-pate Woods.

[from "Handy-Crafts"]

But now he finds this to be "abominable fustian, that is, thoughts
and words ill-sorted, and without the least relation to each other
. . . in the heightenings of Poetry, the strength and vehemence of
figures should be suited to the occasion, the subject, and the
persons."[50]

In fact this particular periwig was Sylvester's contribution; but,
more important, Dryden sees an indecorum or incoherence invisible to those who admired Du Bartas's language. Almost a century
earlier one of Du Bartas's readers had annotated his copy of the
Seconde sepmaine, carefully indexing the tropes and figures.[51] The
description of Baltic Neptune giving "une froide bride / Aux
fleuves debordez" and ornamenting the trees "de flocs de laine,"
just the passage which with its English addition Dryden thought
fustian, is categorized under "metonomia." It would doubtless
have startled this forgotten Elizabethan to read Dryden's objec-
tion, for to him the "relation" of the words was obvious. Modern
readers are likely to share Dryden's distaste for the snow-wigged
trees. Yet it has been argued that in their context (the newly lapsed

and seasonal world) and within that complex of correspondences Renaissance metaphysics and medicine both affirmed, the image makes sense. Dryden is rejecting more than a dated poetic manner.[52]

As a humanist and stylist Du Bartas was linked with poets like Sidney and Spenser, serious writers on important matters but also members of a literary world. Often, however, he was quoted, cited, and praised in contexts that stress his usefulness to religious discourse. One preacher quotes him to illustrate the nature of sin, another borrows some "divinely" composed lines on heathen gods, and James Martin says in his *Via regia* (1615) to read Du Bartas's account of the Israelite escape from Egypt, an event he compares to the defeat of the "Spanish Behemoth" in 1588.[53] Nor was his popularity as a source of illustration confined to the vigorously Protestant, for Elizabeth Grymeston's touching *Miscellanea* (1604) quotes the Catholics Southwell and Verstegan as well as Du Bartas.

English writers seldom refer to Du Bartas as a Protestant, but in Christopher Marlowe's unkempt *Massacre at Paris* (acted 1592/93) he appears onstage as a fierce militant. Guise, of course, is the villain, Henri de Navarre the hero, Ramus among the many victims, and Pleshé (Du Plessis) and Bartus (Du Bartas) attendants to the Protestant leader. Here is the Huguenot partisan missing from most English commentary. Bartus hopes Navarre will "plant the true succession of the faith, / In spite of Spain and all his heresies," and serves a master who says the Popish prelates will curse the day he was ever king of France. Du Bartas plays only a minor role, however; Marlowe's imaginative sympathies, if not his approval, bend toward the ominous and aspiring Guise.[54]

More important than these brief appearances are comments on Du Bartas that touch a subject significant in England's cultural history—the increased thirst for explicitly religious or unfeigned moral verse and the questions that arose when poets tried to satisfy it. Du Bartas's name was firmly attached to such attempts. Thomas Gokin, for instance, marvels in his verse *Meditations upon the Lords prayer* (1624) "that this taske hath not beene undertaken in this kinde by some Du Bartas, who might erect an heaven on earth upon this Basis" (sig. A4). Some writers are simply grateful for morally sound matter. The Scottish dominie Alexander Hume opens his *Hymnes, or sacred songs* (Edinburgh, 1599) by exhorting the youth of Scotland to eschew love toys and romances; like Plato, however, he will not exile "the moderate and trew commendation of the vertuous, and noble actes of good men: nor yet the extolling of liberall sciences: But thou hast notable examples in the French toong set foorth by Salust of Bartas" (sig. A4^v). A generation later William Prynne's *Histriomastix* (1633), an enormous work filled with the sort of language Jonson parodied in Zeal-of-the-land-Busy, grants that poetry is "lawfull, yea useful and commendable among Christians, if rightly used," and admits, among other works, "the modern Distiques of Dubartas." Prynne even allows "some parts of Ovid" (sig. Oooool^v).

Thomas Tomkis does not mention Du Bartas in his university play *Lingua* (1607), a high-spirited drama about the struggle to bring language under rational and moral control, but he borrows from him in many passages. "Lingua" herself has some shady friends. One is Mendacio, born in Greece and nursed in Crete (home of paradoxical liars), who boasts he held Homer's quill, "helped Herodotus to pen some part of his muses, lent Pliny inke to write his history, rounded Rabalais in the eare"; another, Phantastes, tells Psyche how hard he must work to keep "puling Lovers" supplied with themes. The play is funny, but the accusation that Lingua and her companions "made Rhetorique wanton" was serious and widespread.[55] Anthony Stafford, for instance, whose *Niobe* (1611) quotes the epitaph on Sidney someone translated from Du Bellay, was dismayed by his times—"Sodome, thy sinnes were fewe in respect of ours"—and persuaded that modern poets encouraged the wickedness he felt surging around him. These, he says, "are rightly taxed by that last, and everlasting Worthie of the French, divine du Bartas," and he gives the opening lines of the "Second jour" on the "vers pipeurs" which "cachent le venin que les jeunes esprits / Avalent à longs traicts." Stafford scorns excuses that disguise lasciviousness "under a veile of smooth running words," and scolds those who invoke false gods and the muses (sigs. A6–A8).

This desire for religious poetry, however, was not merely pious moralism or grouchy distrust of fiction. Disturbing and serious issues were involved, such as the moral meaning of time and its use, the responsibility of poets to the common weal, and the relationship of feigning to truth, of words to the Word. Spenser might have been amused or irritated to read in *Apollo Christian or Helicon reformed* (1617) that "Wisdome is Queene, who fareth not with Faëries" (sig. C2ᵛ). But even for more capacious spirits than this anonymous author the choices were not simple. Within only a few lines Milton's perspective can shift to disorient the reader, as when, for example, the piercingly lovely description of shining Mulciber falling earthwards from the crystal battlements of Heaven is followed by "Thus they relate / Erring," a painful admission for a humanist poet.[56]

There was little agreement on these issues even among those who admired Du Bartas. Patrick Adamson, for instance, who refers glancingly to him in his *Poemata sacra* (1619), writes that some think no song good if it lack Joves, Venuses, "et fabulosa id genus Graecorum commenta" (sigs. b1, T4ᵛ). On the other hand William Vaughan, equally ready to serve truth, claiming in *The spirit of detraction conjured* (1611) that he will follow "Du Bartas his advice, having Faith for my sailes, the holy Ghost for my Pilot, and the Bible for my starre" (sig. Ii3), bitterly opposed to "baudy ballads," shocked by "scoffing Rabelais," and doubtful that More's Utopia is more than an "ayrie castle," defends his use of names like Apollo in *The golden fleece* (1626): "That Divine Poet Salust Lord of Bartus in many parts of his Books useth this name for the Sunne, as he doth also Minerva and the Muses for Learning, Mars and Bellona for warre, Bacchus for wine, Ceres for Corne, Vulcan for fire, Venus for lust, Diana for chastitie, Neptune for the sea, Æolus for the windes, Styx and Acheron for hell. It is not the bare name but the inward sense, which a discreet Reader should pry into" (sig. V2; these inward senses, however, seem sadly narrow).

One of those fabled muses was Urania, and although references to his poem "Uranie" are surprisingly few, the English praised Du Bartas over and over again for writing "divine" poetry, for following his muse upwards, for shaming those mired in frivolity or lust; even the many books with "Urania" in the title, the many acknowledgments of her starry or religious encouragements, must often have been made with implied reference to him. Urania herself, however, was an ancient and complex figure. The muse of astronomy and, more recently, of inspired Christian verse, she had

long been associated with harmonious sounds and motions, initiation into mysteries, and flight to spiritual freedom in those realms
from which love, knowledge, and vatic power emanate.[57] The
Renaissance Urania often urged the Scriptures upon her chosen
poets, but she did so through images of soaring, radiance, and
ecstasy.

It is true that one element in the atmosphere surrounding Du
Bartas's name derived not from pleasure in such levitations but
from various and, I think, increased anxieties or dislikes such as
social resentment, sexual unease, a sense of time as a commodity
one could in some sense "have" and so lose or waste, and a belief
in, and hence a fear of, the power of words. Inevitably, therefore,
some who like Cyril Tourneur asked God to "Israellize" their
tongues denounced poets debased by libidinous passion.[58] On
occasion the language is so extreme one senses a displaced psychological pressure. Even before the vogue for divine poetry
reached its height, for instance, Bishop William Alley had
suggested in his *Poore mans librarie* (1565) that purveyors of wanton
books be burned alive (sig. L2). And James Cleland's *Institution of a
young noble man* (1607) says "I am so affraid of Poësie, that I dare not
councell you to read much thereof privately, it is so alluring" (1612
ed., sigs. V1^v–V3^v). Sometimes the fear is not of Circe's sty but of
illusion and deceit. "Stage-plays, and pleasures, are but wakeing
dreames" says one doubter in 1631, voicing a widespread
skepticism in words that might have given Prospero and his creator
cause for wry thought.[59]

To such writers Du Bartas had the advantage of working with
improving and true material, yet it is not among such worried
imaginations that one finds his chief admirers. Although those
who loved him often rejected lascivious or petty topics, they turned
to Urania not so much from negation as from positive pleasure or
hope. Nor was their desire always for biblical poetry; "divine"
subjects included the created cosmos as well as Scripture.[60]

For some, the divine muse was a guide to love; she was related,
after all, to Venus Urania. Thus James Day's *New spring of divine
poetry* (1637), which imitates both Du Bartas and Ovid in
describing the Creation, assures boys they will find greater happiness in beholding "A visage that will make thy Venus cold."
Day's own poetry has a delight ignored in some modern dis-

cussions of Du Bartas's influence. He describes that time of love
when

> the Lion with the Lambe did goe,
> And knew not whether blood were sweete or no,
> The little Kids to shew their wanton pride,
> Came dancing by the loving Tigers side. . . .
> The busy Mice sat sporting all the day,
> Meanewhile the Cat did smile to see them play.
>
> [sigs. B1ᵛ–B2]

And in one of the most interesting treatments of the theme, Inigo
Jones's and William Davenant's masque *The temple of love* (1635),
"Divine Poesie, the secretary of Nature"—dressed like Urania in
sky-colored and star-spangled robes—together with Orpheus
restores the temple of chaste love by conquering both lust-
provoking magicians and modern "precise" devils who hate poetry
and music.[61]

Divine subjects, it was said, not only improve the soul but
elevate poetry. Since earthly love is "Common to every ballad-
makers rime," a true poet needs a more important theme. He
knows "No musicke's equall to a Heavenly muse" and that "Wit
choosing the best subjects to worke on, / Shall find glory with God
and grace with man," just the promise Urania had granted Du
Bartas. Such poetry reminds us that "Order and Number set the
World in frame, / Tun'd the harmonious Spheres"; those who
scorn the art cannot have read David. With the Bible before us we
have no excuse for fooleries:

> What? Are our Rils drunke up? Our fountains dry?
> That wee must to such durty puddles fly,
> First shall no Tapers grace the spangled heaven,
> The rough Alps lye as the smooth Vallies even:
> Ere who are conversant in sacred writ,
> Shall faile of Themes to exercise their wit.

In Scripture we find an astonishing store of, for instance, allegories
and enigmas: "Who but the Mother of us all Gods minde / Could
in few words such stronge allusions finde?"[62]

Charles Butler praises Du Bartas precisely in these terms, for
although his relief that "our Marlows are turned into Quarleses"

inspires no faith in his taste, his argument is in part aesthetic. Because the art of language comes from God, he says in *The principles of musik* (1626), Du Bartas rightly condemns its degradation by lascivious authors (five quatrains from Sylvester's "Urania" follow). God's own psalms, as the "sweet Bard Dubartas" claims, are better literature than the songs of the "degenerated Crue."[63]

Many who wrote "divine" poetry mention Du Bartas, whether to justify themselves or to give him credit for inspiring and teaching them. Sometimes the tribute comes in the title—Edward Cooke's brief versified story of the Creation and Fall, for instance, is called *Bartas junior* (1631). Others render fuller acknowledgment. Drayton's original preface to his *Moses* (1604) cites Du Bartas's *Judith* as another work in which material not found in Scripture is nevertheless borrowed "as Jems and exteriour ornaments to beautifie our Subject," and in the poem itself he praises the "hallow'd labours" of the poet who divinely sang "This Alls creation" in "Courtly French."[64] Several years later Giles Fletcher the younger refers to Du Bartas in the preface to his *Christs victorie, and triumph* (1610), a poem that shows the influence of the *Weeks* as well as of Spenser. Some people, he says, have "so left-handed an opinion" of poetry that they think it sacrilegious to "deale with divine and heavenly matters," and others would banish it altogether. But God wrote poetry, and among the moderns we have "thrice-honour'd Bartas, and our (I know no other name more glorious then his own) Mr. Edmund Spencer (two blessed Soules)." Like Urania, Fletcher is in part a Neoplatonist. He reminds us that the purpose of a poet's "heavenly infusion" is to show God's glory, that poets are effective because their harmonious numbers penetrate the soul; Christ, he writes later in the poem, was the true Orpheus. Agreeing that a great subject improves poetry, he tells other authors:

> Your songs exceede your matter, this of mine,
> The matter, which it sings, shall make divine.
As starres dull puddles guild, in which their beauties shine.[65]

The most interesting reaction to Du Bartas's Uranian achievements, however, is that which celebrates or joins his joyful rush upwards. In these tributes one can perceive a widespread and excited longing for an imagined spatial motion which because it moves the point of view up allows the sight to take in more, to include and compress into a single enraptured gaze the entirety of created things. The "encyclopedia" of the learned poet is thus spread out before our eyes, filled with variety and patterned according to some design, such as an allegorical procession or "days." This feeling as much as anything else explains the welcome Du Bartas and his Urania received in England, for the emotion to which the pair appealed was not only a devout hope for Christian poetry but an often intense desire to fly, to mount, to view from on high, even if what one could see there reaffirmed the ordering limits of the cosmos.

Others in different ages had enjoyed journeys aloft—Plato, Cicero in his *Somnium Scipionis*, even worried Geffrey swept up to the House of Fame in the eagle's talons. That there was an increased fascination with such flight in the late Renaissance has, however, been much noted. Du Bartas himself loved unbroken circles—the heavens for him were a divine ceiling painting, not the limitless and homogenous space some other Uranians thought they perceived—but he satisfied a taste even on the part of those who shared his conservative cosmology for what Marjorie Nicolson called "the aesthetics of infinity," although a better phrase for Du Bartas would be "the aesthetics of levitation."[66] One finds this aesthetics throughout the century in major writers like Drayton, Burton, and Milton, and the same note is often heard among the less well known when Urania's name appears.

John Bainbridge, "Doctor of Physicke, and lover of the Mathematicks," for instance, explains in *An astronomicall description of the late comet* (1619) that such studies are fit only "for those who have been rapt up above the elementary regions of vulgar Schooles: and slept not in Parnassus, but Olympus, under the spangled canopy of Urania." He is no whit disturbed by the comet, saying he lies "prostrate at the Almighties power in the globositie thereof" (sigs. B2–B3, E1). At the thought of God's power others did not fall down but sprang up. A prefatory poem to Robert Farley's *Kalendarium humanae vitae* (1638), for example, tells the author Urania has loosed his "fetter'd minde, / Out of the clayeie prison," so that his pure song flows "from the fountaine of the Milkie Way" (sig. A3^v).

Spenser seldom flew as far and fast as some of Du Bartas's other readers, although in the Mutabilitie Cantos of *The Faerie Queene* it is perhaps Urania who leads him on a "high flight" to witness the great dilation of created being through time. In his hymns to Heavenly Love and Heavenly Beauty he does not invoke her as many might have done, but her description of herself in "The Teares of the Muses," whether or not indebted to "Uranie," would win the latter's approval. She teaches "the worlds creation, / How in his cradle first he fostred was" and

> From hence wee mount aloft unto the skie,
> And looke into the Cristall firmament:
> There we behold the heavens great Hierarchie,
> The Starres pure light, the Spheres swift movement,
> The Spirites and Intelligences fayre,
> And Angels waighting on th'Almighties chayre.[67]

According to Harvey, Spenser knew Du Bartas's "Fourth Day," which "he esteemes as the proper profession of Urania."[68] It is unclear whether Spenser meant that while Urania should inspire descriptions of the heavens other muses should guide other "kinds" (Calliope, for instance, might sing of Judith) or whether he thought Urania had done well to teach not only astronomy but gratitude to the Creator. In any case, he admired "Uranie," ending his poem to Du Bellay in the "Ruines of Rome" with the compliment to Du Bartas discussed earlier in this book.

Barnaby Barnes honored "the Urany of du Bartas," he told Harvey in a preface to *Pierces supererogation* (1593, sig. ***2^v), and he soon left writing love poetry to follow her. His preface to his *Divine centurie of spirituall sonnets* (1595) shows the exhilaration he found in this new discipleship:

> If any man feele in himselfe (by the secret fire of immortall Entheusiasme) the learned motions of strange and divine passions of spirite, let him refine and illuminate his numerous Muses with the most sacred splendour of the holy Ghost, and then he shall (with divine Salust the true learned frenche Poet) finde that as humane furie maketh a man lesse then a man, and the very same with wilde and unreasonable beastes: so divine rage and sacred instinct of a man maketh more then man, and leadeth him (from his base terrestriall estate) to walke above the starres with Angelles immortally.
>
> [sig. A3^v]

In the next century such praise intensifies. Less charmingly put than Barnes's Platonic longings but entertaining in its undaunted search for a conceit is an epigram in William Gamage's *Linsi-woolsie* (Oxford, 1613). Like other epigrammatists, Gamage understood the usefulness of names, finding in "Du Bartas" proof of the poet's transcendence:

> Right well Du Bartas may we call thy name,
> For a ªDuw in Welch betokens more then Man.   [ªGod
> So wast, I thinke, then thou thy Laies didst frame,
> Such Heav'nly Muse sole Man could scarsly scan.
>
> [sig. B6ᵛ]

More conventionally elegant, John Leech cites Du Bartas in his *Musae priores* (1620). After erotica, Anacreontics, and elegies, Leech takes his expected farewell of Love, hoping to please the ear of Phoebus while "Astra super positus." Thus stellified he will write of the crusades, the Last Judgment, or the Creation—a work like that which Du Bartas played on his divine lyre in timeproof poetry (sigs. H6–H7).

Phineas Fletcher, too, noted Du Bartas's progress up. In his *Purple island* (1633), twelve cantos on the physical and moral workings of the human person that even more than the *Weeks* (to which they are indebted) deserve Douglas Bush's Albert Memorial prize, a shepherd poet says that he is through with "wanton toyes" and, filled with a higher love, will sing of higher themes. Others have done so, including Du Bartas. Fletcher imagines him now that he has "soar'd to heav'n":

> Ah blessed soul! in those celestiall rayes,
> Which gave thee light these lower works to blaze,
> Thou sitt'st emparadis'd, and chaunt'st eternall layes.[69]

In New England, Anne Bradstreet, herself the author of religious poetry structured by fours, had long loved the *Weeks*. "In Honour of Du Bartas, 1641" touchingly describes how reading his poetry she feels like a child at a fair. Du Bartas is the exemplaɩy learned poet; she tells him she is awed by

> Thy art in natural philosophy,
> Thy saint-like mind in grave divinity,

> Thy piercing skill in high astronomy,
> And curious insight in anatomy,
> Thy physic, music, and state policy,
> Valour in war, in peace good husbandry.

He is also spatially above her, radiant in sunlike lines:

> Reflection from their beaming altitude
> Did thaw my frozen heart's ingratitude.[70]

Two such compliments appear in works themselves informed by the aesthetics of levitation. Despite several "divine" poems Robert Aylett is a minor figure, but his "Urania," published with *The brides ornament* in 1625, prettily illustrates one aspect of Du Bartas's English reputation. Much of the poem paraphrases "Uranie": Aylett wonders what to write—plays? a celebration of the Union? "wanton Venus, and her Bitter-sweet"? Luckily a winged messenger comes singing like the spheres with the zodiac twinkling on her azure skirts. She ravishes souls "above the Firmament / That they in Numbers like the Spheres may move," and what they move in and by is Love:

> Love's her Beginning, and her End is Love,
> Love is the Soule, and Life of Poesie;
> No Poeme without Love did ever prove,
> No more then Musicke without Harmony.

> [sig. H2]

Love of chivalry inspired Homer and Virgil; Ovid loved the scientific secrets behind his fictions; "old rigid Cato" loved virtue, and Lucretius so loved Dame Nature "He turnes all Pliny into Poetry." Spenser's love escalated from pastoral to "high Heroiques of Armes, and Honour" and

> My Darling Bartas, who on Angells wings;
> Beholds the Six Day's of the World's creation,
> Was so in love with Heav'n and heavenly things,
> Hee wholly on them fixt his Contemplation.

> And wen he on the Seventh Day comes to rest,
> He them all orders to his Makers Glory:
> Doubtlesse he fram'd a new world in his brest,
> Whereof he so Divinely sings the story.

(Like many others, Aylett assumes an order and direction in the work, and he too seems impressed by Du Bartas's power to condense multiplicity and hugeness into an inner microcosm.) This same love was in David and in the early Greeks—before myths degenerated from those early versions in which Zeus was faithful and Venus slept only with Vulcan (and not from concupiscence "but for due"). Modern poets might restore those ancient energies if they would sing the love of "the Bridgroome and his Deare" (sigs. H2^v–H4^v).

A generation later Edward Benlowes did sing that love. *Theophila* (1652), a numerologically arrayed story of the lovesick soul, is among the poems of its time most given to levitation. Benlowes passionately desires to rise higher and higher into an almost erotic bliss of elevation. Divine poetry, he says, is "the internal Triumph of the Mind, rapt with S. Paul into the third Heaven"; these holy hymns, he hopes, will "Fly through Arts Heptarchie . . . Eagling 'bove transitory Sphears, / Till ev'n the Invisible appears." The style in which he "eagles" owes more to Sylvester than was wise, and Benlowes adds further preciosity of his own.[71] Here, for instance, grow those snow-wigged trees:

> Betimes, when keen breath'd Winds, with frosty Cream,
> > Peri'wig bald Trees, glaze tatling Stream:
> (For, May-games past, white-sheet-*peccavi* is Winter's Theme).

His charming if silly reference to Du Bartas, moreover, combines thoughts of harmony and a vision of flight:

> Noble Du-bartas, in a high-flown Trance,
> > Observ'd to start from's Bed, and dance;
> Said: Thus by me shall caper all the Realm of France.

> As viscous Meteors, fram'd of earthy Slime,
> > By Motion fir'd, like Stars, do clime
> The woolly-curdled Clouds, and there blaze out their Time.
> > > > > > [sigs. H6^v, G1]

A love for Uranian flight, then, led many to cherish Du Bartas and to see in his poetry an ascent to truth openly proclaimed while wittily expressed and designed. To such imaginations allegory and fiction might be useful, but not the ironies or obliquities of equally devout writers like More and Erasmus in an earlier age. The longing is for overwhelming rapture and wide-angled vision. Others, however, read Du Bartas not for his "fury" but because he seemed to summarize well the information or arguments they were trying to express. Doubtless many who appreciated his lines on modern poetry or the birth of geese also thought of him as did Bradstreet and Benlowes, but the use they made of him was less overtly levitating and more illustrative. As Richard Willes had remarked in his *De re poetica* (1573), poets are useful to quote, as they give the ears relief from the harshness of dialectic, aid the memory, and like witnesses confirm what philosophers have postulated.[72] Du Bartas was admirably helpful in this way, his verse filled with gems of information, morality, description, and comparison.

He was summoned as a witness on a wide variety of topics. Ralegh, who read him in French, refers us to his arguments on the reality and whereabouts of Eden, and Bacon found him pithily clever on flattery, citing his disdain for those who turn "Hecuba into Helena, and Faustina into Lucretia."[73] Several others were taken by the story in the "Sixth Day" of the Persian king who liked to sit enthroned on a working model of the cosmos. His hubris is meant to dismay us, but the image of a monarch atop an epitomized universe may also have appealed to the same taste for patterned inclusion, for a numerically ordered summation of the spacious yet limited All, which in part explains the *First Week*'s popularity.[74]

On certain matters English writers were especially apt to recall Du Bartas. For some reason he particularly drew the attention of those who wrote on women. Anthony Gibson defended the sex in *A woman's woorth* (1599), although women might be discouraged to find the book is a "paradox." It abounds in famous names, including Spenser, Daniel, and "the Lord of Bartas," quoted on the "cunning Tirianes" who first wrote down musical harmonies (sig. C12). William Heale's *Apologie for women* (Oxford, 1609), written against someone who defended wife-beating, recounts how Adam naturally loved Eve because he "perceived himselfe imparted unto her. Wherefore his first words and morning song, were words of amity and a song of love"; a description of the loving "sweet he-shee-coupled one" from the "Sixth Day" follows (sigs. H3–H3^v).

· The woman who defends her sex in the satirically titled *Haec vir* (1620) may not speak for the author when she quotes a tag from Du Bartas (sig. B3ᵛ), but Daniel Toutevile's *St. Pauls threefold cord* (1635) is quite serious about the advice he gives spouses. "Every Adam must love his Eve," he says, and shows why this follows from the various "causes" of women. God turned bone into body, for instance, so that man "might have an Ivory Pallace wherein to recreate his best Affections." Without her "what would hee bee, but a companion for the Hedgehogge, and the Owle? The glory and the grace, which derived upon him from her, is most elegantly expressed by divine Du Bartas, in the sixt day of the week." Toutevile then repeats six lines in French on how man alone "n'est qu'un Loup-garou, du soleil enemi" (sigs. E3–E4ᵛ). Thomas Tuke adopts a sterner tone in his *Treatise against painting* (1616), a sober exhortation enlivened by many epigrams and quotations to show that make-up violates "the Law and order of nature" while—a central point—wasting time. He offers as corroboration a fragment from Hudson's *Judith* and a longer passage from "The Decay" describing Jezebel and her modern sisters whose "borrowed snares" conceal their "stinking breath, swart cheeks, and hanging chaps."[75]

Perhaps because they were pleased that a famous French poet praised their countrymen as "pillars" of language, the English also welcomed "Babylone" with special warmth. Some writers like Hakewill and Lisle were interested in what Du Bartas said about the French.[76] As early as the *Exequiae . . . Sidnaei* (Oxford, 1587), however, the English also noted his "Quatuor Anglorum Musis . . . columnas . . . Morum, Baconem, Sidneium, ac Elizabetham" (sig. K1). In 1592 Nash wrote in *Pierce Penilesse*, "What age will not praise immortal Sir Philip Sidney, whom noble Salustius (that thrice singuler french Poet) hath famoused, together with Sir Nicholas Bacon, Lord keeper, and merry sir Thomas Moore, for the chiefe pillers of our english speech."[77] Daniel Tuvil says in *Asylum veneris* (1616), an interesting defense of women, that as for that glory of her sex Elizabeth, he will "onely utter to the astonishment of Fame, that which the Muse of divine du Bartas sung of hir with admiration, stiling hir, and that without flatterie" (the encomium to "prudente Pallas" follows, sigs. G8–H1). And in *The compleat gentleman* (1622) Henry Peacham, who liked to quote Du

Bartas, recommends More, the essays of Bacon, and the "Arcadia of the Noble Sir Philip Sidney, whom Du Bartas makes one of the four Columnes of our Language."[78]

No one made greater use of "Babylone" than John Eliot in his *Ortho-epia Gallica* (1593). Eliot says that to refresh his readers while they learn French he has "taken a few pleasant conceits out of Francis Rabelais that merrie Grig, an example or two out of Lewis Vives, a score or two of verses out of Bartasius." In fact he takes more than that, although the teacher in the dialogue on languages says, "I am not ignorant how great my sawcines shall be by presuming to take upon me to counterfait by our English his inimitable stile." Du Bartas, we are told, "hath written more in Three [*sic*] Weekes, then all other French Poets, or all other Poets either Pagan or Christian have done in all their life. Besides a man of as great a wit as ever France bred any." The pupil in this dialogue hears nothing about the English "pillars," but in the next section a traveler recites the celebration of the "Bright Northren Pearle," Elizabeth. "Truly," says his friend, "this Bartasius was a man of a rare spirit."

Eliot had read more than "Babylone"; the end of his book quotes some grateful lines on France from the "Colonies" which had already appeared in his *Survey of France* the year before. His verse lacks the ease of his prose, but his efforts—which precede both Lisle's and Sylvester's—are not without vigor:

> O Fruitfull France! Most happie Land, happie and happie
>   thrice!
> O pearle of rich European bounds! O earthly Paradice! . . .
> The Crocidile fierce-weeping-teares annoyeth not thy maine,
> The speckled-race of crawling Serpents hant not thy domaine,
> Not in one Acre of thy land that cursed seed is seene,
> Backs-venimous-twinding to and fro t'infect thy medowes
>   greene.

Eliot's compounds show that pleasure in the sound and shape of words which doubtless drew him to Rabelais and, in a different mood, to Du Bartas's lark in the "Fifth Day":

> The pretie Larke mans angrie mood doth charme with
>   melodie,

Her Tee-ree-lee-ree Tee-ree-lee-ree chippring in the skie,
Up to the court of Jove, sweet bird, mounting with flickering
   wings,
And downe againe, my Jove adieu, sweet Jove adieu, she
   sings.

The speaker's friend is ecstatic, exclaiming that Amphion, Arion,
and Orpheus "have never bene able to counterfait this little bird
singing hir note."[79]

Excerpts from or references to Du Bartas are even more likely to
turn up in works which deal in one way or another with the natural
world and its significance. Sometimes an author means simply to
illustrate a point or enliven the discourse. Thus a sermon may be
likened to the "water wonders" in the "Third Day," or a text on
Africa pause briefly for Du Bartas's appreciation of the versatile
cocoa tree.[80] Thomas de Gray thought the set piece on the horse in
"The Handy-crafts" worth two pages in his lovely *Compleat horse-
man* (1639, sigs. D2–D3), and Peter Heylyn, more concerned with
the human part of creation, found discussions in the "Colonies" on
matters such as international trade, the origins of Galatia, and the
nature of the races for his very popular *Microcosmus* (1621). Some
years later he reprinted the last passage in his *Survey of the estate of
France* (1656). Climate affects national character, says Du Bartas,
and English readers could take dangerous pleasure in his summary
of the results:

The Northern man is fair, the Southern foul;
That's white, this black, that smiles and this doth scowl.
The one blithe and frolick, the other dull and froward,
The one full of courage, the other a fearful coward.

[sig. a4]

On occasion the quotations from Du Bartas, while recreative in
their contrast to the surrounding prose, also support a larger vision
of the cosmos, bearing witness to the interest and delight of the
natural realm. John Hagthorpe's *Visiones rerum* (1623), for instance,
is fascinated by its inhabitants; he tells some good dog stories,
defends unicorns, mentions elephants' thirst for glory, and
reminds us to read Montaigne and Du Bartas on Androcles and the

lion (sig. E6^v). In *Microcosmographia* (1615), which maps the little
world of man, Helkiah Crooke discusses the genitals with a pleasant gallantry toward the gender he reluctantly calls weaker in
sexual intensity (but hotter in temper, as "many of us know by
woeful experience"). The male seed, he explains, "yssueth with
greater violence and with a kinde of Almaine leape or sub-
sultation." For all his pleasure in the microcosm, though, Crooke
knows about the mutability whose ravages necessitate those
Almaine leaps. "The French Poet Salust," he says, expresses this
changeableness "under the comparison of a notorious Strumpet,"
and he quotes the lines on matter as a Lais in whom "new pleasure
of her wanton fire, / Stirs . . . still another new desire" (1631 ed.,
sigs. Aa5^v–A6, S5).

John Swan's *Speculum mundi* (Cambridge, 1635) relies heavily on
Du Bartas. Swan promises to avoid "quaint language, or fragrant
flowers of flowing Rhetorick," but in fact he studs his hexameral
description of the world with a multitude of excerpts from Lucretius, Virgil, and the *Weeks*. His aim is in some ways like that of
the "Nightingale of France"—to imitate the variegated plenty of
an ingeniously wrought cosmos—so he chooses a few set descriptive pieces; but more than the others who drew on Du Bartas to
illustrate their natural history Swan also adopts his arguments,
speculations, and irritated dismissals of opposing scientific views.
He particularly enjoys curiosities like the river with wine and oil or
the rain of wheat, and apparently believes in them. Indeed, a
startling aspect of Du Bartas's career in England is the persistence
of his role as a scientific authority. Use of the *Weeks* to buttress the
assumptions and details of a world view subject to worsening
erosion does not diminish as the seventeenth century wears on but
if anything increases in the 1630s and 1640s. Even in the 1650s, one
finds him summoned to verify data unable to withstand more
skeptical or scientific examination.

Isaac Walton, for one, had no doubt that Du Bartas's information was sound. His *Compleat angler* (1653) shares with the *Weeks*
the aim of showing and making lovable a Providence that works
through even the lowly chub and to whose ordered world human-
kind owes a thankful attention ("Nay, the very colours of caterpillers are, as one has observed, very elegant and beautiful").
Walton's tone is utterly different from Du Bartas's. His "Piscator"

never raises his voice or loses his temper, and the symbolic significance of fish and fishing is indicated with a delicacy he could not have learned from the *Sepmaines*. Yet like Du Bartas Walton enjoys both the quirks of God's imagination and its larger patterns. To please his companion and, I think, expand his meaning beyond the pastoral world in which they walk, Piscator recites from Du Bartas, Montaigne, Herbert, and others. He "sweetens" his discourse, for instance, with Du Bartas's report in the "Fifth Day" that the ocean contains analogues of all land creatures. Piscator wants chiefly to praise water and its inhabitants, but one can also sense his joy in symmetry. A little later he repeats Du Bartas's descriptions of the adulterous sargus, faithful cantharus, and chaste mullet, in whose squamous behavior roving-eyed human spouses may read needed lessons. Our informant is a poet, Walton confesses, but "he hath gathered this, and other observations out of Authors that have been great and industrious searchers into the secrets of nature." One of those secrets particularly intrigues Piscator—the generation of living creatures "without Venus deed" —and he quotes Du Bartas "for a little confirmation." Far from doubting that leaves in Iceland can turn into goslings, he replaces Sylvester's cautious "they say" with a firm "'tis known" (sigs. C2^v–C5, H3–H4).

Many years before the *Angler*, Dr. Thomas Moffett had written a book on insects, finished by 1590 but unpublished until Dr. Theodore Mayerne printed it with his own introduction in 1634; an English version was attached to Topsell's magnificent *Four-footed beasts* in 1658. Moffett often quotes the poet who, for example, "observed a divine power in Caterpillers from their Original," although he cites Du Monin's Latin translation rather than Du Bartas himself. Mayerne's introduction also shows the feeling that led many to applaud the *Weeks*. Citizens do well, he says, to observe monarchical bees and republican ants, and Christians will think of the Resurrection if they "consider how the Silk-worm makes her self a tombe . . . and by a prodigious metamorphosis it is born anew a Butterfly." By studying even a minuscule animal "thy minde may rise to its original, and fastning thy eyes on heaven inspired by God, wilt cry out, O the depth!"[81]

The cause of this particular "O altitudo!" is the cunningly made world itself, not Urania's summons to the stars. If Du Bartas's

flights to see the All, the One, account for a large part of his
reception in England, so does his delight in what we would now call
the close-up, the detailed cherishing of the Many as a means of
spiritual or religious comprehension. Christians had long seen
traces of God in his Creation, understanding the invisible by
contemplating the visible. This world, wrote Calvin, is a theater or
mirror, and although like St. Paul he warns that what we see in the
glass darkly is only enough to deny us excuse for unbelief, he also
expects us to observe, interpret, and praise.[82] God's creative inventiveness, says Charles Butler in *The feminine monarchie* (Oxford, 1623
ed.), may be seen in the beehive. "These wonderful parts and
properties of this little creature," he asks, "what are they but so
many evident proofes of the infinite power and wisdom of the
Creator?" He repeats Du Bartas's admiring words in the "Fifth
Day" on how these tiny animals show the omnipotence

> Which doth within so narrow space dispence
> So stiffe a sting, so stout and valiant hart,
> So loud a voyce, so prudent Wit and Art.[83]

With considerable sweetness and emotion Henry Valentine
expresses similar feelings. His *Foure sea-sermons* (1635), like Walton's Piscator, find divinity in the great waters. He quotes Du
Bartas on the emergence from *nihil* of all "this city," says that the
heaven is "full of wonders as it is of starres," and admits that the
earth, too, shows God's art. But God is "most wonderfully won-
derfull in the Sea, for it is as full of wonder, as it is of water." It is
also an allegorical emblem, with calms of peace, storms of perse-
cution, gulfs of despair, rocks of presumption, and as for weather-
beaten ships "the best men are a little leakie" and need the pump of
repentance. Valentine also shares God's taste for symmetry, quoting the lines from the "Fifth Day" on how the land is reflected in
the ocean:

> And all that in this All is to be found
> As if the world within the Deepes were drown'd.
>   [sigs. C4ᵛ–E2]

In effect Valentine interprets the sea, just as Du Bartas not only
described but *read* God's book of creatures. This metaphor
(although "metaphor" is too pallid a term) was no recent or merely

literary conceit but an analogy rooted deep in the thought of the
Middle Ages and Renaissance. "Omnis mundi creatura," Alanus
had said, "Quasi liber et pictura / Nobis est et speculum." Du
Bartas himself wrote in the "First Day" that

> The World's a Book in Folio, printed all
> With God's great Works in letters Capitall:
> Each Creature is a Page; and each Effect
> A fair Character, void of all defect.[84]

Like many others who were moved by this analogy Milton knew its
dangers, the temptation to peer too closely at the fine print or to
skip ahead merely because of pride or idle curiosity, but the angel
Raphael nevertheless tells Adam he may search the sky as "the
Book of God before thee set, / Wherein to read his wond'rous
Works" and Adam himself had earlier hoped to ascend to God
through "contemplation of created things."[85]

Several who described this volume call Du Bartas as witness.
Among the most persuasive was John Boys, who also helped
prepare the King James version of God's other book. In the early
seventeenth century he wrote a series of tracts on the liturgical use
of Scripture, often powerful in their rhythmic accumulations of
metaphor and filled with excerpts from his wide reading. He often
quotes the *Weeks*, repeating what "the Nightingale of France
sweetly" says about Abraham and Isaac, the Trinity, angels,
music, and the amazing scolopendra fish, but he was especially
moved by the thought of the cosmos as a book—among the analogy's many functions may have been its reconciliation of scholars'
love of words and the implacable presence of God's primary and
material world.[86] His *Exposition of all the principall scriptures used in our
English liturgie* (1609) quotes Du Bartas on God's Creation from
nihil and then reminds us the cosmos is a mirror of God's power, a
school where, as "the divine Poet" tells us, the Almighty teaches us
his glory (1610 ed., sigs. F1–F1^v).

Nor does God assign a difficult text. The world is allegorical, to
be sure, but despite a widespread if perhaps diminishing conviction that veiled truth was not for everybody, many who "read"
the world thought of it as they thought of the other book—it is, or
should be, available to everyone, not hermetically sealed from
common folk. Boys rejoices that "The great book of the creatures in

folio, may be termed aptly the Shepherds Kalender, and the
Plough-mans Alphabet, in which even the most ignorant may run
(as the Prophet speakes) and read." He cites Du Bartas in the
margin and a little later, when showing that God thus makes
himself available to our senses, turns again to the "sweet" poet:

> Therein our fingers feele, our nostrils smell,
> Our palats taste his vertues that excell,
> He shewes him to our eyes, talkes to our eares,
> In the ordered motions of the spangled spheares.[87]

A related emotion if a narrower spirit informs Edward Evans's
Verba dierum, or, the dayes report of Gods glory (Oxford, 1615). Recall-
ing Psalm 19, Evans gives his own version of the old analogy:
"Nights are as it were the Black Inkie Lines of learning, Dayes the
White Lightsome Space betweene the Lines: where God hath
Imprinted a very legible Delineation of his Glorie"; at this point a
marginal note sends us to other works on the subject such as
"Bartas his Elegancy in the First Day of the First Weeke" (sig.
A1^v). Evans later quotes the "First Day" in French (sig. I2^v), so it
was with some firsthand knowledge that he praised the author.

Unlike many who admired Du Bartas, however, Evans had a
certain hostility toward much secular literature, condemning
"Vaine and Prophane, yea and Diabolicall Mottos, Titles,
Devises, Emblems, Impresas, Epitaphes, Epigrams, Anigrams,
Pageants, Playes, Enterludes, Inscriptions, Dedications, and such
like" (sig. P3^v). Perhaps he feared some of these clever pastimes
involve superstition or perhaps he thought they distract us from
God's two books. If one has nature one does not need Alciati (just
as Stella obviates feigned muses). Yet this impatience with worldly
delights or hermetic faddishness is associated not with Uranian
impulses to flight but with a sharpened focus on Creation's legible
meanings. Considering all these significant wonders about us, he
says, it is a shame Christian poets write so little of them; indeed it is
a shame to mention what they *do* write. "And here I cannot but
commend unto you, and to your imitation Saluste Du Bartas, a
Poet above the ordinary levell of the world, for the choice of his
subject most rare and excellent" (sig. K1^v).

The great Puritan preacher Thomas Adams also recommends
God's book of creatures. He quotes a moral tag from Du Bartas in

his *Diseases of the soul* (1616, sig. D3) but warms more eloquently to the passage on God's loving masterpiece of nonfiction: "There is no Creature but may teach a good soule one step toward his Creator. The World is a Glasse, wherein we may contemplate the eternal power and majesty of God. . . . It is that great Booke, of so large a Character, that a man may run and read it. Yes, even the simplest man that cannot read, may yet spell out of this Booke that there is a GOD. Every Shepheard hath this ABC. What that French Poet divinely sung, is thus as sweetly englished:

> The Worlds a Schoole; where in a generall Story,
> God alwayes reades dumbe Lectures of his Glory."
> *[Works*, 1630, sigs. I5–I5^v]

Adams was a Puritan, Nehemiah Rogers a friend of Archbishop Laud, but about this divine primer they could agree. Rogers's *A strange vineyard in Palaestina* (1623) expatiates upon Isaiah's song of his beloved, interpreting the words of this rare rhetorician, as he calls the prophet, and exploring at length the purpose of figurative language. Rogers struggles to justify poetry: God himself wrote it; it stirs yet solidifies the memory; it condenses or compresses; together with music it has "effects" upon the soul; it draws us to God, who pulls us to him by what we most love. Furthermore, we may compare corporal and spiritual things in order to teach those who otherwise might not understand mysteries. In this way Rogers defends allegory, although instead of relying on its veil to conceal truth from the profane he counts on it to reveal and instruct. After all, the world itself is a school. "From the highest Angell to the lowest worme, all teach us somewhat. The Sun, Moone, Starres, are good Schoolemasters." In Eden we understood the creatures from our knowledge of God, but we soon flunked out: "To the schoole of the creature is man now sent, and put backe (like an idle truant) to his A.B.C. to learne the glory, goodnesse, and providence of the Creator." Rogers, too, has read the "First Day," citing it in the margin next to his comparison of "the great booke of the creatures" to a shepherd's calendar and plowman's alphabet (1632 ed., sigs. G2^v–G4).

Every good book filled with important and complicated data needs an index, some sort of table for ready reference. The index to the book of creatures is, of course, ourselves. Not only are we the

readers (so far as we know the only readers); we are both in the text
and a summation of it—a curious paradox indeed, as though
Spenser's letter to Ralegh were found walking in Fairyland
(through the wood of error, some might say) or a mythographical
dictionary were to turn up as a character in the *Metamorphoses*.
Samuel Hinde's *Free-will offering* (1634) discusses Psalm 107,
"They that goe downe to the Sea in ships." He tells of many
amazing works God has performed upon the deep and urges us to
praise "the wonders that he doth for the children of men." For
"This world is a booke in Folio wherein are written the workes and
wonders of Gods omnipotent hand, the acts and monuments of our
maker and preserver in his owne proper characters. . . . Man is no
other but a concise abridgement of this booke of the world, and an
intire Index to shew and point out the capital observations of the
voluminous and massie pile" (sigs. F4^v–F5). A marginal note cites
Du Bartas.

And what of Eve? William Hodson writes in *The divine cos-
mographer* (1640) that as someone once put it Man was the epitome
of the whole world and Woman its second edition. Hodson has also
read Du Bartas. He repeats the description of Moses in the rushes
and is especially excited by the works of the "Fifth Day" such as
the "whirle-about" whale and the dolphin, "Lover of ships, of
men, of melodie," whose sportiveness rebukes dull slugabeds and
whom, he says, Du Bartas depicts in "orient" colors. Indeed, adds
Hodson in words virtually identical to those of Evans, Du Bartas is
"a Poet above the ordinary level of the world, for the choice of his
subject most rare and excellent . . . admirably copious on this
theme" (sigs. B11, C1, F11–G5).

Not all references to the divine Folio, however, appear in such
explicitly religious works. Thomas Nash (not the famous one)
wrote *Quaternio, or a fourefold way to a happie life* (1633), an entertaining conversation among a countryman, citizen, divine, and
lawyer that squeezes its way through margins thick with
quotations from writers like Owen, More, Sidney, and especially
Chaucer—from whose *Canterbury Tales* Nash extracts prudent
morals—and Du Bartas. Along the fourfold path (again one
notices the connection between a liking for Du Bartas and a
particularly strong taste for number and pattern) the reader may
see lines on Adam's curse, the country life, the horse, nightingale,

musical "effects," wine, order, contentment with little, and many other delights. He will also learn that little animals are illustrations in God's book of creatures, and when he reads a passage on how even heathens like sibyls, Turks, and Pythagoras could deduce from the "Creatures in the sublunarie world . . . there must be some predominant power that did guide and governe them," he will find in the margin the well-known lines on the world as a book "With Gods great workes in letters capitall" (1639 ed., sigs. E3^v, N3).

Du Bartas, then, was a "sweet" stylist and a "grave" writer, to be grouped with Homer, Dante, Ariosto, and Spenser. More important, he was a Christian Uranian with whom we can walk among the stars and gaze upon the All while listening to better poetry than the triflers or lechers can offer; and as a student of God's great book of creatures he read this exciting text with close, astonished, and affectionate scrutiny. Thus one can fairly speak of two related emotions or mental conditions to which he appealed—the desire to rise and see or merge with the transcendent, and what seems like a last flowering of one sort of *figura* (scientific or material allegory, one might call it).

As I suggested earlier, however, Du Bartas may also have pleased a quasi-hermetic or Pythagorean taste for occult mysteries, numerical structures, and Neoplatonic emanations, although few Englishmen were as given to these secret understandings as, for instance, Postel or Agrippa, and although Du Bartas himself remains a respectable and conventional Christian. English readers would not have been surprised to find such tendencies in a Huguenot—Mornay's *Christian religion* is quite syncretic and D'Aubigné once dabbled in magic.[88] Those who looked at La Primaudaye's *French academie* (1586–1618) would have seen references to Hermes and Pythagoras; part III, divided into twelve "days" and one hundred chapters, quotes Du Bartas on God's omnipresence before the Creation (sig. B3).

Few explicitly associated Du Bartas with the occult; rather one finds that admiration for his poetry could accompany an interest in cosmic secrets. Many of his English readers, including some I have already discussed, show through their works, libraries, or friendships that they were attracted to the syncretic or hermetic

movements on the Continent. Mornay's friend Sidney was thus
drawn, up to a point, and so were Spenser and Ralegh. Du Bartas's
most perfervid admirer, Gabriel Harvey, acquired books on magic
and, as I have argued earlier, was intrigued by the ancient theology
and veiled truths.

John Eliot borrows from Du Bartas not only his discussion of
modern languages but the more magical thoughts on Hebrew. A
pupil asks, "The Hebrew, is it mysterious, as the Egyptian tongue,
which is Hieroglyphicke and Caballisticke?" The teacher replies,
"In few words it containes many things, is marvellously sig-
nificative, energicall, pure, chast, holy and divine, manifesteth
cleerely and breefely all that any man can thinke in his hart" (sigs.
F1^v–F2). Even more intriguing is a wine-splashed revel in which
one of the party asks, "Is there any one that will dispute with me of
these intricat problemes of thirst and drinking: I have no lesse
studied Magicke, Negromancie, Alchimie, the Caballisticke
science and Geomancie, then the Philosophie of Hermes Tris-
megistus." One companion replies, "These are high matters, and
profound sciences" and another calls wine an "Angelicall,
delicious, celestiall, joious, deifying liquor." Such language may
merely show good spirits fortified with satire, but like the passages
in Rabelais from which Eliot takes these lines it resonates with
other meanings too. The party over, one speaker says in words
there is no reason to believe Eliot thought inappropriate, "Blest be
the good God of heaven for his graces." If you drink enough wine,
another reveller had said, you will never die, and Eliot's readers
who kept their ears open might have agreed that by one of God's
graces this is in fact so.[89]

Daniel Tuvil, to whose quotation from Du Bartas I have
referred, shows unmistakable signs of hermetic interests. The tolerant humor which allows him to find his own age too "Stoicall and
Criticall" lightens the argument of *Asylum veneris* (1616), yet he is
more than merely funny. Toward the end of his book some lines
from Spenser on the masculine courage of ladies like Britomart
lead to a discussion of male and female. Tuvil repeats the Orphic
claim that Zeus was secretly a hermaphrodite—the female to the
left, infinite, and bad (of course), the male to the right, finite, and
good—which he modifies with an eloquent statement of his own to
the effect that the sexes are basically equal and complementary.

Later, when admitting that there is no use arguing with some people, he mentions the rule of Pythagoras against putting good fare in a foul dish. Tuvil was no Dr. Dee, but his interests led him to the *prisca theologia* as well as to Du Bartas (sigs. I7ᵛ–K1ᵛ, K8ᵛ).

Charles Butler, too, must have enjoyed Du Bartas not only for his "reading" of bees and his elevation of poetry but for his fascination with repeated patterns in the cosmos and their mysterious harmonies. Certainly Butler himself was fascinated. His *Feminine monarchie* explores the numerical significance of the arrangement he suggests for hives and finds in the hum of bees ("Melissomelos, or Bees Madrigall") the basis for human music. He transcribes a swarming song, for which he composes his own lyrics, and prints it in four parts suitable for human voices. Bees, we are told, like to end their songs in three-quarter (i.e. perfect) time and quite rightly have a total of eight tones (1623 ed., sigs. K3–L2).

Some others who referred to or quoted Du Bartas were at least intrigued by the hermetic, whatever the degree of their assent to its wisdom. Long before he translated Goulart, Thomas Lodge had noticed Du Bartas's numerology. Although he could also laugh at the occult, he writes Drayton in 1595 that poets should seek high themes like the Magi following the star, for "True science suted in well couched rimes, / Is nourished for fame in after times." He has read Drayton's "learned nines and threes" (presumably a reference to "Endimion & Phoebe"), and adds his own thoughts on trinities and enneads, citing Hesiod, astrologers, the "true Pythagorists," and Du Bartas:

> And first for three, which Bartas wisely names
> The first of ods, which multiplied, frames
> The sacred number nine.[90]

Henry Reynolds, also a friend of Drayton, knew the same passage. It may be remembered that Reynolds had argued in *Mythomystes* (1633?) for an inspired poetry that interprets myth as deep natural philosophy, and had praised "Salust, who may passe among the best of our modernes." A few pages later Reynolds turns to number. The ancients transmitted their knowledge through number, first by word of mouth and later by the "Art of mysticall writing by Numbers . . . called Scientia Cabalae." Unfortunately

this wisdom is now more than half gone; probably the old story of
Orpheus and Euridice secretly warns of this loss—the poet
brought truth and equity from the "darkenesse of Barbarisme and
Ignorance" with his doctrines, but "in the thicke caliginous way to
the upper-earth, she was lost againe, and remaines lost to us that
read and understand him not, for want merely of the knowledge of
that Art of Numbers that should unlocke and explane his Mysticall
meanings to us." Our incomprehension is all the more painful
because God himself works through number, "which taught the
ingenious Saluste" to say,

> Sacred harmony
> And law of Number did accompany
> Th'allmighty most, when first his ordinance
> Appointed Earth to rest and Heaven to daunce.[91]

If not an ancient theologian like Orpheus, Du Bartas is here closer
to vatic understanding than most modern poets.

Even when an author viewed the *prisca theologia* with suspicion as
well as interest he might quote Du Bartas as an authority. In
Purchas his pilgrimage (1613) Samuel Purchas writes about the
"Ancient Religions before the Flood" and the "Heathenish, Jew-
ish, and Saracenicall in all Ages since." His purpose is to show the
unnaturalness of faction and atheism, although his confidence in
the *consensus gentium* does not prevent his finding popish rites
"derived out of Chaldean, Aegyptian, and other fountaines of
Paganisme." He calls upon an enormous number of authorities
from Lactantius to Chaucer, Agrippa, Ficino, More (whose
Utopia is "too good to bee true"), Harriot, Spenser, and Du
Bartas, citing the last's reference in the "Colonies" to black men
found in America and quoting him on the Egyptian religion:

> The Memphian Priests were deepe Philosophers,
> And curious gazers on the sacred Stars;
> Searchers of Nature, and great Mathematickes
> Ere any letter knew the ancient'st Attickes.
>
> [sigs. ¶4ᵛ, Tt3ᵛ, Ggg 3ᵛ]

Martin Fotherby, Bishop of Salisbury, also sought to prove the
foolishness of atheism; his *Atheomastix* (1622) first argues for Providence and then moves to dazzle the reader by the splendor of

God's book of creatures. Fotherby quotes Du Bartas's "Colonies" on the variety of nations and invasions (sig. Z3^v) and turns to him again when attempting to show that "God hath made all his creatures, in Harmonicall proportion, and in a kinde of Musicke." Through this Pythagorean harmony the Creation makes music for God's glory, "The contemplation of which strange effect, so rapt the Poet Bartas, into admiration of it, that it made him to breake out into this passionate exclamation, of the mighty power of Musicke:

> O what is it, that Musicke cannot do?
> Sith th'all inspiring Spirit, it conquer's too:
> And mak'st the same, downe from th'Imperiall pole,
> Descend to Earth, into a Prophets soule:
> With divine accents, turning rarely right,
> Unto the rapting Spirit, the rapted spright."

Some poets try to recapture the creatures' musical praise; thus Du Bartas gives the lark morning and evening hymns "in a notable fiction."[92]

Two translations of Mercator's great *Atlas* show the cast of mind which led many to the *Weeks*. Wye Saltonstall's *Historia mundi* (1635) and Henry Hexham's *Atlas* (Amsterdam, 1636) open with the same discourse on the Creation which argues that cosmography shows "the infinite wisdome of God, and his inexhaust goodnesse," a goodness manifest "by the admirable concordancie of all things." God created the cosmos from an overflowing fecundity and "digested it into that order, nature, and proportion, according to that Idea, which he from all Eternitie had conceived." Pythagoreans deny the Creation, but the Platonic version "hath more appearance of divinity, then all others, and seemeth to come neerest to the Mosaicall truth."[93]

It is in this at least partially syncretic and certainly semi-Platonic atmosphere that one finds inserted several quotations from Du Bartas as translated by "Mr. Joseph Sylvester": a firm reply to the impertinent query as to God's activities before the Creation, a description of Chaos, and a couplet on the primal divine immanence "Before all time, matter, forme and place." The commendatory poems to Saltonstall, moreover, resemble some of the compliments to Du Bartas. One suggests half jokingly that the

study of geography can lead to mystic rapture, another calls the
world "an ample Text, / Whereon to meditate," and a third sees in
the *Atlas* the same extraordinary compression others felt in the
Weeks:

> The World is here contracted, and in this
> Thou shewest us what the lesser world (Man) is,
> And therein work'st a wonder, that the lesse
> Should comprehend the greaters spaciousnesse.

This tendency to associate Du Bartas with the hermetic on
occasion shows up in library lists. Again one can speak only of a
tendency, for popular writers like Du Bartas were bought by a
great variety of people. Sir Thomas Bludder, a cavalier whose
books were seized by Parliament, owned a number of works like
The Faerie Queene, the *Arcadia*, Whitney's emblems, Browne's pastorals, and Du Bartas's *Weeks*, but his library is not particularly
learned. So, too, the library of Lady Southwell and Captain Sibthorpe, collected toward the middle of the seventeenth century or
earlier, includes Spenser, Ariosto, Herbert, Montaigne, and "The
triumph of faith" but little scholarship. Nor was Scipio le Squyer
(1579–1659) drawn to the occult, although he had a fairly large
collection of literary works such as *Astrophil and Stella*, Marlowe's
Hero and Leander, and books by Chaucer, Spenser, Drayton, and
"Bartas."[94]

In some other libraries, though, like those of Lord Lumley and
Drummond, Du Bartas's companions include authorities on the
occult. The magnificent library of Sir Edward Coke (some of
which was collected by Sir Christopher Hatton) gathered Dante,
Chaucer, Daniel, Spenser, Sidney, and Du Bartas as well as some
books on magic. The library at Sion College, catalogued in 1650,
had Chaucer and Ariosto, Daniel and Wither, More and Montaigne, but in general the emphasis was on learned and religious
works; one finds much hermetic material like the Cabala, and also
Du Bartas's *La sepmaine*. Thomas Plume (1630–1704) bought even
less literature, although he owned a *Faerie Queene* and some Dryden
and Milton. He had Hermes' *Pimander*, Porphyry, Dee (as well as
William Prynne and Richard Baxter) and the 1641 folio of Sylvester's works. Even in a very late library like that of George
Lawson, catalogued in 1681, one finds along with a little literature

like Montaigne's essays, Harington's Ariosto, *Paradise Lost*, and "Du Bartus Divine Weeks and Works" many learned books by scholars like Ficino, Pico, Fludd, and Kircher.[95] Du Bartas, then, kept two sorts of company, sometimes at once and sometimes separately—writers of literary texts like the *Arcadia* and the *Faerie Queene* and learned, even occult, authorities like Lull, Dee, and Thricegreat Hermes.

Despite predictions of everlasting renown Du Bartas's reputation began to collapse soon after the Restoration. He did not lose readers or respect all at once, however. Samuel Pepys records that on a November Sunday in 1662 "My wife and I spent a good deal of this evening in reading Du' Bartas's *Imposture* and other parts, which my wife of late hath taken up to read, and is very fine as anything I meet with." A few years later Edward Phillips, Milton's nephew, wrote in *Theatrum poetarum* (1675) that the *First Week* "hath ever had many great admirers among us," and Richard Baxter also liked Du Bartas, saying in the preface to *Poetical fragments* (1681) that he had outdone Wither and Quarles (to Baxter, high praise).[96] William Winstanley could still admire and quote Du Bartas in his *Lives of the most famous English poets* (1687), and although John Oldham's "Satire dissuading from Poetry" mentions Sylvester's increasing oblivion it says nothing derogatory. In the next century neither Addison nor Pope thought much of Sylvester, but the British Museum's catalogue of printed books lists a work by Josiah Burchett called "The Ark. A poem. In imitation of Du Bartas." It is dated 1714.[97]

Soon even these tributes ceased. What had happened? One reason for his downward slide was doubtless the shift in France, where Du Bartas's name, often joined with Ronsard's, was subject to criticism and even ridicule. Englishmen who kept aware of French taste, particularly those waiting out the Commonwealth in Paris, would sooner or later be affected. I doubt they thought of the *Weeks* as tiresomely Puritan poetry, however, for the exiled king's own father and grandfather had admired them.

Taste was now changing in England too. The digressions and inclusions impressive to readers who valued variety more than unity, and a plenitude of inventions more than elegance of shape, would soon make the *Weeks* appear not a numerically arranged epitome of the All but a chaotic heap. Nor could Du Bartas's language suit new definitions of wit; conceits which had relied for their effect on fanciful diversity rather than controlled judgment now seemed silly or crude—fustian. Once he had been praised for compressing masses of material, for saying as much as possible. Pope's brilliance, on the other hand, depends in large part on what he does not spell out. The fear that his Belinda might "stain her honour or her new brocade" would have elicited from Du Bartas a digression on women's vanity filled with invocations and descriptions suitable for quotation.

Other cultural changes were at work. The fervor to rise did not wholly survive the advent of a more ironic and "classical" frame of mind. It is true that Milton could still move those not themselves Uranian in rhetoric or desire, but he wrote in a recognizable epic tradition and although *Paradise Lost* is in many ways a great Renaissance poem, even including some of those numerical patterns Du Bartas admired, it has a restraint few could find in the *Sepmaines*. And those who from pious pride wanted a great Christian poem to rival ancient epics could now put by the *Weeks* with little regret, reflecting that in Milton their hopes were accomplished.

Du Bartas had once been admired as a reader in the book of creatures, but the assumption that the world we see is sign-bearing was in retreat. Even if such a conviction can never be utterly lost—not while we dream in allegory and think almost instinctively in metaphor—its attenuation must have made the *Weeks* appear old-fashioned and even grotesque. Many people continued to believe that "The heavens declare the glory of God; and the firmament showeth his handiwork." Addison beautifully paraphrased that psalm (although Du Bartas would not have added the rational concession: "What tho' nor real Voice nor Sound / Amid their radiant Orbs be found? / In Reason's Ear they all rejoice"). Still, it is hard to imagine that he would have very often or very loudly cried "O the depth!" at the sight of an ant's leg. Pope says Nature tells us, "Go, from the Creatures thy instructions take," but she seems to mean secular lessons like the political science of bees or the caterpillars' art of weaving. Addison and Pope do not deny the religious significance of nature, indeed they both affirm it; but the shift in sensibility together with new scientific views made it harder to marvel enthusiastically at friendly crabs and chaste fish. James Thompson, who owned a copy of Sylvester, declared that all creation sounds God's praise as the quaternity of the seasons circles around, and he cries out "I lose / Myself in HIM, in LIGHT INEFFABLE!" He does not, however, read the individual birds or fish as tropes in the great folio.[98]

Many other poets have written in styles now archaic and with assumptions now strange or even repellent. Dante, Spenser, and Milton all assumed physical realities now denied by everybody and metaphysical realities denied by many. Yet so far they continue to please and move us. Du Bartas's commitments to his world were, I think, too literal and too urgent. He does not simply postulate the Ptolemaic universe; he argues fretfully for it, and its actual existence becomes necessary to his very meaning. Milton never made his basic drama or intention depend upon the physical structure of his cosmos, difficult though it may be to imagine his story taking place in the universe of, say, Jacques Monod.

Perhaps herein lies the *significatio* of Du Bartas's fame and its collapse. On occasion the *Sepmaines* have been called medieval, but in virtually every way Du Bartas was in fact quintessentially of the Renaissance, from his mannered style and lexical innovations to his desire for religious poetry at once Christian and cosmological, scriptural and arranged along lines circling through number while soaring into space. That is his fascination, but also his limitation. One does not have to believe in the inevitable alienation or anxiety of the artist to notice that much of the greatest work of any period is at least slightly off center. Many of Marot's best poems were written out of his various troubles, Du Bellay was at his most moving when he wrote of his quasi-exile, Ronsard's deepest love poetry disturbs even as it celebrates. Spenser wrote in growing awareness of his world's failures and Milton "on evil days though fall'n." All these were of their own time and usually of their own place, but in their works as in their lives they did not entirely reflect those times and places; their poetry is to some degree angled away from such a reflection.

Du Bartas wrote in the provinces while beset by illness and civil war, yet he remained centered in his world and in a vision by no means simple-minded but hardly modified through irony or ambiguity. What he wrote, although in some ways unusual, nevertheless fulfilled the hopes and criteria of his age; his poetry's popularity was no aberration. And therein, I think, lay the cause of his future oblivion. He held a seemingly magic mirror up to his age and showed it its assumptions, its taste, its longings; when the age changed, the image first looked outworn, then foolish, and then faded altogether. For that reason the revival of the Pléiade in the nineteenth century could affect Du Bartas's reputation only slightly, for he remained at the center of his epoch, fixed there. We can go back to visit him and we should, for the visit has its interest and even gives a strange pleasure; but unlike Ronsard, he cannot come to us across the years, at least not nearly as easily and then only to tolerant readers—few of them French.

Afterword

Clear patterns assuredly free from the shaping projections of our own culture's imagination may be difficult to detect in this book. At least, however, the differences in English response to these five poets are tolerably easy to define. Marot, in England, was the author of usable poetry who helped establish a national literature but toward whom reactions might vary widely and whose irony and humor escaped many readers. Du Bellay was a new and fresh writer who fashioned and refashioned clever conceits in both French and Latin, a poet whose work, especially in the 1580s, was very much on the minds of those engaged in experiment, recovery, and innovation; yet only rarely did he seize the English imagination as an impressive figure worth explicit and written recognition. Ronsard's English career was complex; he had a role in political and religious controversy, soon acquired the robes of a *vates*, and although his love toys were studied closely and his great hymns somewhat neglected he was clearly the most important modern French poet except, probably, Du Bartas. Desportes's career in England was rather oddly divided—on the one hand his clear, witty, and mannered sonnets were widely read and translated but on the other neither his work nor his personality provoked much comment; he had virtually no English "image."

Du Bartas, however, drew from the English an excited adulation and even emulation that responded not only to his piety as such but to his capacity to include and arrange the All into significantly shaped poetry that epitomized the larger Book even while examining the creatures and events contained therein. The English admired and sometimes exulted in his power to rise up toward increased vision, not only shaming lesser poets in his flight but exhilarating his readers as they followed his muse-accompanied

movements upwards to the skies, downwards to the oceans, lat-
erally to distant places, and along perspectives reaching back to
Genesis and forward to the world's end. It has often been remarked
that Renaissance Europe was fascinated by space, particularly
space defined by perspective lines, diagrams, or systems. Du Bartas's space was not that of Copernicus or Bruno, but his very
conservatism must have rendered all the more attractive his long
vistas, the many-angled lines of his vision as it took in the Cosmos,
and the schemes in time and space by which he arranged what he
saw. Thus one could, with Barnaby Barnes, learn from Du Bartas
to walk with angels above the stars, aether blowing free, fiery
globes describing patterns below, the entirety of things available to
the sight—and all the while hear the spheres making harmony, not
the silence of infinite spaces that terrified Pascal.

It is this response, of course, which distinguished Du Bartas's
reputation in England from that of the other four poets. His career
there took him far from a strictly literary role, not because his topic
was "religious" and hence made a pious or extraliterary appeal but
because his poetry answered several immensely powerful
desires—to see the created world epitomized and laid out ready to
be admired and interpreted, to move rapidly through space, and to
contain or define those readings and movements in a scheme at
once temporal, spatial, and numerical. It is perhaps this last desire
which, along with his greater ambiguity, explains why Ronsard's
hymns found no such welcome in England. As individual poems
the hymns are better than anything Du Bartas wrote or could have
written, but they do not have Du Bartas's larger pattern, the nearly
Pythagorean deployment of his materials.

Other distinctions suggest themselves. The English seem to
have responded increasingly to visual elements in the French poets
they read, preferring poems that offered inner pictures, or at least
imitating them more often. It has been said that the Renaissance
saw a shift from the aural to the visual, from discourse to "the
display of meaning in space."[1] Such a theory doubtless over-
simplifies the situation, but it receives some corroboration in the
English treatment of these poets. Marot's effect often relies on his
tone, the quality of his voice, and it was the difficulty of *hearing*
Marot (especially if the reader's French was imperfect) that helped
limit or distort his reputation in England. Du Bartas, on the other

hand, is best appreciated if not too closely heard. His images and outlines are splendid—relentlessly urged, perhaps, and ponderously elaborated, yet often effective. But, although he is capable of shifting, for instance, from the satirical to the exclamatory, his tone is rarely nuanced and his rhythms are often stiff. So too, it was the readily imagined *Antiquitez* and "Songe" that interested Spenser, not the tonal complexity of the *Regrets*; and so, too, English writers were often drawn to love poems providing a little emblem, a situation available to the inner eye.

In comparing the reputations of these poets one can also see the impact of their own explicit estimates of themselves. Of all five poets it was Ronsard and Du Bartas who made the loudest and proudest claims for themselves and their poetry, and it was those two who established the firmest reputations in England. This is not in itself surprising, since Ronsard was in any case the greatest of the five and, as I have argued, Du Bartas the closest to the English imagination's requirements at the time. Nevertheless, the misunderstandings of Marot, the muffled quality of Du Bellay's English reputation, and the near silence on Desportes suggest the value of self-promotion in a society impressed by fame itself and likely to accord ever greater glory to a man precisely because he was already well known.

This cumulative fame has some parallels in the modern American fascination with "celebrities" who have in fact done little except be celebrated in fan magazines or television shows after some initial success, but I think the Renaissance version of this human tendency to make a man even more famous simply for being famous already also had roots in a desire to categorize, to arrange into a scheme, which often involved a keen sense of here (poets in England) and now (modern times) as opposed to there (Petrarch, Ronsard, Du Bartas) and then (Homer, Virgil, and their like). Time, as well as space, is thus organized by traceable lines, just as we may sort out "kinds" of literature, tropes, or national characteristics—for despite what Dr. Browne said, a belief in the drunken German, proud Spaniard, and boasting Scot as described by Du Bellay and others derives not only from failures of charity but from an impulse to sort, label, and put in place. This impulse is no doubt human, not merely characteristic of the Renaissance, but it seems to have increased during an age that saw

attempts to group poets by country and type rather than to stress
the unique qualities of a writer (that came later), and which liked,
as I have argued earlier, to select one or two exemplars for a
particular spot in time and place.

This patterning habit may be psychologically or aesthetically
related to a tendency when translating these five poets to push their
conceits further and to clarify their structures. Thus translations
from Du Bellay and Desportes add to an already flamboyant
anaphora, a version of the epitaph on Bonnivet divides Sidney not
into the original six parts but into at least eleven, the pain of a love
sonnet intensifies into despairing tears, and the motion of a lyric
accelerates toward a final defining couplet. Furthermore, such a
taste for arrangements, for even sharper designs, may explain the
particular fondness for sonnets organizing particles of discourse by
figures of repetition which (unlike the oral formulae of the fairy
story, for instance) bring the repetitions to the ear and eye with
scarcely a pause between.[2] Desportes's and Du Bartas's careers in
England were radically different, but the author of trifles and the
priest of Urania shared a passion to arrange, and, especially, to
arrange into inner images. Each of the two poets appealed to a taste
for outlines and patterns rather than for urgency of narrative or
complexity of tone. Even the Petrarchist paradoxes as Desportes
uses them rely more on a double perspective than on a genuine
ambiguity of the sort more likely to be found in Marot and Ronsard. One could almost diagram Desportes's mingled hopes and
fears, his freezings and burnings, just as one can diagram Du
Bartas's cosmos despite the violent doings in it.

And yet, for all the temptation to elaborate a conceit or sharpen
the structure, there was a countering tendency to make the various
poets conform in some degree to what the English wanted or
expected. Thus Marot is "modernized" into a sonneteer even
when his lyric is not a sonnet, Desportes is rendered less neoclassical and often more like Ronsard and Du Bellay, and Du
Bartas's compounds are softened into forms likely to impress but
not startle an English ear. This normalizing, so to speak, appears
in many English translations and adaptations; but we may never
know if it resulted from a *conscious* desire to make the poetry more
familiar and English, or if poets like Daniel simply instinctively
added details or rhythms that made Desportes seem more familiar,

and translators like Sylvester simply assumed that "cloud-chasing" is really the same thing as "chasse-nues."

The English response to these poets, then, illustrates a variety of tendencies mentioned in this book—to be nervous, even if appreciative, when faced with verse describing unsublimated sexual passion, to ignore, neglect, or misunderstand ambiguities (particularly since these are sometimes inaudible in a foreign language), to relish fame, to sort, compare, arrange and deploy, to enjoy small units of discourse whether as details in an emblematic inner image or as useful lines to quote, and to soar up to the heavens and travel far over the earth noting its wonders and observing its significance.

And yet there is so much we can never know. The limits of Renaissance criticism define what people in those days could say of these poets, and our own limits define the very categories by which we can now coherently say what they said. The exact meaning of their words, the assumptions behind those words, the deeper motivations of the translators, are hard if not impossible to determine. The precise availability of editions to particular people at particular moments, what travelers to France heard and never recorded, the impact of friendships and of volumes shared with acquaintances—all this is necessary to a full knowledge of English reaction and yet largely unavailable to modern investigation.

Even if we had full records, however, or through a magic spell could obtain a sample of genuine Renaissance Englishmen to poll and interview, some mystery would remain, for few human beings are themselves entirely sure why they prefer this, are bothered by that, or feel kinship and pleasure toward one poem and not another. Behind the assured statement that such and such a poet is a great writer, for example, may lie not so much a felt personal experience as a desire to show one is *au courant*, that one likes writers one's parents have not heard of, or that one still appreciates the greatness now scorned by the ignorant young. The English response to these five poets cannot be outlined or arranged as neatly as some people in those days would themselves have liked. If this study shows that tastes and feelings modern scholars have detected elsewhere manifest themselves here as well, it is also a useful reminder, I hope, that such tastes and feelings were shifting and contradictory—like our own.

Notes

1 In quotations, whether from published works or from manuscripts, I have retained the original spelling and punctuation, except with regard to i and j, u and v, and italics.

Chapter 1: Marot

1 For Marot's life and career, see Pauline M. Smith, *Clément Marot* (London, 1970), C. A. Mayer, *Clément Marot* (Paris, 1972), and the latter's persuasive treatment of Marot's literary role in his introduction to Marot's *Oeuvres diverses* (London, 1966). Whenever possible I shall cite Mayer's edition. Mayer outlines the history of Marot criticism in "Clément Marot and Literary History," *Studies in French Literature Presented to H. W. Lawton*, ed. J. C. Ireson, I. D. McFarlane, and Garnet Rees (Manchester, 1968), pp. 247–60. Robert Griffin, *Clément Marot and the Inflections of Poetic Voice* (Berkeley, 1974), offers a nuanced reading.

2 See Walther de Lerber, *L'influence de Clément Marot aux XVIIe et XVIIIe siècles* (Paris, 1920). Lerber cites a study of eighteenth-century libraries that shows Marot's popularity; my own limited investigation of eighteenth-century English booksale lists turned up Marot's works in four of twelve catalogues.

3 See Pierre Villey, "Tableau chronologique des publications de Marot," *RSS* (1920): 46–97, 206–34; 8 (1921): 80–110, 157–211; and his *Marot et Rabelais* (Paris, 1923). See also Mayer, *Bibliographie des oeuvres de Clément Marot* (Geneva, 1954), II, and his *Marot*, for the date of the *Suite*.

4 Marot's poetry does not often appear in sixteenth- and seventeenth-century library catalogues, but Mary Stuart owned his works (see Julian Sharman, *The Library of Mary Queen of Scots* [London, 1889]), and Thomas James's *Catalogus librorum bibliothecae publicae quam T. Bodleius . . .* (Oxford, 1605) records a 1551 edition.

5   No one thinks Marot was a conservative Catholic, but the nature and extent of his disaffection is disputed. Griffin, pp. 117–19, has some sensible things to say on the difficulty of pinning down his position. Here as elsewhere Marot was syncretic and ambiguous.

6   On Marot in England see Sidney Lee's inaccurate but still helpful *French Renaissance in England* (Oxford, 1910); Alfred Upham, *The French Influence in English Literature* (New York, 1908); Lois Borland, "The Influence of Marot on English Poetry of the Sixteenth Century" (unpub. M.A. thesis, University of Chicago, 1913); my own "The Reputation of Clément Marot in Renaissance England," *SRen* 18 (1971), which includes much of the material in this chapter; and Dana Bentley-Cranch, "La réputation de Clément Marot en Angleterre," *Studi Francesi* 17 (1973), 201–21, which deals primarily with the imitations by Surrey, Spenser, Gifford, and Davison and with the references by "E. K.," Gascoigne, and the *Mirror for Magistrates*.

7   Marot, *Les épigrammes*, ed. C. A. Mayer (London, 1970), p. 133. The epigram, which is probably not in Wyatt's hand, is discussed by A. K. Foxwell, *A Study of Sir Thomas Wyatt's Poems* (New York, 1911; 1964), pp. 7–8.

8   See Joseph Kerman in "An Elizabethan Edition of Lassus," *Acta Musicologica* 27 (1955), 71–76. The "Quinta pars" has been filmed for University Microfilms; the "Quarta pars," not in the *STC*, is in the Folger Library.

9   Lassus, *Sämtliche Werke*, ed. F. X. Haberl and A. Sandberger (Leipzig, 1894–1927), XIV, 15–17; Vautrollier, "Quinta pars," sig. A2^v. Music to accompany Marot's poetry was also printed in Le Roy's *A briefe a. plaine.instruction*, trans. "F. Ke." (1574), but only the first few words of the texts and no authors' names are given. For other sacred parodies of Marot see Jean Rollin, *Les chansons de Clément Marot* (Paris, 1951), and for a discussion of their fashion see E. Droz, "Simon Goulart, éditeur de musique," *BHR* 14 (1952), 266–76 (although Vautrollier's parodies precede those cited as the earliest) and H. P. Clive, "The Calvinist Attitude to Music," *BHR* 19 (1957), 80–102, 294–319; 20 (1958), 79–107.

10 Rollin, pp. 70–71. Downe's original is in *Much Ado*, II, iii.

11 William Nelson, *Fact or Fiction* (Cambridge, Mass., 1973), explores the doubts about "feigning."

12 Abraham Fraunce, *The Arcadian Rhetorike*, ed. Ethel Seaton (Oxford, 1950), pp. 61–62 and the Introduction; *Oeuvres lyriques*, ed. C. A. Mayer (London, 1964), p. 177.

13 Many of Harward's extracts are very brief and it is quite possible

several by Marot simply escaped me. It remains evident that he did not know Marot well.

14 Pasquier, sig. P4; the translator may have been W. Watson. Estienne, 1608 ed., sigs. E7, M5^v–M6, and R3^v; I quote the French from the edition of 1735, sig. Cc7. Maupas, trans. W. Aufield, sig. X7^v; the original is even more dismissive: "un Poëte François assez estimé en son temps" (1607; 1625 ed., sig. L6).

15 Sergio Baldi, *La Poesia di Sir Thomas Wyatt* (Florence, 1953).

16 *Oeuvres diverses*, pp. 122–23; Surrey, *Poems*, ed. Emrys Jones (Oxford, 1964), p. 10.

17 *Plays and Poems of William Cartwright*, ed. G. Blakemore Evans (Madison, Wisc., 1951), p. 476.

18 *Tottel's Miscellany*, ed. H. R. Rollins (Cambridge, Mass., 1965), I, 2, 179, 178.

19 *Oeuvres lyriques*, pp. 321–37, 343–53. Spenser, *Works*, ed. Edwin Greenlaw, C. G. Osgood, F. M. Padelford, Ray Heffner, et al. (Baltimore, 1932–49), VII, 104–20. Spenser may have known of Marot for some time, for he used Marot's translation of Petrarch when he Englished the poetry in van der Noot's *Theatre for worldlings* (1569).

20 Patrick Cullen, *Spenser, Marvell, and Renaissance Pastoral* (Cambridge, Mass., 1970), p. 147. Marot was not old by modern standards, but see Creighton Gilbert, "When Did a Man in the Renaissance Grow Old?", *SRen* 14 (1967), 7–32.

21 For the precise extent of Spenser's borrowings see Owen J. Reamer, "Spenser's Debt to Marot—Re-examined," *TSLL* 10 (1968/9), 504–27.

22 There has been disagreement as to the tone of Colin's last remarks and his future intentions; will he give up poetry altogether? move on to a higher "kind"? In either case his mood is more complex and somber than Marot's.

23 *Oeuvres lyriques*, no. 20. See also Christine M. Scollen, *The Birth of the Elegy in France, 1500–1550* (Geneva, 1967). In *Les élégies de Clément Marot* (Paris, 1952) V.-L. Saulnier plausibly suggests this elegy is about Renée of France, miserably married to the duke of Ferrara. The elegy was also translated into Scottish pentameter couplets by "G. H." sometime in the mid 1580s; it is in *The Maitland Quarto MS*, ed. W. A. Craigie (Edinburgh, 1920; Scottish Text Society, 2nd ser. IX), 208–13.

24 *The Poems of Sir Arthur Gorges*, ed. H. E. Sandison (Oxford, 1953), p. 23 and the full notes; see also nos. 26 and 40. *Epigrammes*, p. 181; Spenser, VIII, 233. Spenser's "As Diane hunted on a day," p. 233, is based on Marot's "L'Enfant Amour," *Epigrammes*, pp. 146–47.

25 *Epigrammes*, p. 145; *Rhapsody*, ed. H. E. Rollins (Cambridge, Mass., 1931–32), I, 268–69. Davison wrote his poems in the 1590s. "My love in her Attyre" shows some similarity to Marot's sly epigram "Qui cuyderoit desguiser Ysabeau."

26 Drayton's possible debts to Marot are noted in his *Works*, ed. W. J. Hebel (Oxford, 1931–41; 1961), V, 4, 6, 9, 185, and 187. The influence he may have exerted on English literature is difficult to determine. Various claims have been made about the sonnet, elegy, pastoral, and experiments with metrical variety.

27 The literature on the English psalm and its relationship to European psalters is vast. Most useful for a study of Marot's influence are Orentin Douen, *Clément Marot et le psautier huguenot* (Paris, 1879); John Julian, *A Dictionary of Hymnology* (London, 1907); Waldo Pratt, *The Music of the French Psalter of 1562* (New York, 1939); Hallett Smith, "English Metrical Psalms in the Sixteenth Century," *HLQ* 9 (1945/6), 249–71; L. B. Campbell, *Divine Poetry and Drama in Sixteenth-Century England* (Cambridge, 1959); John Stevens, *Music and Poetry in the Early Tudor Court* (Lincoln, Neb., 1961). The best edition of Marot's contributions is *Les psaumes de Clément Marot*, ed. Samuel Jan Lenselink (Bâle, 1969). For more bibliographical information and a discussion of sources see M. Albaric, "Le psautier de Clément Marot," *Revue des Sciences Philosophiques et Théologiques* 54 (1970), 227–43. William Ringler's introduction to Sidney's poetry (Oxford, 1962) and the introduction to *The Psalms of Sir Philip Sidney and the Countess of Pembroke*, ed. J. C. A. Rathmell (New York, 1963) give useful summaries. Both the music and the French texts are in Pierre Pidoux's *Psautier huguenot* (Bâle, 1962).

28 Michel Jeanneret provides an extended and subtle examination of Marot's translation in *Poésie et tradition biblique au XVIe siècle* (Paris, 1969).

29 The 1592 edition is mentioned by Julian and Douen but appears lost. Douen also lists two other English translations. One is based only on Beza, by Anthony Gilby. The other is the *Psalmes of David (in English meter)* (Middleburgh, 1598), which I have not seen. Sir Robert Ker wrote his son from Paris in 1624 that the French and Dutch had better translations than others and that their singing in two tongues to the same tunes "with one hart and voice" showed a providential undoing of the curse of Babel. His own translations seem to owe more to Buchanan than to Marot or Beza. See *The Correspondence of Sir Robert Ker, First Earl of Ancram* (Edinburgh, 1875), II, 487–506.

30 For the price of a French psalter in the 1580s see Robert Jahn, "Letters and Booklists of Thomas Chard (or Chare) of London,

1583–4," *Library*, 4th ser. IV (1923), 219–37. G. Delamothe, author of *The French alphabet* (1595), urges his readers to attend Huguenot churches to improve their French.

31 See Michel Jeanneret, "Marot traducteur des psaumes entre le néo-platonisme et la réforme," *BHR* 27 (1965), 629–43. Francis Yates, *The French Academies in the Sixteenth Century* (London, 1947), discusses the motives behind much Renaissance psalmody.

32 Sidney, *The Defense of Poesy*, ed. Lewis Soens (Lincoln, Neb., 1970), p. 8. Sidney is praising the most mysterious and divine poetry, not that "right" poetry to which he devotes most of his book. Alexander Gil wrote of Sidney's translation in his *Logonomia anglica* (1621 ed., sig. T2) that you will find there almost all the lyric genres of Roman poetry. On Sidney see particularly D. P. Walker, *The Ancient Theology* (Ithaca, N.Y., 1972).

33 Churchyard then praises authors like Chaucer, Surrey, and Phaer. The description of this passage in my article on Marot in England is inaccurate; I was misled by a confusing reference. There is similar praise for Marot in *Churchyardes chance* (1580), sig. B3.

34 Harvey, *Marginalia*, ed. G. C. Moore Smith (Stratford-upon-Avon, 1913), p. 162.

35 William Browne, "Britannia's Pastorals," *Works*, ed. W. C. Hazlitt (1868–69), I, 192.

36 Robert Sempill, in *Satirical Poems of the Time of the Reformation*, ed. James Cranstoun (Edinburgh, 1891; Scottish Text Soc. 1st. ser. XX and XXIV), 386. Marot, *Les épîtres* (London, 1958), pp. 171–76. One of the obscure "coq-à-l'âne" satires was noted in England; Bentley-Cranch quotes a letter from the unhappy Arabella Stewart to her husband William Seymour in 1610 or 1611 while both were imprisoned for their imprudent marriage: "And no fortune, I assure you, daunts me as much as that weakness of body I find in myself, for si nous vivons l'âge d'un veau, as Marot says, we may, by God's grace, be happier than we look for in being supposed to enjoy ourselves with his majesty's favour."

37 Facsimile reproduction (Kent State University, 1970) of Put-tenham's *Arte*, ed. Edward Arber (1906), p. 32.

38 From a MS of Roger's epigrams now in the Huntington Library, f. 135a. Hoyt Hudson, *The Epigram in the English Renaissance* (Princeton, 1947), p. 137, gives the Latin and the translation I quote. The scribe writes in some alternative words such as "Tusca . . . Suada" for "Itala . . . lingua." Roger's epigrams were for the most part written in the 1560s and 1570s.

39 James Howell, *Epistolae Ho-elianae*, ed. Joseph Jacobs (London, 1892),

II, 591–92. The same remarks appear in Howell's introduction to his *Lexicon tetraglotton* (1660). Most of his letters were probably written in the 1640s. His literary opinions sometimes echo Estienne Pasquier's *Recherches de la France*; see, e.g., *Les oeuvres* (Amsterdam, 1723), I, sig. Bbb3ff.

40   Du Bartas, *Works*, ed. U. T. Holmes, J. C. Lyons, and R. W. Linker (Chapel Hill, 1935–40), III, 142; (Simon Goulart) *La seconde sepmaine* (Geneva, 1593), sig. S7.

41   On Eliot's debts to Du Bartas see C. B. Beall, "John Eliot's *Ortho-Epia Gallica* and Du Bartas–Goulart," *SP* 43 (1946), 164–75, and David Thomas, "John Eliot's Borrowings from Du Bartas in his Minor Works," *RLC* 43 (1969), 263–76. Eliot's poem for Robert Greene's *Perimedes* (1588) saying Greene refines English as Marot refined French also derives from "Babylone."

42   Thomas Blenerhasset's defense of an unrhymed "complaynt" in *Parts Added to the Mirror for Magistrates*, ed. L. B. Campbell (Cambridge, 1946), p. 450. In *The scholemaster* (1570) Roger Ascham, too, traces "rude, beggarly rhyming" to France, although its ultimate origins, he believes, lie in the Gothic invasions of Italy.

43   Spenser, VII, 10, 17. E. K. says the November eclogue imitates Marot, "But farre passing his reache . . ." (p. 104).

44   George Gascoigne, *The Posies*, ed. J. W. Cunliffe (Cambridge, 1907), p. 33; this is the later edition of a collection he now claims to have "gelded" and for which he feels both affection and embarrassment. Timothy Kendall, *Flowers of Epigrammes* (London, 1577), Spenser Society reprint XV (1874), p. 159. English readers, however, might have noted Montaigne's more affectionate reference to Marot as an authority on venereal matters. Thanking God that French ladies would not prefer death to dishonor he says "suffit qu'elles dient *nenny* en le faisant, suyvant la reigle du bon Marot." See the *Oeuvres complètes*, ed. Albert Thibaudet and Maurice Rat (Paris, 1962), p. 338. Florio catches Montaigne's humor but omits the ambiguous "bon": let the ladies "say, *No, and take it*, following the rule of Marot" (1603; Everyman Edition, London, 1897), III, 44. Montaigne is quoting one of Marot's most popular lyrics, "De Ouy & Nenny"; I can find no English version, but Montgomerie translated it into delightful Scots. Cf. Buckingham's advice to Richard in Shakespeare's *Richard III*, III, vii: "Play the maid's part, still answer nay, and take it."

45   Thomas Brice, *Against filthy writing* (1562; a broadside); I. H., *This worlds folly* (1615), sigs. B2^v–B3.

46   *Oeuvres lyriques*, p. 205. Even in our own day we seem more comfortable with interpretations of Renaissance sonnet sequences that

stress psychological or philosophical exploration and complexity. Such indeed plausible approaches rescue Renaissance love poetry for our own ideas of importance but for one reason or another they were unused by critics at the time. For a comment on Sidney's evasion of the issue see T. G. A. Nelson, "Sir John Harington as a Critic of Sir Philip Sidney," *SP* 67 (1970), 41–56.

47 Joseph Hall, *Collected Poems*, ed. A. Davenport (London, 1949), pp. 93, 257. In a book of paradoxes translated from the French by Anthony Munday as *The defence of contraries* (1593) we read of those learned men "of our time" who came to troubled ends, including "The French Poet . . . by the miserable and implacable sute of the court, even in his coldest years" (sig. E3^v), which sounds like a reference to Marot.

48 *Pierces supererogation* (1593), sig. V4^v. "Bellay" is almost certainly not the poet but one of his learned relatives, such as the general and diplomat Guillaume du Bellay.

49 Thomas Coryate, *Coryat's Crudities* (Glasgow, 1905), I, 31, 42.

50 Marot, *Oeuvres satiriques*, p. 15. Theodore Beza, *Icones* (Geneva, 1580), sig. Y4. Beza's complaints about Marot's "mores parum Christianos," he might have reflected, were not unlike the scattered attacks on his own life. See my "English Writers and Beza's Latin Epigrams," *SRen* 21 (1974), 83–117.

51 *Calendar of Letters and Papers*, Foreign and Domestic, XVI, no. 488. Mayer discusses the passage in *La religion de Marot* (Geneva, 1960), pp. 93–94. Such references make one doubt the accuracy of Lee's statement that Marot's difficulties "could but evoke sympathy in England" (*Renaissance*, p. 113).

52 Foreign Series, V, no. 1413.

53 *The Poems of John Donne*, ed. Herbert Grierson (Oxford, 1912), I, 349. Hall, p. 271.

54 On the complex shifts of opinion toward psalm translation see Jeanneret, *Poésie et tradition* and Yates, *French Academies*.

55 George Wither, *A Preparation to the Psalter*, Spenser Soc. Reprint XXXVII (1884), p. 8. Henry Parrot wrote in *Laquei ridiculosi* (1613) of how a selfish clergyman rode along singing "Geneva Psalmes" not "knowing better how to spend the day" (sig. I5). Harington has a similar epigram.

56 Quoted from Zachary Boyd in J. Holland, *Psalmists of Britain* (London, 1843), I, 257–58. Boyd is citing someone else's report.

57 Michel Coyssard in *Hymnes sacrez* (1600), quoted by Jeanneret, *Poésie et tradition*, pp. 193–94. Florimond de Raemond, *Historiae de ortu, progressu, et ruina haereseon huis saeculi* (trans. from French, Cologne,

1614), II, sig. Kkkk3. His slanders did not go unnoticed in England. Thomas Rymer's "Short view of tragedy" (1692) quotes them. Rymer had already remarked in his preface to his translation of Rapin (1674) that Marot and Baïf attempted a little criticism but there was no "noble Contest" among the French until the "Royal Academy was founded. . . . Then Malherb reform'd their ancient licentious Poetry." See *The Critical Works of Thomas Rymer*, ed. Curt A. Zimansky (New Haven, 1956), pp. 102–3, 2.

58   Lyons, 1583, sig. B2; the language is Michel Coyssard's, but since Hay signs the new introduction the comments doubtless had his blessing. Hay was a Scottish Jesuit whose "demands" were addressed to the kirk back home.

59   Puttenham, p. 97.

60   C. A. Mayer, "Notes sur la réputation de Marot au XVIIe et XVIIIe siècles," *BHR* 25 (1963), 404–7.

61   From a prefatory poem in *A banquet of jests* (1630), 1640 ed., sig. A5^v.

62   On the significance of this connection and its relation to conceptions of the self see Robert Klein, "Un aspect de l'hermeneutique à l'âge de l'humanisme classique: Le thème du fou et l'ironie humaniste," *Archivio di Filosofia* (Padua, 1963), pp. 11–25. On Skelton's clowning and its subsequent effect on his reputation see Michael West, "Skelton and the Renaissance Theme of Folly," *PQ* 50 (1971), 23–35. Even More's "image" on occasion took a similar turn, accumulating those funny stories and quick answers which More himself relished and told but which suggest some found his humor more comfortable when leveled and made less disconcerting.

63   *Les épîtres*, p. 133.

64   *Epigrammes*, p. 280.

CHAPTER 2: DU BELLAY

1   The great biography is Henri Chamard, *Joachim Du Bellay* (Lille, 1900); shorter and more recent are Frédéric Boyer, *Joachim Du Bellay* (Paris, 1958) and V.-L. Saulnier, *Du Bellay* (4th ed., Paris, 1968). My summary of Du Bellay's publications is based on Chamard, "Bibliographie des éditions de Joachim Du Bellay," *Bulletin du bibliophile* (1949), 400–15; 445–63.

2   *Oeuvres poétiques*, ed. Henri Chamard (Paris, 1908–31, 6 vols.), I, 123. Unless otherwise identified all references to Du Bellay's poetry cite this edition.

3   As Henri Weber says in *La création poétique au XVIe siècle en France* (Paris, 1955), the literal meaning of the Pléiade's love poetry usually matters less than the images and what they suggest, such as "la fusion

de la femme aimée avec les grandes forces cosmiques qui animent l'univers" (p. 291).

4   On this visit see G. Dickinson, *Du Bellay in Rome* (Leiden, 1960).

5   The irony is pointed out in *Les regrets et autres oeuvres poëtiques*, ed. J. Jolliffe with introduction and commentary by M. A. Screech (Geneva, 1966), p. 15. See also John C. Lapp, "Mythological Imagery in Du Bellay," *SP* 61 (1964), 109–27. W. D. Elcock, "English Indifference to Du Bellay's 'Regrets,'" *MLR* 46 (1951), 175–84, concludes that the English were not attracted by the poetry's intimacy and introspection.

6   Richard A. Katz, *Ronsard's French Critics: 1585–1828* (Geneva, 1966), esp. p. 100; Saulnier, *Du Bellay*, pp. 170–72.

7   Du Bellay, III, 52–53. As Chamard's note says, the swan image in fact derives from Horace.

8   Du Bellay, V, 45. For a witty exploration of what such myths meant to Du Bellay and how his use of them differed from that of earlier poets and from Ronsard's see Françoise Joukovsky-Micha, *Poésie et mythologie au XVI⁰ siècle* (Paris, 1969).

9   The best antidote to anachronistic readings of Du Bellay is Robert Griffin, *Coronation of the Poet: Joachim Du Bellay's Debt to the Trivium* (Berkeley, 1969).

10 Except for Sidney Lee, *The French Renaissance in England* (Oxford, 1910), Alfred Upham, *The French Influence in English Literature* (New York, 1908), and Elcock's article, there has been little on Du Bellay in England. I note some articles on individual authors below; for broader surveys see Sidney Lee's introduction to *Elizabethan Sonnets* (Westminster, 1904), L. E. Kastner, "The Elizabethan Sonneteers and the French Poets," *MLR* 3 (1907/8), 268–77, Janet Espiner-Scott, *Les sonnets élisabéthains* (Paris, 1929), and her "Some Notes on Joachim Du Bellay," *MLR* 36 (1941), 59–67.

11 *L'Olive* XIX; *Tottel's Miscellany*, ed. H. R. Rollins (Cambridge, Mass., 1965), I, 99; "naamkouth" means famous. See J. C. Arens, "Du Bellay's Sonnet *Face le Ciel* Adapted by Nicholas Grimald," *PLL* 1 (1965), 77–78. Du Bellay's poem was popular, quoted in Tabourot's *Bigarrures* and Pasquier's *Recherches*.

12 Screech denies the *Antiquitez* "valeur visuelle" (*Regrets*, p. 32), but to Spenser and many of his contemporaries they and the "Songe" would have had great visual value; the "vision" is of an idea contemplated by the mind's eye. See Daniel Russell, "Du Bellay's emblematic vision of Rome," *Yale French Studies* 47 (1972), 98–109.

13 It was reprinted with an introduction by Louis S. Friedland and a bibliographical note by William Jackson (Scholars' Facsimiles and

Reprints, New York, 1939). For Spenser's text see the *Works*, ed. Edwin Greenlaw, C. G. Osgood, F. M. Padelford, and Ray Heffner (Baltimore, 1932–49), VIII, which has the pictures and material on Spenser's authorship. See also W. J. B. Pienaar, "Edmund Spenser and Jonker van der Noot," *ES* 8 (1926), 33–44, 67–76; Harold Stein, *Studies in Spenser's Complaints* (New York, 1934); and A. W. Satterthwaite, *Spenser, Ronsard, and Du Bellay* (Princeton, 1960). A less conventional and quite persuasive view of the *Theatre* is in J. A. van Dorsten, *The Radical Arts* (London and Leiden, 1970). For what the "idea" of Rome and its collapse meant to Spenser see Millar MacLure, "Spenser and the ruins of time," in *A Theatre for Spenserians*, ed. Judith Kennedy and James Reither (Toronto, 1973), pp. 3–18.

14 V.-L. Saulnier, "Commentaires sur les *Antiquitez de Rome*," *BHR* 12 (1950), 114–43, penetrates many of the "Songe"'s opacities.

15 Van Dorsten discusses the artist, p. 76. Leonard Forster, in *Janus Gruter's English Years* (Leiden & London, 1967), p. 52, says the artist was probably M. Geeraerts. Satterthwaite, pp. 255ff, argues Spenser did not translate the Apocalyptic sonnets. Leonard Forster discusses the identity of Theodore Roest, who Englished the commentary, in "The Translator of the 'Theatre for Worldlings,'" *ES* 48 (1967), 27–34.

16 Van der Noot was soon to rejoin the Catholic church. On the *Theatre*'s possibly eirenic aims see van Dorsten, pp. 77–78.

17 Van der Noot, *Het Bosken en Het Theatre*, ed. W. A. P. Smit (Amsterdam, 1953), which gives his sources.

18 Van Dorsten suggests the blank verse results from an impulse to neoclassical experiments leading later to attempts at quantity. In *The Poetry of Edmund Spenser* (New York, 1963), p. 65, William Nelson says it could be due to a "humanist contempt for rhyme as a barbaric ornament," and Derek Attridge, in *Well-Weighed Syllables* (Cambridge, 1975), shows how for some Elizabethan writers merely to omit rhyme was, in a sense, to write quantitative verse. Spenser's translations of Petrarch rhyme, but Petrarch was not writing about ancient Rome.

19 The Variorum edition sets the Apocalyptic sonnets off from the others, but the *Theatre* had printed them as a unit of fifteen.

20 *La deffence et illustration de la langue françoyse*, ed. Henri Chamard (Paris, 1948), pp. 156–57. "Fifteen," like "ten," can make an equilateral triangle or pyramid if arranged spatially; if left to progress linearly the center is emphasized, although here the result is not to celebrate a triumph but to dramatize a defeat. For the background to such speculations see Alastair Fowler, *Triumphal Forms* (Cambridge, 1970).

Gunnar Qvarnström is probably right, furthermore, to associate Renaissance numerology with an awareness of mutability. See his "Poetry and Numbers," *Scripta Minora* (Lund, 1964/65), p. 13 and A. Kent Hieatt, *Short Time's Endless Monument* (New York, 1960).

21 St. Augustine, *Opera Omnia* (Paris, 1841), IV, 1144 (in a discussion of Psalm 89); 1960, VI, 749–50; *On the Psalms*, trans. Scholastica Hebgin and Felicitas Corrigan (London, 1960), I, 62–64. Petrus Bongus, *Numerorum mysteria* (Bergamo, 1591; first ed., 1585), "De Numero XV," sigs. Ccl^v–Cc3. Spenser may be playing with "seven" and "eight" in the "Mutabilitie Cantos" of the *Faerie Queene*; the seventh shows us time's rotation and the eighth points to eternity.

22 On Du Bellay's apocalyptic overtones in the "Songe" see Gilbert Gadoffre, "Structures des mythes de Du Bellay," *BHR* 36 (1974), 273–89.

23 Rosemary Freeman, *English Emblem Books* (London, 1948), p. 73, says Peacham imitates Du Bellay, but I see no certain indication. William Browne, *Works*, ed. W. C. Hazlitt (1868–69), II, 329–32.

24 Spenser, *Complaints*, ed. W. L. Renwick (London, 1928), p. 244.

25 The *Aeneid*, I, 278–82; cited in Chamard's notes.

26 Garlands often had this significance. Abraham Fraunce, for instance, said of them that "through their circular figure might be signified victory or eternity" (*Insignium*, 1588, sig. G4^v).

27 Bongus, sigs. Hhl^v–Hh2^v. The *Antiquitez* have thirty-three sonnets if one includes the introductory poem to Henri II, so it is also possible Spenser wanted to restore the original total as well as to praise a poet to whom he owed so much.

28 *Ruines*, 11. 583–85, 682. For specific parallels see the Variorum edition's notes.

29 Du Bellay, IV, 3–26, esp. lines 37–120. See also Gerald H. Snare, "The Muses on Poetry: Spenser's *The Teares of the Muses*," *Tulane Studies in English* 17 (1969), 31–52.

30 In the preface to *Daphnaida* (1591).

31 *Poems*, ed. H. E. Sandison (Oxford, 1953) and notes.

32 No. 45. Other English poems pursue this gloomy thought. See, for instance, similar poems in William Corkine's *Airs* (1610) and John Dowland's *Second book of airs* (1600).

33 After kindly reading some poems by Gorges and Soowthern I sent him, Dr. Attridge wrote me he thinks neither poet is working with classical meters but is clearly experimenting in some fashion, perhaps with Italian or French models. Gorges tends to make such experiments when writing on Roman subjects, so perhaps to him non-accentual verse sounded "classical."

34   Caroline Ruutz-Rees describes several borrowings in "Some Debts of
     Samuel Daniel to Du Bellay," *MLN* 24 (1909), 134–37. See also Joan
     Rees, *Samuel Daniel* (Liverpool, 1964) and Pierre Spriet, *Samuel Daniel*
     (Paris, 1968).

35   Rees, pp. 26–30. As she says, Daniel does better with Desportes, for
     weaker poems submit more easily to refashioning.

36   Samuel Daniel, *Poems and A Defence of Ryme*, ed. A. C. Sprague
     (Chicago, 1965; first pub. 1930), pp. 191, 17. Kastner, "Elizabethan
     Sonneteers," cites a similar poem by Bartholomew Griffin.

37   *Delia*, XXXVII, IV, and XLIV. Upham, p. 119, says "At the
     Authors going into Italie" (Daniel, p. 187) echoes the *Regrets*.

38   It is most probable, of course, that other writers during the Renais-
     sance imitated Du Bellay, although conceits passed so quickly from
     hand to hand it is hard to read on such well-fingered currency the
     features that would show its origin. In *The Flaming Heart* (Gloucester,
     Mass., 1958; 1966), pp. 272–76, Mario Praz compares Sidney's pro-
     testations of sincerity to Du Bellay's "J'ay oublié l'art." Espiner-Scott
     finds the 25th sonnet to Stella like *Regrets* CLXXVII; Ringler says the
     thought was commonplace, but the sonnets do seem similar in
     movement. Drayton's ode to the new year may owe something to Du
     Bellay's ode to Robert de La Haye in IV, 178; see Anthony La
     Branche, "The 'Twofold Vitality' of Drayton's *Odes*," *CL* 15 (1963),
     116–29.

         Other echoes sound from time to time. Joseph Rutter's *Shepheardes
     holy-day* (1635) includes an invocation to sleep (sig. D7^v) which shares
     a line with *L'Olive* XLVII: "Clore mes yeulx d'une eternelle nuit"
     parallels "Wrappe up mine eyes in an eternall night." An intriguing
     trace of Du Bellay can be seen, I think, in John Dickenson's *Greene in
     conceipt* (1598). One quantitative poem tells of a lover awash in his
     inner tempest who glimpses the eyes of his lady appearing through
     the storm like Castor and Pollux, a conceit he may have found in
     L'Olive XI. If he did (although he might also have read it in Ariosto),
     then here is one more example of how attention to Du Bellay often
     accompanied attempts at metrical experiment.

39   Du Bellay, V, 366. He also wrote a Latin version; see *Poésies françaises
     et latines*, ed. E. Courbet (Paris, 1918), I, 531.

40   William Bond, in "The Epitaph of Sir Philip Sidney," *MLN* 58
     (1943), 253–57, cites the references to the epitaph by Eliot, Stafford,
     Camden, Weever, and one by Churchyard that I cannot trace. See
     also Henry Holland, *Monumenta sepulchraria Sancti Pauli* (1614), sig.
     C4. I have also seen the epitaph in several of the seventeenth-century
     commonplace books in the Folger Library.

41 *The Poems of Sir Walter Ralegh*, ed. Agnes Latham (Cambridge, Mass., 1951), p. 7 and notes.

42 One of Henry Constable's sonnets on Sidney, probably written before 1590, says "every vertue now for part of thee doth sue"; see his *Poems*, ed. Joan Grundy (Liverpool, 1960), p. 169. Gorges's "Mars and the Muses" derives eventually from the same conceit. There is a canceled epitaph for Alençon in Gorges's MS (the duke's soul goes to heaven, his body to France, and his "love was faire Elyzabeths whoe bredd the same"); a note in Gorges's hand says, "q^d Churchyarde." See p. 75 and notes, although Sandison does not cite Du Bellay.

43 *Poems*, ed. Thomas Crockett (Edinburgh, 1913, S. T. S. 2nd ser., V), p. 189. See too his "Fairweill to the Musis," p. 267. Du Bellay's "Adieu" (IV, 190–200) is itself based on one by Buchanan, but Stewart uses Du Bellay's meter. On Stewart's debts to Du Bellay, see Matthew P. McDiarmid, "Notes on the Poems of John Stewart of Baldynneis," *RES* 24 (1948), 12–18.

44 *Works*, ed. Henry W. Meikle (Edinburgh, 1914, S. T. S. 2nd ser., VI), pp. 5, 328. The introduction describes Fowler's career. Other Scots knew Du Bellay. Alexander's debts are described by L. E. Kastner, "The Scottish Sonneteers and the French Poets," *MLR* 3 (1907), 1–15, and by R. D. S. Jack, "Imitation in the Scottish Sonnet," *CL* 20 (1968), 313–28, although some examples seem dubious to me. Fowler's nephew William Drummond borrowed little if anything from Du Bellay but he owned the *Jeux rustiques*; see Robert Mac-Donald, *The Library of Drummond of Hawthornden* (Edinburgh, 1971). Ronsard and Du Bartas were more to his taste.

45 *Essayes*, trans. John Florio (London, 1897), I, 182.

46 *The Works of Sir Thomas Browne*, ed. Geoffrey Keynes (London, 1928–31), I, 78–79. The source of his "opprobrious Epithets" was first identified by H. G. Ward, "Joachim Du Bellay and Sir Thomas Browne," *RES* 5 (1929), 59–60.

47 W. L. Renwick, "The Critical Origins of Spenser's Diction" and "Mulcaster and Du Bellay," *MLR* 17 (1922), 1–16, 282–87. Not everyone admired the pamphlet. Barthélemy Aneau's scornful and occasionally acute remarks in his *Quintil horatian* are printed in Chamard's edition of the *Deffence*. Alert English readers of Beza's preface to his *Abrahams sacrifice*, trans. A. Golding(?) in 1577, might have recognized a reference to Du Bellay and his friends in the complaint that some "intending to inrich our tongue, do powder it with Greeke and Latine tearmes" (sig. A3^v).

48 Julian Sharman, *The Library of Mary Queen of Scots* (London, 1889). She also had *L'Olive*. According to Brantôme Mary liked to read Du

Bellay; see his *Oeuvres complètes*, ed. L. Lalanne (Paris, 1864–82), VII, 406.

49   G. G. Smith, ed., *Elizabethan Critical Essays* (Oxford, 1904), I, 209 and notes.

50   Facsimile reproduction (Kent State University, Ohio, 1970), intro. Baxter Hathaway, pp. 122–23; *Deffence*, pp. 150–55. Smith, *Critical Essays*, II, 417, identifies Du Bellay as Puttenham's source, but the same anagrams are in Tabourot arranged in an order closer to that of the *Arte*. Dee's copy is mentioned by Frances Yates, *Theatre of the World* (Chicago, 1969), p. 12.

51   Du Bellay, *Deffence*, p. 14; Daniel, *Poems*, pp. 139, 135. The *Deffence* may lie behind some of Daniel's *Musophilus*; compare the speculation that "The treasure of our tongue" may "in time" enrich "unknowing Nations" with Du Bellay's more explicitly imperialist fancy that "Le tens viendra" when France and French will dominate the world (Daniel, *Poems*, p. 96; *Deffence*, pp. 27–28).

52   For the Somerset swans see the article on Sanford in the *DNB*. For the next few years those with an interest in European criticism seem to have ignored the *Deffence*. Much later, however, Thomas Rymer mentioned Du Bellay in a preface to Rapin's *Reflections* on Aristotle (1674); see *Critical Essays of the Seventeenth Century*, ed. J. E. Spingarn (1908–09; Bloomington, 1957), II, 167.

53   *Deffence*, pp. 74–83.

54   Whitney, *A choice of emblemes*, ed. Henry Green (first pub. London, 1866; reissued New York, 1967), p. 230.

55   Du Bellay, ed. Courbet, I, 514; the poem is an epitaph for a youth, adapted from Alciati. It says,

> Love and Death have changed each one's arms for the other's:
> So Love now bears a scythe, now bears Death a torch;
> Death now touches the mind, but Love now strikes the flesh:
> Thus do young men die, thus do old men dote.
> Love now strikes at the throat, but Death now blinds the eye.
> As Death now teaches to love, so Love now orders to die.
> Learn hence what mocking jests are found in human life:
> Death prepares the couch, but Love prepares the bier.
> You also, Nature, learn to pervert your very laws
> If thus the young men die and thus the old men dote.

For Whitney's version see *Choice*, pp. 132–33. Some permutations of the conceit are described by Joseph Fucilla, "De Morte et Amore," *PQ* 14 (1935), 97–104; he does not mention the versions treated in this chapter or the quotations from Du Bellay.

56 Francis Thynne, *Emblemes and Epigrames*, pub. for the Early English
    Text Soc., orig. ser. 64 (London, 1876), pp. 7–8. Henry Peacham,
    Minerva Britanna (Scolar Press Facsimile, Leeds, 1966), p. 172. There
    is a modern version by Kipling.
57 *The Anatomy of Melancholy*, Part III, Sect. 2, Memb. 3. I have not found
    the passage before the fifth ed. (1638).
58 Du Bellay, ed. Courbet, I, 458: "You gave to your book the name
    Trifles, my Paul— / In all the whole book the best title of all." H. H.
    Hudson points out Owen's source in *The Epigram in the English Renais-
    sance* (Princeton, 1947), p. 125.
59 Du Bellay, ed. Courbet, I, 477, 511:

    > The Thracian to Euridice would sing
    > And drew the stones, the trees, wild boars and bears.
    > But filled with your harsh din the woods now ring—
    > And frightened beasts take refuge in their lairs.

    > With silence I greeted the lover, with barking the thief;
    > And thus gave I joy to my master, and thus to his wife.

60 Sigs. W3–W4. Pasquier also praised Du Bellay in his *Jesuites catechisme*
    (1602), sig. F3; William Watson, the probable translator, gives the
    epithet "gallant" for Pasquier's "gentil."
61 Montaigne, trans. Florio, I, 255 ("Of the institution and education of
    Children"). There is a reference to him and "la pleiade" in Henri
    Estienne's *World of wonders* (1607; 1608 ed., sig. C6) and in Robert
    Tofte's *Honours academie* (1610), translated from Book V of Nicolas de
    Montreux's *Bergeries de Juliette* (1598), a suave lover tells his skeptical
    beloved that she is "farre more fairer then the Cassandra of great
    Ronsard, more chaste then the Oliva of Hunny, mother Bellay [*sic!*]
    and more perfect then, the Diana of courteous De Reports [*sic* for
    Desportes]" (sig. Ii2). As the printer warns the reader, Tofte's
    translation was hasty and unrevised.
62 Sigs. L2, Q1^V, R2^V. According to H. R. Plomer, "A Cavalier's Li-
    brary," *The Library* new ser. 5 (1904), 158–72, the distinguished
    doctor Sir Theodore de Mayerne wrote Viscount Conway in 1651
    thanking him for "Bellay's macaronic verses," but this is almost
    certainly an error for Belleau, whose macaronics were published that
    year in *L'Eschole de Salerne*. Thomas Bancroft's *Time's out of tune* (1658),
    sig. B7^V, refers to "Those Eulogies that did our Moor advance, / And
    learned Bellay in the Realm of France," but it is impossible from the
    context to know if he means eulogies by Joachim or eulogies about one
    of his cousins.

Collectors, even in the early eighteenth century, continued to buy Du Bellay's works. I have found records of sales in the catalogues of John Bridges (1725/26), who had the *Oeuvres*, *Poemata*, and translations from Virgil—the *Poemata* went for 6s 6d but the *Oeuvres françaises* for only about half that; William Dickenson (1719); John Dunton (1733), whose copy of the *Poemata* brought a mere 1s 6d. Years later the *Oeuvres* turns up in the catalogue of Joseph Spence and William Duncombe (1769); it cost 2s 6d.

63   Ronsard, in "Response aux injures et calomnies"; for Du Bartas's proudest claims see his "L'Uranie."

64   *The Selected Poems of George Daniel of Beswick*, ed. Thomas B. Stroup (Lexington, Ky., 1959), p. 11.

Chapter 3: Ronsard

1   On Ronsard's life Raymond Lebègue's *Ronsard* (Paris, 1966, 4th ed.) is short and useful. For the trips to Scotland see esp. Michel Dassonville, *Ronsard* (Geneva, 1968), I, 70–106.

2   Quotations in my text cite the *Oeuvres complètes*, ed. Paul Laumonier, completed by Isidore Silver and Raymond Lebègue (Paris, 1914–75, 20 vols.); they are indicated by "L." followed by the volume and page. See also Laumonier's *Tableau chronologique des oeuvres de Ronsard* (2nd ed., Paris, 1911; 1969).

3   Gustave Cohen, *Ronsard* (1924; Paris, 1956), p. 134; Isidore Silver, in a review of F. Desonay's *Ronsard poète de l'amour*, *Romanic Review* 45 (1954), 134–41.

4   André Gendre, *Ronsard: poète de la conquête amoureuse* (Neuchâtel, 1970), pp. 466–72; Donald Stone, *Ronsard's Sonnet Cycles* (New Haven, 1966), pp. 37–38. Brian J. Mallett, "Some Notes on the 'Sensuality' of Ronsard's *Amours de Cassandre*," *Kentucky Romance Quarterly* 19 (1972), 433–46, stresses the subjectivity of such responses. See also Henri Weber, *La création poétique* (Paris, 1956) and I. D. McFarlane's suggestive "Aspects of Ronsard's Poetic Vision," in *Ronsard the Poet*, ed. Terence Cave (London, 1973), pp. 13–78.

5   Cohen, p. 176.

6   For a similar comment see *Sonnets pour Helene*, ed. Malcom Smith (Geneva, 1970), p. 62.

7   Besides the articles mentioned below see Sidney Lee, *The French Renaissance in England* (Oxford, 1910); Alfred Upham, *The French Influence in English Literature* (New York, 1908); and Isidore Silver, "Ronsard in European Literature," *BHR* 16 (1954), 241–54.

8   Paul Laumonier, "Ronsard et l'Ecosse," *RLC* 4 (1924), 408–28.

9   Brantôme, *Oeuvres complètes*, ed. L. Lalanne (Paris, 1864–82), VII,

406. Crichton is quoted in Claude Binet's *Vie de Pierre de Ronsard*, ed. Laumonier (Paris, 1910), p. 177. The story of Mary's present, on pp. 28–29, was added in 1597.

Crichton, who lived in Paris, contributed to Ronsard's *Tombeau*; he tells how one urn contains the ashes of Homer, Virgil, Pindar, Hesiod, and Ovid—for in Ronsard they all had lived again. The *Tombeau* is printed with Ronsard's *Oeuvres*, ed. P. Blanchemain (Paris, 1855–67), VIII. Crichton was probably the author of an obscene Latin epigram on Elizabeth and those "who plow and pierce the English wolf," including Leicester prompt "in veneram," "membriosor" Hatton, and salacious Ralegh. See J. E. Phillips, *Images of a Queen* (Berkeley, 1964), pp. 146, 290. In his notes to Binet, p. 209, Laumonier quotes another Scot, Alexander Boyd, who called Ronsard a new star, chief of those he admired. Laumonier also says Ronsard was read abroad in "French schools," but cites little firm evidence.

10 Phillips, *Images*, explores this propaganda. Mary owned Ronsard's *Discours des miseres*, *Nues*, and an "Abridgement of the Art Poetik in Frenche"; see Julian Sharman, *The Library of Mary Queen of Scots* (London, 1889).

11 M. C. Smith, "Ronsard and Queen Elizabeth I," *BHR* 29 (1967), 93–119, describes Ronsard's motives.

12 S. P. 70/76, no. 817. The writing is hasty; "the redyng" could be "their redyng" and "Ronsarde" could be "Ronsards." The summary in the *Calendar of State Papers*, Foreign Series VII, 297, omits the pun on "news." Ronsard's poem is in L. XIII, 267–77.

13 S. P. 70/77, no. 908; "Le procés" is in L. XIII, 17–29.

14 S. P. 70/79, no. 1128; Smith, "Ronsard," gives a transcription.

15 Binet, p. 28, added in 1597. John Underhill, *Spanish Literature in the England of the Tudors* (New York, 1899), p. 234, says Smith and Chaloner corresponded about Ronsard, but I have not been able to confirm this.

16 J. A. van Dorsten, *The Radical Arts* (London, 1970), appends a text of *Troobles*, which he believes was published in 1567, although the title page says 1568.

17 J. B. Leishman, "Variations on a theme in Shakespeare's 'Sonnets,'" *Elizabethan and Jacobean Studies Presented to F. P. Wilson* (Oxford, 1959), 112–49. Sidney's editor William Ringler, however, is not sure he read Ronsard, and adds he may have been "guided more by his Protestant sympathies than by aesthetic considerations"; see *The Poems* (Oxford, 1962), p. xxxv. In *Poets, Patrons, and Professors* (Leyden, 1962), p. 120, though, van Dorsten remarks of Sidney and others "how singularly

unrelated politico–religious principles and literary friendships could be."

18 For Sidney's reaction see James Osborn, *Young Philip Sidney* (New Haven, 1972), pp. 215–27.

19 H. M. Richmond, "Ronsard and the English Renaissance," *Comparative Literature Studies* 7 (1970), 141–60.

20 Cohen, esp. pp. 269–70, 284; Laumonier, *Ronsard, poète lyrique* (Paris, 1932, 3rd ed.), p. 205; Lebègue, pp. 152–55. Mark Whitney, *Critical Reactions and the Christian Element in the Poetry of Pierre de Ronsard* (Chapel Hill, 1971), outlines the discussion. A complicating factor is Ronsard's own shifts on issues like the Creation; see Isidore Silver, "Ronsard's Reflections on Cosmogony and Nature," *PMLA* 79 (1964), 219–33, although I am not sure Ronsard (or his English readers) would have thought his lines clearly opposed to Scripture.

21 Marc-René Jung, *Hercule dans la littérature française du XVIe siècle* (Geneva, 1966), p. 125. There are similar remarks in Albert Py's *Ronsard* (Paris, 1972).

22 These and other attacks are reprinted in F. Charbonnier, *Pamphlets protestants contre Ronsard, 1560–1577* (Paris, 1923).

23 Van Dorsten speculates on Jeney's motives in *Arts*, ch. 7; my quotations are from his text of *Troobles*. The stationers' register describes a search on Feb. 21, 1569, for John Stow's unlawful books, including "A Discourse of the trow[b]les in Ffrance in print, translated by Thomas Jeney gent Dedicate[d] to the Ffrench quene." Perhaps the dedication misled the authorities into thinking the book Catholic. Phillips, *Images*, pp. 34–37, describes his earlier pamphlet.

24 For the Latin see van Dorsten, *Arts*. In fact, Ronsard's style in the *Discours* is less Parnassian, more oratorical and popular; see Francis Higman, "Ronsard's political and polemical poetry," *Ronsard the Poet*, pp. 241–85.

25 Phillips, *Images*, pp. 71–73. Barnaud had the aid, perhaps, of other writers.

26 Phillips, *Images*, p. 73.

27 Sig. B6^v; L. XVI, 150–51. Jacques Ferrand, too, quotes the *Franciade* in his *Erotomania*, trans. E. Chilmead in 1640, and credits Ronsard.

28 See J. E. Phillips, "Daniel Rogers: A Neo-Latin Link Between the Pléiade and Sidney's 'Areopagus,'" *Neo-Latin Poetry of the Sixteenth and Seventeenth Centuries* (William Andrews Clark Memorial Library, University of California, 1965), pp. 5–28, and F. J. Levy, "Daniel Rogers as Antiquary," *BHR* 27 (1965), 444–62, who mentions the poems to Ronsard.

29   In Dronysiacis nuper victoria campis,
      Ad fortes quod se flexerit Huguenothos,
    Qui pauci numero, pugna campoque positi
      Militis innumeri sustinuere manum,
    Mirari Ronsarde soles: haecque anxia mentem
      Cura nam pariter detinet atque dolet.
    Scilicet ignoras, (a quo victoria pendet)
      Quod Deus Huguenotis ex pietate favet.

From a manuscript of Rogers's poetry (HM 31188) now in the Huntington Library, San Marino, California; I quote this and other poems from the MS with the kind permission of the Library. I have worked from a microfilm copy provided to Columbia University by the Marquess of Hertford, to whom the MS belonged until recently. This epigram is on f. 99a. The epigrams were mostly written in the 1560s and 1570s so far as I can tell. The anonymous Huguenot poem is reprinted in Charbonnier, p. 223. In fact the battle of Dreux went badly for the Huguenots.

30   Ronsarde Aoniae magister artis
    O princeps patriae lyrae arbiterque,
    Cui Phoebi varios modos poeta
    Dircaeo melius canis poeta:
    Hos aequo capias favore versus
    Non aequo pede quos Thalia mittit,
    Et vultu inspicias peto benigno
    Amor scribere quae iubet benignus.
    Virtutis cupidus tuae Rogerus
    Iam pridem celebri perenniclari
    Fama nominis excitatus, ardet
    Sic Ronsarde tui poeta amore
    Nil illi potius sit, aut prius quid
    Notos quam queat ut tibi esse, teque
    Observet propius, tuam et medullis
    Virtutem hauriat ebriosus imis.
    Hanc ergo referat vicem precatur,
    Eius tyro chori esse possit unus
    Cui tu ceu clarius praeis Apollo.
    Sic Musae faveant tuo furori
    Sic sacro foveant suo liquore
    Divinae fluvium tuae perennem
    Venae, sint faciles tibi et vocanti.
    Ronsarde Aeoniae magister artis
    O princeps patriae lyrae arbiterque.   [fol. 294b]

31   O quae lux adeo mihi benigna
      Fulsit, sorte adeo mihi benigna,
      Nuper, quum peterem tuos Baifi
      Penates, legeres mihi tuae quum
      Musae delicias venustiores.
      Sic me crede tuis inebriasti
      Doctis illecebris leporibusque
      Abundas adeò quibus venustis,
      Curae ut sollicitae anxii et timores
      Queis vestrae modò Galliae ob tumultus
      Turbatae implicor et malè et malignè,
      Confestim fugerent meosque sensus
      Non iam conficerent malè aut malignè.
      Hùc accessit et id boni videre
      Possem tempore quod beatus uno,
      Ronsardi faciem sacram poetae,
      Poetae illius illius poetae,
      Phoebus plus oculis suis amat quem ...
      Illum dùm video audio tuasque
      Cantantem lepido sono camoenas
      Conscriptas lepido stylo camoenas.
      Phoebum credo vagum tuis camoenis
      Perculsum lepidis polo relicto
      Descendisse tuas, Baifi in aedes.
                                              [fols. 291a–291b]
      "Poetae illius illius poetae" recalls Catullus's brutal poem to "Lesbia
      illa, / Illa Lesbia" (*Carmina* LVIII), but it is hard to believe Rogers
      meant his echo as the ironic modification a modern poet might
      intend.

32   *The Works of Edmund Spenser*, ed. Edwin Greenlaw, C. G. Osgood,
      R. M. Padelford, et al. (Baltimore, 1932–49), IX, 6, 442.

33   Phillips, "Rogers," esp. pp. 24–27, and Gerald Snare, "The Muses on
      Poetry: Spenser's *The Tears of the Muses*," *Tulane Studies in English* 17
      (1969), 31–52. On friendships see also J. A. van Dorsten, *Poets*. In one
      letter to Rogers in 1575, quoted p. 203, Dousa thanks him for Ron-
      sard's *Franciade* and Belleau's pastorals. It may also be significant, in
      view of Spenser's interests, that Rogers was intrigued by numbers; he
      writes in an epigram reprinted by H. H. Hudson in *The Epigram in the
      English Renaissance* (1947; New York, 1966), p. 136, that Salisbury
      Cathedral has 365 windows, a pillar for each hour of the year, and 12
      doors.

34   Spenser, IX, 462. The graces, of course, were a major Neoplatonic

symbol. Harvey's "Non multis dormio" adapts a proverb used, for instance, in Cicero's letter to Gallus (and in a later one to Atticus); Cicero asserts his canny independence, saying "Cipius opinor, olim: 'Non omnibus dormio.' Sic ego non omnibus, mi Galle, servio." From *M. Tulli Ciceronis Epistulae*, ed. L. C. Purser (1901; Oxford, 1957), I, Book VII, xxiv. "Non omnibus dormio" was the punchline to a story about a husband who "slept" while rich suitors courted his wife but "woke up" with a shout of "I'm not asleep to everybody" when a slave tried to steal his wine. The anecdote is funny but implies discrimination.

35 Et vos grandiloqui vates, tragiciqúe Poëtae,
    Qui Ligerim incolitis, Rhodanumque, Araremqué, et Iberum
    Et Rhenum, et Tamesim, et quotquot floretis ubique
    Carmine foelices; quorum Ronsardus in albo
    Obtinuit primas.

    [sig. C1]

36 Harvey, *Marginalia*, ed. G. C. Moore Smith (Stratford-upon-Avon, 1913), pp. 161–62. A reference to Du Bartas's *Premiere sepmaine* gives a *terminus a quo* of 1578. On his books see Virginia Stern, "The *Bibliotheca* of Gabriel Harvey," *RenQ* 25 (1972), 1–62. I refer to "inner workings" but "upper" might be better—where we tend to go "in" or "down" to the subconscious, Ground of Being, or subatomic "level," Renaissance poets tended to rise.

37 . . . linguae Ciceronis flumina tanta
    Ausoniae Arpinum celebrat, Ronzardus honori est
    Natalique solo, cultae Italiaeque Petrarcha.

    [sig. D4^v]

    In his edition of Willes's *De re poetica* (Oxford, 1958) A. D. S. Fowler speculates that he was Spenser's shepherd "Willey"; if so, he provided yet another link between Spenser and French poetry.

38 *Critical Essays of the Seventeenth Century*, ed. J. E. Spingarn (1908–1909; Bloomington, 1957), I, 141–79. He exaggerates Desportes's depth. Reynolds's views on myth may seem reductive (it is disappointing to read that the powerfully archetypal story of Persephone is merely about human agriculture) but for him his "scientific" interpretations are mystic and exciting.

39 *The Library of Drummond of Hawthornden*, ed. Robert MacDonald (Edinburgh, 1971). An appendix gives Drummond's notes on "Books red be me." Also in his library was a "Ronsardi vita," possibly Binet's. L. E. Kastner's edition of Drummond's *Poetical Works* (Manchester, 1913) includes material on his sources.

40 Drummond, II, 37–47; L. VIII, 246–54.

41 Spingarn, *Critical Essays*, I, 216 (he means the poems on Marie). Drummond, *Works*, ed. Bishop Sage and Thomas Ruddiman (Edinburgh, 1711), pp. 143, 115, 230; L. XVII, 67–68.

42 Drummond, II, 268. Ronsard was well known in Scotland. The king himself borrowed from his criticism; see R. D. S. Jack, "James VI and Renaissance Poetic Theory," *English* 16 (1967), 208–11, and G. G. Smith's notes to the *Schort Treatise* in *Elizabethan Critical Essays* (Oxford, 1904). Alexander Montgomerie was Ronsard's ablest imitator; of his seven or so adaptations the best paraphrases with even greater sensuosity a lyric to Marie (L. VII, 287) on how

> So suete a kis ʒistrene fra thee I reft,
>   In bouing doun thy body on the bed,
>   That evin my lyfe within thy lippis I left;
>   Sensyne from thee my spirits wald never shed.

See his *Poems*, ed. J. Cranstoun (Edinburgh, 1885–87; S. T. S. 1st ser. IX, X, XI), p. 109, and the supplementary volume ed. George Stevenson (Edinburgh, 1910; S. T. S. 1st ser. LIX). William Alexander's youthful poems to "Aurora" recall Ronsard; see the notes to his *Poetical Works*, ed. L. E. Kastner and H. B. Charlton (Edinburgh, 1929; S. T. S. 2nd ser. XXIV). Alexander Craig borrowed some of his odd *Amorose songes* (1606), addressed to a whole spectrum of ladies from Idea to Lais (thus differentiating the mixed love felt by an Astrophil into its constituent parts). Jack, "The Poetry of Alexander Craig," *Forum for Modern Language Studies* 5 (1969), 377–84, finds the poems to the shepherdess Kala like those to Marie, and one to "grave Lithocardia" on Cupid's fishing trip ("Love set his Bow") also seems to me like Ronsard (L. VII, 181); see Craig's *Poetical Works*, introd. David Laing (1873; New York, 1966), p. 28. None of these writers, however, referred to Ronsard or seems to have thought him a *vates*.

43 Julien Tiersot, *Ronsard et la musique de son temps* (Paris, 1903?), p. 66; E. H. Fellowes, *English Madrigal Verse* (3rd ed., Oxford, 1967, revised F. W. Sternfeld and David Greer), p. 744.

44 Thomas Watson, *The Hekatompathia*, introd. S. K. Heninger (Gainesville, 1964). The Latin is on p. 12 and Heninger provides a translation on pp. xii–xiii. He thinks Watson probably wrote his own notes.

45 Grahame Castor, "The Theme of Illusion in Ronsard's *Sonets pour Helene* and in the Variants of the 1552 *Amours*," *Forum for Modern Language Studies* 7 (1971), 361–73, traces Ronsard's treatment of erotic fantasy; Gendre, *Ronsard*, explores its literary advantages.

46 For his fifty-fourth passion Watson "imitateth here and there a verse of Ronsardes, in a certaine Elegie to Janet Peintre du Roy" (L. VI, 152).

47 Sig. A4ᵛ. Cf. "A Caliope," L. I, 174–79: "Si des mon enfance / Le premier de France / J'ai pindarizé." Robert Shafer, *The English Ode to 1660* (Princeton, 1918) discusses Soowthern, pp. 44ff.

48 George Puttenham, *The arte of English poesie*, introd. Baxter Hathaway (Kent State University, Ohio, 1970), pp. 259–60. Puttenham also seems to have read Ronsard's criticism, as had George Gascoigne for his *Certayne notes of instruction* (1575). See Smith, *Elizabethan Critical Essays*, II, 75, 415 and I, 359–61.

49 L. IV, 23–24. I give a later version, for that was the source of Lodge's poem quoted below. I am not sure which version Gorges used. See his *Poems*, ed. H. E. Sandison (Oxford, 1953), pp. 55–56. "Erect thy flighte" closely resembles Ronsard's sonnet to Cassandre, "Haulse ton aiṣle" (L. IV, 104–5).

50 On Spenser and Ronsard see A. W. Satterthwaite, *Spenser, Ronsard, and Du Bellay* (Princeton, 1960). The variorum edition cites many parallels. Besides the more obvious similarities such as a love for mythological figures inhabiting a countryside at once mysterious and familiarly local, one feels in both poets an impulse toward inner-ness—the center of a circle, the cave, the well, the grove. Ronsard's ode to L'Hospital shares with Spenser's Garden of Adonis a sense of the occult sources of the world's abundance: the young muses are led down to a fountain-filled ocean palace to see the vessels in which are enclosed "Les semences de toutes choses" (L. III, 126).

51 L. VII, 259–62. See Leo Spitzer, "Spenser, *Shepheardes Calendar, March*," *SP* 47 (1950), 494–505, and D. C. Allen, "Three Poems on Eros," *CL* 8 (1956), 177–93. Spenser must have used an early edition, for he refers to Cupid's peacock feathers, a detail Ronsard dropped after 1560. Spenser's Anacreontic poem on Cupid, published with the *Amoretti*, resembles "Le petit enfant Amour" (L. VII, 106–7), but there were many versions of this little story of Love's misadventure. In his edition of *Helene* Smith finds some parallels with the *Amoretti*; "Je ne veux comparer tes beautez à la Lune" does seem similar to "Long-while I sought to what I might compare" (no. IX).

52 T. P. Harrison, "Spenser, Ronsard, and Bion," *MLN* 49 (1934), 139–45, and Peter Bondanella and Julia Conaway, "Two Kinds of Renaissance Love: Spenser's 'Astrophel' and Ronsard's 'Adonis,'" *ES* 52 (1971), 311–18, which well points out differences in tone but, I think, neglects the deeper suggestions of Ronsard's mythology. For another comparison of feminine infidelity with the receptivity of

lasting matter to temporary forms see Du Bartas's *Premiere sepmaine*, "second jour."

53 *Poems*, ed. Ringler, pp. 166–67. A. W. Osborn, *Sir Philip Sidney en France* (Paris, 1932), p. 49, suggests that old King Basilius in the *Arcadia* borrows from a sonnet to Hélène the argument that dry wood burns better than green, but Laumonier cites a similar thought in Petrarch.

54 L. IV, 35–36; Fletcher, *English Works*, ed. Lloyd E. Berry (Madison, Wisc., 1964), p. 109. *Licia* seems to play with numbers. Fifty-two sonnets followed by 7 poems of which the last is in 12 stanzas hint at a game with days, weeks, and months. Indeed, he says in sonnet XXXII, "Yeares, months, daies, houres, in sighes I sadlie spend." Fletcher had told Licia he was building her a "temple"; perhaps, like Daniel Rogers, he knew about Salisbury Cathedral's reputation as frozen numerology. In any case such patterning symptomizes a sensibility that despite its lightheartedness might have been drawn to the more vatic aspects of Ronsard.

55 See Marion Grubb, "Lodge's Borrowing from Ronsard," *MLN* 45 (1930), pp. 357–60. Ronsard's poems are in L. IV, 152–53 (itself from Horace) and L. II, 1–5. On Lodge's other sources see *Elizabethan Sonnets*, ed. Sidney Lee (Westminster, 1904), I, introduction; Janet Espiner-Scott, *Les sonnets élisabéthains* (Paris, 1929); and N. Burton Paradise, *Thomas Lodge* (New Haven, 1931).

56 Lodge, *Complete Works*, ed. Edmund Gosse (1883; New York, 1963), II, 51. Lodge's word "lappe" and other details show he worked from an edition of Ronsard after 1552 but before 1584. The other borrowings in *Phillis* are no. 9 (from "De ses cheveulx," L. IV, 79), no. 30 (from "Je parangonne," L. IV, 102), no. 31 (from "Franc de raison," L. IV, 89–90), no. 32 (from "Cent et cent foys," L. IV, 25–26), no. 33 (from "Quand au premier," L. IV, 35–36), and no. 35 (from "J'espere et crain," L. IV, 16).

57 Lodge, II, 19; Ronsard, L. VI, 199. Some details show Lodge may have used both the *Meslanges* and a later edition of the *Oeuvres*.

58 Lodge, II, 22–23.

59 See, for instance, Sidney Lee on Lyly in *Renaissance*, p. 218; C. S. Lewis on Barnes in *English Literature in the Sixteenth Century* (Oxford, 1954), p. 495; and Douglas Bush, "Notes on Shakespeare's Classical Mythology," *PQ* 6 (1927), 295–302. H. M. Richmond's "'To be or not to be' and the *Hymne de la Mort*," *Shakespeare Quarterly* 13 (1962), 317–20, and his "Ronsard and the English Renaissance" both note some interesting verbal parallels (e.g. "sea of troubles" and "mer des ennuis"). Richmond probably exaggerates both the hymn's popu-

larity in England and its conventional character. (Although doubt-less some Scots were impressed or puzzled when Mary Stuart's would-be lover Chastelard read it on the scaffold just before his death; see Brantôme, VII, 451–53.)

60   *Works*, ed. J. W. Hebel (Oxford, 1931–41; 1961), II, 349; see also Anthony LaBranche, "The 'Twofold Vitality' of Drayton's *Odes*," *CL* 15 (1963), 116–29.

61   The flea is in L. XVII, 302-3; Smith's *Helene* cites the parallel (flea poems were not uncommon, but these two seem especially similar). "Foudroye moi le cors" was first published in the *Meslanges* and withdrawn in 1584. The poem to Marie is in L. X, 238–44. These two parallels (if not always my examples) are suggested by H. M. Richmond, "Donne and Ronsard," *NQ* 203, new ser. V (1958), 534–36, and "Ronsard and the English Renaissance." He cites others I find less compelling but I am sure he is right to stress the importance of Ronsard's tone of voice.

62   Evelyn M. Simpson prints the passage in "More Manuscripts of Donne's *Paradoxes and Problems*," *RES* 10 (1934), 288–300, 412–16. On its significance see Clayton D. Lein, "Donne and Ronsard," *NQ* 219, new ser. XXI (1974), 90–92.

63   "Si la beauté se perd," L. XVII, 313–14; Thomas Carew, *Poems*, ed. Rhodes Dunlap (Oxford, 1949), p. 16. The notes cite other resemblances.

64   L. II, 33–35; Thomas Stanley, *Poems and Translations*, ed. G. M. Crump (Oxford, 1962), pp. 49–50. See Mario Praz, "Stanley, Sherburne and Ayres as Translators and Imitators of Italian, Span-ish and French Poets," *MLR* 20 (1925), 280–94.

65   *Complete Poems*, ed. David Vieth (New Haven, 1968), pp. 52–53 ("Vulcan, contrive me such a cup") and L. V, 80. Ronsard's poem ("Du grand Turc") combines two lyrics from the Anthology linked in the edition he used; Rochester adapts the second only.

66   L. XII, 284–92 and I, 243 ("Donque, forest," revised as "Couché sous tes umbrages vers"). Richmond discusses these parallels and others I find less convincing in "Ronsard and the English Renais-sance." I also disagree that Marvell's use of the after all familiar concept of nature as a "source of divine revelation" is more daring than Ronsard's. On Ronsard and Milton's "L'Allegro" and "Il Penseroso" see Richmond, "'Rural Lyricism': A Renaissance Muta-tion of the Pastoral," *CL* 16 (1964), 193–210.

67   *The Works of William Fowler*, ed. H. W. Meikle (Edinburgh, 1914; S. T. S. 2nd ser. VI), p. 19.

68   Sylvester, *Complete Works*, ed. A. B. Grosart (1880; Hildesheim,

1969), I, 144. In 1596, it may be remembered, Simon Harward referred to Ronsard as "eruditissimus" in the preface to his *Encheiridion* (sig. A3ᵛ).

69   Browne, *Works*, ed. W. C. Hazlitt (1868–69), I, 192.

70   Sigs. G3ᵛ–G4ᵛ. Hakewill might have read Pasquier's epigram in the 1587 edition of Ronsard; Pithou's epitaph was published in the *Tombeau* (Ronsard, ed. Blanchemain, VIII, 252).

71   Quoted in Jonson's *Works*, ed. C. H. Herford and Percy Simpson (Oxford, 1925–52), XI, 332–33.

72   Sig. Qqqqq4ᵛ. The poem, by J. Héroard, says "Traveler beware, this is sacred soil; depart, the earth you tread is holy, for Ronsard lies here, with whose rising the muses wished to rise and with whom fallen they wish to be buried. Let those who come next not envy this nor posterity hope an equal destiny." See Pierre Dufay, *Le portrait, le buste et l'épitaphe de Ronsard* (Paris, 1907).

73   Sigs. Ff5ᵛ–Ff6ᵛ. Saltonstall says Anacreon was born in La Perche and was called the "Remigium Bellaquium" of his age, either an unusually ignorant statement or a subtle compliment.

74   *The Diary of John Evelyn*, ed. E. S. de Beer (Oxford, 1955), II, 147. Evelyn may confuse the chapel at Plessis with the nearby priory of St. Cosme, which he also visited.

75   Jonson, *Works*, VIII, 181–82; Drummond's notes are in I, 134 (for his own opinion of the *Amours* see above, p. 99). For Jonson's library see I, 250–71 and XI, 593–603. His "plain style" did not stop him from adopting postures and tones quite like those of Ronsard's early odes (e.g. "Arise Invention, / Wake, and put on the wings of Pindars Muse," VIII, 176). Because of his presumed ignorance of French, Herford and Simpson doubt he used Ronsard as a model but the evidence for that ignorance is not wholly firm.

76   Sigs. F2–F3. Upham, p. 124, and Lee, *Renaissance*, p. 212, say the poem parodies a song in Lodge's *Rosalynde* (1590; "Phoebe sate / Sweete she sate / Sweete sate Phoebe when I saw her," *Works*, I, 48–49). Either the author saw the poem in manuscript or he worked fast.

77   *The Three Parnassus Plays*, ed. J. B. Leishman (London, 1949); I *Return*, IV, i.

78   II *Return*, III, iii.

79   Howell, *Epistolae Ho-elianae*, ed. Joseph Jacobs (London, 1892), II, 591–92. Similar remarks appear in his *Lexicon* (1660).

80   Charles Maupas, *A french grammar and syntaxe*, trans, W. Aufield (1634), sig. C5.

81   *The choyce letters of Jean Louis Guez Sieur de Balzac* (1658), sigs. L8,

M1–M1ᵛ. Balzac, however, quotes the ode to M. L'Hospital with no visible discomfort in a letter on March 2, 1645.

82 "Of Poetry," in *Critical Essays*, ed. Spingarn, III, 98–99; *The Critical Works of Thomas Rymer*, ed. C. A. Zimansky (New Haven, 1956), p. 79. Another indication of Ronsard's reputation in the late seventeenth century may be deduced from the substitutions Dryden made in revising William Soame's translation of Boileau. For Ronsard, who Boileau says muddled French verse "en français parlant grec et latin," Dryden puts Davenant (for Marot, whom Boileau liked, Dryden has Spenser). See his *Poems*, ed. James Kinsley (Oxford, 1958), I, 334–35 and IV, 1943.

83 Of the eighteen or so catalogues I have seen for the late seventeenth and the first half of the eighteenth centuries Ronsard appears in two: those of Elijah Fenton (1730/31) and Thomas Coke (1687–1759), who added the poetry of Ronsard, Marot, and Jamyn to the library he inherited from Sir Edward Coke; see C. W. James, "Some Notes on the Library of Printed Books at Holkham," *Library*, 4th ser. XI (1931), 435–60.

84 *The Poems of Alexander Pope*, general ed. John Butt (London, 1963, 3rd ed.), V (ed. James Sutherland), 339–40; *The Works of Alexander Pope* (London, 1797; 1806 ed.), VII, 96, and VI, 231.

CHAPTER 4: DESPORTES

1 Jacques Lavaud, *Un poète de cour au temps des derniers Valois, Philippe Desportes* (Paris, 1936), pp. 428–29. On Desportes's bibliography see Lavaud and also Victor E. Graham, "Supplément à la bibliographie des oeuvres de Desportes," *BHR* 19 (1957), 485–88.

2 *Oeuvres de Philippe Desportes*, ed. Alfred Michiels (Paris, 1858), pp. 491–92.

3 Michel Jeanneret, *Poésie et tradition biblique au XVIᵉ siècle* (Paris, 1969), discusses Desportes's psalms.

4 The poems are printed with *Diverses amours et autres oeuvres meslées*, ed. Victor Graham (Paris, 1963). Unless indicated otherwise my references to Desportes's poetry cite Graham's edition (5 vols. in 6, 1958–63); my arabic numerals cite the page, roman numerals the sonnet number. Graham omits the imitations of Ariosto, the religious poetry, and some minor poems.

5 Philippe Desportes, *Les imitations de l' Arioste*, ed. Jacques Lavaud (Paris, 1936), which also includes his unpublished and uncollected verse.

6 Helmut Hatzfeld, "The Style of Philippe Desportes," *Symposium* 7 (1953), 262–73, says Desportes is often ironic and parodic, which may

be too charitable. Robert M. Burgess, "Mannerism in Philippe Desportes," *L'Esprit createur* 6 (1966), 270–81, argues for some variety in Desportes's "manner," but the poems in which Burgess finds a new style were not much imitated in England.

7   *Diane* II, 306: "Pédanterie, en parlant aux femmes." Graham prints Malherbe's comments as footnotes.

8   Lavaud, p. 376.

9   On Desportes in England see A. H. Upham, *The French Influence in English Literature* (New York, 1908); Sidney Lee, *The French Renaissance in England* (Oxford, 1910), and his Introduction to *Elizabethan Sonnets* (Westminster, 1904); Janet Espiner-Scott, *Les sonnets élisabéthains* (Paris, 1929); and L. E. Kastner, "The Elizabethan Sonneteers and the French Poets," *MLR* 3 (1907/8), 268–77.

10 *Poems*, ed. H. E. Sandison (Oxford, 1953), no. 1. The notes cite Gorges's sources. I think he worked from an edition of 1577 or a little later, so in quoting the French I will use the earlier variants.

11 No. 10, on the dream, is from *Diane* II, "Songe," pp. 239–40; no. 16, on reputation, is from a sonnet now in *Diverses amours*, pp. 25–26, first published with the poems to Diane. Nos. 32 and 22, which include passages on mutability, are from a "Chanson" in *Hippolyte*, pp. 59–63, and the "Rymes tierces" in *Diane* I, 184–86.

12 My references to Lodge cite his *Complete Works*, ed. E. Gosse (1883, reissued New York, 1963); most of his debts to Desportes were pointed out by Kastner, "Thomas Lodge as an Imitator of the French Poets," *Athenaeum*, Oct. 22, 1904, pp. 552–53.

13 *Phillis* (1593), in *Works*, II, nos. 2 and 10.

14 *Works*, I, 44. The French reads,

> Si je me siez à l'ombre, aussi soudainement
> Amour, laissant son arc, s'assied et se repose;
> Si je pense à des vers, je le voy qui compose;
> Si je plains mes douleurs, il se plaint hautement.
>
> [*Diane* II, iii]

"Most happie blest the man" (I, 34–36) is from the "Bergeries" in *Diverses amours*, as is "Wearie am I."

15 *Works*, I, 74–75, 101, 109, 117–18. The conceit and first stanza of another lyric, "First shall the heavens," derive from *Diane* II, lxviii.

16 *Works*, II, 55. Two other poems to Phillis are from Desportes. No. 37, on tears as alchemical distillations, is from *Diane* I, xlix; no. 36, from *Diane* II, iii, is the same sonnet on Cupid's omnipresence printed with *Scillaes metamorphosis* and revised for *Rosalynde*.

17 J. W. Lever, *The Elizabethan Love Sonnet* (1956; London, 1966), p. 150.

See also Joan Rees, *Samuel Daniel* (Liverpool, 1964) and Pierre Spriet, *Samuel Daniel* (Paris, 1968).

18   Samuel Daniel, *Poems and A Defence of Ryme*, ed. Arthur C. Sprague (Chicago, 1965, first pub. 1930). For these lines see *Delia*, nos. 42 and 4.

19   *Delia* 9 is from "Si c'est aimer" (*Diane* I, xxix) and no. 15 probably from *Diane* I, viii. No. 35 may be compared with "Pour mettre devant un Pétrarque" in *Diverses amours* and no. 49 with *Cléonice* lviii.

20   Henry Constable, *Poems*, ed. Joan Grundy (Liverpool, 1960), p. 131. Grundy says, p. 76, that Constable's affinities are with the "less lyrical, more drily intellectual sonneteers"; his fidelity to Desportes, "unmodified by any influence from the Pléiade, makes him in some ways Desportes' purest English imitator."

21   Constable, p. 208. "I Doe not now complaine," p. 198, seems based on *Diane* I, xxviii; "To live in hell," pp. 203–4, more or less follows the structure and conceit of *Diane* I, xxix; "Unhappy day" paraphrases *Diane* I, xlvii. Because of these poems Constable's debt to Desportes has sometimes been exaggerated.

22   See L. E. Kastner, "Spenser's 'Amoretti' and Desportes," *MLR* 4 (1908), 65–69 and the notes in the variorum edition of Spenser, ed. E. Greenlaw, C. G. Osgood, F. M. Padelford, et al. (Baltimore, 1932–49), VIII.

23   Sidney Lee, who does not reprint the sequence, identifies Emaricdulfe as Marie Cufeld anagrammed (*Elizabethan Sonnets* I, cv).

24   Janet Espiner-Scott, "Encore un imitateur de Desportes," *RLC* 5 (1925), 471–73, specifically notes the debts to the "Procez contre amour" in *Diane* I. The 1595 edition is not in the STC. See *Some Longer Elizabethan Poems*, ed. A. H. Bullen (New York, 1964), p. 320.

25   Joshua Sylvester, *Complete Works*, ed. A. B. Grosart (1880; Hildesheim, 1969), I, 11.

26   Sylvester, II, 324. "Looke crueller" is from *Hyppolyte* lxxvii and "Love, doe thy worst" from *Hippolyte* ix. Perhaps Elizabeth herself had read Desportes; see her "I grieve" in *Poems*, ed. Leicester Bradner (Providence, 1964), p. 5, and compare with *Hippolyte* ii and *Diane* II, xix.

27   *Poems*, ed. Agnes Latham (Cambridge, Mass., 1951; reissued 1962), pp. 11–12 and notes. For the anonymous poem in fourteeners see *The Phoenix Nest*, ed. H. R. Rollins (Cambridge, Mass., 1931), p. 171.

28   *Brittons Bowre of Delights*, ed. H. R. Rollins (New York, 1968; first pub. 1933), p. 21. On Lyly see Ernst G. Mathews, "Gil Polo, Desportes, and Lyly's 'Cupid and my Campaspe,'" *MLN* 56 (1941), 606–7.

29   *Bowre*, p. 47 and notes. Rollins's notes to the *Bowre* and *The Phoenix Nest* cite other traces of Desportes here and in other collections. William Alabaster, too, may have been reading Desportes in the 1590s, for in a sonnet he asks Christ to write on his soul with the quill of His passion and the ink of His blood, much as Desportes had told his Savior "D'un de tes cloux je veux faire ma plume, / Mon encre de ton sang" (*Oeuvres*, ed. Michiels, p. 503). But he may have found this striking conceit in Vittoria Colonna. See John W. Dickinson, "Vittoria Colonna, Philippe Desportes and William Alabaster," *RLC* 35 (1961), 112–14. Edward Benlowes uses the same image in *Theophila* (1652), sig. F5ᵛ.

30   E. H. Fellowes, *English Madrigal Verse* (3rd ed., Oxford, 1967, revised F. W. Sternfeld and David Greer), p. 305. A lyric set by Morley, pp. 136–37, recalls Desportes's anticipations of Hell.

31   During the same decades of his popularity in England Desportes was read in Scotland. See L. E. Kastner, "Scottish Sonneteers and the French Poets," *MLR* 3 (1907), 1–15, and R. D. S. Jack, "Imitation in the Scottish Sonnet," *CL* 20 (1968), 313–28 (which cites some parallels I find dubious). On Stewart, who made a splendid translation of "Ceste fontaine est froide" from *Diverses amours*, see G. A. Dunlop, "John Stewart of Baldynneis, The Scottish Desportes," *Scottish Historical Review* 12 (1914/15), 303–10, and M. P. McDiarmid, "Notes on the poems of John Stewart of Baldynneis," *RES* 24 (1948), 12–18. William Fowler borrowed a conceit or two; see the discussion of his sources in *Works*, ed. H. W. Meikle (Edinburgh, 1914, S. T. S. 2nd ser. VI).

   William Alexander imitated rather than translated him, and even when probably indebted has an energy quite his own—when his lady comes to "cure" him in a dream she says "I am the Eccho that your sighs resounds, / Your woes are mine, I suffer in your wounds"; see his *Works*, ed. L. E. Kastner and H. B. Charlton (Manchester, 1929, S. T. S. 2nd ser. XIV), II, 486. William Drummond owned the *Premières oeuvres* as well as a *Roland furieux* and *Quelques prieres et meditations chrestiennes*, probably by Desportes. If in several poems Drummond was thinking of Desportes, as his editor supposes, then what usually interested him was not a conceit's content but its diagram or outline, its logical structure. See *The Library of Drummond of Hawthornden*, ed. Robert MacDonald (Edinburgh, 1971), and L. E. Kastner's notes to the *Poetical Works* (Manchester, 1913).

32   *The Poems of Thomas Carew*, ed. Rhodes Dunlap (Oxford, 1949), p. 41. Desportes's source was Tebaldeo, but since some of Carew's other poems echo Desportes it seems likely he found his conceit in *Hippolyte*.

See Dunlap's notes to "My mistress commanding me to returne her letters" and "To the Painter."

33 *Imitations*, p. 162; *The Works of Sir John Suckling*, ed. Thomas Clayton and L. A. Beaurline (Oxford, 1971), I, 54–55. See also "Suckling and Desportes," an exchange between H. E. Berthon and L. E. Kastner in *MLR* 6 (1911), 221–24. Neither Berthon nor Kastner was sure the French poem is by Desportes, although it was credited to him when first printed in *Le Parnasse des plus excellens poètes de ce temps* (1607). Lavaud has no doubts as to its authenticity.

34 In *The Works of the English Poets*, ed. Alexander Chalmers (Vol. VI, London, 1810), 722.

35 John Eliot, *Ortho-epia Gallica* (1593), sig. B1. *The Works of Michael Drayton*, ed. William Hebel (1931–41; Oxford, 1961), I, 96.

36 See Davison's *Poetical Rhapsody*, ed. A. H. Bullen (London, 1890–91), I, 1. H. Reynolds, *Mythomystes* (1633?) in *Critical Essays of the Seventeenth Century*, ed. J. E. Spingarn (1908–9; Bloomington, Ind., 1957), I, 146. Howell, sig. C11.

37 *Apollo shroving: composed for the Schollars of the Free-schoole of Hadleigh in Suffolke for Shrove-Tuesday* (1627), sig. F5ᵛ, said by a diligent student to a flighty friend.

CHAPTER 5: DU BARTAS

1 See his *Pierces supererogation* (1593) in *Elizabethan Critical Essays*, ed. G. G. Smith (Oxford, 1904), II, 265–66; Harvey's copy of John Eliot's *Ortho-epia Gallica* (1593) filmed for University Microfilms, sig. H1; Caroline Brown Bourland, "Gabriel Harvey and the Modern Languages," *HLQ* 4 (1940/41), 85–106; and the *Marginalia*, ed. G. C. Moore Smith (Stratford-upon-Avon, 1913), p. 115.

2 *English Literature in the Earlier Seventeenth Century* (Oxford, 1945), p. 73.

3 *Crowell's Handbook of Elizabethan and Stuart Literature*, ed. James E. Ruoff (New York, 1975).

4 For Du Bartas's life, bibliography, sources, and reputation in Europe, see his *Works*, ed. Urban T. Homes, John C. Lyons, and Robert W. Linker (Chapel Hill, N. C., 1935–40, 3 vols.). All my quotations from Du Bartas in French cite this edition unless otherwise indicated. Another recent edition is *La Sepmaine ou Creation du Monde*, kritischer Text der Genver Ausgabe von 1581, ed. Kurt Reichenberger (Tübingen, 1963). My description of the *Muse* is based on the 1579 edition, the version known in England.

5 His irritated poems on Du Bartas are in his *Oeuvres complètes*, ed. Paul Laumonier (Paris, 1914–75), XVIII, 358–59.

6 James's letter to Du Bartas is printed with the latter's *Works*, I, 203–4.

For the presents and invitations see the *Extract from the Despatches of M. Courcelles* (Bannatyne Club Publications no. 22, Edinburgh, 1828), p. 80.

7   E.g., A. E. Creore, "Du Bartas: a Reinterpretation," *MLQ* 1 (1940), 503–26, and Bruno Braunrot, *L'Imagination poétique chez Du Bartas* (Chapel Hill, 1973). There are some suggestive comments on his style in Georges Poulet's "Poésie du cercle et de la sphère," *Cahiers de l'Association Internationale des Etudes Françaises* 10 (1958), 44–57. As a classicist friend, Prof. Agnes Michels, pointed out to me, Lucretius also uses the word "omnis" over and over, and he too seeks to include a multitude of things as a way of apprehending that All.

8   See, for instance, Henri Weber, *La création poétique au XVIe siècle en France* (Paris, 1956), esp. pp. 540ff, for a subtle discussion of Du Bartas's prosody, and Odette de Mourgues, *Metaphysical, Baroque and Précieux Poetry* (Oxford, 1953), pp. 39–40. Yet Goulart's commentary on the "Second Day" of the *Premiere sepmaine* asks the reader to compare the description of the heavens with "a Hymne that Ronsard hath made of Heaven, and he shall finde, that what the one hath dilated in one hundreth Verses, the other hath cunningly related, and concluded, in a very few words which omit nothing" (Thomas Lodge's trans., *A learned summary*, 1621, sig. M4).

9   James Craigie's introduction to Thomas Hudson's *Historie of Judith* (Edinburgh, 1941, S. T. S. 3rd ser. no. XIV), xxvii; Alfred Upham, *French Influence in English Literature* (New York, 1908) p. 218; Robert MacDonald, *The Library of Drummond of Hawthornden* (Edinburgh, 1971), p. 137; C. S. Lewis, *English Literature in the Sixteenth Century* (Oxford, 1954), p. 544. See also Francis Haber's introduction to *Bartas, his divine weekes and workes* (Scholars' Facsimiles and Reprints, Gainesville, Fla., 1965); S. K. Heninger, "Tudor Literature and the Physical Sciences," *HLQ* 32 (1969), 101–33; and E. R. Gregory, "Du Bartas and the Modes of Christian Poetry in England," unpublished dissertation, University of Oregon, 1965, who discusses his Christian skepticism.

Other material on Du Bartas's English reputation may be found in Sidney Lee, *The French Renaissance in England* (Oxford, 1910); Arthur Nethercot, "The Reputation of Native versus Foreign 'Metaphysical Poets' in England,"*MLR* 25 (1930), 152–64; William Abbot, "Studies in the Influence of Du Bartas in England 1584–1641," unpublished dissertation University of North Carolina at Chapel Hill, 1931; James Carscallen, "English Translators and Admirers of Du Bartas, 1578–1625," unpublished B.Litt. thesis, Oxford, 1958, which the author kindly lent me; and my own "The Reception of Du

Bartas in England,"*SRen* 15 (1968), 144–73. See also, when it is available, the forthcoming edition of Sylvester's *Weeks*, edited by Susan Snyder.

10 On this aspect of Du Bartas's imagination see Jean Dagens, "Du Bartas humaniste et encyclopédiste dévot," *CAIEF* 10 (1958), 9–29, and François Secret, "La kabbale chez Du Bartas et son commentateur Claude Duret," *Studi Francesi* 3 (1959), 1–11.

11 E.g., I. D. McFarlane, *A Literary History of France: Renaissance France* (London and New York, 1974), pp. 387–88, says wittily that Du Bartas's poems sometimes seem "a vast Parnassian and humanist junk-shop."

12 Jonson said this to Drummond; see his *Works*, ed. C. H. Herford and Percy Simpson (Oxford, 1925–52), I, 133. Du Perron's similar criticism is quoted by Braunrot, p. 23.

13 S. K. Heninger, *Touches of Sweet Harmony: Pythagorean Cosmology and Renaissance Poetics* (San Marino, 1974), argues for an approach to poetic form in the Renaissance that deals not with "a continuum of parts . . . but rather with a series of discrete parts each of which relates directly to the whole" (p. 390). Du Bartas's readers were in fact aware of a continuum, as one would expect from their training in rhetoric, but Heninger's argument makes sense of the *Sepmaines*' structure in a way conventional readings cannot. Richard Willes remarks in his *De re poetica* (1573), ed. A. D. S. Fowler (Oxford, 1958), p. 120, that a feigning poet is like a mathematician who abstracts shapes from matter.

14 For bibliographical information I have consulted Abbot's dissertation, the fullest study until Snyder's edition appears. Craigie discusses Hudson as a translator and the reception of his work. See also Ian Ross, "Verse Translation at the Court of King James VI of Scotland," *TSLL* 4 (1962/63), 252–67.

15 *The Poems of James VI of Scotland*, ed. James Craigie, 2 vols. (Edinburgh, 1955 and 1958; S. T. S. 3rd ser. XXII and XXVI), I, 27, 25. James includes the French text.

16 James, I, 97–195; James also includes a fragment of "Eden." The "Premier jour" and French poem are in II, 148–55, 102. See also Ian Ross, "Verse Translation" and *New Poems of James I of England*, ed. A. F. Westcott (New York, 1911).

17 Craigie, in James, I, 274–80, gives many compliments although not the anagram or Vaughan's *Caroleia*. Harvey's statement (from *Pierces supererogation*) is in *Elizabethan Critical Essays*, II, 265. For Drummond, see his *Works*, ed. L. E. Kastner (Manchester, 1913), I, 146. Charles, too, seems to have liked Du Bartas. The British Museum's catalogue

of printed books records a copy of the 1605 *Weekes and workes* with two lines of Latin and an epigram in the prince's hand and a manuscript dedication to him by Sylvester.

18   The evidence for the translation is summarized in Sidney's *Poems*, ed. William Ringler (Oxford, 1962), p. 339. A. C. Hamilton calls Du Bartas the real "enemy" of Sidney and Spenser in *The Structure of Allegory in the Faerie Queene* (Oxford, 1961), pp. 124–27, 223–24. E. R. Gregory takes the opposite view in "Du Bartas, Sidney, and Spenser," *CLS* 7 (1970), 437–49, and Alan Sinfield argues in "Sidney and Du Bartas," *CL* 27 (1975), 8–20, that Sidney's position on divine poetry evolved from uncertainty to a desire to write or at least translate it.

19   *The Lumley Library*, ed. Sears Jayne and F. R. Johnson (London, 1956). My suggestion is based on materials in the *DNB*. Neither this translation nor Churchyard's appears in Abbot's dissertation.

20   Listed in Pollard and Redgrave as Sylvester's, but see Ernest A. Strathmann, "The 1595 Translation of Du Bartas' *First Day*," *HLQ* 8 (1945), 185–91.

21   The *Belvedere* was published for the Spenser Society (1875; New York, 1967). Craigie identifies the lines from Hudson and James in his editions of their works.

22   Charles Crawford's edition (Oxford, 1913) describes Allott's methods and identifies his many errors. There must have been a multitude of quotations from Du Bartas in a huge miscellany of which we now have only fragments. It was called "Hesperides" and was put together some time around 1660; the catalogue of authors included many works by Sylvester and Hudson's *Judith*. See Gunnar Sorelius, "An Unknown Shakespearean Commonplace Book," *The Library* 5th ser. XXVIII (1973), 294–308.

23   By John Vicars. For the sake of convenience all references to the commendatory poems quote Sylvester's *Works*, ed. Alexander Grosart (1880; reprinted Hildesheim, 1969, 2 vols). Unless otherwise identified, my quotations from Sylvester are from this edition.

24   Drayton's epistle to Henry Reynolds in his *Works*, ed. J. W. Hebel (Oxford, 1931–41; 1961 ed.) III, 230. Drummond's opinion is in *Critical Essays of the Seventeenth Century*, ed. J. E. Spingarn (1908–1909; Bloomington, 1957), I, 217. In the same conversation Jonson retracted his earlier praise of Sylvester (p. 211).

25   On Sylvester see Philipp Weller, *Joshuah Sylvesters Englische Übersetzungen der Religiösen Epen des Du Bartas* (Tübingen, 1902), who stresses his "nationalisierung und popularisierung" (p. 37); Katherine Jackson, "Sylvester's 'Du Bartas,'" *Sewanee Review* 16

(April, 1908), 316–26, who collects many references to the translator; and Vagn Lundgaard Simonsen, "Joshuah Sylvester's English Translation of Du Bartas' 'La Première Sepmaine,'" *Orbis Litterarum* 8 (1950), 259–85, unsympathetic to Sylvester. H. Ashton's *Du Bartas en Angleterre* (Paris, 1908, reprinted Geneva, 1969) includes a discussion of Sylvester.

26 For a brief description of the MS, now at the Folger Library, see my article, "An Unknown Translation of Du Bartas," *Renaissance News* 19 (1966), 12–13. The Folger has kindly given me permission to quote the MS. "The sacred warr" is described by Thomas Corser, *Collectanea Anglo-Poetica*, Chetham Soc. 52 (1860), 193–99.

27 L. B. Campbell, "The Christian Muse," *HLB* 8 (1935), 29–70, and her *Divine Poetry and Drama in Sixteenth-Century England* (Cambridge, 1959) describe Du Bartas's influence on this vogue. Despite exaggerations G. C. Taylor's *Milton's Use of Du Bartas* (1934; New York, 1968) demonstrates Milton knew the *Weeks*.

28 Hall, *Poems*, ed. Arnold Davenport (Liverpool, 1949), p. 113; *The Three Parnassus Plays*, ed. J. B. Leishman (London, 1949), II *Return*, III, iii; Thomas Digges, *Foure paradoxes* (1604), sig. K2^v; *Coryat's Crudities* (Glasgow, 1905), I, 113; John Wodroephe, *The spared houres of a souldier. Or, the true marrowe of the French tongue* (1623), sig. Mm4. Alexander himself refers briefly to Du Bartas in his critical work *Anacrisis* (1634?), and borrowed heavily from him for *Doomes-day* (1614, 1637, written first in 4 and then in 12 "hours"). Drummond said Alexander had done more in a "day" than Tasso in a lifetime and Du Bartas in "two weeks" (quoted in T. H. McGrail, *Sir William Alexander* [Edinburgh, 1940], pp. 40–41).

29 Susan Snyder, "Donne and Du Bartas: *The Progresse of the Soule* as Parody," *SP* 70 (1973), 392–407, argues that Donne laughs at the *Weeks*, although some of what she says he found funny in Du Bartas was so widely believed I cannot be sure Donne was thinking specifically of him or even that he seriously questioned what he supposedly parodied. Snyder's citations of stylistic similarities, however, do suggest a parody of some sort.

30 See above, p. 120. Churchyard, sig. E4. On sig. G3^v he praises Du Bartas's "excellent verse."

31 *Works of John Taylor the Water Poet Comprised in the Folio Edition of 1630*, Spenser Soc. Reprint (1869), pp. 513, 217 (*Taylors motto*, 1621); see p. 386 for a reference to Du Bartas's "heavenly all admired Muse."

32 William Browne, *Works*, ed. W. C. Hazlitt (1868–69), I, 192.

33 *Selected Poems of George Daniel*, ed. Thomas B. Stroup (Lexington, Ky.,

1959), pp. 10–14; Howell, *Instructions*, sig. C11; Nash, *Have with you to Saffron-Walden* (1596) in *Works*, ed. R. B. McKerrow (1904–1910; Oxford, 1958), III, 130.

34 *Works*, ed. Walter R. Davis (London, 1969), p. 299. Campion's essay, *Observations in the art of English poesie*, was published in 1602 but entered in the stationers' register in 1591.

35 Hall, *Poems*, p. 16; Fitzgeffrey, *Affaniae* (1601), sigs. N2–N2^v ("nec tu Bartasse triumphas / Ulteriùs"). See also William Covell, *Polimanteia* (1595), sigs. L2, R2^v.

36 *Pierces supererogation*, in *Elizabethan Critical Essays*, II, 265–66.

37 For these and many other annotations see *Marginalia*, ed. Moore Smith, p. 168; Eleanor Relle, "Some New Marginalia and Poems of Gabriel Harvey," *RES* n.s. 23 (1972), 401–16; Harvey's *Marginalia* (several of his books bound together at the Folger Library), quoted with the permission of the Library.

38 Folger *Marginalia*, fols. 2, 39^v.

39 For a comparison of Ronsard's and Du Bartas's cosmological thought and feeling see the stimulating study by Luzius Keller, *Palingène, Ronsard, Du Bartas* (Berne, 1974).

40 Spingarn, *Critical Essays*, II, 4–6.

41 Sig. H4^v. Alberta Turner, "French Verse in the Oxford and Cambridge Poetical Miscellanies," *MLQ* 10 (1949), 458–63, mentions Du Bartas's influence on such collections.

42 *The Anatomy of Melancholy* (1st ed., 1621), ed. Floyd Dell and Paul Jordan-Smith (1927; New York, 1955), p. 275. Burton owned the "Colonies" (London, 1598, presumably Lisle's translation); it is mentioned in "Two lists of Burton's Books," ed. S. Gibson and F. R. D. Needham, *Oxford Bibliographical Soc. Proceedings and Papers* I (1922–26), 222–46.

43 Quoted by Abbot, p. 73.

44 Abraham Holland, "A continued inquisition" (1625), published with John Davies of Hereford's "Sourge for paper-persecutors," in his *Works*, ed. A. B. Grosart (Edinburgh, 1878), II, 80–81.

45 Sigs. E6^v–E7. Earlier, Zouch had said of France, in lines recalling the start of Shakespeare's *Henry IV* Part I,

> Yet Mars short-winded angry accents breaths,
> Late basely of great Henry dispossest,
>   And scarce Apollo hath lamenting left,
>   Of his divine Du Bartas quite bereft.

[sig. D5]

46 Catullus, *Carmina*, LXIII, 1. 72; Hall, p. 95.

47 *Works*, ed. Edmund Gosse (1883; New York, 1963), IV, 76. Lodge's is the only translation I have seen in blank verse.

48 E.g. Marston in *Poems*, ed. Arnold Davenport (Liverpool, 1961), p. 82. He is attacking those who rail against James VI and Du Bartas (not a large or vocal group, one imagines).

49 Sig. V4. In his *Aphorismes civill and militarie* (1613) Dallington quotes several passages from the "Furies" in French. For textbooks that cite Du Bartas see John Sanford, *Le guichet françois* (Oxford, 1604), sig. E3; Pierre Erondelle, *The French garden* (1605, 1621 ed.), sigs. O3ᵛ–O4; John Wodroephe, *The marrow of the French tongue* (1625), sig. F5; and Peter Bense, *Analogo-diaphora* (Oxford, 1637), sig. D3ᵛ. All these except Erondelle cite him specifically on grammar. Cotgrave also used Du Bartas; see Vera Smalley, *The Sources of A Dictionary of the French and English Tongues by Randle Cotgrave (London, 1611)* (Baltimore, 1948).

50 From the dedication to *The Spanish Friar*, in *Essays of John Dryden*, ed. W. P. Ker (New York, 1961), I, 247. When polishing William Soame's translation of Boileau, Dryden added similar denigrations; see *The Poems of John Dryden*, ed. James Kinsley (Oxford, 1958), I, 332–34 and IV, 1943.

51 Carscallen, pp. 213–17, describes the annotations by James Bisse. To John Prideaux, in *Hypomnemata* (ca. 1650), Chaucer, Spenser, and Du Bartas offer examples of the "cryptic method" in rhetoric (discourse arranged in arbitrary order for emotional effect). His position is thus somewhere between that of Fraunce and Dryden. The passage is quoted by W. S. Howell, *Logic and Rhetoric in England, 1500–1700* (Princeton, 1956), pp. 315–16.

52 John Illo, "Dryden, Sylvester, and the Correspondence of Melancholy Winter and Cold Age," *ELN* 1 (1963/64), 101–4.

53 Sig. C7ᵛ; see also John Crompe, *Collections out of S. Augustine* (1638), sig. D2ᵛ, and Nicholas Hunt, *The new-borne Christian* (1631), sig. T3ᵛ. Although a recusant, Richard Rowlands (Verstegan) quotes Du Bartas twice in his *Restitution of decayed intelligence* (Antwerp, 1605), sigs. G2, M4ᵛ.

54 *The Jew of Malta and The Massacre at Paris*, ed. H. S. Bennet (1931; New York, 1966), pp. 223, 252. But J. R. Glenn, "The Martyrdom of Ramus in Marlowe's *The Massacre at Paris*," *PLL* 9 (1973), 365–79, argues that Marlowe treats the Huguenots ironically.

55 Sigs. D1–D3ᵛ, F3ᵛ; M. P. Tilley, "The Comedy *Lingua* and Du Bartas' *La Sepmaine*," *MLN* 42 (1927), 293–99. There may have been a stage version of Du Bartas; Henslowe's *Diary* records "The vii dayes of the wecke" for the summer of 1595 and "The 2 wecke" for Jan., 1596.

56   *Paradise Lost*, I, 740–47. The dilemma is not exclusively Christian; cf. Lucretius's magnificent set piece on the great mother goddess which concludes suddenly that although "they tell" such things, "longe sunt tamen a vera ratione repulsa" (*De Rerum Natura*, II, 645).

57   John Steadman, "'Meaning' and 'Name': Some Renaissance Interpretations of Urania," *Neuphilologische mitteilungen* 64 (1963), 209–32. Steadman argues that Milton's Urania is more complex than a "Christian muse," but Uranie is also complex.

58   Tourneur, *The transformed metamorphosis* (1600), sig. B4, whose hero follows Urania; in this very sentence, however, Tourneur calls God "Jove."

59   John Done, *Polydoron* (1631), sig. D7. Done enjoyed Erasmus and Chaucer, however.

60   This is all the more true because for many people at that time, as Keller argues in *Palingène, Ronsard, Du Bartas*, to think religiously was virtually to think cosmologically.

61   Printed with stage designs and costumes in Stephen Orgel and Roy Strong, *Inigo Jones* (Berkeley, 1973), II, 599–629.

62   Peter Pett, *Times journey to seeke his daughter truth* (1599), sig. A4^v (he also admires Spenser); Augustine Taylor, *Divine epistles* (1623), sig. M6; anon., *Davids troubles remembered* (1638), in an opening poem by R. Sybthorp; J. A. [Rivers], *Devout rhapsodies* (1647), sigs. B1^v–B2^v.

63   Sigs. N4^v, R2–R3; sig. ¶ 2^v refers to Du Bartas's section on music in the "Columnes." See also Nan Cooke Carpenter, "Charles Butler and Du Bartas," *NQ* 199 (1954), 2–7; she describes the two writers' shared taste for music and Platonism.

64   Drayton, *Works*, V, 227, III, 358. See II, 489 and V, 178 for a quotation from Du Bartas. "Endimion" (1595) has a vision of the cosmos and number not unlike Du Bartas's raptures.

65   *The Poetical Works of Giles Fletcher and Phineas Fletcher*, ed. F. S. Boas (Cambridge, 1908–1909) I, 10–13, 59. For another tribute see Edward Browne's *Brief meditations of the day in general* (1641), in effect a condensation of Du Bartas's "None such and holy weeke."

66   Marjorie Nicolson, *The Breaking of the Circle* (Evanston, Ill., 1950), p. 141. See also Beverly S. Ridgely, "The Cosmic Voyage in French Sixteenth-century Learned Poetry," *SRen* 10 (1963), 136–62. Françoise Joukovsky-Micha, *Poésie et mythologie au XVIe siècle* (Paris, 1969), describes the increased use of flights with the muse to symbolize initiation.

67   Spenser, *Works*, ed. E. Greenlaw, C. G. Osgood, F. M. Padelford, et al. (Baltimore, 1932–49), VIII, 77.

68 Harvey, *Marginalia*, ed. Moore Smith, p. 161. H. G. Lotspeich, "Spenser's Urania," *MLN* 50 (1935), 141–46, argues that she owes much to Du Bartas. L. B. Campbell, "Muse," thinks the muse of the Mutabilitie Cantos is Urania.

69 *Poetical Works*, II, 15. A. B. Langdale, *Phineas Fletcher* (New York, 1937), describes his debts to Sylvester.

70 *The Works of Anne Bradstreet*, ed. Jeannine Hensley (Cambridge, Mass., 1967), pp. 192–94. In her prologue to *The tenth muse* (1650) Bradstreet mentions "Great Bartas' sugared lines" (p. 15). A prefatory poem calls her "a right Du Bartas girl" and another friend makes the anagram "Anna Bradestreate—Dear neat An Bartas." Her affection for Du Bartas persisted; see Kenneth Requa, "Anne Bradstreet's Use of Du Bartas in 'Contemplations,'" *Essex Institute Historical Collections* 110 (1974), 64–69.

71 Sig. B3; Harold Jenkins, *Edward Benlowes* (Cambridge, Mass., 1952), describes his debts to Sylvester. See also Thomas Bancroft, *Time's out of tune* (1658), who complains that poets no longer aspire like "rich-soul'd Salust" to the "roof of Heaven in noble flights of wit" (sigs. B8–C3).

72 Willes, *De re poetica*, ed. Fowler, p. 87.

73 Ralegh, who may well have read Du Bartas more for Goulart's commentary than for the verse itself (his own theories are heavily indebted to such compendia), four times refers to "Eden" or "L'imposture" in his notes to Book I of his *History of the World*; see his *Works*, ed. Oldys and Birch (1829, reissued New York, 1966), II, 66, 67, 129, and 137. His line references make it clear he used a French edition. It is not surprising Ralegh read Du Bartas; the two shared a strong tendency to skepticism and a Christianity that responded more to the cosmos and the pattern of history than to Christ himself and the Redemption. Bacon refers to Du Bartas in *The Advancement of Learning* (1605), ed. G. W. Kitchin (1915; London, 1958), p. 21; the lines are from the opening of the "Second Day."

74 Matthew Stoneham, *Two sermons* (1608, sig. B2); see also Henry Peacham, note 78 below. Hakewill, *Apologie*, sig. Ii4ᵛ, and Rowlands, *Restitution*, sig. G2, cite the related account in the "Sixth Day" of the silver model of the cosmos the emperor Ferdinand had made for "Soliman the great Turck."

75 Sigs. G4ᵛ, E4ᵛ, B2. Richard Brathwait, *The English gentleman* (1630), sig. Ll2ᵛ, quotes the same fragment from *Judith*.

76 See pp. 23–24. John Molle's introduction to Mornay's *Treatise of the church* (1579) quotes "great" Du Bartas on that "notable Champion" (1606 ed., sig. A2).

77 Nash, *Works*, I, 193–94. Nash is correct in saying Sir *Nicholas* Bacon; Du Bartas's editors wrongly assume he meant Francis.

78 1634 ed., sig. Il. Later he cites Du Bartas's descriptions in the "Sixth Day" of the mechanical eagle in Nuremburg and the Persian king's glass model (sigs. L3^v–L4^v). In *Graphice* (1612) and *Prince Henrie revived* (1615) he quotes a tag on artisans who have their wits "au bout des doigts."

79 Sigs. B3, E4^v–H4^v, L2, y4, t2–t3. Gratitude that one's own country is free from frightening animals derives ultimately from Virgil's second Georgic. In Eliot's scene in the bookstore, sigs. i2–i3, a university student requests both *Weeks* in French. It is possible Shakespeare knew the lines Eliot quotes from Du Bartas; see J. W. Lever, "Shakespeare's French Fruits," *Shakespeare Survey* 6 (1953), 79–90.

80 Paul Baynes, *An epitome of mans misery* (1619, in an opening letter from a friend); Thomas Herbert, *Some yeares travels into Africa and Asia* (1634; 1638 ed., sigs. B3, Xx4).

81 Moffett praises the *Premiere sepmaine* in *Nobilis, sive Vitae Mortisque Sydniadis* (1593), ed. and trans. V. B. Heltzel and H. H. Hudson (San Marino, 1940), p. 74. *The theater of insects* (vol. III of *The history of four-footed beasts*, 1658, reprinted in a facsimile edition, New York, 1967), pp. 882–84, 1039.

82 *Institutes of the Christian Religion*, ed. John T. McNeill and trans. F. L. Battles (Philadelphia, 1960), Book I, ch. 5, and notes.

83 Sigs. D3^v–D4. See also Archibald Simson, *Heptameron . . . that is, meditations and prayers, upon the worke of the lords creation* (St. Andrews, 1621), who paraphrases St. Paul on the Creation as a mirror of God and cites among his own sources St. Ambrose and "the woorthie D. Bartas" (sig. A5).

84 E. R. Curtius, *European Literature and the Latin Middle Ages*, trans. Willard Trask (1953; New York, 1963), pp. 319–26. He quotes the lines by Sylvester but assigns them to Quarles.

85 *Paradise Lost* VIII, 67–68; V, 511–12.

86 John Boys, *Works* (1638), sigs. Sss3, Ee6, Ddd2, Dddd6, Y6.

87 Ibid., sigs. Vvv8–Vvv8^v. Drummond knew the passage, paraphrasing it in "Of this faire Volumne"; see Fernand Baldensperger, "Un Sonnet de W. Drummond et son point de départ dans 'La semaine' de Du Bartas," *MLN* 55 (1940), 493–95. Drummond owned Du Bartas's works, including two Latin translations, and listed him among the authors he read; see his *Library*, ed. MacDonald.

88 Robert Griffin. "Agrippa D'Aubigné and Sixteenth-Century Occultism," *Romanische Forschungen* 79 (1967), 114–32.

89 Sigs. e2–g1^v. Frances Yates, "The Importance of John Eliot's *Ortho-*

epia Gallica," *RES* 7 (1931), 419–30, finds the juxtaposition of lively Rabelais and pious Du Bartas "subtly ironical," but it is not surprising Eliot enjoyed both authors. Harvey and Dallington did so.

90 "A Fig for Momus," *Works* III, 60–63.

91 Spingarn, *Critical Essays*, I, 146, 158–59. On Du Bartas and numbers see Christopher Butler, *Number Symbolism* (London, 1970). For another view of Du Bartas as a *vates* see Thomas Gainsford, *The vision and discourse of Henry the seventh* (1610), sig. A2ᵛ.

92 Sigs. Dd5–Ee5. Captain John Smith borrowed from Fotherby for his *Generall historie of Virginia* (1624) and took over some quotations from Du Bartas. See Philip Barbour, "Captain John Smith and the Bishop of Sarum," *HLQ* 26 (1962/63), 11–30. Dr. Barbour kindly drew my attention to *Atheomastix* and its use of Du Bartas.

93 My quotations from the prefatory discourse cite Hexham. R. A. Skelton, editor of the facsimile edition of Hexham (Amsterdam, 1968), says Hexham took his translation of the opening discourse from Saltonstall, who in turn worked from the large Latin folio editions of the *Atlas*; the ones I have seen do not quote Du Bartas.

94 John Lievsay and Richard Davis, "A Cavalier Library—1643," *Studies in Bibliography* 6 (1954), 141–60; Sister Jean C. Cavanaugh, "The Library of Lady Southwell and Captain Sibthorpe," *Studies in Bibliography* 20 (1967), 243–54; F. Taylor, "The Books and Manuscripts of Scipio le Squyer," *Bulletin of the John Rylands Library* 25 (1941), 137–64.

95 On Lumley see above, p. 179; for Drummond see his *Library*, ed. MacDonald; *A Catalogue of the Library of Sir Edward Coke*, ed. W. O. Hassall with a preface by Samuel Thorne (New Haven, 1950); *Catalogus universalis librorum omnium in Bibliotheca collegii sionii* (1650); *Catalogue of the Plume Library*, compiled by S. G. Deed (Maldon, Essex, 1959); George Lawson, *Catalogus librorum* (1681).

96 *The Diary of Samuel Pepys*, ed. Robert Latham and William Matthews (London, 1970–74), III, 247; Phillips, *Theatrum* (1800), p. 277; Baxter is quoted by Weller, *Sylvester*, p. 108.

97 Winstanley, *Lives*, ed. William Parker for Scholars' Facsimiles and Reprints (Gainesville, 1963), sigs. G3, H6ᵛ; John Oldham, *Poems*, introd. Bonamy Dobrée (London, 1960), pp. 231–32. In *The Spectator* Addison criticizes the shaped poems in the translation of Du Bartas; perhaps he was thinking of some of the prefatory verse (1907; London, 1957) I, 178. For Pope's opinion see J. Spence's *Anecdotes*, ed. S. W. Singer (London, 1964), p. 45. Prof. Susan Snyder informs me that Burchett's work is in fact a translation.

98 Addison, *Spectator*, III, 438–39; Pope, *An Essay on Man*, ed. Maynard

Mack (New Haven, 1951), pp. 110–11; for James Thomson, see *English Romantic Poetry and Prose*, ed. Russell Noyes (Oxford, 1956), p. 10. His library is described in *Sale Catalogues of Libraries of Eminent Persons*, Vol. I, ed. A. N. L. Munby (London, 1971), 45–66. Vol. V, ed. Stephen Parks, includes the library of Lawrence Sterne, who also owned a Sylvester.

AFTERWORD

1 Walter Ong, "From Allegory to Diagram in the Renaissance Mind," *The Journal of Aesthetics and Art Criticism* 17 (1959), 423–40. From this point of view it is not surprising that two of Du Bartas's earliest admirers were Fraunce and Harvey, both rhetoricians interested in the new visually arranged systems of Ramus.

2 The taste for complex tropes and schemes doubtless goes back as far as poetry itself and must have sources deep in the psyche. It is the specific passion for anaphora, series, and emblems that seems noteworthy in many of the borrowings from French poetry. These devices rely on phrases or comparisons which although united by participation in a significant pattern are themselves less interrelated than the phrases used in other popular devices like ploche or climax.

Index